Responses to Naturalism

This volume offers critical responses to philosophical naturalism from the perspectives of four different yet fundamentally interconnected philosophical traditions: Kantian idealism, Hegelian idealism, British idealism, and American pragmatism. In bringing these rich perspectives into conversation with each other, the book illuminates the distinctive set of metaphilosophical assumptions underpinning each tradition's conception of the relationship between the human and natural sciences. The individual essays investigate the affinities and the divergences between Kant, Hegel, Collingwood, and the American pragmatists in their responses to philosophical naturalism. The ultimate aim of *Responses to Naturalism* is to help us understand how human beings can be committed to the idea of scientific progress without renouncing their humanistic explanations of the world. It will appeal to scholars interested in the role idealist and pragmatist perspectives play in contemporary debates about naturalism.

Paul Giladi is Senior Lecturer in Philosophy at Manchester Metropolitan University, an affiliate of the UCD Centre for Ethics in Public Life, and an honorary research fellow at the University of Sheffield. He has published numerous articles in leading philosophical journals and edited collections on Hegel, pragmatism, critical social theory, feminism, and Anglo-American philosophy.

Routledge Studies in Contemporary Philosophy

Responses to Naturalism
Critical Perspectives From Idealism and Pragmatism

Edited by Paul Giladi

Routledge
Taylor & Francis Group

NEW YORK AND LONDON

First published 2019
by Routledge
52 Vanderbilt Avenue, New York, NY 10017

and by Routledge
2 Park Square, Milton Park, Abingdon, Oxon OX14 4RN

*Routledge is an imprint of the Taylor & Francis Group, an
informa business*

© 2020 Taylor & Francis

Library of Congress Cataloging-in-Publication Data
A catalog record for this book has been requested

ISBN: 978-1-138-74474-5 (hbk)
ISBN: 978-1-315-18085-4 (ebk)

Typeset in Sabon
by Apex CoVantage, LLC

To two sorely missed colleagues: Lynne Rudder Baker (1944–2017) & Hilary Putnam (1926–2016)

Contents

PART II
Pragmatist Responses to Naturalism   165

Acknowledgements

First and foremost, I would like to thank all of the contributors to this volume—Shannon Dea and Nathan Haydon, Mario De Caro, Katerina Deligiorgi, Willem A. deVries, Giuseppina D'Oro, Gabriele Gava, Johannes Haag, Steven Levine, David Macarthur, Alexis Papazoglou, and Paul Redding—for their hard work and unfailing support throughout work on this edited collection.

Secondly, this volume was made possible in part through the support of a grant from the John Templeton Foundation/the University of Cambridge's *New Directions in the Study of Mind* initiative for the co-investigated project 'Idealism and the Philosophy of Mind', https:// idealismsite.wordpress.com/, which was led by Giuseppina D'Oro, Alexis Papazoglou, and me. The respective opinions expressed in this collection are those of each project investigator, and do not necessarily reflect the views of the John Templeton Foundation.

Special thanks to Andrew Weckenmann at Routledge for his warm embrace of the project from the beginning; Allie Simmons; and Routledge's two diligent readers of the proposal.

My thanks also to all the conference delegates at the Idealism and Metaphilosophy of Mind Conference held in London at Senate House in 2016. I also wish to thank all the participants in the Idealism and Philosophy of Mind Summer School held at Keele University in 2017. Both events were philosophically fruitful and enjoyable, and many of the contributions to this volume were enriched by the discussion at both events.

For help and encouragement along the way on the naturalist, idealist, and pragmatist side of things, I would like to thank Carl Sachs, and my colleagues at University College Dublin during my time there as a teaching and research fellow in philosophy in 2017–2018. I also want to thank my colleagues at Manchester Metropolitan University for their sustained support of my research here.

Above all, I wish to thank the two special women in my life who are a constant source of joy and wisdom: my mum, Mona, and my partner, Eleanor.

Introduction

Paul Giladi

I

The Warring Drives

One of the legacies of modernity, typified by significant breakthroughs in natural scientific inquiry, is the way in which philosophy's self-image—at least in the Anglo-American analytic tradition—has increasingly become naturalistic. However, the naturalisation of philosophy goes beyond the purely negative and somewhat banal claim that there is no supernatural reality. In other words, the naturalistic transformation of philosophic inquiry involves something more *important*, more *interesting*, and more *compelling* than just a model of ontological taxonomy in which transcendent deities, Jedi Knights, and spooky and occult things, are not included in the inventory of what there is. I think what makes the *basic* tenet of naturalism important, interesting, and compelling is the complex ways in which it construes that *the image of the world provided by the natural sciences as all there is to the world*.[1] Naturalism, therefore, has metaphysical *and* methodological dimensions: (i) at the most fundamental ontological level, reality is just what the natural sciences deem it to be;[2] (ii) our ways of intelligibly articulating reality, the ways in which we make sense of things, are ultimately justifiable only by the methods and practices of the *Naturwissenschaften*. The conjunction of (i) and (ii) is often referred to as 'scientific naturalism'.[3]

A significant consequence of the naturalisation of philosophic inquiry and the ascendancy of scientific naturalism is that the defence of the autonomy of the *Geisteswissenschaften* has also changed, to the extent that in the Anglo-American analytic tradition, defending the autonomy of philosophy is *almost* exclusively articulated from some kind of naturalistic standpoint. For, even though one might deem philosophy as irreducible to natural science, one often still maintains a naturalistic bent that philosophy must be practised in such a way that is supportive of or continuous with physics, chemistry, and biology. To put this another way, given how rapid and entrenched naturalisation has been, it is reasonable to claim that the *default* position for mainstream analytic philosophers is naturalism *tout court*, insofar as the burden of proof is automatically on those who are critical of or resistant to naturalism *tout court*. In terms of one's philosophical coming-of-age in many analytic departments, one is baptised a naturalist, to remove the original sin of supernaturalism. And in terms of one's aspirations to be taken seriously in the Anglophone philosophical world and maintain good working relationships with the relevant powers-that-be, naturalism must be a doctrine which demands absolute loyalty on pain of some kind of intellectual *auto da fé*. To quote Hilary Putnam:

> [t]oday the most common use of the term "naturalism" might be described as follows: philosophers—perhaps even a majority of all the philosophers writing about issues in metaphysics, epistemology, philosophy of mind and philosophy of language—announce in one or another conspicuous place in their essays and books that they are "naturalists" or that the view or account being defended is a "naturalist" one; this announcement, in its placing and emphasis, resembles the placing of the announcement in articles written in Stalin's Soviet Union that a view was in agreement with Comrade Stalin's; as in the case of the latter announcement, it is supposed to be clear that any view which is not "naturalist" (not in agreement with Comrade Stalin's) is anathema, and could not possibly be correct.[4]

Ironic religious inflections aside, there is something almost *irresistible* to naturalism. As Barry Stroud phrased it, there is a *charm* to it.[5] Crucially, what makes naturalism so appealing and enduring is that its charming qualities are deep-rooted in our psychological architecture and cognitive make-up: as human beings, we are *sense-making creatures*. We inquire into things, to render the world around us rationally intelligible and meaningful. From an anthropological perspective, then, naturalism's charm consists in appealing to our basic cognitive *drive* to render reality discursively accessible. However, if this is *all* there is to naturalism, then it seems difficult to plausibly claim—let alone *motivate*—any kind of legitimate philosophical tension or even antinomy. For, under such a conception of naturalism, the idea of bringing into question such an orientation of thinking, one which taps into our *need* as a species to rationally make sense of things, seemingly countenances blocking the way of inquiry. This would be anathematic to the very function of philosophical reflection, leaving *reality* not only discursively inaccessible, but also leaving *us* radically alienated from our *own* nature. Furthermore, naturalism is not just charming at the primitive anthropologic-psychological level; naturalism is also appealing because of just how successful and emancipatory the natural sciences have undeniably been. Questioning naturalism, then, would be tantamount to disputing the remarkable epistemic successes of physicists, chemists, and biologists. As Peirce famously wrote: "[a] man must be downright crazy to deny that science has made many true discoveries" (*CP*: 5.172).

However, construing naturalism *tout court* as the exclusive ally of our anthropological disposition for sense-making is rather problematic. For, in many respects, the most sensitive, reflective, and nuanced responses to naturalism are motivated precisely by *(i) wanting to render reality intelligible and meaningful; and (ii) wanting to help us feel at home with our sense-making nature.* This is why there *is* philosophical tension, why there is an antinomy of sorts when developing a critical perspective on naturalism. Such philosophical problematisation can be most clearly evidenced (at a general level) in our struggles to balance the naturalistic drive with our default commitment to phenomena which *eo ipso* seem to *radically* differ from leptons, quarks, and quantum fields. The phenomena in question range from first-person intentional states, reasons, and meaning, to numbers and moods. In many respects, this class of phenomena are integral parts of the manifest image of the world, a humanistic perspective which is indispensable for human beings *qua* enquirers. The subsequent situation, then, is one in which the conflict between the naturalistic drive and the humanistic drive gives rise to a fundamental *aporia*—one which is famously expressed in C. D. Broad's *The Mind and its Place in Nature*.[6] As John McDowell puts it:

> Modern science understands its subject matter in a way that threatens, at least, to leave it disenchanted, as Weber put the point in an image that has become a commonplace. The image marks a contrast between two kinds of intelligibility: the kind that is sought by (as we call it) natural science ["the kind we find in a phenomenon when we see it as governed by natural law"] and the kind we find in something when we place it in relation to other occupants of "the logical space of reasons" ["the kind of intelligibility that is proper to meaning"].[7]

Under ever-increasing naturalisation, the task of philosophy has moved from a Collingwoodian self-image concerned with uncovering the presuppositions underpinning different forms of experience, and showing how they enable different ways of knowing.[8] With Quine as the lead prophet of naturalisation in Anglo-American philosophy—particularly in epistemology—*"the task of philosophy in mainstream analytic discourse involves assuming the methodological superiority of the natural sciences and then articulating positions that do not upset the presuppositions of scientific knowledge"*.[9] As Putnam writes:

> Analytic philosophy has become increasingly dominated by the idea that science, and only science, describes the world as it is in itself, independent of perspective. To be sure, there are within analytic

philosophy important figures who combat this scientism. . . . Nevertheless, the idea that science leaves no room for an independent philosophical enterprise has reached the point at which leading practitioners sometimes suggest that all that is left for philosophy is to try to anticipate what the presumed scientific solutions to all metaphysical problems will eventually look like.[10]

Herein lies the rub, though: I recognise one does not find it easy to accommodate manifest image phenomena such as self-consciousness, norms, and intentionality, within the world as presented to us by physics, chemistry, and biology. Because of this *real* difficulty, either one is inclined to place these outside the natural order, or one feels *forced* to either eliminate them from one's explanatory scheme or somehow reduce them to naturalistic materials, such as atoms and neural mechanisms. However, if we place such these oddities outside nature, we commit ourselves to regard consciousness, normative relations, etc. as *spooky*, which robs them of having any *serious* value. Equally, if we reduce them to naturalistic materials or even eliminate them altogether, their special status is robbed and the space of reasons loses all of its *normative lustre*. To quote Stroud here:

> a natural world conceived of only as the totality of all the physical facts obviously does not contain any psychological facts. There are no truths to the effect that someone believes, knows, feels, wants, prefers, or values anything. Of course, anyone who holds that the physical is all there is might hold that everything we think along those lines is really just physical facts in disguise. In any case, that would leave no psychological facts for a naturalistic theory of the world to explain. The study of human beings on such a restricted physicalist conception would be just a study of physical goings-on, including some that happen to go on in human organisms.[11]

Clearly, this *aporia*, which has been formalised in the literature as The Location/Placement Problem, appears to force enquirers into an antinomial conflict: *one must either adopt the scientific image of humanity-in-the-world, i.e. adopt the results of the empirical and natural sciences and conform to their standards; or adopt the manifest image of humanity-in-the-world, i.e. conform to the standards of how we understand ourselves and our world that is not justified by appeal to the scientific method and the results of the empirical and natural sciences.* One can quickly see how The Placement Problem is the manifestation of the intractable conflict between the naturalistic drive and the humanistic drive, since one cannot have one's hermeneutic cake and eat it here—something has to give.

II

Peace in Our Time? The Rise of and Reaction to Liberal Naturalism

However, rather than attempt to *solve* the Placement Problem, which arises when one assumes the natural sciences enjoy either ontological or explanatory priority over the human sciences, some philosophers have recently sought to relax the notion of *nature* in such a way that removes the spectre of reduction or elimination. For example, Lynne Baker,[12] Akeel Bilgrami,[13] Mario De Caro and David Macarthur,[14] John Dupré,[15] Fiona Ellis,[16] Susan Haack,[17] Jennifer Hornsby,[18] John McDowell,[19] Huw Price,[20] Hilary Putnam,[21] Thomas Scanlon,[22] Barry Stroud,[23] and David Wiggins[24]—to name but a few—have all respectively argued for more commodious forms of naturalism. Rather than maintain that the basic tenet of naturalism is *best* realised in the doctrine of *scientific* naturalism, the development of 'liberal' forms of naturalism—whether post-Kantian idealist or neo-Aristotelian or naïve realist or analytic pragmatist iterations—aims both to improve on scientific naturalism, and to carefully navigate between supernaturalism and scientific naturalism.

The broad tradition of liberal naturalism *as an intellectual orientation for coordinating non-eliminativist, non-reductionist discourse about normative kinds* often claims to have significant advantages over its more conservative (or 'hard' naturalist) cousin. Importantly, liberal naturalists *explicitly* maintain their naturalist credentials, but do so in such a way that aims to make a clear demarcation between them, supernaturalists, and scientific naturalists. As Mario De Caro and David Macarthur write:

> [liberal naturalism is a new form of naturalism] that wants to do justice to the range and diversity of the sciences, including the social and human sciences (freed of positivist misconceptions), and to the plurality of forms of understanding, including the possibility of non-scientific, nonsupernatural forms of understanding (whether or not these also count as forms of knowledge).[25]

Since liberal naturalism is conceived as occupying the conceptual space between supernaturalism and scientific naturalism, liberal naturalism has been traditionally met with two contrasting intellectual reactions: firstly, on the other hand, liberal naturalism has been met with enthusiastic acclaim. This is because its pluralism and capaciousness are not cognitively chauvinistic, supremacist, and imperialist, since liberal naturalism deems both the manifest image and the scientific image to be indispensable *for their respective purposes of inquiry*. To this extent, then, our drives to render reality intelligible by doing naturalistic work as well as humanistic work would suggest Platonic psychic harmony, insofar as one can finally have one's naturalist and humanist cakes and eat them. For, insisting that normative kinds are conceptually irreducible to purely causal and descriptive kinds in no way disqualifies oneself from regarding the natural sciences as authoritative ways of making sense of things. In other words, the advantage of liberal naturalism over conservative naturalism is that *one can be scientific with all the accompanying epistemic virtues without being scientistic.* Conceived in such a manner, philosophy is not monogamous with the *Naturwissenschaften* but *polyamorous* with both the natural sciences *and* the human sciences. To quote Bernard Williams here:

> I very much prefer that we should retain the category of philosophy and situate ourselves within it, rather than pretend that an enquiry which addresses these issues with a richer and more imaginative range of resources represents "the end of philosophy." The traditions of philosophy demand that we reflect on the presuppositions of what we think and feel. The claim which I am making, from here, from inside the subject, is that in certain areas, at least, this demand itself cannot be adequately met unless we go beyond the conceptions of getting it right that are too closely associated with the inexpressive models drawn, perhaps unconsciously, from the sciences. . . . We can dream of a philosophy that would be thoroughly truthful and honestly helpful. . . . It would need resources of expressive imagination to do almost any of the things it needed to do. . . .[26] Philosophy is, rather, in these fields, the extension of our most serious concerns by other means, but at least it should introduce our ordinary concerns in a humanly recognisable form. . . .[27] But we should remember that work may be unimaginative not because it is badly argued but because it is arguing with the wrong people; not because it has missed an argument, but because it misses the historical and psychological point.[28]

Liberal naturalism's more inclusive stance towards different modes of discourse providing a more expressive imagination is not the only reason for finding liberal naturalism attractive. What also makes liberal naturalism appealing is that it offers objections, certainly at least on Dupré's own version, to what one might dub a further 'dogma of empiricism'. Such a potential further dogma of empiricism is central to scientific naturalism's *own* plausibility and appeal: the monism which is definitive of scientific naturalism involves the principle of causal closure of the physical, and the idea that higher-level, nonphysical properties are reducible to, or at least supervene on, lower-level, physical properties. For Dupré (1995), this monism is something that one has no compelling reason to accept on *empirical* grounds. In other words, liberal naturalism's extra attractiveness here consists in how it allegedly offers an *immanent critique* of scientific naturalism, by suggesting that scientific naturalism is not plausible on *scientific* terms.[29]

On the other hand, however, liberal naturalism has been met with scepticism. A particularly evocative critique has been levelled by Ram Neta, who has argued that there is no logical space for liberal naturalism to occupy:[30]

> What if digestion, or respiration, or reasoning are natural kinds, their nature consisting simply in the mechanisms that enable them to occur? Is the liberal naturalist committed to denying this possibility? If so, then I confess I can see no good reason to accept Liberal Naturalism. And if not, then I confess I do not understand just what Liberal Naturalism is.[31]

For Neta, under liberal naturalism, either manifest image phenomena are reducible to the ontological features of the natural sciences, or that manifest image phenomena are irreducible to the ontological features of the natural sciences. If manifest image phenomena are reducible, then liberal naturalism collapses into scientific naturalism; if the manifest image phenomena are irreducible, then liberal naturalism collapses into supernaturalism. Therefore, there is no logical space for liberal naturalism to occupy: liberal naturalism is *either* masquerading as scientism[32] *or* it is masquerading as supernaturalism.

III

The Resumption of Conflict: Drawing Analogies With Critical Theory

I have found the view of liberal naturalism as either incoherent or decidedly duplicitous rather curious. Perhaps one helpful way of unravelling why exactly some view liberal naturalism in such ways lies in drawing an analogy between Neta's dilemma and Habermas's critique of social democracy. This is because both liberal naturalism and social democracy are examples of *via media*, and therefore share important *formal* features: the modern liberal-welfare state is an essential institution of social democracy, which principally structures the provision of welfare under the framework of reifying capitalist practices. For Habermas, since the structure of a social democracy is constituted by the systems of money (market capitalism) and formal power (the state), the provision of welfare will invariably fail to fulfil the function of mitigating conflict.[33] Under the liberal-welfare state, there is little or no way to resist ideological encroachment and colonisation by systems, since what is the *base* of the societal *superstructure* is the capitalist mode and relations of production. If the base is constituted by systems, then the entire whole is vulnerable to encroachment by systems. Securing and protecting the lifeworld, therefore, is effectively impossible under social democracy.

Equally, under the Sellarsian *synoptic vision of fusing the manifest and scientific images together into one coherent image*, as James O'Shea correctly notes, "[Wilfrid] Sellars does indeed want to hold that the ontology of persons as rational agents and conceptual thinkers within the space of reasons is in principle successfully accommodated *within* the comprehensively physicalist ontology of the ideal scientific image of the world".[34] To a critic of *both* scientific and of liberal naturalism, since the Sellarsian synoptic vision is *primarily* structured by the comprehensively physicalist ontology of the ideal scientific image, the purely naturalistic vocabulary will invariably fail to fulfil the function of mitigating conflict with the grammar of the *manifest* image. Under Sellars's liberal naturalist synoptic vision, so the argument goes, there is little or no way to resist colonisation by the scientific image, since what is the *base* of the synoptic vision *superstructure* is purely naturalistic vocabulary. If the base is constituted by the comprehensively physicalist ontology of the ideal scientific image, then the synoptic vision is vulnerable to systemic encroachment by scientistic forms of naturalism. Securing and protecting the ontology of persons as rational agents and conceptual thinkers within the comprehensively physicalist ontology of the ideal scientific image of the world, therefore, is effectively impossible.

I would maintain that drawing further analogies between critical theoretic concerns about the compatibility of capitalism with democracy and metaphysical and epistemological concerns about the compatibility of the manifest image with the scientific image bears philosophical fruit: for Habermas, social conflict in late modernity is rooted in the struggle to resist the colonisation of the lifeworld by systems. Conflict is not now *principally* resulting from dissatisfaction with the material distribution of goods and services in a given society, but rather resulting from dissatisfaction with the encroachment by systems on the lifeworld's territory. Between *The Theory of Communicative Action* and *Between Facts and Norms*, the language Habermas uses to articulate how the lifeworld can and should resist the pathological effects of juridification is primarily *defensive*. As he writes:

> The goal is no longer to supersede an economic system having a capitalist life of its own and a system of domination having a bureaucratic life of its own but to erect a democratic dam against the colonising encroachment of system imperatives on areas of the lifeworld.[35] . . . it is a question of building up restraining barriers for the exchanges between system and lifeworld.[36]

As I understand Habermas, the way in which one can effect *resistance* to the system's colonial oppression is to act as a border-patroller and to maintain a protective barrier. Crucially, though, Habermas appears to be committed to the claim that instrumental capitalist structures must be accepted as having primacy over communicative ones and that the best one can hope for is to maintain the integrity of the democratic dam.

By analogy, the way in which one can effect resistance to scientism's colonisation of the normative space of reasons is to act as a conceptual border-patroller and to maintain a protective hermeneutic barrier. Recognising the hegemony of the natural sciences and nomothetic rationality's dominance requires those wishing to resist the totalising encroachment of the space of reasons by purely naturalistic vocabulary to erect a hermeneutic dam and maintain its structural integrity as best as one reasonably can. Crucially, though, this defensive strategy appears to be committed to the claim that nomothetic rationality must be accepted as having *primacy*. For example, the notions of *finding a place for mind in the natural world* and *making elbow room for intentionality in the world described by physics* both seem to presuppose that one ought to accept from the very outset the vocabulary and general *Weltanschauung* of the natural sciences, and then find some meaningful and coherent way of *fitting* phenomena such as intentionality and normativity into that nomothetic picture.

Habermas himself recognised the deficiency of overly defensive attitudes to system-encroachment, and the way he shifts to a far more positive and ambitious model of resistance in *Between Facts and Norms* is one which can and should be extended to the goal of decolonising the normative space of reasons from scientistic encroachment. For Habermas in *Between Facts and Norms*, if one is to resist and eventually overcome juridification, one must develop deliberative democracy, in which legal power can be rooted in the communicative power of the lifeworld, especially a well-functioning public sphere and civil society.[37] Traversing "the long march through the institutions"[38] is progressively transformative, because debunking the legal positivist framework in favour of a discourse theory of law involves combatting and reversing the *un*official circulation of power in constitutional democracies. The official circulation of power in a constitutional democracy involves the public voting and providing input to legislative assemblies; legislative assemblies then makes laws; the executive enacts these laws; and the judiciary reflects on these laws in cases of conflict. The unofficial circulation of power, by contrast, involves political parties, etc. manipulating the public. For Habermas, "in a perceived crisis situation",[39] the flow of power can be reversed to its official state once the public become *actively* aware of its unofficial circulation. This form of social consciousness reveals how one no longer deems current frameworks as *rationally satisfying*, thereby compelling agents to radically revise their socio-political sense-making practices.

By analogy, to resist and eventually get over scientism involves combatting and reversing the circulation of *epistemic* power. Paraphrasing Walter

Mignolo somewhat, this decolonial way of thinking is "nothing more than a relentless analytic effort to understand, in order to overcome the logic of [epistemic] coloniality underneath the rhetoric of modernity, the structure of management and control that emerged out of the transformation of the [epistemic] economy".[40] From this perspective, scientific naturalism is guilty of a *cognitive* variety of imperialism, one which is the theoretical equivalent of Iris Marion Young's concept of *cultural* imperialism:

> In societies stamped with cultural imperialism, groups suffering from this form of oppression stand in a paradoxical position. They are understood in terms of crude stereotypes that do not accurately portray individual group members but also assume a mask of invisibility; they are both badly misrepresented and robbed of the means by which to express their perspective. Groups who live with cultural imperialism find themselves defined externally, positioned by a web of meanings that arise elsewhere. These meanings and definitions have been imposed on them by people who cannot identify with them and with whom they cannot identify.[41]

In the 1990s, the politics of difference focused on questions concerning nationality, ethnicity, and religion. Under this approach, the value of cultural distinctness is *essential* to individuals and not something accidental to them: their personal autonomy depends in part on being able to engage in specific cultural practices with others who identify with one another as in the same cultural group. For Young, most modern societies contain multiple cultural groups, some of which unjustly dominate the state or other important social institutions, thus inhibiting the ability of minority cultures to live fully meaningful lives in their own terms. The dominant group in society can limit the ability of one or more of the cultural minorities to live out their forms of expression. In other words, the dominant culture threatens to swamp the minority culture to the extent that particular cultural practices and different hermeneutic spheres—ways in which members of cultures interpret their experiences—get crowded out or erased. Under this analogy, the concern about scientific naturalism is that the vocabulary of the ideal scientific image becomes epistemically authoritarian and imperialistic by forcing other forms of inquiry to adopt the *discursive recourses and grammars* of formal disciplines that are fundamentally different in various ways to the manifest image's 'web of meanings'.

IV

Why 'Responses to Naturalism': Idealism and Pragmatism

In recent decades, naturalism's orthodoxy has been mainly challenged by phenomenologists, particularly those of a Husserlian persuasion.

Interestingly, just like there has been a split between left-wing Sellarsians,[42] who focus on Sellars's rejection of the Myth of the Given and commitment to the conceptual irreducibility of the manifest image, and right-wing Sellarsians,[43] who focus on Sellars's strong scientific realism, some phenomenologists are increasingly *less* resistant to seeing the naturalistic vocabulary of cognitive science integrating with phenomenology.[44] To my mind, the most important hermeneutic lesson to draw from such complexity is that one should pause before thinking that traditions which have historically been viewed as *opposed* to naturalism *in toto* necessarily continue to oppose naturalism *in toto* now. In this respect, it would be erroneous to think a response to naturalism from phenomenology *just* means a rejection of naturalism by phenomenology. This is where idealism and pragmatism come into the story.

On one side, idealism—when crudely understood—has historically been interpreted as *the* exemplar of supernaturalism or *anti*-naturalism. For example, immaterial minds have ontological primacy over material objects; transcendental inquiry has logical priority over naturalistic inquiry; God created the physical universe in order to achieve self-consciousness; and one can establish general scientific laws without recourse to experimentation by transcendentally reflecting on our discursive architecture. On the other side, pragmatism—when crudely understood—has historically been regarded as *the* paradigmatic hardheaded naturalist. For example, the only legitimate form of inquiry is the scientific method; the *a priori* is an unfortunate relic of a non-scientific disposition; our beliefs and theories must be subjected to constant experimentation to determine their legitimacy; and meaningfulness consists in accounting for the demonstrable effects of discursive practices in the world. However, as with the case of phenomenology, neither idealism nor pragmatism should be construed as towing *one* party line, according to which idealists are whipped into *scorning* naturalism, and pragmatists are whipped into *deifying* naturalism. Matters are a lot more complicated here.

To this end, the motivation of this volume is precisely (i) to do justice to the discursive complexity *within* idealist responses to naturalism and to the discursive complexity *within* pragmatist responses to naturalism; (ii) to put idealist and pragmatist responses into conversation with one another about how best to respond to naturalism. What is especially attractive about creating dialogue between all these rich perspectives together on the subject of naturalism and its prospects, something which has never been done before, is that idealism and pragmatism offer some of the most interesting and philosophically sensitive responses to naturalism. This is not in the least because Kantian idealism, Hegelian idealism, British idealism, and pragmatism all have sophisticated and enduringly relevant views about modernity, rationality, human mindedness, and the nature and function of philosophic inquiry.

Specifically, this volume is an effort to respond to naturalism from the perspectives of Kantian idealism, Hegelian idealism, British idealism, and pragmatism in order to illuminate the distinctive set of *metaphilosophical* assumptions underpinning it. The volume investigates the affinities and the divergences between Kant, Hegel, Collingwood, and those who are part of the pragmatist tradition. Crucially, not only will significant points of convergence and contestation be established *within and between* idealism and pragmatism in their particular responses to naturalism, but such is the enduring philosophical attractiveness of idealism and pragmatism that they can help move this substantive and significant debate forward, heralding new directions for the analytic tradition in making sense of nature and normativity.

V

The Structure of the Edited Volume

The volume is divided into two parts: Part I concerns idealist responses to naturalism, and comprises two essays on Kant, two essays on Hegel, one essay on Kant/Hegel/Husserl, and one on Collingwood/Heidegger. Part II concerns pragmatist responses to naturalism, and comprises two essays on Peirce, one essay on common sense and Putnam's variety of liberal naturalism, two essays on Sellars, and one essay on neopragmatism. I recognise that no idealist chapter in the volume focuses on Fichte or Schelling, but this is not due to any intention to erase the Fichtean or Schellingian perspective. Rather, the absence of Fichte and Schelling is due to wanting to keep Part I as wieldy as possible. I very much hope the chapters on idealist responses to naturalism provoke further publications on Fichte and Schelling. Equally, I recognise that no pragmatist chapter in the volume focuses on James or Dewey, but this is not due to any intention to erase the Jamesean or Deweyan perspective. Rather, as before, the absence of James and Dewey is due to wanting to keep Part II as wieldy as possible. I very much hope the chapters on pragmatist responses to naturalism provoke further publications on James and Dewey.

In 'Moral Natural Norms: A Kantian Perspective on Some Neo-Aristotelian Arguments', Katerina Deligiorgi focuses her attention on a strand of neo-Aristotelianism—beginning with Philippa Foot and finding contemporary support in Michael Thompson—that is of special interest from a Kantian perspective. While both Aristotelian ethics and Kantian ethics are objectivist; Kantian ethics, at least as it is usually articulated, is construed as rationalist, absolutist, and wholly abstract, whereas the neo-Aristotelian picture addresses human beings as natural beings and seems more attentive to the historical, social, and embodied particularities of human life. In this respect, Aristotelian ethics raises a challenge: it professes to have the conceptual resources to address a range of first-order as well as second-order ethical questions *precisely* in those areas in which Kantian ethics is traditionally supposed to be weak. From a contemporary perspective, neo-Aristotelianism is particularly attractive because it allows for a naturalistic defence of moral value that fits within liberal naturalism. This is most clearly evidenced in McDowell's concept of 'second nature'. Deligiorgi develops a non-naturalist Kantian response to the neo-Aristotelian challenge, in which there is nothing 'queer' or 'spooky' about the anti-naturalistic position attributed to Kant.

Johannes Haag's chapter, 'Naturalism and the Primacy of the Practical: Kant on the Form of Theoretical and Practical Reason', focuses on Kant's *Critique of the Power of Judgement*. Haag argues that Kant's concept of *nature* lies at the foundation of a non-reductive or liberal form of naturalism. It is a *naturalism*, insofar as everything that counts as empirical is subject to *constitutive* (rather than reflective) judgment, and therefore can, at least in principle, be describable by natural science. It is *non-reductive* or liberal, insofar as the drawing of these boundaries is itself grounded in the cognitive activity of rational subjects, an activity irreducible to empirical kinds, and necessarily relying on *a priori* conceptual structures. Hence, for Haag, Kant's naturalism is a 'normative naturalism'. Since the reflection on these normative structures underpinning nature in various ways requires a special form of philosophical methodology, i.e. transcendental philosophy, it is a unique form of *philosophical* naturalism. According to Haag, for Kant, the naturalisation of the world ultimately has to submit to the *practical interest* of reason, given the regulative operations of God and the immortality of the soul. However, at the same time, naturalisation is *tempered* in such a way that does not breach the conceptual barrier between the theoretical and the practical—the respective domains of Nature and Freedom. While the power of judgment brings the *practical* form of reason and its characteristic causality to bear on the description of nature, it does so only at a *regulative* level.

In Paul Giladi's contribution to the volume, 'The Placement Problem and the Threat of Voyeurism', he moves away from Kantian responses to naturalism, and instead offers a more polemical Hegelian position. Rather than *solve* the Placement Problem by arguing in favour of either reductionism or eliminativism or supernaturalism, Giladi contends one should *dissolve* the Placement Problem in an Hegelian manner. He proposes that the explanation for why the Placement Problem grips the philosophic imagination with such force is that rational activity is exclusively articulated in terms of the kind of inferential patterns definitive of analytical thinking, namely the kind of thinking symptomatic of *Verstand*. This, in turn, leads to conceiving of the space of reasons and the space of nature as *fundamentally* in tension with another, and to regarding the manifest image and scientific image as metaphilosophical *antagonists*. However, central to Hegelianism is a committed opposition to treating the nomothetic qualities of the Laplacian model of rationality which

Verstand instantiates most explicitly as exhaustive of critical think-ing. This is because Hegel places significant emphasis on the dialectical function of *Vernunft*, which does not conceive of rational activity as a detached, voyeuristic critical reason. Why *Vernunft* is favoured here over analytical reflection is that *Verstand* fails to be completely illustrative of our *geistige Einstellung* phenomenology. Understood in this Hegelian way, the attempt to translate the vocabulary of the manifest image into the vocabulary of the pure and ideal scientific image amounts to a debili-tating variety of alienation in which humanity is estranged from its *Geis-tig* and therefore necessarily pluralist matrix of sense-making practices. For Hegel, one must go beyond a particular kind of naturalism, namely a *narrow* naturalism which alienates us from our 'amphibian' nature.

The fourth chapter focusing on idealist responses to naturalism is by Alexis Papazoglou, who offers an idealist challenge to naturalism. Papa-zoglou claims that scientific naturalism has come under a lot of criticism, primarily because of the placement problems it creates. This has led influ-ential philosophers, such as McDowell and Price, to propose alternatives to scientific naturalism, without, however, veering off to the supernatural or undermining the priority of the natural sciences. For Papazoglou, both the McDowellian and Pricean strategies involve finding an underlying assumption of scientific naturalism's position, exposing it as problem-atic, and proceeding to reject it, thus leaving behind only the redeeming qualities of naturalism, without any of the negative features. However, for Papazoglou, admirable as these attempts at redefining naturalism are, they seem to fall short of the job: McDowell struggles to show in what sense his position should count as naturalism, since he lacks a clear picture of what is to count as nature; and Price struggles to convince that his position is *really* all that different from scientific naturalism. For Papazoglou, idealist thought starting with Kant offers a better line of thought than liberal naturalism. Where scientific naturalism suggests we take the results of natural science as the starting point of our inquiries into the world and ourselves, idealism asks what the philosophical pre-suppositions of scientific inquiry are in the first place. Papazoglou then develops two arguments: (i) a transcendental argument against scientific naturalism, which claims that if the conditions for the possibility of natu-ral science cannot themselves be given a scientific account, then scientific naturalism's claim about the priority of scientific accounts cannot hold; and (ii) an idealist argument against scientific naturalism.

Paul Redding in 'An Hegelian *Actualist* Alternative to Naturalism' defends Hegel's alternative to Spinozist naturalism, focusing on Hegel's approach to modality. Critical of Spinoza's strict necessitarianism, Hegel insisted on finding a place for possibility in the actual. For Redding, this means that there is good reason to compare Hegel with some contemporary actualists who, despite affirming the reality of possibility, oppose David Lewis's commitment to other possible worlds. As the actual is all there is, alternate possibilities must be, somehow, internal to it—unrealised states or properties of the actual. Drawing on this parallel, Redding interprets Hegel's idealism as consequential to his brand of actualism. If 'actual' functions as a type of indexical, Redding then asks if the actualist is obligated to have commitments to minds and their subjective points of view that in some sense escapes our conception of nature. If so, actualism seems to presuppose a type of idealism. For Redding, this position would be toxic only if the necessity of mindedness in reality were meant in a stronger sense—for example, were the mind thought of as necessary *per se*—i.e. as present in every possible state of the world.

The sixth and final chapter in Part I, 'How to (and Not to) Defend the Manifest Image', is by Giuseppina D'Oro, who focuses on R. G. Collingwood's claim for the irreducibility of actions to events in relation to Heidegger's argument for the irreducibility of the ready-to-hand to the present-at-hand. D'Oro argues against the attempt to save the manifest image by invoking the relation of entailment (whether that implied by the notion of *supervenience* or by the more traditional notion of analytic *entailment*) on the grounds that the manifest image is *sui generis*. The defence of the manifest image that D'Oro proposes as an alternative here rests on the Kant-inspired idealist assumption that *knowledge makes a difference to what is known*, and that since the manifest and the scientific image are the correlative of two different ways of knowing they do not compete with one another. For D'Oro, the need to legitimise the manifest image in the light of the scientific image arises because the relation between the scientific and the manifest image has not been properly conceptualised. Once the scientific and the manifest image are understood as the correlative of different ways of knowing, the problem which the location strategy seeks to solve is shown to rest on a misconception of the relationship holding between different kinds of knowledge. D'Oro then contrasts her approach with Frank Jackson's strategy for saving the manifest image from elimination, which relies on a modest conception of the role of conceptual analysis in metaphysics and presupposes a hierarchical view of the relation between the sciences, with physics as the most basic science. For D'Oro, the role of conceptual analysis in metaphysics is *not* modest: conceptual analysis establishes what the subject matter of different kinds of knowledge is by making explicit the inferences or judgments which they deploy to generate their own *distinctive* kinds of knowledge claims. There is therefore no need to espouse the location strategy advocated by the modest conception in order to save the manifest image from the eliminativist's guillotine, and avoid conflict between philosophy and natural science.

Shannon Dea and Nathan Hayond's 'From the Experimentalist Disposition to the Absolute: Peirce's Pragmatic Naturalism is the first of Part II's six chapters on responses to naturalism from pragmatism. Dea and Haydon examine the avant-la-lettre naturalism of Peirce.

They argue that Peirce was both a methodological and a metaphysical naturalist. For Dea and Haydon, he was also a theological naturalist and a naturalistic idealist. That Peirce's naturalism is at once realist and idealist lends support to viewing idealism as neither anti-realist nor anti-science. Dea and Haydon characterise Peirce's pragmatic maxim as an attempt to formalise 'the experimentalist disposition'. They then discuss Peirce's metaphysical naturalism, and trace connections between his famous injunction against blocking the path of inquiry, and the second tenet of 19th-century naturalism—that all of reality is, in principle, commensurable. For Dea and Haydon, while Peirce preceded the 20th-century baptism of naturalism, attending to the historical precursors of Peirce's naturalistic thought and to Peirce himself helps us understand the sources of contemporary philosophical naturalism.

In 'Common-sense and Naturalism', according to Mario De Caro, some of the main opponents of the strict naturalists are traditionally philosophers who assume that (i) barring special conditions, perception gives us access to the external world as it really is; (ii) middle-size objects have properties that are not identical to whatever microphysical properties constitute them; and (iii) empirically adequate scientific theories that appeal to unobservable entities may be useful heuristic tools, but are not true descriptions of the world. Among these philosophers (and barring some obvious differences between them) are most of the Aristotelians, Reid, James, Duhem, Austin, van Fraassen, and, in some relevant aspects, Husserl, G. E. Moore, Bergson, and Wittgenstein. In his chapter, De Caro argues that common-sense realists have excellent reasons for arguing against the reductive or eliminativist views of the strict naturalists regarding the common-sense view of the world, but they are unjustified in defending scientific anti-realism. De Caro contends that the most reasonable view is Putnam's form of pragmatist liberal naturalism, since it is realist in regard to both the common-sense and the scientific views of the world.

Gabriele Gava, in 'Peirce and Methodological Naturalism', flags two ambiguities in the term 'naturalism' that have consequences for how we should approach the question whether Peirce is a naturalist or not. As far as the first ambiguity is concerned, Gava claims asking in general whether Peirce is a naturalist seems unhelpful and potentially misleading. The risk is that the issue simply becomes that of putting a general label on Peirce, in a way that obfuscates his specific positions. As far as the second ambiguity is concerned, for Gava, even when we focus on one or a set of the issues that the question might involve, it seems that the question cannot be taken as having a clear 'yes' or 'no' answer. Rather, according to Gava, the task is to clearly represent Peirce's position on one topic and place it within (or without) the spectrum of positions that can plausibly be described as naturalist. The key question for Gava is where one ought to place Peirce's views with respect to different forms of methodologi-cal naturalism. Gava distinguishes 'moderate' methodological naturalism from 'extreme' methodological naturalism, and argues that while Peirce in 1877 defends a form of 'extreme' methodological naturalism, Peirce's position becomes more complex between the end of the 19th century and the beginning of the 20th century. For Gava, Peirce seems to endorse a form of 'extreme' methodological naturalism regarding the human sci-ences (excluding philosophy), while Peirce appears to be committed to an anti-naturalist view concerning the method of philosophy.

Willem deVries's 'Picturing: Naturalism and the Design of a More Ideal Truth' centres on how Sellars's notion of *picturing* plays a crucial role in his attempt to find a stable middle-ground between 'crass naturalism' and the 'sophisticated idealism' that flourished in the Germanic states between the publication of the first version of the *Critique of Pure Reason* in 1781 and Hegel's death in 1831. In his chapter, deVries tries not only to isolate those insights of the German Idealists that Sellars thought needed to be *permanent* parts of the philosophical tradition, but also to develop an argument for why Sellars thought he needed a special notion of a picturing relation that holds between (some) intentional represent-ings and the items they represent. For deVries, picturing should be best interpreted as a design-level provision (à la Dennett) that provides a nec-essary condition for the existence of properly intentional-level activity.

For Steven Levine in his chapter, 'Rethinking Sellars's Naturalism', per-haps the most difficult issue in Sellars's scholarship concerns the question of how normativity fits into a naturalistic picture of the world: on the one hand, Sellars takes it that the norms that articulate the framework of per-sons—the framework at the heart of the manifest image—are irreducible. On the other hand, Sellars is a scientific realist for whom the physical sci-ences are the ontological measure of all things. In an ideal scientific frame-work, there are no norms. So the question is: how can Sellars square the seeming indispensability of the normative with its apparent reducibility in an ideal scientific framework? In his chapter, Levine examines James O'Shea's answer to this question. Levine agrees with O'Shea's reading of Sellars's strategy to fit normativity into a naturalistic picture of the world. But he argues that this strategy cannot work because the notion of causal reduction at play in it admits of two interpretations, both of which lead to unacceptable theoretical consequences. The first, which interprets the concept of causal reduction in a weak way, leads to what O'Shea calls a 'separated-off' account of persons-in-the-world, while the second stronger interpretation leads to certain paradoxical conclusions.

David Macarthur's chapter, 'Pragmatic Naturalism: The Authority of Reason, The Agrippan Trilemma and the Significance of Philosophising *in medias res*', argues that the only hope for a satisfying response to the Problem of the Criterion in epistemology is if one disavows the inferentialist model of entitlement that it presupposes from a naturalistic normativist perspective. For Macarthur, both pragmatism and German Idealism are forms of normativism, that is, both involve commitments to a conception of rational normativity that is indispensable and not reducible to categories recognised by scientific naturalism. Given their joint commitment to normativism, then, one can construe the debate between pragmatism and German Idealism in terms of the Dummettian notion of competing *explanatory* (as opposed to *suasive*) arguments for normativism. For Macarthur, the German Idealist response to the Problem of the Criterion reveals how hard it is to respond to Agrippa's Trilemma if one accepts its account of entitlement and then tries to show that there is some sort of supernaturalist super-entitlement. As such, Macarthur endorses the pragmatist's normative naturalism as opposed to what he deems as the normative non-naturalism of German Idealism. Macarthur's chapter also aims to show how pragmatism was able to naturalise Kant's anti-foundationalist strategy for achieving rational authority. Crucially, moreover, Macarthur argues that scientific naturalism faces its *own* dilemma in confronting Agrippa's Trilemma: either scientific naturalism hopelessly tries to answer the problem by appeal to reliable processes we need know nothing about; or scientific naturalism attempts to block the regress by an appeal to nature to stop the regress. However, the latter strategy only makes the problem worse. For Macarthur, the issue of *responsibility for belief* cannot be avoided in these ways.

Notes

1. I think the approach of Finn Spicer (2011) and Alison Stone (2013) to naturalism as a *cluster concept* is helpful. Spicer, with support from Stone, identifies the following claims that make up the various strands of naturalism:

   1. Rejection of the idea of first philosophy.
   2. Belief that philosophy is continuous with the sciences.
   3. Disbelief in supernatural entities/processes.
   4. Physicalism about the mind.
   5. Opposition to non-naturalism about ethics/values.
   6. Rejection of a priorism.

   Given this way of understanding naturalism, then, we can assert the following: someone is a naturalist if they are committed to all six claims. However, as Stone correctly writes, "naturalism is also a matter of degree in that, for each strand of the cluster naturalism that a philosophy exhibits, it will exhibit that strand to greater or lesser degrees: for instance, one might uphold the continuity of science in stronger and weaker forms" (Stone 2013: 63).
   See also Ritchie (2008) and Giladi (2014a).

2. Alex Rosenberg puts forward a stronger claim here:

   > What is the world really like? It's fermions and bosons, and everything that can be made up of them, and nothing that can't be made up of them. All the facts about fermions and bosons determine or "fix" all the other

facts about reality and what exists in this universe or any other if, as physics may end up showing, there are other ones. Another way of expressing
this fact-fixing by physics is to say that all the other facts—the chemical,
biological, psychological, social, economic, political, cultural facts supervene on the physical facts and are ultimately explained by them. And if
physics can't in principle fix a putative fact, it is no fact after all.

(Rosenberg 2014: 19)

3. Cf. Papineau (1993).
4. Putnam 2004b: 59.
5. Cf. Stroud (1996).
6. Cf. Broad (2008).
7. McDowell 1994: 70.
8. See D'Oro (2017) for further on this.
9. https://philosophynow.org/issues/123/Defending_Humanistic_Reasoning.
10. Putnam 1992: x.
11. Stroud 1996: 48.
12. See Baker (2013, 2017).
13. See Bilgrami (2012).
14. See De Caro and Macarthur (2004a, 2004b).
15. See Dupré (1995, 2004).
16. See Ellis (2014).
17. See Haack (2007).
18. See Hornsby (2001).
19. See McDowell (1996).
20. See Price (2004).
21. See Putnam (1992, 2002, 2004b, 2012, 2015, 2016a).
22. See Scanlon (2003).
23. See Stroud (1996).
24. See Wiggins (2009).
25. De Caro and Macarthur 2010: 9.
26. Williams 2006: 211–212.
27. Ibid., 206.
28. Ibid., 212.
29. This takes us to the question about whether the scientific image is unified or disunified, which puts Rosenberg and Don Ross (the latter at least to some extent) on one side of the distinction, and Nancy Cartwright and Dupré on the other.
30. Gardner (2007) offers a similar critique, by arguing that anti-reductionism fails to supplant reductionism or just collapses into supernaturalism.
31. Neta 2007: 662.
32. "Scientism is, rather, a misunderstanding of the relations between philosophy and the natural sciences which tends to assimilate philosophy to the aims, or at least the manners, of the sciences" (Williams 2006: 182).
33.

Capitalist societies are distinguished from all others not by the problem
of their reproduction, that is, the reconciliation of social and system inte-
gration, but by the fact that they attempt to deal with what is in fact the
basic problem of all societies in a way that simultaneously entertains two
solutions which logically preclude one another: the differentiation or pri-
vatisation of production and its politicisation or socialization. . . . The two
strategies thwart and paralyse each other.

(Offe 1984: 85)

34. O'Shea 2009: 194.
35. *TCA* II: 364.
36. Habermas 1992: 444.
37. The Democratic Principle: "Only those statutes may claim legitimacy that can meet with the assent of all citizens in a discursive process of legislation that in turn has been legally constituted" (*BF&N*: 110).
38. *TSTPS*: 210.
39. *BF&N*: 380.
40. Mignolo 2011: 10.
41. Young 1990: 59.
42. Richard Rorty, John McDowell, and Robert Brandom are some of the most prominent of left-wing Sellarsians.
43. Patricia Churchland, Paul Churchland, Daniel Dennett, Ruth Millikan, William Lycan, and Jay Rosenberg are some of the most prominent right-wing Sellarsians.
44. Important figures here include Francisco J. Varela, Jean-Michel Roy, Jean Petitot, Bernard Pachoud, Dan Zahavi, and Shaun Gallagher.

Part I

Idealist Responses to Naturalism

1 Moral Natural Norms

A Kantian Perspective on Some Neo-Aristotelian Arguments

Katerina Deligiorgi

We are human beings. That is to say, we are an organic life form, living, breathing, moving, hurting and mending, doing and suffering beings. It would be an odd moral philosophy that loses sight of this fact. This chapter is concerned with a contemporary Aristotelian position in moral philosophy, defended originally by Philippa Foot (2001) and subsequently by Michael Thompson (2003, 2004, 2008), that aims to put this fact at the heart of our philosophical reflections about morality. This strand of neo-Aristotelianism[1] is of special interest from a Kantian perspective for a number of reasons. Both ethics are objectivist. Whereas Kantian ethics, at least as it is usually presented, is rationalist, absolutist and abstract, the neo-Aristotelian version has its roots in nature, addresses human beings as natural beings, and is attentive to the particulars of human life.[2] Perhaps the best way to capture the difference from which others flow is that nature and reason are not contraries in the neo-Aristotelian account; rather, it is natural for human beings to be rational, to reason about the good, and act on the basis of practical reasoning. From a contemporary perspective, this is particularly attractive because it allows for a naturalistic defence of moral value that fits within the broader trend towards 'liberal' or 'expansive' naturalism.[3] Finally, because natural goodness rather than moral legislation is the guiding notion, the problem of the authority of the moral law, a problem originally identified by Elisabeth Anscombe (1958) as being particularly tricky for Kant's moral philosophy, simply does not arise for Aristotelianism.

In summary, Aristotelian ethics has the resources to address a range of first- as well as second-order ethical questions precisely in those areas in which Kantian ethics is traditionally supposed to be weak. My aim in this chapter is to examine some of these questions, narrowing my remit to those concerning the nature of the good and the authority of norms. In particular, I want to motivate and sketch a non-naturalist Kantian response to the neo-Aristotelian challenge that targets specifically its meta-ethical and meta-normative naturalistic assumptions.[4]

I

The Idea of the Good

Kant begins his ethics with the good. Clearing the ground for a meta-physics of morals, he states that it is "impossible to think of anything at all in the world, or even beyond it, that could be considered good with-out limitation except a **good will**" (GW 4:393; emphasis in original). So before even philosophy starts properly, when the topic is simply common human reason, Kant asks his readers to think about a good that is "with-out limitation" (GW 4:393) and "absolutely good" (GW 4:394). The answer, 'good will', leads to the further question: 'what makes the will good?' to which Kant replies, it is not good on account of the "effects or accomplishes" (ibid.), but rather because of its form. The question then is how to characterise this form apart from saying that it is good. Kant's imagined interlocutor, someone endowed with common human reason, must be thinking of *something* when thinking of the good will *as* abso-lutely good. The idea of a will that can be 'good in itself' and favoured above everything else simply in itself (ibid.) seems slippery, however.

Not only does Kant not allow any content to be thought here, such as effects produced by the will, he gives no clues as to how to direct thinking about such a good; indeed he grants that there is something strange in this train of thought, which could be a "mere high-flown fantasy" (ibid.). Some would agree straightaway; abstracting the will from its "fitness to attain some proposed end" (ibid.) takes away from us the resources to think about the good. More seriously this abstraction signals a "break with the concept human",[5] because seeking to imagine a perfectly abstract willing as good willing means already imagining a disembodied willing and this is an early and decisive wrong turn.[6] I shall return to this shortly. First, I want to pursue another obvious line of attack.

In these opening lines of the *Groundwork*, Kant talks about the good as such, good without qualification, limitation, condition. This kind of talk, however, is possibly questionable and should be done away with. Follow-ing Geach (1956), Foot recommends an 'attributive' understanding of adjectives such as 'good' and 'bad'.[7] It is important to dwell on this point because it plays a foundational role in shaping Foot's position. Accepting Geach's argument is a first move intended to provide a further, more fine-grained analysis of the 'logical grammar' of moral evaluative terms.[8] This is a long-standing commitment. In 'Goodness and Choice' (1961), Foot develops an account of the good that is tied to function. She argues that there is a very large range of words which are not 'functional' in the sense that philosophers use—e.g. 'knife', 'pen', 'eye', 'root'—"whose meaning determines criteria of goodness".[9] Her examples include 'farmer', 'rider', 'liar', 'daughter', 'father'. The criteria of goodness in this latter category are not fixed by the use the thing is put to, but rather by the kind of interest we have in something and "what we expect from it".[10] This takes us towards the point that Thompson then develops about goodness having human form. Given its significance for both Foot and Thompson, it is important to attend to the original Geachian point.

Geach's target is the search for *the* good, principally exemplified in G. E. Moore's non-reductivism. Geach aims to show that 'good' behaves in a way that is not compatible with non-reductivism. Descriptive adjectives as in the sentence 'this is a red shoe' can be parsed as 'this is red' and 'this is a shoe'; attributive ones, such as 'this is a good horse' cannot be so parsed, because for 'good' ascriptions to be meaningful there need be always something to which they are attributed (' . . . is a good A', 'A' is a placeholder for a noun term). The argument is also applicable here, since I attribute to Kant the view that he has a good without qualification in his sights. Although it looks as if he is making attributive use of it, as in the good *will*, what guides the enquiry is the search for something that is good without qualification. 'Something' functions grammatically as placeholder for a noun term but conceptually the enquiry belongs with the tradition that searches for *the* good. So, the Geachian point still has a target in Kant. The way to respond to this challenge is to show that the idea of the good is conceptually well-defined, that it has a shape by which we can recognise it. This is exactly what Kant does when he tries to show that the good can be a form and connects the form of goodness with duty. Duty captures the common moral notion that moral goodness is about doing the right thing just because it is the right thing to do. Our pre-philosophical moral life then allows us to capture a form of goodness that is not dependent on anything external to it, such as inducements or consequences. Therefore, the thought of goodness we started with is not empty, or fantastical. It is rather common. It may be that Kant's further attempt to specify this thought through the notion of law as an elucidation of the principle of duty goes wrong. But, so far we have no reason to abandon the path Kant opens for us.

We may decide to part ways when confronted with the issue of locating the form of goodness. Foot aims to show that "evaluations of human will and action share a conceptual structure with evaluations of characteristics and operations of other living things, and can only be understood in these terms";[11] and again: "moral judgment of human actions and dispositions is one example of a genre of evaluation itself actually characterised by the fact that its objects are living beings".[12] The point is forcefully made by Thompson, who argues that what keeps us "from accepting a naïve Aristotelianism or a practical naturalism or a natural goodness theory" of the sort Foot presents is the idea that the concept *human* does not have the right sort of relation to knowledge to "count as anything relevant to fundamental ethical theory".[13] This is why he thinks Kant "is so emphatic about dispensing with (what I am calling) the concept *human* within practical philosophy; it is something alien, impure, empirical" that must be replaced with "the *pure* concepts of a *rational being in general* or of a *person*".[14]

To address these points, I propose to proceed as follows. First, I want to respond to the negative claim implicit in Thompson's discussion of Kant and it concerns Kant's motivation for the move to pure ethics. Once this is cleared, and it is shown that it is not excess fastidiousness with the messiness of humanity that moves Kant, I will turn to Foot's positive doctrine about natural goodness, taking into account Thompson's eloquent elaboration of it, on the importance of the 'concept of human', of keeping in our sights the life form that has arisen "on this planet, quite contingently, in the course of evolutionary history".[15]

Kant explains the move to pure moral philosophy and the need for such a move in different but compatible ways. In the *Groundwork* he presents it as a result of a *"natural dialectic"* (GW 4:405); it is not speculation, he writes, but "practical grounds themselves" that push us to step from our common practical assumptions to "the field of practical philosophy" (ibid.). The natural dialectic consists in this, that on the one hand we have the notion of goodness that fits our various purposes and then also the notion of doing the right thing just because it is the right thing to do. This latter, Kant says, is perfectly perspicuous to common human reason and without need for philosophy; common human reason distinguishes what is good and what is evil in a way that fits this notion of duty (cf. GW 4:404). We may challenge Kant that he has not shown that *all* such evaluations are indeed translatable into the vocabulary of duty. I think this is true. However, if we think of duty as a stand-in for the "condition of a will that is good in itself, the worth of which surpasses all else" (GW 4:403), then duty and ordinary judgments of moral goodness do seem to coincide in that they capture goodness that shapes behaviour that can go against someone's interest at least narrowly conceived. The thought is that there is a good that is not translatable by saying 'in my interests', and which more generally does not take the form of qualified goods. Happiness promoting goods are of that sort. This is merely a conceptual distinction at this juncture, and it is a conceptual distinction Kant detects in ordinary moral thinking.

So why leave this happy place? What Kant thinks creates the need for philosophy—which, like Socrates makes common reason "attend to its own principle" (GW 4:404)—is what happens when one "feels within himself a powerful counterweight to all the commands of duty" (GW 4:405). If we stay at the level of common reason, there are solutions to this; we can either train ourselves better or try to fit better with the moral teachings we have been given, by attending to exemplars and so on. However, none of these addresses the philosophical worry about the ground of morality and the validity and authority of its commands. So practical philosophy is introduced to help us learn about the 'source of its principle' (ibid.). This is not the full explanation of why Kant then adduces an *a priori* ground for moral laws, but at least it shows that it is not the idea Thompson (2004, 2013) attributes to him, namely that the natural kind 'human' is alien and external and so unable to contribute anything fundamental to ethical theory. The concern, rather, is with identifying a domain of a goodness that is moral and can serve as "ground", "source" (GW 4:405) or "basis" (MM 6:125) for such good. That the search turns to an *a priori* and not natural domain has to do with the question of authority of morality and the nature of agency, issues to which Foot is highly alert as I will now try to show.

Let us now turn to examine Foot's positive proposal. In *Natural Goodness*, Foot offers a systematic argument for the thesis about moral evaluations being a species of evaluations of natural goodness and defect in a human being. In what follows, I will reconstruct the basic steps. The first step is to say that moral evaluations connect to ideas of goodness that gain their meaning—and sense—from human nature. The point of this is to alert us to the distinctive grammar of goodness judgments that apply to living beings. Things can be good or defective with respect to what they are supposed to do; living beings can be good or defective with respect to the sort of being they are supposed to be. Foot wants us to attend to the set of judgments we pass on individual living beings with respect to their life form, so they can be good or defective in some such respect. Specifically the evaluation of the goodness of individual living beings is possible without reference to the aims and interests of other beings. Such evaluation is natural, given the assumptions so far, and, following the previous point, it is also intrinsic.

To elaborate: the evaluation is natural because it relies on what Foot, after Anscombe, calls "Aristotelian necessities".[16] These necessities are expressed in sentences about living beings, their habits, and life cycles that need not be true of each individual yet are true of the natural history story one wants to tell of the living being in question. Thompson, who has given a detailed analysis and defence of this species of necessity, calls these sentences "Aristotelian categoricals",[17] and Foot has a similar account.[18] Further, the evaluation is also intrinsic because it relates to goodness or badness with respect to the life cycle of the individual we judge. Life cycles include facts about nourishment and reproduction, from which norms are derived that characterise the life-form, e.g. co-operative hunting in wolves.[19] In this way, we arrive at norms that are explicable "in terms of facts about things belonging to the natural world".[20] This broad schema of natural normativity is recommended because it allows us to make sense of judgments of goodness through interrelated notions of function and purpose that we commonly extend to non-moral evaluations of natural beings. In the case of human beings, the evaluations do not refer to features of the individual, say her ears or feet, but to the dispositions of her will. Foot is in agreement with Kant here. She states that "moral goodness is goodness of the will",[21] where by 'will' she does not mean a piece of human mechanics, like a valve, say, which pushes us to action, but rather a manifestation of practical rationality. Will is a term that captures how humans act, which is by having some reason to do things. Natural goodness sets the context for the employment of practical rationality or, what amounts to the same thing, for exercises of the will.

This is the position in essence. I will now discuss briefly John McDowell's response to this, partly because of its importance for any discussion of Foot's views and partly because it helps bring into the argument a certain Kantian family of views.

McDowell's basic point is also the starting point for Christine Korsgaard's *Sources of Normativity*, namely that rational reflection is both a condition for posing normative questions and also the source of our continuing difficulties in settling with an answer:

> normativity is a problem for human beings because of our reflective nature. Even if we are inclined to believe that an action is right and even if we are inclined to be motivated by that fact, it is always possible for us to call our beliefs and motives into question.
>
> (Korsgaard 1996: 49, also 119)[22]

McDowell's argument is important because it picks on a point that is internal to Foot's account, namely that humans have practical rationality. McDowell says that "we cannot make sense of *logos* as manifesting itself in agency without seeing it as selecting between options, rather than simply going along with what is going to happen anyway" (McDowell 1998: 170). He illustrates the point with the example of the speaking reasoning wolves, what the wolves 'acquire is the power of speech, the power of giving expression to conceptual capacities that are rationally interlinked in ways reflected by what it makes sense to give as a reason for what' (McDowell 1998: 169).[23] Practical rationality works in a context of reasons in the plural; having acquired reason, a wolf 'can contemplate alternatives, he can step back from the natural impulse and direct critical scrutiny at it', he can ask 'Why should I do this?'. Once *this critical question has arisen*, McDowell argues, the most pertinent question then seems to be, how can it help to appeal to what wolves need? 'Why should I pull my weight?', says our reflective wolf, wondering whether to idle through the hunt but still grab his share of the prey. Suppose we respond, truly enough: 'Wolves need to pool their energies, if their style of hunting is to be effective'. If our wolf has stepped back from his natural impulse and taken up a critical stance why should what we say impress him?[24] The point of the story is that though it is possible to include in a natural history of humanity practical rationality, once you have accounted for its functioning, then you have allowed for a gap to emerge between the individual who makes use of his reason and the natural goodness that is explicable in terms of facts about things that belong to the natural world.

McDowell and Foot share a conception of living nature that is not just a sum of biological facts. These facts are the substratum for the exercise of skills and abilities that can be exercised more or less well.[25] Foot is not unaware of the point about reasons McDowell raises. She says that "while animals for the good (thing) *that they see*, humans go for *what they see as good*",[26] and she continues that human beings have the power to *see grounds* for acting "and if told that they should do one thing rather than another they can ask *why* they should".[27] She also goes as far as to acknowledge that the "[h]uman good is *sui generis*".[28] However, she also insists that there is a "natural-history story [about how human beings] achieve this good".[29] But this 'achieving' of the good, even if there is a natural history story that gives content to goodness, is not the same as *seeing* in the natural history story grounds for acting. McDowell's point is that 'reason' is a normative notion and if we are concerned with normative force, then facts about what rational wolves or humans need to survive and flourish need not tell us what individuals in either species ought to do; in short, the ought is guided by a conception of norm that does not follow goodness.[30] The worry is not about how facts bear on goodness but how goodness bears on norms.

Let me explain. When Foot tackles the question 'Why should I do this?',[31] she sees it primarily as a question of how objective evaluative standards bear on individual first-person normative perplexity or outright scepticism. But the issue I think McDowell is raising here is of a rather different sort, namely that norms, on Foot's account, are just means for bringing about the good. In that sense, and that sense alone, she has not revised her original thought about the hypotheticity of imperatives, given some good (now of course including objective natural sorts of good, goods that tend to matter to us) the norm is just a way to reach it. By contrast, if I read McDowell correctly, he is suggesting that norms have a life apart from their connection to goodness. This is why when he develops his own positive views, he thinks of norms becoming visible to us and having authority over us within a certain culture or way of life they help constitute. Following this line, morality itself would be a *sui generis* institution that generates oughts that are connected to but not identical to the human good. Because of this McDowell's neo-Aristotelianism is not vulnerable to the sort of criticisms standardly levelled against Foot's natural goodness position, namely that virtues do not promote fitness; such criticisms show the need for a clear boundary between substantive conceptions of goodness that can be drawn from the natural history story and formal conceptions tied to norms human beings follow, revise, contest, and so on.

Thompson (2003) addresses just this issue, albeit briefly, when he discusses what he calls "logical Footianism".[32] He appears to be tackling head on the idea of instrumentality. He denies however that Foot only allows for such norms and considers this to be an extreme Humean position.[33] Instead, he argues that there is no *a priori* way of saying what "routes or forms that the practical application of thought can take in a practically reasoning animal" and that the idea of practical reasoning simply demands that someone does A "on the strength of a consideration about doing A".[34] What form these considerations take is left open, the sorts of ought and should that are available to practical reasoners are context specific. I do not think this is a satisfactory position. It may be a good position to have on the nature of ought because it cleaves between functional and agential interpretations of the ought.[35] However, it is not clear that this general position helps with the moral ought: the criticism is that moral oughts have a way of slipping out of their moorings in conceptions of goodness and so they need special attention.[36] When Foot (2004) addresses Humeanism she is much clearer about the target, and much closer to Kant in fact. She argues that there are different types of practical rationality not reducible to each other. The first two are recognisable types of what Kant calls hypothetical imperatives: there is the 'Humean' or 'neo-Humean' "that refers all rational decisions to the base of the agent's present desires",[37] and the 'prudential' that refers to broader conceptions of self-interest and the agent's good.[38] Foot's aim, just like Kant's aim which I sketched earlier, is to make space for a third type, which is of special relevance to morality, the normativity involved when we "*speak of reasons for doing a certain action or not doing it*".[39] She then argues that these reasons have their roots in the natural history story of human beings and refers the reader to the idea of natural goodness she develops in her book.[40]

If the dialectic I presented so far is on the right lines, then the natural history story of goodness can indeed provide content for evaluative judgments and for exercises of practical rationality. However, it faces a problem when it comes to getting to grips with the specific normativity of the moral terms 'should' and 'should not'. Another way of putting this is that the problem is not a problem of content but of form. Within the neo-Aristotelian tradition I have been discussing there is talk of a form of life, but the emphasis is on the sorts of contents that make the life good for such-and-such living being, and in the case of humans the good that informs their practical reasoning. The talk of 'form' in other words takes us to a very abstract notion of goodness of the living being in question, a notion that can be filled by whatever life necessitates or a flourishing life necessitates. And I made the point that ought and good—even at that general level—can come apart. They can come together if the ought can connect with an idea of goodness that is formal. This is the direction Kant is going: his insistence on law and ought is not a kind of rule fetishism, but rather the idea that the moral law, or better, an ought that has the characteristic of being categorical, that is, for all rational beings and not admitting of exceptions, is expressive of the moral good, a good without limitation.

But, it has to take an imperatival form because it is the form the good takes *for* human beings, that is, for finite beings capable of practical rationality but who also have all sorts of other ends to do with their current desires or longer term prudential aims. So, the idea of a moral law in the form of a categorical imperative is intended to help identify or clear out a space for ends which Kant calls ends of reason, that are ends proper to moral beings. But, going in this direction seems to place Kantian ethics at the crosshairs of Anscombe's criticism about law and authority.

II

The Idea of Law

Anscombe (1958) offers a subtle diagnosis of modern moral philosophy, because of her brevity of expression, some care is needed in reconstructing her argument. On my reading, she is opening a two-front attack: on the one hand, she shows that a moral philosophy that directs us to care for the consequences of our actions only risks leaving us with an ethics that is conditional, allowing no sense of something that is simply wrong to do full stop; on the other hand, she argues that the notion of the 'ought' current in modern moral philosophy, while it has force, just like the prescriptivists and emotivists believe, it has no moral authority; it is like a verdict that "retains its psychological effect, but not its meaning".[41]

I want to start by examining the notion of the force of the ought. One thing Anscombe can mean by force in this context is motivating force or some such notion that speaks to the belief/desire debate. Taking a step back to consider her contribution to this debate, an obvious point of reference is her use of the metaphor of the direction of fit.[42] In her description of the contrast between a man using a shopping list and a detective jotting down what the man puts in his shopping basket she appears to endorse a recognisably Humean psychology, in which beliefs aim at fitting with the world (the detective's role) whereas desires aim at realisation (the shopper's role). Such interpretation is not decisive, however. The broader context of this brief discussion is given by the aim to say something about actions that is specific to them and so say something about human behaviour such that it is not just like any other causal phenomenon (which is not to say whether it is non-causal or anything of the sort).

This project is perfectly consistent with the moral point she makes about consequentialist ethics, but seen from the other side so to speak: the point is that a certain kind of naturalist commitment only allows us to look at behaviour as a cause for certain consequences, which leave out what we might want to have in view, when trying to understand what someone is doing, namely the practical attitudes of the person.[43] If we now look at the direction of fit remarks with this larger context in mind, we can see that the initial Humean resemblance fades away to some extent, at least insofar as we may not speak of individual desires as aiming at this or that, but of desiring as something that makes sense if we open our eyes to things such as the practical attitude of a person who has certain ends in view and is guided by them in doing whatever it is they are doing, when they act intentionally.

Having now bracketed the motivational or narrowly psychological interpretation of the notion of the force of the ought, we may now turn to what I think Anscombe's real topic is, the authority of the ought. This comes out clearly in her criticism of Kant. Her argument is basically this: Kant's attempt to secularise the ought, to transpose legislation from divine to human agency, is not working because self-legislation is a bogus notion. And it is bogus precisely because it is short on authority. If I can make the law, I can also break it: I'm above it. The whole point of the authority of the law, however, is that it works if I am *under* it. The relation is not supposed to be symmetrical.[44] This is a perfectly good point. I will now outline Kant's position in order to show how it is not touched by this version of the criticism.

Kant is alert to the question of the authority of moral demands. This is what drives the argument that the ground of moral laws must be *a priori*. Understanding Kant's apriority claims then will serve two functions in the context of this discussion: first it ties up with the earlier discussion about the search for a non-natural ground for the form of moral goodness, and so it speaks to Thompson's argument; and second it explains how Kant aims to secure the authority of the moral ought, so as not to make it a matter of mere caprice.

The way Kant presents the relation of grounding in the first *Critique* is by separating the moral ought from anything in nature: "The **ought** expresses a species of necessity and a connection with grounds which does not occur anywhere else in the whole of nature" (A547/B575; emphasis in original).[45] This is of a piece with Kant's justification for the need for a metaphysics of morals, a pure philosophy of morals and with the specific claim that moral commands have *a priori* grounds. I shall isolate the apriority claim and seek to explain what is at stake here, with a view to justifying this move.

Apriority is a claim that moral commands are moral as a matter of a *sui generis* primitive fact, what Kant calls a fact of reason. It is a fact of reason, because of the nature of the reasons morality gives us, which are objective in the sense that they have objective form, which is to say that they are universalisable and holding for all rational beings. If we follow Kant then, or at least this interpretation of his argument, we have a top-down authority relation between a primitive ground, which is not opaque, but on the contrary has rational shape and is accessible by individual rational thinkers, and a grounded. The authority question is separate both from that concerning the goodness of the law. What Kant is saying effectively is that morality generates reasons for us to do things. The positive argument does not give us any more than that. Kant is not providing us with the *a priori* ground. He simply describes the relation of ground to grounded and argues that it is not a brute fact but a fact of reason. Reason gives us both the shape of authoritative commands—they are obligating unconditionally—and connects these with the formal idea of goodness, as I argued previously.

Where does self-legislation come into this account then? Self-legislation, or more accurately, rational self-legislation, is a metaphor for rational order of moral norms.[46] Essential for understanding self-legislation is the claim that, in moral matters, "reason does not follow the order of things as they present themselves in appearance, but frames for itself with perfect spontaneity an order [*eine eigene Ordnung*] of its own according to ideas" (A548/B576). Of course, insofar as they reason morally and try to figure out what to do, individual agents self-legislate in an etiolated sense of the word, that is, they check whether their reasons can be a law for all agents. Individual moral self-legislation is a co-legislation and drives home the idea that we are citizens in the moral commonwealth, not kings or dictators.

Still, one may argue, what is special about the fact of reason with respect to the authority question? It is fine to answer Anscombe's criticism by pointing at reason as legislating, but why reason rather than nature? In other words, how about Thompson and Foot's points: why should reason frame for itself its own moral order rather than turn to nature and seek guidance there? I think for this we need to look at the negative version of the argument about apriority, namely the claim that the ground for the moral ought, that by virtue of which the law is a moral law, is not reducible to natural facts. Here is how one may challenge the Kantian view: Kant, especially in the first *Critique* passages I have been quoting, is assuming a value-free conception of nature as a domain of efficient causes. Such an assumption is not necessary; worse, it is misleading when it comes to living beings. Here then is a root problem with the original grounding argument.

While it is true that one of the notions of nature Kant presents fits the accusation, it is also true that this is far from the only notion he holds and defends. Not only is he aware of teleological judgments when it comes to living beings, but he also seeks to incorporate them systematically into his philosophy. In principle then, functional naturalistic explanations, where some features of the living being or its life cycle are judged to be good for something, are available to him. That the ground of moral demands is not to be sought there is justified by the conceptual distinction he makes between what is in the interests of the agent (or the species) in the widest sense and what is moral. It is not that Kant would be unable to entertain the idea that there is natural goodness—this is exactly how he thinks of happiness—it is just that he thinks this is the wrong *kind* of goodness for morality.

I now want to return to Anscombe's argument and see how it stands with respect to this interpretation of Kant and self-legislation and to the earlier discussion of Foot. Anscombe introduces the point about divine command to point at a deficit in current uses of 'ought', the lack of proper appreciation of the authority of morality yields commands that are at best *pro tanto*. This is a very Kantian thought as I hope to have shown. What I want to discuss now is whether divine authority adds something to the argument that the Kantian picture I have presented lacks. There are two ways of going here: one is to take Anscombe's use of divine command as a model solution to the problem of authority and either criticise it or show that it is not mandatory; the other is to focus on her recommendation that we learn from Aristotle.

One area that the Kantian apriority argument, the irreducibility to a fact of reason, may have an advantage over divine command, is that these norms are accessible to reason and amenable to rational reflection, so the ought relates intelligibly with the form of goodness. Stephen Darwall (2006) offers an interpretation of Puffendorf's solution to the problem of divine command, which he argues is also relevant to Anscombe. In order to distinguish between moral obligation and coercion, Darwall argues, "Pufendorf required an account of moral agents' distinctive capacity for self-censure from a shared second-person and its role in free rational deliberation. But this also effectively assumes that to be accountable to God, moral agents must be accountable to themselves".[47] He takes this point to be sufficient to turn Anscombe's claim 'on its head': while morality is indeed inconceivable without "addressable demands",[48] these are not divine demands, or they are divine to the extent that human beings "can enter (individually) into moral community with God only if we have the authority to form a moral community ourselves as mutually accountable free and rational persons".[49] I think Darwall is right in pointing at the relevance of moral community—and I sought to gesture in that direction when explaining how self-legislation works at the individual level. However, his point about coercion is convincingly refuted by Robert Stern, who argues, on Anscombe's behalf, that virtues are precisely the sorts of things that make sense "prior to God's law-giving" and so "justify his authority".[50]

It remains to ask then whether divine command is necessary for securing authority. Sabina Lovibond argues that the non-theist need not be worse off than the theist. In the context of a sympathetic reading of Anscombe, Lovibond uses Cavafy to show what it takes to "keep the commandments of morality" without thinking of God.[51] The exact same point can be made in a Kantian context; what is needed is recognition of the existence of a *special* domain of norms that are not like other norms, in that their command is categorical. Categoricity implies a number of things about the distinctive shape of such demands, i.e. they are unconditional, their relation to agents, bearing on their deliberations and decisions, claim to be taken seriously and so on.

Let us now turn to the recommendation that we turn to Aristotle. It seems to me that Anscombe, and, following her, Foot look to Aristotelean ethics in order to have substantive things to say about what we ought to do without. Still there is a subtle difference of emphasis between Anscombe's and Foot's approach to Aristotle. Anscombe is interested in alerting her contemporaries to a rich resource substantive normative ethics that does not seek to hide the modern problem of the authority of moral norms behind empty invocations of 'law' (empty because they lack an authoritative Law-giver). In contrast, for Foot, Aristotelian ethics can help us reconnect with the ways in which we think about goodness in general and also re-align ourselves with the idea of the good of living beings. That is, irrespective of where we stand on the issue of the role of God in ethics, Aristotle can give us a context in which to use so-called 'thick' concepts, such as 'just', or 'unjust' and so on, and so help us say something about what we should be doing morally besides calculating outcomes, the relative merits of action in accordance with their foreseen or foreseeable consequences.

This is why, I take it, Anscombe argues that instead of thinking of being bound, or obligated, to do such and such, we can think, with Aristotle's help, of failures of action as instances of *hamartanein* of "missing the moral mark" (Anscombe 1958: 30).[52] The question is what happens if we keep the Aristotelian thinking about goodness without the divine command. My concluding point in the previous section, which is now made more vivid in the present context, is that while Foot recognises and argues forcefully for a form of practical rationality that is neither hypothetical/instrumental nor prudential/interest-based, it is not obvious how natural goodness can sustain it. This leaves Kantian ethics in a relatively strong position on this count. In addition, if we take seriously Kant's conception of the law as given here rather as mere historical leftover that is reduced to individual self-determination, then it would appear that there are other ethical environments not necessarily ruled by God that can account for authoritative moral commands.[53]

In the final section, I turn to the deeper issue raised by McDowell about rational reflection and whether it is in fact damaging for the argument about authority I sketched here.

III

Reason and Reasons

The traditional concern with Kantian ethics is its non-naturalism. I tried to show that there is nothing 'queer' or 'spooky' about the anti-naturalistic position I attributed to Kant. I want now briefly to consider a naturalistic Kantian ethics such as that defended by Korsgaard to show its proximity to Foot's naturalistic Aristotelianism. This will help to address an issue that can arise from the previous discussion, namely that for beings endowed with rational deliberative abilities, reasons shall always appear in the plural and such plurality does not fit the appeal to reason in the singular as a ground for moral demands. Strictly speaking, this is not a concern that features in Foot or Thompson. Still it is relevant to the broader discussion, because of the important role that pure reason plays in Kant's ethics, a role that I sought to defend and which is integral to the non-naturalist meta-ethical and meta-normative elements of the Kantian position, as presented here.

Korsgaard's naturalism consists mainly in her rejection of the grounding trajectory I sketched. This is motivated by an acceptance of the sort of metaphysical commitments popularised by expressivists, though not unique to them, namely that there are no facts that are prior and ought to guide our deliberation about what to do. There are facts that are relevant to our moral deliberations, those that Korsgaard counts as formative of our practical identities, but they are subject to rational reflection which is fundamentally about picking reasons that enable one to move on, and, in later writings, constitute oneself as agent. Not just anything will do, however, in this effort at self-constitution; what matters is that we apply principles and ultimately the moral law. My aim in outlining this basic thought, which of course Korsgaard (1996, 2009) develops and defends with great subtlety, is to show a parallel with Foot.[54] It is conceivable that an agent may constitute herself on the basis of principles without making the further move to the idea of a moral law. What happens if an agent does this? She is not a non-agent, because ex hypothesis she uses principles, it is just that they need not be moral principles. That is, it is perfectly possible to be acting with some good in view, without any particular orientation or care even for a specifically moral good. How can we appeal to such an agent to make them see this? In some versions of her argument, Korsgaard seems to answer that if reflection goes deep enough then it shall reach moral form. But this would mean that moral form is ultimately a conceptual necessity for agency. This has not been shown however, and a good thing too, since on both Kantian and Aristotelian ethics *the form of goodness, and the ought that is intelligibly connected with it, reaches out to us but it is not just us.*[55] Whereas naturalism appears equipped to do justice to this objectivist thought, its limitation in both Korsgaard and Foot is that there is nothing in our form of life that makes morality a necessary feature of it. Our form of life could have evolved without any conception of or orientation to a moral form of goodness.

Is Kant justified in putting his faith in reason, though? McDowell writes about freedom of action as essentially a freedom of choice between options—what Kant calls *Willkür*. He says: "freedom of action as inextricably connected with a freedom that is essential to conceptual thought".[56] The point on which I want to focus is that we find ourselves with certain abilities, connections, impressions, and so on and then we reflect and once we reflect we think of possibilities, of options. But, options and possibilities are not categorical and unconditional things. So maybe the Kantian position is not better off here than the alternatives. I will answer this in a roundabout way starting with the role of practical reasoning in Foot and Thompson.

I wrote at the start that the role of practical reasoning in neo-Aristotelian ethics is one of the points in its favour; this is because we do not face a problematic relation to some external standard we have to meet. Aristotle, on Anscombe's interpretation, gives us a good way of thinking about what it takes for humans to do things *intentionally*: we are practical thinkers, we do things for reasons. This is something that Aristotle tries to capture in his account of practical syllogism, which is both reconstructive of how one goes about doing things, so that they have an answer to give if asked 'why did you do this?' and it is also action guiding when one has to put some thought into what one is to do, so they consider different ways of attaining the end they have. Thompson (2013) shows why this is an advantageous position to have when it comes to moral matters because you do not need to apprehend some form of the good in order to act well, human goodness comes with the assurance that what it is to be human is known through being human.

Let us put to one side the earlier worry about our form of life to have developed without regard for goodness. After all, here we are now doing moral philosophy and inheritors of a rich tradition of thinking about moral goodness. Here is the problem though: Aristotle describes practical syllogisms as "syllogisms of things to be done have a starting-point, viz. 'since the end, or what is best, is such-and-such', whatever that may be" (*NE* II 12, 1144a31–3). The significance of this quote is that we already have the end in view. Practical syllogism is not about choice of ends. If we have the end, then we can deliberate strategically, contextually, defeasably about reasons. The reason why this is a problem is that, if we follow the authority-categoricity-reason line of thought, then what we want is not a model of strategic reasoning; what we want is to pick ends that are in accordance with reason in the singular, that is, the reason that issues to us categorical demands, the reason that grounds our distinctly moral conception of goodness. This is what Kant seeks to give us with the formulations of the categorical imperative and its distinction from the various forms of hypothetical imperatives (including prudential ones).

I want to conclude with a word about the Martians that seem so troublesome to Thompson (2004). Here is a different way of looking at Kant's rational legislative ambitions: when it comes to following reason's command, individual self-legislators are, as I said before, bound by their context; specifically they address others whom they recognise as members of their moral community. What is gained by labelling them all 'rational'? It sounds like ethical empire building so when those Martians—or maybe angelic hosts—materialise in our lonely planet we can all know where we stand.[57] I beg to differ. I think the underlying thought, which is also crucial to understanding the universalisation test, is that who is to count as a member of our moral community is not given; rational being is not a natural kind or at least it is not something stamped on our hide so we can tell who is rational just by looking. This is where rational reflective doubt plays a positive role: reason asks us not to take for granted its constituency, those who have a claim on our attention and can be expected to answer back when we set off pursuing the ends we stringently examined and decided that they are moral. Reason here guards us against becoming complacent. Maybe no Martians will come and no angelic hosts will manifest among us, but we have wronged many in the past and continue so to do, those we consider and those we have considered not our own. So maybe in order to lead a moral human life we cannot rest content with just the human form, maybe we need to keep the door that reason wedges open so as not to be left with a diminished form of the human.

Notes

1. Thompson calls his view 'naïve Aristotelianism' (2008). Foot in the early 'Virtues and Vices' paper sees herself as part of a fresh movement in analytic moral philosophy that concerns itself with virtues, citing Geach and von Wright, and argues that Aristotle and especially Aquinas can offer valuable resources to think about these matters (Foot 1978: 1). Anscombe (1958) is an obvious point of reference. For a philosophical treatment of this conceptual family see Vogler (2013).
2. This is a description of Kant's ethics, which I endorse; at the same time, I hope to show that these characteristics are defensible and not just useful as critical targets.
3. The term 'liberal naturalism' is used in this sense by Putnam (2016), though antecedents can be found in Stroud (1996) 'expansive' naturalism. For discussion, see De Caro and Macarthur (2010).
4. There is by now a long tradition of Kantian commentary that focuses on substantive issues, and I have made my own contribution to this, partly inspired by pioneers such as Herman (1996) and Baron (1996). For a systematic, thorough, and practically detailed argument, see Varden (2018).
5. Thompson 2013: 704.
6. Compare Aristotle's opening of the *Nicomachean Ethics*: "Every craft and every inquiry, and likewise every action and every pursuit [or, better, choice, *proairesis*], are thought to aim at some good; for which reason the good has rightly been declared to be that at which all things aim" (*NE* I, 1094a).
7. Foot 2001: 3.
8. Ibid., p. 3.
9. Foot 1978: 137.
10. Ibid., p. 139.
11. Foot 2001: 5.
12. Ibid., p. 3.
    Foot's naturalism, originally at least, does not appear to be motivated by the usual attractions of naturalism, chiefly avoiding supernaturalism (see e.g. Stroud 1996). Rather, she is interested in showing that moral evaluations

belong to a larger family of evaluations of "natural goodness and defect in living beings" (Foot 2001: 3). This is also obvious in Foot's early work, in which Aristotelean and Aquinian notions of goodness and virtue are not sought out explicitly for the purpose of constructing a naturalistic ethics but because they seem to provide better answers to moral questions than alternatives (see e.g. 'Virtues and Vices' and 'Goodness and Choice'). The concern with avoiding supernaturalism seems to be more of a worry for McDowell than for Foot.

13. Thompson 2013: 704.
14. Ibid., p. 704.
15. Thompson 2004: 12.
16. Foot 2001: 15.
17. Thompson 2008: 29.
18. Cf. Foot 2001: 29.
19. Cf. ibid., p. 34.
20. Ibid., p. 37.
21. Ibid., p. 14.
22. C. Korsgaard 1996: 49. See also 119.
    Korsgaard goes on to say that this is the reason we are pushed to do moral philosophy. While the point resembles Kant's, it is not Kant's. Kant speaks of moral doubt arising in a context in which we feel the pull of contrary inclinations. This doubt may be called self-serving from a moral point of view, but more benignly it is a temptation to wheel and deal when it comes to moral matters doing what suits us because 'maybe there is nothing special about doing the right thing; maybe there is no overarching right thing I ought to be doing'. The difference is subtle but important because this latter enquiry leads to a justification of the nature of moral demands whereas the 'why should I do this?' which Kant also addresses leads to a justification of the authority of moral demands in relation to the agent to whom they are addressed. I think Kant's point is rather closer to what Foot calls a 'tight corner' (Foot 2004: 1), though her example of the 'Farm Boy from the Sudetenland' does not illustrate this, on the evidence she cites from the letter she uses from the anonymous farm boy, the young man seems remarkably clear about what is to be done, why it should be done, and at peace with his choice; he possesses enviable clarity of vision and calm.
23. Cf.: "Suppose some wolves acquire reason. I mean this as something one might say in Greek with the word 'logos'. What the wolves acquire is the power of speech, the power of giving expression to conceptual capacities that are rationally interlinked in ways reflected by what it makes sense to give as a reason for what" (McDowell 1998: 169).
24. Cf. McDowell 1998: 171.
25. 'Substratum' is not quite right because it implies something neutral and rigid, whereas natural traits can affect the exercise of skills and abilities. In humans, for example, pathological forgetfulness would make it very hard to keep promises. Where the boundary is between, say, between purely physical facts and normative facts, is an issue that Foot does not address.
26. Foot 2001: 56.
27. Ibid., p. 56.
28. Ibid., p. 51.
29. Ibid., p. 51.
30. Cf: 'Reason does not just open our eyes to nature, as members of the animal species we belong to; it also enables and even obliges us to step back from it, in a way that puts its bearing on our practical problems into questions.

With the onset of reason, then, the nature of the species abdicated from a previously unquestionable authority over the behaviour of the individual animal' (McDowell 1998: 172). McDowell's own way of addressing this issue is through the concept of second nature which "open[s] our eyes to reasons" (McDowell 1996: 88) and allows us to navigate a properly normative domain (and therefore assert, reject, assess, comply with reasons). A similar point is made by Rosalind Hurstouse on the importance of upbringing, which I take it is a kind of becoming initiated into the normative domain properly speaking, not just how virtuous people do things, but that there is such a thing to which virtuous people respond, namely moral oughts; see Hursthouse 1999: 79–80.

31. Cf. Foot 2001: 52–65.
32. Thompson 2003: 2.
33. Ibid., p. 4.
34. Ibid., p. 4.
35. I take Kant to have a typically agential conception, the ought is something that addresses and needs uptake by agents, and I take Judith Jarvis Thompson (2008) to have a functional conception; see (Thompson 2008: 211) especially.
36. I think this is a point that Darwall also makes when he says "[m]oral *obligations, I* argue, are not just what there are good (or even compelling) moral reasons for us to do; they are what members of the moral community have the authority to demand that we do, what we are accountable to one another and ourselves for doing" (Darwall 2007: 891). However, our right to use the notion of obligation needs to be established or at least something more needs saying about it. I do this in the following section, where I also look at some other points Darwall raises in connection to Anscombe.
37. Foot 2004: 3.
38. Cf. ibid., p. 3.
39. Ibid., p. 3.
40. Cf. ibid., p. 9.
41. Anscombe 1958: 33.
42. Viz. Anscombe 2000: 56.
43. We might even want to include here for moral appraisal other less well-defined items, that are not to do with overt choices or deliberations with a view to make a choice, items which Iris Murdoch groups under "texture of being" (Murdoch 1956: 39). For relevant and very illuminating analysis of just these issues, see Morris (1998).
44. The point is made succinctly by Teichmann: "A law is not a request, nor yet a cooperative agreement. In fact, one cannot make requests of oneself, or make agreements with oneself, any more than one can legislate for oneself; but in the case of legislation, as Anscombe indicates, the main problem for Kant's view is that one cannot punish oneself for breaking one's own 'laws' " (Teichmann 2008: 109). The passage is cited in Stern (2014), and I engage with Stern in what follows.
45. I take the argument here to be about the moral ought rather than any ought, given the context. I also read this as continuous with the following thought from the *Groundwork*: "Everyone must grant that a law, if it is to hold morally, that is, as a ground of an obligation, must carry with it absolute necessity" (GW 4:389). This is a point that Kant picks up also later when drawing a contrast between laws of physics and of chemistry: "But it is different with moral laws. They hold as laws only insofar as they can be *seen* to have an *a priori* basis and to be necessary" (MM 6:215). Put together, the three quotes give us a conceptual point to which corresponds a metaphysical commitment

about the nature of deontic grounding, a connection with ground and author-ity, and finally how this relation of ground to law must be visible to agents that fall under the law.

46. The idea of the self-legislation of reason involves also claims of metaphysical and epistemic priority, which exceed the scope of this discussion; I provide further detail in my (2017); I discuss the meta-ethical commitments of the position in my (2012).

47. Darwall 2006: 114.

48. Ibid., p. 115 n.

49. Ibid.

50. Stern 2014: 1120.

51. Lovibond 2004: 158. I have argued in a different context, criticising Foot, about the availability of this perspective, that of keeping the commandments of morality in messy surrounds by those who may not even have the words, or perhaps inclination, to describe their action or stance in this way (viz. Deligiorgi 2012: 128–129).

52. Anscombe 1958: 30.

Whether this is an accurate representation of Aristotle is debatable. Roger Crisp, for example, has argued that Aristotle has a use for concepts that are much closer to the moral should and ought than Anscombe suggests, and gives the example of dei, 'one ought', 'one should', which, he argues, are plausibly derived from the impersonal form of 'deo' 'to need' (viz. Crisp 2004: 83). Crisp goes on to make the interesting point that *dei* came to be used in the fifth century, in contrast to *chre,* for 'objective' necessities or constraints and gives a reference to Williams (1993) who in turn refers to Bernardete (1965). Nonetheless, if I am right, Anscombe is not seeking such a notion in Aristotle, in the first place.

53. I am tempted to say that the autonomy of morality as such is at stake in Kant's discussion that starts with duty and so the possibility of recognising as authoritative a distinctly moral ought, the moral law.

54. I treat Korsgaard's views in much more detail in Deligiorgi (2012).

55. Perhaps this is the point Thompson is making when he is saying "our confi-dence in the validity of considerations of justice and other fundamental forms of practical thought must, at a certain level, be groundless" (Thompson 2003: 7).

56. McDowell 1998: 171.

57. Millgram (2005) has a similar diagnosis, namely that Kant's practical rea-soning is fundamentally shaped by Kant's commitment to the principle of sufficient reason (PSR). Kant is as a matter of fact suspicious of the PSR but Millgram's point still has a target if the picture Thompson paints is correct.

References

Anscombe, G. E. M. 1958. 'Modern Moral Philosophy'. *Philosophy* 33: 1–19.

———. 2000. *Intention.* Cambridge, MA: Harvard University Press.

Aristotle. 2009. *Nicomachean Ethics.* L. Brown (ed.) and D. Ross (trans.). Oxford: Oxford University Press.

Baron, M. 1996. 'Kantian Ethics'. In M. W. Baron, P. Pettit and M. Slote (eds.) *Three Methods of Ethics.* Oxford: Blackwell.

Bernardete, S. 1965. 'XRH and DEI in Plato and Others'. *GLOTTA* 43: 285–298.

Crisp, R. 2004. 'Does Modern Moral Philosophy Rest on a Mistake?' *Royal Institute of Philosophy Supplement* 54: 75–93.

Darwall, S. 2006. *The Second Person Standpoint: Morality, Respect, and Accountability.* Cambridge, MA: Harvard University Press.

———. 2007. 'Law and the Second-Person Standpoint'. *Loyola of Los Angeles Law Review* 40: 891–910. Available at: http://digitalcommons.lmu.edu/llr/vol40/iss3/2

De Caro, M., and D. Macarthur (eds.). 2010. *Naturalism and Normativity*. New York: Columbia University Press.

Deligiorgi, K. 2012. *The Scope of Autonomy: Kant and the Morality of Freedom*. Oxford: Oxford University Press.

———. 2017. 'Interest and Agency'. In J. M. Rasmussen, M. Gabriel and J. Rometsch (eds.) *German Idealism Today*. Frankfurt: De Gruyter.

———. 2018. 'The "Ought" and the "Can"'. *Con-Textos Kantianos. International Journal of Philosophy* 8: 6–30.

———. forthcoming. ' "Why Be Moral?" How to Take the Questions Seriously (and Why) from a Kantian Perspective'. In C. Yeomans and A. Lyssy (eds.) *Dimensions of Normativity: Kant on Morality, Legality, Humanity*.

Foot, P. 1978. *Virtues and Vices*. Oxford: Blackwell.

———. 2001. *Natural Goodness*. Oxford: Clarendon Press.

———. 2004. 'Rationality and Goodness'. *Royal Institute of Philosophy Supplement* 54: 1–13.

Geach, P. T. 1956. 'Good and Evil'. *Analysis* 17: 33–42.

Herman, B. 1996. *The Practice of Moral Judgement*. Cambridge, MA: Harvard University Press.

Hursthouse, R. 1999. *On Virtue Ethics*. Oxford: Oxford University Press.

Kant, I. 1998. *Critique of Pure Reason*. P. Guyer and A. W. Wood (eds. and trans.). Cambridge: Cambridge University Press.

———. 2012. *Groundwork for the Metaphysics of Morals*. M. Gregor and J. Timmermann (eds. and trans.). Cambridge: Cambridge University Press.

———. 2017. *The Metaphysics of Morals*. L. Denis (ed.) and M. Gregor (trans.). Cambridge: Cambridge University Press.

Korsgaard, C. M. 1996. *The Sources of Normativity*. Cambridge: Cambridge University Press.

———. 2009. *Self-Constitution. Agency, Identity, Integrity*. Oxford: Oxford University Press.

Lovibond, S. 2004. 'Absolute Prohibitions Without Divine Promises'. *Royal Institute of Philosophy Supplement* 54: 141–158.

McDowell, J. 1996. *Mind and World*. Cambridge, MA: Harvard University Press.

———. 1998. *Mind, Value, and Reality*. Cambridge, MA: Harvard University Press.

Millgram, E. 2005. *Ethics Done Right: Practical Reasoning as a Foundation for Moral Theory*. Cambridge: Cambridge University Press.

Morris, M. 1998. 'Mind, World and Value'. In A. O'Hear (ed.) *Current Issues in the Philosophy of Mind*. Cambridge: Cambridge University Press.

Murdoch, I. 1956. Symposium: 'Vision and Choice in Morality'. Aristotelian Society, *Dreams and Self-Knowledge*. Supplementary Volume XXX: 32–58.

Putnam, H. 2016. *Naturalism, Realism, and Normativity*. M. De Caro (ed.). Cambridge, MA: Harvard University Press.

Stern, R. 2014. 'Divine Commands and Secular Commands: Darwall on Anscombe'. *Mind* 123: 1095–1122.

Stroud, B. 1996. 'The Charm of Naturalism'. *Proceedings and Addresses of the American Philosophical Association* 70: 43–55.

Teichmann, R. 2008. *The Philosophy of Elizabeth Anscombe*. Oxford: Oxford University Press.

Thompson, M. 2003. 'Three Degrees of Goodness'. *Iride* XVI: 179–200.

———. 2004. 'Apprehending Human Form'. In A. O'Hear (ed.) *Modern Moral Philosophy*. Cambridge: Cambridge University Press.

———. 2008. *Life and Action*. Cambridge, MA: Harvard University Press.

———. 2013. 'Forms of Nature: "First", "Second", "Living", "Rational", and "Phronetic"'. In G. Hindirchs and A. Honneth (eds.) *Freiheit*. Frankfurt: Klostermann.

Varden, H. 2018. *A Kantian Theory of Sexuality*. Oxford: Oxford University Press.

Vogler, C. 2013. 'Aristotle, Aquinas, and the New Virtue Ethics'. In T. Hoffman, J. Müller and M. Perkams (eds.) *Aquinas and the Nicomachean Ethics*. Cambridge: Cambridge University Press.

Williams, B. 1993. *Shame and Necessity*. Berkeley, CA: University of California Press.

2 Naturalism and the Primacy of the Practical

Kant on the Form of Theoretical and Practical Reason

Johannes Haag

In his *Critique of Practical Reason*, Kant emphasises that "it is ... always only one and the same reason which, whether for a theoretical or a practical aim, judges according to *a priori* principles" (CPrR 5:121). And yet the form of practical judgment clearly is different from the form of theoretical judgment: in theoretical judgment, the object of representation precedes the representation; whereas in practical judgment the representation of the object precedes the object. Theoretical judgment thus is tailored to the description of nature and its specific (i.e. mechanistic) causality, whereas practical judgment serves to articulate the intentions of finite rational beings and their specific (i.e. teleological) causality.

Kant argues that there is a primacy of practical reason that affords some theoretical propositions (that cannot be validated by theoretical reason alone) to be sufficiently authenticated by practical reason if they belong to the latter's (morally founded) interest, notably the existence of God and the immortality of the soul. Furthermore, it does not suffice for theoretical reasons to simply accept these propositions; it is required on the grounds of the primacy of practical reason "to compare and connect them with everything that it has within its power as speculative reason" (CPrR 5:121).

In this chapter, I will show that the far-reaching results of this claim are worked out no earlier than in the completion of the *Critique of the Power of Judgement*. In this culminating work of Kant's Critical Philosophy, we can observe how much the naturalistic description of the empirical world in the end has to submit to the practical interest of reason without at the same time transgressing the ultimate conceptual barrier between the theoretical and the practical. While the power of judgment even brings the practical form of reason and its characteristic causality to bear on the description of empirical reality, it does so only in its reflective or regulative mode. A teleological description of nature, consequently, cannot afford us a theology and the barrier between theoretical and practical reason can be shown to be upheld by the ethicotheology of the third *Critique*.

In his *Critique of Practical Reason* (CPrR) Kant emphasises that "it is . . . always only one and the same reason which, whether for a theoretical or a practical aim, judges according to *a priori* principles" (CPrR 5:121). And yet the form of practical judgment clearly is different from the form of theoretical judgment: in theoretical judgment the object of representation precedes the representation whereas in practical judgment the representation of the object precedes the object. Theoretical judgment thus is adequate to the description of nature and its specific (i.e. mechanistic) causality, whereas practical judgment serves the articulation of intentions of finite rational beings and their specific (i.e. teleological) causality.

Nevertheless, Kant argues that there is a *primacy* of practical reason that affords some theoretical propositions (that cannot be validated by theoretical reason alone) to be sufficiently authenticated by practical reason if they belong to the latter's (morally founded) 'interest', notably the existence of God and the immortality of the soul. Furthermore, it does not suffice for theoretical reason to simply accept these propositions; it is required on the grounds of the primacy of practical reason "to compare and connect them with everything that it has within its power as speculative reason" (CPrR 5:121).

The guiding question of the following considerations will be on the one hand to determine the true extent of this 'comparison and connection' in Kant's critical philosophy at least in broad outline, and on the other hand to determine whether the results of this process of comparing and connecting threaten the specific form of naturalism that I take to be the principled result of the *Critique of Pure Reason* (CPR).

I will show that the far-reaching results of this comparison and connection are not given in the second *Critique*, but are worked out no earlier than the completion of the *Critique of the Power of Judgement* (CPJ). In this 'completion of the critical enterprise'[1] we can observe how much the naturalistic description of empirical reality in the end has to submit to the practical interest of reason. The question, however, remains as to how it can do so without at the same time transgressing the ultimate conceptual barrier between the theoretical and the practical. The answer, in a nutshell, will have to be that, while the power of judgment even brings the practical form of reason and its characteristic causality to bear on the description of empirical reality, it does so only in its reflective mode. A teleological description of nature, consequently, cannot afford us a theology and the barrier between theoretical and practical reason can be shown to be upheld in the critical distinction between physical teleology and moral teleology[2] that results from the ethicotheology of the third *Critique*.

I will begin my considerations with (i) an elucidation of Kant's use of the concept of nature in the *Critique of Pure Reason*. From there, (ii) I will proceed with introducing the primacy of the practical, as it is discussed in the *Critique of Practical Reason* and its potential implications for theoretical reason. (iii) These implications, as we will then see, get a lot more substantial with Kant's discovery of the principle of purposiveness as a synthetical *a priori* principle for the power of judgment. In particular, the discussion of objective purposiveness and natural ends at first glance seems to effect a teleological revision of the concept of nature as well as an expansion of the limits of knowledge as conceived in the first *Critique*. Therefore, such discourse needs to be appropriately constrained by tying it to the merely reflective (as opposed to constitutive) power of judgment. Nevertheless, this teleological turn allows us to adhere to the interest of practical reason in a way that was not envisaged in any of Kant's earlier writings. Consequently, in the *Critique of the Power of Judgement*, Kant can be seen as walking a tightrope between the interest of practical reason and the safeguarding of his own transcendental idealist version of philosophical naturalism.

I

Kant's Concept of Nature

As a point of departure, let me turn to Kant's *concept of nature* that lies at the foundation of what I take to be a non-reductive or a 'liberal' form of philosophical naturalism. It is a *naturalism* in that the boundaries of Kant's empirical reality are drawn in such a way that everything that counts as an empirical fact is subject to constitutive judgment and therefore can at least, in principle, be described by natural science. Furthermore, whatever counts as an empirical fact is not only describable by natural science, but also conceived mechanistically. It is *non-reductive* (or liberal) insofar as the drawing of these boundaries is itself grounded in a synthetic activity by finite rational subjects of experience that itself is not reducible to empirical fact, but is necessarily relying on *a priori* conceptual structures that in turn are conceived as *rules*. This view of concepts as rules transfers to *empirical* concepts. Hence, Kant's naturalism is essentially what one might call a 'normative naturalism'. Since the reflection on these normative structures underpinning nature in various ways requires a special form of specific philosophical methodology, i.e. transcendental philosophy, it is a unique form of *philosophical* naturalism. At the level of abstraction relevant for our question, we find two different, but closely interwoven conceptions of nature: *natura materialiter spectata* and *natura formaliter spectata*.[3] Materially conceived nature (*natura materialiter spectata*) is defined as the "sum total of all appearances" (CPR B163), whereas nature formally conceived (*natura formaliter spectata*) is "nature [considered merely as nature in general] . . . as the original ground of its [nature's] (necessary) lawfulness" (CPR B165).[4] These characterisations, of course, need a lot of unpacking before their value for a non-reductive philosophical naturalism can be assessed.

First of all, notice that the definitions of *totals* (of *all* appearances and nature *in general*) rest on more basic definitions of material and formal nature. Thus, Kant notes at a later point of the *Critique of Pure Reason*:

> 'Nature' taken adjectivally (*formaliter*) signifies the connection of determinations of a thing in accordance with an inner principle of causality. Conversely, 'nature' taken substantively (*materialiter*) is understood the sum total of appearances insofar as these are in thoroughgoing connection through an inner principle of causality.
>
> (CPR A418–9 / B446 n.)

And he gives an example for this distinction:

> In the first sense one speaks of the 'nature' of fluid matter, of fire, etc., and employs this word adjectivally; conversely, if one talks about the 'things of nature,' then one has in mind a subsisting whole.
>
> (CPR A 418/9 / B 446)

In other words, every object has its own formal nature—its own 'inner principle of causality'. It is itself a material (substantive) nature *qua* sum total (*Inbegriff*) of specific appearances, in the subsisting whole that it is. Interestingly, the *material* nature of a thing is a subsisting whole *in virtue of* ('through') the inner causal principle that is its *formal* nature. Formal nature, consequently, functions as an inner principle of material nature.[5]

Accordingly, we have altogether four different concepts of nature that at the same time seem closely related and, as we will see shortly, cannot be understood separately:

1a. Material nature as a particular sum of appearances (united in a representation of an object).
1b. Formal nature of a particular sum of appearances (united in a representation of an object).
2a. Material nature as the sum total of all appearances.
2b. Formal nature of this sum total.

The question, then, is how the conception of a material nature of *particular* objects and their formal principle of being is to be understood and how it transfers to a conception of a *nature in general* as a principle of all appearances. The nature in question is both in the particular and the general case a nature *of appearances* that are considered according to their lawfulness—a lawfulness accounted for *either* by the particular principle or law that grounds the 'thoroughgoing connection' in the particular *or* by the laws of a nature in general that accounts for the 'necessary lawfulness' of the sum of all particulars. Accordingly, it is the two concepts of appearance and law that underlie both the concepts of individual or particular nature and the concept of a nature taken as a whole of particular natures. Consequently, it is these two concepts that we have to turn to, in order to understand the different conceptions of nature and their interaction.

Appearances are, in first analysis, that which sensibly appear, i.e. that which is empirically represented in an intuition. Appearances, in other words, are the content of empirical representations that are intuition. Intuitions differ from other empirical representations by being immediate representations of these appearances: intuitions, as Wilfrid Sellars often puts it, do have an irreducibly demonstrative aspect to their way of representing.[6] They are ways of perceptually taking the world to be so-and-so.

Appearances, however, are this very content only insofar as the content is *undetermined* (cf. A 20 / B 34), i.e. only in abstraction from the content representing the world thus-and-so. Considered as appearances, they do not yet refer to anything existing differently (and independently) from these representations. Nevertheless, they are not simply arbitrary aggregates of a sensibly given manifold. The sensible manifold is already structured in a synthetic process. The result of this structuring are intuitions of essentially perspectival, three-dimensional images (or, as Sellars has it, image-models) of objects, considered, again, in *abstraction* from their reference to objects taken to be existing independently from these very representations.

The details of this process of synthesis are contentious and need not detain us for the purpose of this chapter.[7] What we need to concentrate on is the conception of appearances as structured sensible content of representations (*Vorstellungen*) that is considered in *abstraction* from the intuition's being a representation, i.e. the intuition's object-directedness. Even considered as appearances, i.e. as *products* of a synthetic process, the content of intuitive representations as such already has to be thought of as subjected to the pure concepts of the understanding.

However, not to all of the categories; Kant carefully distinguishes between the mathematical and the dynamical categories: the former responsible for the possibility of qualitative and quantitative structuring of sensibly given content, the latter for the relation between different intuitions. Only the former are, as Kant puts it "constitutive" (CPR A664 / B692) with respect to intuitive representations, while the latter are constitutive with respect to experience (*Erfahrung*).

I will elucidate on this second class of categories later. Right now, it is the first class that is of the main interest for the purpose at hand: the mathematical categories are the *a priori* prerequisites for an intuitive representation having even undetermined, i.e. non-referential, content. Since we already identified this content with the appearance, we can conclude that appearances are the *sensible content of intuitions considered merely as subjected to the mathematical categories and in abstraction from its being subjected to the dynamical categories.*

It should be clear that appearances as such cannot be sufficient for any *interesting* concept of nature. Whatever this concept ultimately comes to, it certainly should include the claim to *objectivity* that we normally associate with the idea of nature: nature and its objects should be conceived as existing independently of our perceiving them (though, ultimately not of our conceiving them). Appearances are, by definition, not such objects. As content of a representation they are themselves representations, albeit singled out *via* the objects they represent, not as acts of representation. If anything, they are the paradigm of merely subjective entities.

However, since appearances enter the definitions of nature under consideration in a substantial way, we need to clarify how the necessary objectivity comes into the picture.[8] With respect to our definitions that means turning to the 'thoroughgoing connection' of the appearances whose sum total is constitutive of the material nature by means of a principle, i.e. a *law* or a set of laws. Take Kant's example of an intuitive representation of a house at the beginning of the 'Second Analogy of Experience' in the *Critique of Pure Reason*. The perception of the house is something that takes time. As Kant puts it: "The apprehension of the manifold in the appearance of a house that stands before me is successive" (CPR A190 / B235). Intuiting something happens in time: it is extended in time. The succession of subjective states with a certain content, as we have seen, is a succession of appearances. The question we are concerned with right now is the question how these subjective representative states can be conceived as representations of an object existing independently of being thus perceived. Or as Kant puts it: "Now the question is whether the manifold of this house itself is also successive, which certainly no one will concede" (CPR A 190 / B 235). And he goes on to invoke the concept of an appearance just elucidated:

> Now, however, as soon as I raise my concept of an object to transcendental significance, the house is not a thing in itself at all but only an appearance, i.e., a representation, the transcendental object of which is unknown; therefore what do I understand by the question, how the manifold may be combined in the appearance itself (which is yet nothing in itself)?
>
> (CPR A190/1 / B235/6)

The transcendental significance invokes the perspective of the transcendental philosopher that is relevant for us. In what sense the house ultimately is, from a transcendental perspective, *only* an appearance is a question we will have to come back to. Right now it suffices that, properly speaking, we have not brought anything apart from representations into the picture. Our question is how we get from appearance to reality even if this reality, ultimately, from a transcendental perspective turns out to be nothing but (the sum total of) appearance.

His answer to this question merits closest scrutiny and will be with us until the very end of my considerations:

> Here that which lies in the successive apprehension is considered as representation, but the appearance that is given to me, in spite of the fact that it is nothing more than a sum (*Inbegriff*) of these representations, is considered as their object, with which my concept, which I draw from the representations of apprehension, is to agree.
>
> (CPR A191 / B236)

What "lies in the successive apprehension" is the succession of subjective representative states *qua* acts with a certain content. This content, the appearance, is "given to me", as Kant puts it, echoing the phenomenological passivity claim that at this point of the history of philosophy already has become a standard move in order to justify a causal theory of perception.

The content thus given is, Kant then claims, nothing but the "sum total of these representations". This claim refers to the already-established unity of a *succession of appearances that constitutes one complex appearance* in accordance with the mathematical categories.

However, we now have to turn to the question of how we can conceive of this complex of representations (which already is a representation of a unified complex) as the representation of an object existing independently from these very representations that constitute its matter. It is only if we take the dynamical categories into consideration that we can take appearances to *be* such objects. We achieve that by structuring the (successive) content of our intuitions in accordance with these dynamical categories, in particular by taking them to be representations of substances—bearers of properties—that are extended over time and by ascribing them causal and dispositional properties.

But, importantly, in doing this we cannot ascribe these properties to the content of the representations (i.e. the appearances) *as such*. For, only something conceived as a substances can be ascribed causal and dispositional properties—and contents are not substances. Consequently, in subjecting them to the dynamical categories we 'consider these appearances'—the content of the successive representations—'as their objects'—i.e. as the objects of these representative acts. In this way, we are forced by subjecting the appearances to the dynamical categories to make the all-important conceptual transition from *appearance* to *experience*.

At the same time, this *first* transition corresponds to a *second* transition from the *material* to the *formal* concept of the nature of particulars that serves as the 'inner principle' of the material concept of this nature. This inner principle, I would argue, is no other than the sum of the causal and dispositional properties characteristic of the object in question.[9] The specific causal properties are ascribed to this object by the perceiving subject in virtue of the concept the subject subsumes this object under—in our example the concept of a house.

This concept, of course, is an *empirical* concept. As an empirical concept, it had to be "drawn from empirical representations". Once we are in possession of an empirical concept it can be applied to give an object of experience the specific (causal) unity that it has in virtue of being conceived *as* an object of the relevant kind—in our example, as a house. But this specific unity, in turn rests on a broader, in fact, universal unity that, Kant claims, cannot be drawn from experience, but is necessarily presupposed by any discursive experience, i.e. by the categories or pure concepts of the understanding.

We will have to come back to this claim shortly, but for now, I wish to note that the necessary application of the categories afford us a *third* transition: namely, the transition from the form of *particular* objects of nature to the form of nature in *general* insofar as it is lawful—i.e. *natura formaliter spectata*. For, the categories are universal principles that necessarily underlie *any* conceiving of appearances as objects of experience. And since there can be no conception of an object of experience without the categories, these principles have to be formal principles of a *nature in general*. *Qua* principles of a nature in general these principles at the same time include yet a (simultaneous) *fourth* transition of the material nature of particulars to a material nature in general—the sum of all appearances qua sum of all objects of experience, i.e. *natura materialiter spectata*.

With this clarification in mind we thus can turn back to the elucidation of the definitions of nature with which we have been concerned. I have claimed that *material* nature is either the sum total of particular appearances, or of all appearances; whereas *formal* nature refers to the *principle of unity* of either the sum total of appearances that thereby constitute concrete objects of experience or, as nature in general, as the sum total of *all* appearances.

One can understand now how it is possible to speak of 'a 'sum total' in *both* cases, while only in the second case it is *all* appearances we are considering: it is *not* every possible appearance we have to consider in referring appearances to an object conceived of as being distinct from them. It is only the relevant consecutive sequence of appearances *all of whose parts* are referred to as one and the same object that thereby becomes an object of one (coherent) *experience* by means of an interplay of mathematical and dynamical categories. In contrast, as soon as we consider the sum total of *all* experiences, *we turn to a conception of* nature as a whole that can be conceived both formally (concentrating only on the necessary *a priori* principles that characterise it) or materially (by considering these principles in application). *Natura materialiter spectata* therefore is, indeed, 'the sum total of all appearances'. It is this concept that, at a later point of his argument in the *Critique of Pure Reason*, Kant tentatively equates with the concept of a *world* (cf. A419 /

B447), that is the subject matter of experience and, thus, natural science. With this in mind, I would now like to turn to the challenge posed by the primacy of the practical and the resulting demands on theoretical reason that otherwise would be seemingly content with the sparse conception of nature just elucidated.[10]

II

The Primacy of the Practical and the Interest of Reason

Though the two forms of the employment of reason—theoretical and practical—do not (at least not necessarily (cf. CPrR AA.5:120)) contradict each other, there might arise between them a *question of authority* or, as Kant puts it, of *primacy*. This question of primacy arises as soon as one of the two is, as it were, trespassing into the realm of the other. Whereas theoretical reason will ordinarily be prohibited from this kind of trespassing as long as it is subjected to the rigorous scrutiny with respect to the validity of its own assumptions resulting from the first *Critique*, practical reason might not be that easy to restrict. And this is exactly the situation that arises in the course of the *Dialectics* of the *Critique of Practical Reason*: An "original principle *a priori*" (AA. 5:120) of practical reason, i.e. the moral law, is given as a fact of reason (*Faktum der Vernunft*). And as such, according to Kant, it turns out to be "inseparably bound up with certain theoretical positions [*Positionen*]" (CPrR AA. 5:120), i.e. God and the immortality of the soul. Kant concludes from the fact that it is "one and the same reason which . . . judges according to a priori principles" (CPrR AA. 5:121) that with respect to pure *a priori* judgments of practical reason that are not contradictions any propositions of theoretical reason "as soon as these same propositions belong inseparably to the practical interest of pure reason, it must assume them—although as a foreign offering not grown on its soil but yet sufficiently authenticated" (CPrR AA. 5:121). It is this reasoning that leads Kant to the claim we started with: that theoretical reason indeed has to 'seek to compare and connect' these theoretical propositions that are 'a foreign offering', with everything that it has within its power as theoretical reason.[11]

Theoretical reason, in other words, is not justified in simply rejecting these normative propositions as extravagant (*überschwenglich*), but must assume them as 'sufficiently authenticated' by their following from the moral law. How they follow from the moral law will be a question that I am going to address only in passing and only insofar as it serves my main topic. I will instead concentrate on the second qualification of the task of theoretical reason—the comparison and connection with everything in its power—that follows from this primacy of the practical. What are the propositions in question? As I already indicated, it is the idea of

God and the idea of the immortality of the soul. In order to understand why these propositions are inseparably bound up with the moral law, we have to turn to the critical solution of the *Antinomy of Practical Reason* in the *Dialectics* of the second *Critique*. The antinomy arises in the context of the introduction of the highest good as the necessary object of an action under the more law. The highest good can be characterised, in first approximation, as a state of the highest virtue, i.e. the highest deservedness for happiness, that is at the very same time a state of the highest happiness.[12] Since the two concepts of virtue and happiness are thus necessary determinations of the concept of the highest good and since, there is, furthermore, no *analytic* connection between the concepts of virtue and happiness there must be a *synthetic* and *a priori* connection between the two determinations. For, unless there were such a connection, Kant reasons, the concept of a highest good itself would turn out to be an impossible concept—and, given its being the necessary intentional object of an action under the moral law, it would thus make the moral law, the fact of reason, itself a mere illusion.

If, therefore, the highest good is impossible according to practical rules, then the moral law which commands us to further this good must also be fantastic and aimed at empty imaginary purposes, and hence in itself false (CPrR AA. 5:114).

The conceptual options for the thinking of the sought-after synthetic *a priori* relation are introduced by Kant as the two theses of an antinomy:

> *Thesis*: [The striving for] happiness is generating (*hervorbringen*) a reason (*Grund*) for (or is the efficient cause (*Bewegursache*) of) a virtuous attitude (*tugendhafte Gesinnung*) (or the maxim of virtue).
> (cf. 5:113/114)[13]

> *Antithesis*: A virtuous attitude (or the max-im of virtue) is (necessarily) generating (or is the efficient cause of) happiness.[14]

As Kant makes clear without much further ado, the thesis from the standpoint of the *Analytics of Practical Reason* can be seen as immediately false since the maxims funded in the strife for happiness cannot serve as the basis for morality. The antithesis, however, can ultimately be defended and the antinomy thus be resolved—provided one does not understand it as a proposition about the direct causality of virtue in the sensible world:

> it is not impossible that the morality of one's attitude should have a connection, and moreover a necessary one, as cause with happiness as effect in the world of sense, if not a direct connection then still an indirect one (by means of an intelligible originator of nature), a linkage which in a nature that is merely an object of the senses can

never take place except contingently and cannot be sufficient for the highest good.

(CPrR AA. 5:115)

It is this indirect linkage that is provided by the postulates of God and the immortality of the soul. They are, consequently, introduced in the context of the discussion of the conditions of the possibility of the highest good in the *Dialectics* of the *Critique of Practical Reason*. This discussion is structured by the differentiation between conditions "directly under our control" (CPrR AA. 5:119) on the one hand, and conditions that are "presented to us by reason to compensate our inability (*Unvermögen*)" (CPrR AA. 5:119) to realise this idea of a highest good. These conditions, as Kant puts it, are necessary according to practical principles. The ideas of God and the immortal soul, naturally, belong into the latter category. It is significant that the reflections on the primacy of practical reason directly follow this plan for structuring the discussion. One might expect that these reflections are themselves part of this discussion—and, I think, rightly so. For, what is 'directly under our control' with respect to the will as pursuing the highest good is the principle that reason gives itself in order to determine the will with respect to its "ultimate and complete (*vollkommenen*) purpose" (CPrR AA. 5:120). This principle constitutes the interest of practical reason, i.e. it contains the conditions "under which alone [this power's]exercise is furthered" (CPrR AA. 5:119). Primacy, as we have seen, is introduced as a primacy of such interests vice versa each other—in the case at hand the interests of practical vs. the interests of theoretical reason.

Consequently, it is indeed vital for the thriving of practical reason in terms of self-determination and thus for its pursuing the highest good in acting autonomously under the moral law that its interest is not trumped by a theoretical reason 'stubbornly pursuing its own interest'. After all, even if the underlying form or trajectory is radically different in the theoretical and practical exercise of reason, it *is* one and the same reason that is so exercised in *a priori* judgment—whether the judgment is theoretical or practical. One interest, consequently, has to be subsumed under the other—and it cannot be the other way round, since, as Kant points out *every* interest is "ultimately practical" (CPrR AA. 5:121), since every interest is defined *via* the exercise of a capacity.

One of the most prominent features of the conception of the highest good in the second *Critique* (and an important change from the brief account in '*Canon*' chapter of the first *Critique* is the realisability of the highest good in the sensible world:[15] we have to ascribe to us the duty of making *nature* such that as much in it is balanced adequately with respect to happiness and morality even if our factual powers can never be sufficient to achieve such a balance. As Kant puts it in the *Critique of the Power of Judgement*, the highest good has to be conceived as the

> world-best (*Weltbeste*) that consists in the conjunction of the highest welfare (Wohl) of the rational beings in the world (*Weltwesen*) with the highest condition of the good with respect to them (*an denselben*), i.e. general happiness together with morality conforming to the law.
>
> (CPJ AA.5:453.17–20)

It is, indeed, in the '*Doctrine of Methods*', towards the very end of his third *Critique*, that Kant first takes up the questions of the highest good and the postulates again. He has to go back to these questions, I will try to show in the remainder of this chapter, since only in the course of this work he not only finishes his 'critical enterprise', but at the same time the task of 'comparing and connecting the theoretical propositions that result from the interest of practical reason with everything that it has within its power as speculative reason'. The purpose of the following considerations, accordingly, will be to show how this task is carried out in the *Critique of the Power of Judgement* in a way that does full justice to the interest of practical reason without at the same time endangering the non-reductive philosophical naturalism that Kant first delineated in his first *Critique*. The presentation of the concept of objective purposiveness in natural ends will play a decisive role in achieving this twofold aim.

III

The Presentation of the Concept of Purposiveness

In order to show this we have to start with an exposition of the role of purposiveness within the *Critique of the Power of Judgement*. The third *Critique* is Kant's attempt to bridge the chasm between theoretical and practical philosophy—or, to put it more positively, to show how the form of theoretical reason and the form of practical reason can be seen as but two forms of what is ultimately *one and the same* reason, though the real ground of this unity must, as Kant claims, ultimately be elusive for us.

At the very beginning on the next to last section of the published *Introduction* Kant writes:

> We can regard natural beauty as the presentation (Darstellung) of the concept of formal (merely subjective) purposiveness and natural ends as the presentation of the concept of a real (objective) purposiveness, one of which we judge through taste (aesthetically, by means of the feeling of pleasure), the other through understanding and reason (logically, in accordance with concepts).
>
> (CPJ AA. 5:193)

So, what is meant by Kant's claim that natural beauty and natural ends are the *presentation* (*Darstellung*) of subjective and objective purposiveness respectively? In order to analyse the meaning of this passage, we have to become clear about the central concepts of *presentation* on the one hand and of (subjective vs. objective) *purposiveness* on the other.

Let me start with *purposiveness*. The distinction between subjective and objective purposiveness is ultimately responsible for the architectonic of the third *Critique* as a whole: upon the distinction between subjective or formal purposiveness (a purposiveness that we represent aesthetically) and objective or real purposiveness (represented logically) rests the central sub-division of the book between the critique of the *aesthetical power of judgment* and the critique of the *teleological power of judgment*.[16]

Purposiveness took centre stage in Kant's critical thought during the development of the third *Critique* as he discovered a new *synthetic a priori principle* for the power of judgment that necessitated a critique of this epistemic capacity.[17] According to the account of our epistemological powers in the *Critique of the Power of Judgement*, the power of judgment can be divided in a heteronomous *constitutive* power of judgment and an autonomous *reflective* power of judgment: the first applies laws of the understanding or reason to nature, the second gives a law to itself. This law must be fit to guide the subsuming activity of the power of judgment in its quest for the general to subsume the given particular, i.e. in its quest for constitutive judgment with respect to objects in nature and the laws that govern them.

This proves necessary since the epistemic situation the power of judgment faces is an *underdetermination* of the special laws or concepts[18] by the most general laws given by the pure concepts of the understanding and the transcendental principles resulting from them. For, in its reflective activity, the power of judgment, consequently, has to successively find more general laws to subsume the laws under that in relation to them are more particular. It thereby engages in a process that could only be brought to an end in case the sequence of laws would be complete and continuous—a merely regulative ideal, of course, that we will never be able to achieve.

The ideal result of this process would thus be a sequence of laws that has properties closely resembling the totality we think through the *transcendental ideas of reason* familiar from the *Appendix* to the Transcendental Dialectic in the *Critique of Pure Reason*, namely the Soul, God, and the World. It is in particular the totality that Kant refers to as the idea of *world* that is important here. Indeed, it is the very idea that was the culmination of the preceding discussion of the concept of nature.

The newly discovered synthetic *a priori* principle of the power of judgment is first introduced in the following way:

> The principle of the power of judgement in regard to the form of
> things in nature under empirical laws in general is the purposiveness

of nature in its multiplicity. I.e., nature is represented through this concept as if an understanding contained the ground of the unity of the manifold of its empirical laws.

(CPJ AA. 5:180/1)

In order to understand this *principle of purposiveness* and its relation to the concept of nature in the first *Critique* it is extremely important to keep in mind that Kant's model for purposiveness always is the purposiveness to an end that is set intentionally by a will.[19] This is a general point, but a crucial one for the understanding of the principle of purposiveness (and of the concept of a natural end as well): we can (and must) abstract from this will in using the concept of purposiveness in the context of the transcendental principle of the power of judgment. But the regulative "as if" mode we *have* to use in this context is a constant reminder that, while we are aware of the *merely* regulative use we can make of the representation of such a will, we *cannot* conceive of purposiveness without it.

As such, according to Kant, we must consider the particular empirical laws of nature as if an (infinite) intellect was responsible for their unity *for the sake of our epistemic capacity*.[20] It is through this change of perspective that Kant now can make plausible that purposiveness can be found in the structure of empirical knowledge *without* looking for *teleological explanations* of empirical objects. The *mechanical* structure of reality *as such* can now express purposiveness *with respect to our epistemic powers*, i.e. *subjective purposiveness*.

One might even say that the technical distinction between subjective and objective purposiveness was introduced *exactly* to this end: Purposiveness, we learn in the introduction to the third *Critique*, can be differentiated in purposiveness that is represented in an object of experience either on a *subjective* or an *objective* ground. We must distinguish, accordingly, between *subjective* and *objective* purposiveness—a distinction that, of course, is forcefully reiterated in the very first section of the *Critique of the Teleological Power of Judgement* (§61).

In the case of subjective purposiveness, the representation of the purposiveness of the object is thus based on a merely *subjective* ground. In contrast, in the case of objective purposiveness an object would be represented as corresponding with respect to its form "with the possibility of the thing itself, in accordance with a concept of it which precedes and contains the ground of this form" (CPJ AA. 5:192). The representation of the object's purposiveness in this case would be based on an *objective* ground.[21]

The newly found principle of purposiveness, however, has its ground in the *experience* of something we might call actualised experience of subjective purposiveness:

So it is actually only in taste, more precisely, only in taste concerning objects of nature, that judgement reveals itself as a faculty that has its own principle and hence is justified in claiming a place in the general critique of the higher cognitive faculties—a place one might otherwise not have expected for it.

(*First Introduction* AA. 20:244)[22]

It was a real discovery for Kant that nature itself not only must be considered as if it was purposively ordered (something that could be learned already from the *Appendix* to the Transcendental Dialectic and its analysis of reason's regulative ideas), but that, *in exhibiting beauty*, nature was indeed purposive with respect to the peculiar constitution of human epistemic faculties.[23]

Nature consequently in fact exhibits *subjective* purposiveness for us. It exhibits this purposiveness through the beautiful. It is, so we judge by means of our reflective power of judgment, *as if* nature was responding to our specific epistemic constitution. The transcendental principle of purposiveness of nature is in this way *forced upon us* and, consequently, has an application in judgments about nature in its relation to us. This is something no merely regulative principle of reason could afford us. Kant makes clear that it is not *another* principle that is applied in aesthetic judgment, but the very same principle of purposiveness that we have to apply since the suitability of nature to our epistemic faculties[24]—found in natural beauty and looked for in the laws of nature[25]—must otherwise seem purely accidental.

With this in mind, we have arrived at a point where it is reasonable to get back to the passage about natural beauty and natural ends as being *presentations* of subjective and objective purposiveness, respectively.[26]

For Kant, in nearly all instances, the "faculty of presentation is the imagination" (CPJ AA. 5: 232). Presentation, indeed, is the main function of imagination. Imagination is a "formative faculty" (AA. 28.1:235 ff.) that by means of its synthetic function gives us conceptually informed intuitive representation of objects of experience *as* objects of a certain kind.

Now, natural beauty and natural ends *qua presentations* of the concepts of subjective and objective purposiveness must be the products of the imagination in its synthesising function, i.e. presentations the imagination is construing in accordance with certain discursive rules. Indeed, it is the very concepts that are presented by the imagination in an intuitive representation that must themselves provide the conceptual resources in accordance with which the presentation is construed.[27] Consequently, the imagination, in presenting the concepts of subjective or objective purposiveness, constructs intuitions in accordance with those concepts.

Since subjective purposiveness is important for my purposes only insofar as it gives rise to the new transcendental principle of purposiveness discussed previously, I will concentrate on objective purposiveness that, at first glance, appears more threatening for the mechanistic-lawful concept of nature underlying the non-reductive philosophical naturalism developed in the *Critique of Pure Reason*.[28]

Subjective purposiveness does not threaten this naturalism, since it builds on the experience that—though it is an experience *on occasion* of natural objects, i.e. natural beauty—is not an experience of something that could not be explained qua natural object by means of the mechanistic laws. What *cannot* be explained is its perfect fit for our epistemic capacities. However, these capacities are not themselves construed in Kant's Critical Philosophy as themselves parts of nature. Rather, they are construed as capacities whose activity is *the condition of the possibility of nature*. They are, as such, not accessible to a treatment of an *empirical* psychology that only ever can investigate their effectuations in the *empirical* subject. Importantly, this distances Kant's naturalism from most contemporary forms of naturalism;[29] but it is a naturalism, nevertheless, in carefully restricting the realm of knowledge to empirical knowledge and the conditions of its possibility.

The case of *objective* purposiveness is different: in this case, the entities that serve as presentations of this concept really are objects of a certain kind: they are intuitions of objects that represent them *as natural ends*. Consequently, these intuitions are presentations of the concept of objective purposiveness *in nature* not—as in the case of subjective purposiveness—in nature *in relation to us*. However, it is worth remembering that, since the concept of a natural end is an empirical concept, acquired only through the systematic experience that Kant calls observation (*Beobachtung*), there must in this case be an *antecedent* intuition of the relevant objects that does *not* yet represent them as natural ends. With this in mind, let us now turn to the objective purposiveness in nature and, hence, to Kant's discussion of natural ends.

IV

Objective Purposiveness and Natural Ends

Let me start by noticing the striking difference with subjective purposiveness with respect to the consequences for a Kantian naturalism. The subjective purposiveness we find in natural beauty clearly does not commit us to conceive of nature as a whole as if it was the product of an infinite will. Nature in the experience of beauty seems to be answering to our specific human epistemological powers—but this does not mean that we must conceive of everything in nature as being purposive, let alone to conceive of ourselves as a final end of nature. No merely subjective purposiveness could justify that.

Only the discovery of objective purposiveness in nature could count as at least a *first step* into this direction. Consequently, at the heart of Kant's *Critique of the Teleological Power of Judgement* lies the concept of a natural end. It is this concept that not only constitutes the central topic of the *Analytic of the Teleological Power of Judgement*, but, at first glance, seems to shake the very ground on which the analysis of purposiveness and its *a priori* principle up to the introduction of natural ends in §65 of the third *Critique* was founded: the status of the principle of purposiveness as a principle for the *reflective* power of judgment that, as such, can only result in *reflective* judgments.

It is of the utmost importance to note that the concept of a natural end is introduced not for heuristic purposes, but is *necessitated* by the confrontation with certain objects of experience. These particular phenomena, on closer "observations" (*Beobachtung*) (§66, 5:376)) turned out to be objects of a particular kind, i.e. organisms or "organised products of nature". The concept of natural end, in other words, is *not a concept born out of choice, but out of necessity*.

Organisms withstand mechanical explanation: mechanical explanation is always an explanation that explains a given entity as the sum of its parts. But, for Kant, organisms are not mere sums of their parts. Organisms exhibit a mutual causality of whole and part—a self-organisation that distinguishes them from all other appearances, including artefacts:

> In such a product of nature each part is conceived as if it exists only through all the others, thus as if existing for the sake of the others and on account of the whole, i.e., as an instrument (organ), which is, however, not sufficient (for it could also be an instrument of art, and thus represented as possible at all only as an end); rather it must be thought of as an organ that produces the other parts (consequently each produces the others reciprocally), which cannot be the case in any instrument of art, but only of nature, which provides all the matter for instruments (even those of art): only then and on that account can such a product, as an *organised and self-organising* being, be called a natural end.
>
> (CPJ AA. 5:373–4; my emphasis)

This mutual causality of whole and part we encounter in organisms is "not thinkable and not explicable (*denkbar und erklärlich*) even through an exact analogy with human art" (CPJ AA. 5:375.15/6; cf. CPJ AA. 5:375.5–7). It is, for a discursive understanding like ours, only graspable by a "remote analogy" (CPJ AA. 5:375.20) with a causality we *do* know, i.e. a final causality, closely connected with the form of *practical* reason, in which the representation of the end precedes the result of the process of production: to conceive of something as an end involves an essential appeal to the faculty of reason as the faculty that is responsible for the explanation of intentional action, i.e. the faculty responsible for teleological explanations. In the case of intentional action, the representation of the whole does indeed precede the existence of the parts: one first forms the idea and only afterwards works on its realisation.

However, the analogy, Kant clarifies, on closer looks is not only remote, but, "strictly speaking" (CPJ AA. 5:375), not an analogy at all, since the object in question is at the same time represented as a *natural* object, i.e. as an object that is not caused by a rational being external to it. As Kant makes very clear in the *Dialectic* (§74), for the description of natural organised beings we not only need the concept of an end (i.e. "contingency of the form of the object (in relation to mere laws of nature)") (CPJ AA. 5:396.26/7), but, additionally, the concept of a *natural product*. And this concept "includes natural necessity" (CPJ AA. 5:396.26).[30]

Thus, the concept of an end, which has its home in the explanatory discourse surrounding intentional action, on occasion of the observation of organised products of nature, seems to be in need of a synthesis with a concept of natural necessity associated with mechanical explanation. But these two concepts are in tension with each other, if not in outright opposition. There is no causal concept 'we know' which can adapt to this situation. We therefore *conceptually struggle* with this phenomenon, since the mutual causality of whole and part does not fit within the constraints of our conceptual system and we consequently have to content ourselves with the construction of an auxiliary, mongrel concept that does fit this framework—at least by remote analogy with the familiar concept of intentional final causation. This concept, of course, is the *concept of a natural end*: organisms have to be conceived as *ends*. Yet since organisms, unlike artefacts, are natural objects, i.e. products of nature and not products of thinking beings, we have to think of organisms as *natural* ends.[31]

But our use of the concept of a natural end is not only *necessary*, given our cognitive constitution, it is, at the same time, experienced as ultimately unable to fully do justice to the phenomena to be explained (and, subsequently, to be synthesised in accordance with this concept).[32] The mongrel concept of a natural end is a concept which we cannot help but construct in the face of certain phenomena that the imagination presents us with in intuition. It, therefore, "includes natural necessity and yet at the same time a contingency of the form of the object (in relation to mere laws of nature) in one and the same thing as an end" (CPJ AA. 5:396). This concept of a natural end, even if it does not contain an outright contradiction, can be only a "problematic concept" (CPJ AA. 5:397) in the Kantian sense, since it cannot be abstracted from experience.[33]

If that is right, we find ourselves compelled to introduce forms of teleological explanation not only in our overarching scientific pursuit of a unified empirical reality according to a principle of subjective purposiveness, but even in the synthetic construction of some of our intuitions of *appearances* (viz. organisms): we now have to present objective purposiveness in objects of experience, i.e. *in nature*.

It thus turns out that we are confronted in experience with a product of nature that exhibits a purposiveness that is found *neither* in the purposiveness we encounter in the beauty of nature *nor* in nature's responsiveness to our search for the systematic unity of its laws. In the latter cases, we could conceive of the purposiveness in question as formal or *subjective* purposiveness. But, the case of organisms is not amenable to the same treatment, since in this case purposiveness is *found* in nature that is not subjective and formal but objective and real: We observe purposiveness *in nature*, not *in nature in relation to us*.

Kant emphasises the dramatic consequences of this discovery in the sections following his discussion of organisms. In particular, he emphasises in Section 68 that, once we have judged a subclass of natural objects as objectively purposive, this allows for judging nature *as a whole* as a system of ends:

> we may go further and also judge to belong to a system of ends even those things (or their relation, however purposive) which do not make it necessary to seek another principle of their possibility beyond the mechanism of blindly acting causes; because the former idea already, as far as its ground is concerned, leads us beyond the sensible world, and the unity of the supersensible principle must then be considered as valid in the same way not merely for certain species of natural beings but for the whole of nature as a system.
>
> (CPJ AA. 5:380/1)

However, given this reversal of philosophical fortunes *what reason do we have to argue for the mere reflectivity of the teleological judgments?* Are not these judgments with this transition becoming themselves *constitutive* judgments? In other words, is not the (merely) heuristic status of the principle of purposiveness jeopardised by the introduction of the concept of a natural end?

Kant, of course, denies just that repeatedly and consistently. The motive for this claim is obvious: Understanding teleological judgments as constitutive means to interpret them as applications of an objective principle for the *constitutive* power of judgment, i.e. the principle that the generation of material things is not possible through mechanical laws alone (CPJ AA. 5:387). But this principle stands in an antinomic relation to the principle that the generation of material things is possible solely by the laws of mechanics.[34] It therefore would pose a serious challenge to the non-reductive philosophical naturalism so carefully delineated in the first *Critique*: not only would the mechanical closure of the explanation of nature be threatened, but the limitation of knowledge to empirical matters of fact and the conditions of their possibility would be seriously different from the picture given in the earlier work.

The reason for this is rooted in our conception of teleological causality: it requires us to think of a purpose as a representation of the would-be effect of an intentional activity. Given that the concept of a natural end leads to the conception of nature as a whole as a system of ends, we have to think of its intentional cause as well. In this way, an infinite being that created nature (God) would have to be thought as the condition of its possibility. However, that only follows, if we had to conceive of organisms as natural ends (and nature as a system of ends) by way of constitutive judgment. If we restrict this reasoning to the *reflective* power of judgment, we are free to abstract from the purposes involved in our way of conceiving teleological causality.

However, although Kant's *motive* for the claim that judgments of objective purposiveness are merely reflective and not constitutive may be obvious, the *justification* for this claim is less so. In fact, Kant does not argue for this claim before the *Dialectic of the Teleological Power of Judgement*. I would go so far as to suggest that the justification of this claim is the main purpose of the *Dialectic*. For, Kant is ultimately entitled to this claim only after the solution of the antinomy of the power of teleological judgment—a solution that is given no earlier than in Section 77 of the third *Critique*.[35]

Let me offer the following brief summary of the complicated argument in this section: The organisms we find ourselves confronted with in nature, give rise to an antinomy for us, inasmuch as they seem to demand incompatible explanations—a *mechanistic* explanation, insofar as they are parts of nature (blind mechanism), and a teleological explanation insofar as they are thoroughly organised wholes. In order to reconcile mechanistic with teleological explanation, Kant introduces the contrastive concept of an intellectual intuition *qua* productive unity of thought and being (in an infinite being, i.e. God as creator). The cognitive activity of such a faculty would serve to *ground* a supersensible substratum in which teleology and mechanism are one. Due to the discursive nature of our cognitive architecture, we have to think of nature as an *end* of this supernatural ground. The further contrastive concept of a *higher* finite understanding that can schematise the categories according to a different, in particular: non-temporal kind of sensibility (and hence could manifest an alternative to the uni-directionality of or temporally schematised causality), on the other hand, serves to *restrict* this assumption—and with it the necessity of a teleological description of the phenomenal world—to finite beings *of a certain kind*, i.e. finite beings like us that are incapable of this kind of alternative intuitive access to the world. In this way, the contrast between mechanical and teleological description of nature can justifiably be ascribed to the reflective as opposed to the determining use of our power of judgment, for it is tied to our special kind of sensibility that cannot be assumed the same for all possible finite rational beings. Only together can these concepts of limiting faculties dissolve the antinomy of teleological judgment while at the same time offering an explanation for the fact that, despite all possible progress in the mechanical explanation of nature, we are "never to lose sight of the fact that those (products in nature) which, given the essential constitution of our reason, we can . . . subject to investigation only under the concept of an end of reason, must in the end be subordinated to causality in accordance with ends" (CPJ AA. 5:415).

V

Physical Teleology, Ethicotheology, and the Primacy of Practical Reason

Natural ends thus show that there can be necessary conceptual reactions to certain phenomena that still are not conceptually necessary simpliciter. Other finite rational beings with a non-temporal schematization of causality could explain mechanistically. And that is why the framework of teleological explanation even can be part of teleological reasoning: it is necessary not only in the application of the principle of (subjective) purposiveness of the (particular) laws of nature, but also in order to press forward with mechanical explanation with respect to organisms as far as possible, still conscious of the fact that they necessarily escape a *complete* mechanistic explanation:

> indeed this is so certain that we can boldly say that it would be absurd for humans even to make such an attempt or to hope that there may yet arise a Newton who could make comprehensible even the generation of a blade of grass according to natural laws that no intention has ordered; rather, we must absolutely deny this insight to human beings.
>
> (CPJ AA. 5:400)

Since the reaction is, however conceptually necessary for beings like us (forms of sensibility), we can go on from there doing the bidding of practical reason explore how far it can conceptually take our reflective mode of being: it is this reflective mode that guarantees that we ultimately accept the fact that it is in the end only the 'foreign offering' born out of the interest of practical reason that gets us over the threshold to justifiably postulating God (along with the immortality of the soul)—and not teleology in nature. Let me close by outlining this transition from physical teleology as conceived by the reflective power of judgment to the 'offering' of practical reason.

As we have seen, the fact that we have to classify an important and large class of objects in nature as ends, according to Kant "necessarily leads to the *idea of the whole of nature as a system in accordance with the rule of ends*, to which idea all of the mechanism of nature in accordance with principles of reason must now be subordinated" (CPJ AA. 5:379). Once our reflective judgment is *forced* to accept objective purposiveness in *some* things in nature, there is no good reason anymore to not broaden the teleological perspective to the whole of nature.[36]

Even the concept of a natural end, as we have seen, is already pointing to an entity *beyond nature*, i.e. to an intelligible ground of nature. And the same holds all the more for the teleological interpretation of nature as a system is: It invokes the idea of an "architectonic intellect (*architektonischer Verstand*)" (CPJ AA. 5:420) that is intentionally responsible for the objective purposiveness of nature taken as a whole.

In this way, the *teleological* perspective on nature seems to lead quite naturally to a *theological* perspective. However, as the solution to the Antinomy of the Teleological Power of Judgement has shown this holds only for the reflective power of judgment. The teleological perspective, consequently, does not by itself have the means to determine either the 'original ground' or the *final end* of a nature thus conceived. But that is what a perspective requires in order to be truly teleological. Indeed, here we touch upon the limits of teleological reasoning not only with respect to its epistemic reach, but as well with respect to its moral implications: physical teleology is physicotheology only insofar as it needs, in accordance with needed epistemic limitation of our reflective power of judgment, to assume a supersensible substratum conceived of as an architectonic understanding.[37] It must leave undetermined whether this architectonic understanding is truly acting teleologically or merely as an artistic intellect that, as it were, acts instinctively 'from its own nature'. Physical teleology is, therefore, a mere "propaedeutic of theology" (CPJ AA. 5:442).[38]

Nevertheless, the physical teleological perspective forces us to thematise not only the beginning of the chain of final causes, but as well its ultimate or final end:

> Once an understanding has been conceived that must be regarded as the cause of the possibility of such forms as they are really found in things, then we must also raise the question of the objective ground that could have determined this productive understanding to an effect of this sort, which is then the final end for which such things exist.
>
> (CPJ AA.5:434/5)

However, this final end cannot be *in* nature, since it must be unconditioned, yet everything in nature even according to the teleological perspective is conditioned (i.e. a means to an end). The final end, by definition, can only be an end, not a means. It can only be dependent on "the idea of it" (CPJ AA. 5:435).

It is this concept of a final end that brings moral philosophy into focus once more, since the final end can only be a human being insofar as it is a moral, autonomous finite rational being. We are such beings only if "considered as a noumenon"" (CPJ AA. 5:435) as Kant points out.

> Now of the human being (and thus of every rational being in the world), as a moral being, it cannot be further asked why (*quem in finem*) it exists. His existence contains the highest end itself, to

which, as far as he is capable, he can subject the whole of nature, or against which at least he need not hold himself to be subjected by any influence from nature.

(CPJ AA. 5:435)

In the end, it thus is the teleological perspective that affords a transition to the supersensible ground of nature and hence to theology as well as to the supersensible being of moral agents and hence to moral philosophy: Not by supplying itself the conception of a final end, but by pointing to an undetermined (and, as far as the power of judgment is concerned, undeterminable) *vacancy* that can only be filled by a determination of pure *practical* reason.

While the presentation of objective purposiveness in objects of nature (natural ends) affords a way of pointing towards the intelligent world-cause and its final end, this concept is not *introduced* by this reasoning: Indeed, in the *Critique of Practical Reason* it has been introduced by the reflections on the highest good and the postulates necessary for its realisability.[39]

And indeed it is exactly at this point of his argument in the *Doctrine of Methods* of the *Critique of the Power of Judgement* that Kant takes up his doctrine of the highest good and the postulates.[40] It is only through practical reason that the idea of a final end *in nature* can get objective reality through its identification with the highest good. Kant nicely summarises this connection towards the very end of the third *Critique*:

In contrast, the highest final end that is to be realised by us, that through which alone we can become worthy of being ourselves the final end of a creation, is an idea that has objective reality for us in a practical relation, and is an object, but since we cannot provide objective reality for this concept from a theoretical point of view, a mere matter of faith of pure reason, together with God and immortality, as the conditions under which alone we can, given the constitution of our (human) reason, conceive of the possibility of that effect of the lawful use of our freedom.

(CPJ 5:469/70)

It thus turns out that only by aiming to realise the highest good as a final end *in* nature we can be considered worthy of being the final end *of* nature. The primacy of practical reason has thus been done full justice, while at the same time theoretical reason has come as far as conceptually possible in order to 'compare and connect the self-determination of practical reason with everything that it has within its power'.

The peculiar teleological perspective that is necessitated by the objective purposiveness of natural ends thus necessitates the transition from theoretical to practical reason without being able to actually itself be part of the actual transition that transcends its conceptual scope. Therefore, the teleological considerations of the third *Critique* bring theoretical reasoning right to the threshold of its reaching into the realm of the nominal, without, however, ever transgressing this threshold in a way that would endanger the limits of experience that Kant so carefully draws in the *Critique of Pure Reason* in order to make room for his naturalism of empirical reality.

Hence, while this transition indeed can indeed bridge the chasm between theoretical and practical reason, we have to keep in mind that this whole reasoning is reasoning of the reflective, not the constitutive power of judgment. (That was exactly what the solution of the *Antinomy of the Teleological Power of Judgement* with its extensive and intricate use of negative limiting concepts was intended to show.) In this way, we cannot lend the resulting view of an objectively purposive nature and its creator (a creator with will and intellect having purposes and final ends) any kind of theoretical reality. These ideas can get whatever reality they have only through *practical* philosophy. Kant remains adamant about the limits of theoretical knowledge, thereby saving his transcendental idealist version of philosophical naturalism.

Notes

1. Cf. CPJ AA 5:170. On the question of completion cf. Förster 2012, Ch. 7.
2. Cf. CPJ AA 5:447.
3. Cf. CPR B163.
4. Parallel considerations an be found in CPR A125–6.
5. This is in line with hylomorphic readings of Kant's transcendental idealism. Cf. e.g. Engstrom (2006), Pollok (2014). On the general Kantian use of the form-matter distinction that is presupposed here, see Haag 2007: 108f.
6. Cf. e.g. Sellars 1978: §48.
7. Cf. for the details Haag 2007, Chs. 6–8.
8. The following considerations are heavily indebted to Sellars (1976).
9. For a similar line of thought, see Pollok (2001).
10. One might ask here if the formal sparseness and pure mechanism of nature in the first *Critique* (as well as in the *Prolgeomena*) amounts to a *disenchanted* conception of nature—what John McDowell calls a 'bald' naturalism. Given my characterisation of Kantian naturalism at the beginning of the first section of this chapter, I think the answer to such a question is that Kantian naturalism is not a disenchanted or 'bald' naturalism.
11. In a way, the following sections are an attempt to describe a non-reductivist approach to this fact that leaves the 'oddness' of Kant's normativism from the perspective of a contemporary (mainstream) analytic naturalism largely intact.
12. The concept of a highest good has received intense discussion over the last years. I cannot go into these for the purpose of this paper. Cf. e.g. Aufderheide and Bader 2015; Höwing 2016.
13. This is a merger of the two formulations Kant gives on CPrR AA. 5:113 and 5:114, respectively.
14. Again a merger of the two formulations. Since Messer's seminal study of Kant's Ethics (1904) the antinomy has often been recast in the following way:

thesis: the highest good is possible. Antithesis: the highest good is impossible. This formulation, while it cannot be found at the surface of the text has several advantages and can be seen in line with the spirit of the Kantian argument. Cf. Förster 2012: 120. However, for reasons of exposition of the concept of a highest good I decided to stick more closely to Kant's own exposition of the antinomy.

15. For this cf. e.g. Förster 2000, Ch. 1, Guyer 2003: 209.
16.

> On this is grounded the division of the critique of the power of judgement into that of the aesthetic and teleological power of judgement; by the former is meant the faculty for judging formal purposiveness (also called subjective) through the feeling of pleasure or displeasure, by the latter the faculty for judging the real purposiveness (objective) of nature through understanding and reason.
>
> (CPJ AA. 5:193)

17. For a sketch of this development, see Förster 2012, Ch. 6.
18. Again, the difference is ultimately not that important for Kant's conception of knowledge.
19. Cf. CPJ AA. 5:220.
20. Cf. CPJ AA. 5:180.
21. Cf. CPJ AA. 5:192.
22. Cf. Förster 2000: 10.
23. Cf. 5:2010. Förster emphasises that point repeatedly.
24. Cf. CPJ AA. 5:193.
25. Cf. CPJ AA. 5:359.
26. For the purpose at hand, I will mostly ignore the highly significant fact that the faculty of presentation is the *imagination*.
27. This holds at least for schematic presentation.
28. That means that I will ignore the relevance of the aesthetically considerations in relation to the question of an *interest of practical reason*. Cf. e.g. CPJ AA. 5:300. This interest, for the purpose at hand, is only relevant in as such as it relates to the conception of nature.
29. See, for example, McDowell (2009), Price (2013, 2015).
30. Otherwise, it would indeed be a mere "analogue of art" (CPJ AA. 5:374).
31. This is the point at which Hannah Ginsborg's influential criticism of Peter McLaughlin's interpretation goes astray. She writes:

> For, to put the point very simply, the mechanical inexplicability of organisms in that sense is supposed to be a ground for regarding them teleologically: it is because organisms are, to us, mechanically inexplicable, that we must regard them as ends or purposes. But for Kant there is no less of a need for teleology in understanding a machine such as a watch, than there is in understanding an organism. And this means that—unless, implausibly, the need for teleology in the two cases stems from two quite different sources—it cannot be the non-machine-like character of organisms which makes them mechanically inexplicable. Rather, what makes them mechanically inexplicable has to be something they share with machines and other artifacts.
>
> Ginsborg 2004: 37

This would only be right, if organisms would exhibit a causality 'analogous to a causality we know', i.e. the final causation of intentional action.
32. James Kreines makes a similar point in Kreines 2005.

33. Cf. CPJ AA. 5:408.28/9. Since the concept could not simply be abstracted from the objects in question—organisms—it had to be formed, as we have seen, by an analogical transformation from the concept of an end.
34. The resulting antinomy would be an antinomy of reason, not of the power of judgment, as Kant makes clear. Cf. CPJ AA. 5: 387.
35. What follows is a mere outline of this complex argument. For a more detailed account along the lines suggested cf. Haag 2013. The suggested reconstruction of course relies heavily on Eckart Förster's account as presented in chapter 6 of his *The 25 Years of Philosophy* (2012).
36. Against this background even beauty in nature can now be considered objectively purposive. Cf. CPJ AA. 5:380
37. Cf. for example CPJ AA. 5:437
38. CF. as well CPJ AA. 5:444.
39. Cf. CPrR AA. 5:129. The extreme brief remarks at the end of the *Paralogisms*-chapter in the B-edition of the CPR (cf. B 425) can be read as anticipating the much more explicit introduction in the CPrR.
40. Kant refers back to these considerations in the CPJ AA. 5:446.

References

Kant's works are quoted in the usual manner after *Kants gesammelte Schriften*, vols. 1–22 ed. Preußischen Akademie der Wissenschaften, Berlin 1902 ff., vol. 23 ed. Deutschen Akademie der Wissenschaften, Berlin, 1956, vols. 24–29 ed. Akademie der Wissenschaften zu Göttingen, Berlin 1966 ff. The translation for the most part follows the *Cambridge Edition of the Works of Imanuel Kant*, eds. P. Guyer and Allen W. Wood.

Aufderheide, J., and Bader, R. M. (eds.) 2015. *The Highest Good in Aristotle and Kant*. Oxford: Oxford University Press.

Engstrom, S. 2006. 'Understanding and Sensibility'. *Inquiry* 49: 2–25.

Förster, E. 2000. *Kant's Final Synthesis*. Cambridge, MA: Harvard University Press.

———. 2012. *The Twenty-Five Years of Philosophy*. Cambridge, MA: Harvard University Press.

Ginsborg, H. 2004. 'Two Kinds of Mechanical Inexplicability in Kant and Aristotle'. *Journal of the History of Philosophy* 42: 33–65.

Guyer, P. 2003. 'Beauty, Systematicity, and the Highest Good'. *Inquiry* 46: 195–214.

Haag, J. 2007. *Erfahrung und Gegenstand*. Frankfurt: Klostermann.

———. 2013. 'Grenzbegriffe und die Antinomie der teleologischen Urteilskraft'. In J. Haag and M. Wild (eds.) *Übergänge, diskursiv oder intuitiv? Essays zu Eckart Försters Die 25 Jahre der Philosophie*. Frankfurt: Klostermann.

Höwing, T. (ed.) 2016. *The Highest Good in Kant's Philosophy*. Berlin: De Gruyter.

Kreines, J. 2005. 'The Inexplicability of Kant's Naturzweck: Kant on Teleology, Explanation and Biology'. *Archiv fur die Geschichte der Philosophie* 87: 270–311.

McDowell, J. 2009. *Having the World in View: Essays on Kant, Hegel, and Sellars*. Cambridge, MA: Harvard University Press.

Messer, A. 1904. *Kants Ethik*. Leipzig: Veit.

Pollok, K. 2001. *Kants "Metaphyissche Anfangsgründe der Naturwissenschaft".* *Ein kritischer Kommentar.* Hamburg: Meiner.

———. 2014. ' "The Understanding Prescribes Laws to Nature": Spontaneity, Legislation, and Kant's Transcendental Hylomorphism'. *Kant-Studien* 105: 509–530.

Price, H. 2013. *Expressivism, Pragmatism, and Representationalism.* Cambridge: Cambridge University Press.

———. 2015. 'Idling and Sidling Toward Philosophical Peace'. In S. Gross, N. Tebben and M. Williams (eds.) *Meaning Without Representation: Essays on Truth, Expression, Normativity, and Naturalism.* Oxford: Oxford University Press.

Sellars, W. 1976. 'Kant's Transcendental Idealism'. *Collections of Philosophy* 6: 165–181, reprinted in: Sellars, W. 2002, *Kant's Transcendental Metaphysics. Sellars's Cassirer Lectures Notes and Other Essays.* J F. Sicha (ed.) Atascadero, CA: Ridgeview.)

———. 1978. 'The Role of Imagination in Kant's Theory of Experience'. In H. Johnstone (ed.) *Categories: A Colloquium.* University Park, PA: Pennsylvania State University Press, reprinted in: Sellars, W. 2007. *In the Space of Reasons: Selected Essays of Wilfrid Sellars.* K. Scharp and R. B. Brandom (eds.) Cambridge, MA: Harvard University Press.

3   The Placement Problem and the Threat of Voyeurism

Paul Giladi

We see that the intellect, so skilful in dealing with the inert, is awkward the moment it touches the living. . . . [The intellect] proceeds with the rigour, the stiffness and the brutality of an instrument not designed for such use.

—Henri Bergson

The apparent force of the Placement Problem appears to lend considerable weight to philosophical projects such as reductionism, eliminativism, and instrumentalism. These theories, it is thought, are united by vocabularies and conceptual schemes better suited than their more metaphysically inclined rivals to make sense of things,[1] since reductionism and eliminativism are thought to be prices very much worth paying to avoid supernaturalism. However, rather than *solve* the Placement Problem by arguing in favour of either reductionism or eliminativism or supernaturalism,[2] I think we should *dissolve* the Placement Problem in an Hegelian manner: I argue that the explanation for why the Placement Problem grips the philosophic imagination with such force is that rational activity is exclusively articulated in terms of the kind of inferential patterns definitive of analytical thinking, namely the kind of thinking symptomatic of *Verstand*. This, in turn, leads to conceiving of the space of reasons and the space of nature as fundamentally in tension with another, and to regarding the manifest image and scientific image as metaphilosophical antagonists.

However, central to Hegelianism is a committed opposition to treating the nomothetic qualities of the Laplacian model of rationality which *Verstand* instantiates most explicitly as exhaustive of critical thinking. This is because Hegel places significant emphasis on the dialectical function of *Vernunft*, which does not conceive of rational activity as a detached, voyeuristic critical reason. Why *Vernunft* is favoured here over analytical reflection is that *Verstand* fails to be completely illustrative of our *geistige Einstellung* phenomenology, our *Erlebnis*, and our sense of ourselves as self-interpreting rational agents engaging in multifaceted forms of enquiry. For Hegel, one must go beyond a particular kind of naturalism, namely a narrow naturalism which alienates us from ourselves.

I

For Occidental cultural theory, the guiding principle of modernity, typified by the Enlightenment, was the expectation that the emancipation of natural and normative sciences from religion would, as Habermas phrases it, "promote only the control of natural forces but also understanding of the world and of the self, moral progress, the justice of institutions and even the happiness of human beings".[3] Given the macrosociological dimension and scope of the project of the Enlightenment, Weber famously argued that modernity involves the interrelation of *rationalisation* and *disenchantment*. The process of rationalisation involves humanity's attempt to make all features of reality intelligible, so much so that the cognitive desire to make sense of things invariably morphs into the "desire to increase mastery, control, over every aspect of the world".[4] However, the general process of the rationalisation of the world crucially involves increased exercises of discursive sub-processes: developments in 'substantive rationality' involve rendering values traditionally associated with religious forms of life and value-systems more coherent; and developments in 'formal rationality' involve methods and practices that increasingly codify and quantify attitudes and institutions.

Under the Weberian framework, there are particular kinds of action necessarily associated with formal rationality and substantive rationality respectively: instrumental rational (*zweckrational*) action involves using discursive reason for the sake of achieving some particular goal. Instrumental/formal reason aims at controlling/dominating the objects of one's concern. However, by contrast, value-rational (*wertrational*) action is not modelled on any kind of subject-object relationship and means-end framework. This is because value-rational action is the variety of activity discursively constituted by communicative reason, to use Habermasian terminology: since the function of substantive rationality is to bring about the *intelligibility* of normative concepts such as justice and goodness under a coherent and rationally justified system, value-rational action is directed at ends-in-themselves and to realising an intersubjective relationship between agents as much as possible.

The relationship between drives for substantive rational action and drives for instrumental/formal action invariably causes friction *within* reason, to the extent that the question for modernity would not be whether or not reason will be sovereign but *which specific pattern of rationality and action would emerge hegemonic in the general process of rationalisation*. For Weber, the task of sociology is to explore why instrumental/formal rationality has come to dominate in modern Western society, and why, by consequence, has nature been disenchanted (*entzaubert*) and culture faces "extirpation".[5] Construing modernity as eventually culminating in a state of "mechanised petrification"[6] in an "iron cage" (*stahlhartes Gehäuse*),[7] Weber articulates the connection between rationalisation and disenchantment in terms of a tragic dialectic of religion.

While, of course, providing a complete explication of Weber's social anthropology of religion goes far beyond the scope of this chapter, I think it would be helpful to briefly sketch his central narrative: in an effort to satisfy non-biological means of self-preservation,[8] pre-historical human beings developed fetishist religious practices. Primitive societies often tended to imbue ordinary objects with spiritual and magical significance under a form of polytheism, so much so that nature was enchanted as the living embodiment of divine beings. However, over the course of the development of societal psychology and the ways in which human societies considered how to satisfy their *cura animarum*, the fetishist framework gradually gave way to intellectualised monotheistic religions underpinning the Abrahamic faiths. As Keith Breen writes, "Judaism, Christianity and Islam . . . sought to render suffering comprehensible".[9] This turn to rationalisation, as Weber put it, was motivated by showing that the world "in its totality is, could, and should somehow be a meaningful 'cosmos'".[10]

With Christianity at least, the kind of systematisation of doctrine and the challenges raised to Catholicism by the Protestant movement during and since the Reformation establish the ironic grounds for the progressive secularisation of modern Western society: although the rise of institutionalised religion and its correlative theological schema led to the abandonment of primitive fetishism, the disenchantment of the world is effected by the power of Protestantism and Puritanism, which did not simply wish to reject papal authority and revise Christian theology by rejecting divine mysteries.[11] These movements also wished to construe religion as *allied* with formal reason and not merely residing within the bounds of sense:[12] explanation-bearers were no longer an esoteric group of priests endowed with magical capacities for disclosing "mysterious incalculable forces".[13]

Rather, as a result of the spectacular and rapid expansions in scientific knowledge and enquiry, that title now belonged to those engaging in formalised rational practices. The mathematical paradigm of scientific explanation that had initially been articulated by Laplace[14] and refined by the German Materialists during the mid-1800s[15] had enabled nomothetic reason to achieve hegemony due to how the formalisation and mathematisation of the complexities in nature were being met with enthusiastic acclaim:[16] with Helmholtz's landmark 1847 monograph, *Über die Erhaltung der Kraft*, leading from the front, one explained natural events and processes by subsuming them under general laws of mechanics, specifically in the reduction of all changes in the physical world down to the movements of atoms.[17] To quote Frederick Beiser on this subject:

> Since the laws of such mechanics are mathematically formulable, they have all the certainties of mathematics. Following this paradigm, the

ideal of knowledge is a system of differential equations from which we can determine, with complete precision and accuracy, what happens in the universe at any given place and time. If we know these equations, and if we also know the position, velocity, and direction of all the atoms in one moment of the universe, we can determine with complete precision their position, velocity, and direction at every other moment, whether in the past or future. Ultimately, we could formulate for the system of equations a single mathematical formula to express the whole of these mechanical relations.[18]

Nature is thus conceived as a refined aggregate of physical objects and processes, following strict universal and necessary laws. Anything that is natural must conform to these laws. For Helmholtz, as Michael Friedman writes, "the possibility of reducing all of the appearances of nature to this basis, in accordance with the law of causality, is then 'the condition for the complete conceptualisability of nature' [*Die Bedingung der vollständigen Begreiflichkeit der Natur*]".[19]

If advances in modern physics and chemistry had not already proclaimed nomothetic rationalisation as sovereign,[20] the revolutionary impact of Darwinism in biological science guaranteed the *complete* disenchantment of the world by construing humanity in *purely* causal and naturalistic vocabulary with traditional onto-theological concepts and categorisations consigned out of the scientific image.[21] As Windelband elegantly wrote:

> Transcending the limited domain of phenomena to which their original fruitful application was restricted, these [nomothetic] methods have been generalised as much as possible in the attempt to comprehend the entire circumference of human knowledge.[22]

Such was the totalising effect of nomothetic reason's transformation of enquiry (and social relations and practices) that the Laplacian model of scientific explanation became the foundational schema of what contemporary Anglo-American philosophers tend to call the 'Placement Problem'.[23]

As Huw Price (2004) suggests, the Placement Problem can be expressed in the following way:[24]

1. All reality is ultimately natural reality.
2. Whatever one wishes to admit into natural reality must be placed in natural reality.
3. *Modality, meaning, universals, norms, intentionality,* and so on do not seem admissible into natural reality.
4. Therefore, if they are to be placed in nature, they must be forced into a category that does not seem appropriate for their specific

characters; and if they cannot be placed in nature, then they must be either dismissed as non-genuine phenomena or at best regarded as parasitic second-rate phenomena.[25]

The Placement Problem problematises where 'odd' phenomena, such as norms and intentionality, might 'fit' in the world described by physics, chemistry, and biology. Natural science and fundamental physics *in particular*, therefore, are hegemonic,[26] to the extent that they have become the focal points of dialectic.[27] Why these 'odd' phenomena are viewed as *problematic* is principally because their status as central concepts of the *manifest* image's web of belief means there is invariably *foundational* friction between them and the mathematisable and quantifiable features of the *scientific* image.[28] Such is the latter's epistemic authority that the Placement Problem, from the very outset, aims to *level out the idiosyncratic dimensions of the manifest image and the space of reasons in order for them to be deemed legitimate.* This is because both the structure and the discursive grammar of the Placement Problem frame the legitimacy of modality, meaning, universals, norms, and intentionality *in terms of whether or not they can be placed/located in the world described by the natural sciences.*[29] As Sellars writes:

> The naturalistic 'thesis' that the world, including the verbal behaviour of those who use the term 'ought'—and the mental states involving the concept to which this world gives expression—can 'in principle', be described without using the term 'ought' or any prescriptive expression, is a logical point about what it is to count as a description *in principle* of the world. . . [N]aturalism presents us with the ideal of a *pure* description of the world (in particular human behaviour), a description which simply says what things *are*, and never, in any respect, what they *ought* or *ought not* to be; and it is clear (as a matter of simple logic) that neither 'ought' nor any other prescriptive expression *could* be *used* (as opposed to *mentioned*) in such a description.[30]

Since purely naturalistic vocabulary is given *priority for arranging our way of making sense of things*, modality, meaning, universals, norms, and intentionality must be *forced* into a quantitative category that does not seem appropriate for their *specific* characters;[31] and if they cannot fit in the world described by the natural sciences, then they must be either dismissed as non-genuine or at best regarded as parasitic. Alex Rosenberg makes the latter point particularly proudly here:

> What is the world really like? It's fermions and bosons, and everything that can be made up of them, and nothing that can't be made up of them. All the facts about fermions and bosons determine or

"fix" all the other facts about reality and what exists in this universe or any other if, as physics may end up showing, there are other ones. Another way of expressing this fact-fixing by physics is to say that all the other facts—the chemical, biological, psychological, social, economic, political, cultural facts supervene on the physical facts and are ultimately explained by them. And if physics can't in principle fix a putative fact, it is no fact after all.[32]

Given the *levelling* nature of nomothetic rationality and its naturalistic vocabulary, anything that resists conforming is thereby labelled 'odd'— by being labelled in such a manner, 'odd' phenomena become 'problematic' and are thereby *ultimately* construed in terms of *strict alterity*.

The Laplacian model of *quantitative* rationality gives rise to the Placement Problem; and the *force* of the Placement Problem lends considerable weight to philosophical projects such as reductionism, eliminativism, instrumentalism, and nonfactualism. This is why under the Placement Problem, anything that is opposed to reductionism and eliminativism is *ipso facto* understood to have a penchant for the supernatural or the irrational. Such labelling, of course, serve as a *prima facie* reason to be particularly concerned that the occult and the non-scientific are being surreptitiously smuggled through customs.

However, rather than *solve* the Placement Problem by arguing in favour of either reductionism or eliminativism or supernaturalism, I think we should *dissolve* the Placement Problem in a Hegelian manner: central to Hegelianism is a committed opposition to treating the nomothetic qualities of *Verstand* as exhaustive of critical thinking. This is because Hegel places significant emphasis on the dialectical function of *Vernunft*, which does not conceive of rational activity as a detached, voyeuristic critical reason. Why *Vernunft* is favoured here over analytical reflection is that *Verstand* fails to be completely illustrative of our *geistige Einstellung* phenomenology, our *Erlebnis*, and our sense of ourselves as self-interpreting rational agents engaging in multifaceted forms of enquiry. For Hegel, one must go beyond a particular kind of naturalism, namely a *narrow* naturalism which alienates us from ourselves. The ultimate advantage of this *broader* naturalism is that it is a remarkable improvement over the emaciated empiricism of reductionism and eliminativism,[33] as it is defended as part of a properly scientific understanding of the world.

II

Unlike Kant, Hegel does not claim that "[*Verstand* and *Vernunft*] . . . designate completely independent functions or faculties. Reason is simply the necessary result of the immanent movement of the understanding".[34] In other words, reason is a "form of holistic explanation, which shows how all finite things are parts of a wider whole".[35] For Hegel, the advantage of drawing this distinction between reason and understanding is that we can be in a position to not be wrapped up in the various dualisms which are the inevitable consequence of reflecting *only* from the perspective of *Verstand*, i.e. purely *analytical* forms of reflection. What *Vernunft* provides consciousness with is the means to avoid the pitfalls of dualisms and the problems of analysis by thinking dialectically, i.e. by drawing distinctions yet establishing interconnectedness to a whole:

> What man seeks in this situation, ensnared here as he is in finitude on every side, is the region of a higher, more substantial, truth, in which all oppositions and contradictions in the finite can find their final resolution, and freedom its full satisfaction. . . . The highest truth, truth as such, is the resolution of the highest opposition and contradiction. In it validity and power are swept away from the opposition between freedom and necessity, between spirit and nature, between knowledge and its object, between law and impulse, from opposition and contradiction as such, whatever forms they make take. Their validity and power *as* opposition and contradiction is gone. . . . The ordinary consciousness, on the other hand, cannot extricate itself from this opposition and either remains despairingly in contradiction or else casts it aside and helps itself in some other way. But philosophy enters into the heart of the self-contradictory characteristics, knows them in their essential nature, i.e. as in their one-sidedness not absolute but self-dissolving, and it sets them in the harmony and unity which is truth. To grasp this Concept is the task of philosophy.
>
> (Hegel 1975; LA I: 99–100)

The arguments Hegel gives in this engaging passage—namely that the task of philosophy is to lead our ways of understanding all aspects of our world away from purely dualistic and oppositional ways of thinking, and to enable us to reflect on the intelligibility of both difference *and* unity in our world—serve as a powerful critique of strategies that ignore (whether wilfully or not) the *philosophical* nature of certain problematics. If one applies this general metaphilosophical riposte to the development of *strict* scientific naturalism since Quine in the Anglo-American world, I think there is good reason to suppose Hegel would agree with the following claim by Lynne Baker, namely that "[s]cientific naturalism often seems like a change of subject that lacks respect for the peculiar projects and puzzles that traditionally occupy philosophers".[36] Crucially, however, the lack of respect for the peculiarity and *sui generis* features of the normative space of reasons does not *necessarily* find its expression in *only* reductionist and eliminativist philosophical projects: the expressions *finding a place for mind in the natural world* and *making elbow room for intentionality in the world described by physics*, which seem to be staples of more liberal and pluralistic conceptual attitudes, both seem to presuppose that one ought to accept from the very outset the vocabulary and general *Weltanschauung* of the natural sciences and *then* find some meaningful and coherent way of quite literally *fitting* in phenomena such as intentionality and normativity into that nomothetic picture.

The Hegelian concern about such a model is a crisis of communication: the model remains locked in the viewpoint of *the understanding* and is therefore dialectically inhibited from *radically revising the very notion of how sense-making ought to be constituted and practised*. For all of the indisputably important and impressive noetic achievements of the natural sciences,[37] the march to scient*ism*[38] constitutes a type of 'self-renunciation' and a *failure of rationality*. I think a particularly helpful way of seeing how this works is provided by reflecting on Hegel's arguments in 'Observing Reason'.

The form of consciousness in this chapter of the *Phenomenology of Spirit* is concerned with achieving at homeness in the world *only* through the natural sciences. Since the natural sciences are serving as *the* cognitive guide here, the phenomenological subject is interested in making sense of things *only* nomothetically, by subsuming individuals under general categories or universal laws of nature:

> Previously, its perception and *experience* of various aspects of the Thing were something that only *happened* to consciousness but here, consciousness *makes its own* observations and experiments. 'Meaning' and 'perceiving', which previously were superseded *for us*, are now superseded by and for consciousness itself. Reason sets to work to *know* the truth, to find in the form of a Notion that which, for 'meaning' and 'perceiving', is a Thing; i.e. it seeks to possess in thinghood the consciousness only of itself. Reason now has, therefore, a universal interest in the world, because it is certain of its presence in the world, or that the world present to it is rational. It seeks its 'other', knowing that therein it possesses nothing else but itself: it seeks only its own infinitude.
>
> (*PS*, §240: 145–6)

However, the practice of purely observing nature and aiming to 'carve reality at the joints' through the exercise of nomothetic rationality quickly sees the phenomenological subject finding *Verstand* rationally unsatisfying. As Hegel writes:

> Observation, which kept [its biological categories] properly apart and believed that in them it had something firm and settled, sees principles overlapping one another, transitions and confusions developing; what it at first took to be absolutely separate, it sees combined with something else, and what it reckoned to be in combination, it sees apart and separate. So it is that observation which clings to passive,

unbroken selfsameness of being, inevitably sees itself tormented just in its most general determinations—e.g. of what are the *differentiae* of an animal or a plant—by instances which rob it of every determination, invalidate the universality to which it has risen, and reduce it to an observation and description which is devoid of thought.

(*PS*, §247: 150)

For Hegel, to properly develop a conception of nature, one must go beyond a particular kind of empiricism, namely an empiricism which only, as Cinzia Ferrini writes,

> analyses objects by distinguishing and isolating their various features, [where] these features [then] acquire the form of universality by being separated. Yet this highlights the first inconvenience of description, the superficiality of abstracting universals from particulars and then consequent instability and arbitrariness of these general forms under which things are merely subsumed.[39]

Hegel's critique of *Verstand* is made especially complex by how he seems to blend his metaphysical concerns about a non-dialectical relationship between the categories of individuality/universality/particularity with a phenomenologico-hermeneutic concern about the *practices* of nomothetic enquiry *simpliciter*. However, while Hegel's objections to abstract universality are well documented in the literature, there seems to be comparatively *less* attention devoted to his objection to the *practice of observation*. For example, Robert Stern's analysis of 'Observing Reason' principally focuses on Hegelian worries about universals, but only hints at what *might* be construed as the *more* philosophically striking objection to scientific naturalism in that chapter of the *Phenomenology*: "Observing Reason thus finds itself constructing laws that are increasingly general and removed from the concreteness of the experimental situation".[40]

An advantage of diagnosing scientism et al. as cognitive pathologies lies in how the one-sided conceptual structure that constitutes the framework of scientism reveals underpinnings of the eliminativist and reductionist attitudes that serve as steering drives of nomothetic practice. I think one has compelling reason to think that positions such as eliminativism exhibit marked degrees of anthropological self-hate, to the extent that the desire for a purely nomothetic account of the world conveys a fear of complexity and a corresponding loathing of the necessarily qualitative features of embeddedness and embodiment. Such theories, as Nicholas Rescher writes, "turn Occam's razor into Robespierre's guillotine".[41] From a Hegelian-Husserlian perspective, purging the lifeworld of all its idiosyncratic and unique *Geistig* features, to quote Tim Mooney, involves a self-refuting "secularised Platonism",[42] for scientism necessarily *presupposes* the grammar of the *lifeworld* in an effort to excise it *in favour* of the pure scientific image. As Robert Hanna writes:

> the basic natural sciences, as rational human cognitive achievements, and also natural scientists themselves, as fully engaging in pre-exact-scientific and trans-exact-scientific human rationality at every moment of their conscious and self-conscious lives, are necessarily irreducible to the physical facts known by those very sciences and those very scientists.[43]

Such a position is broadly shared by Baker, but her unique critical perspective on contemporary scientific naturalism extends the polemic beyond Hanna: "[i]n a world without first-person properties . . . there could be no second-order (or reflective) mental processes at all; so, a scientist who wants to study second-order (or reflective) mental processes must presuppose that her subjects have first-person properties".[44] Baker's argument hinges on the claim that first-person phenomena and, what I would call, *the hermeneutic textures* of the robust first-personal perspective are irreducible and ineliminable,[45] to the extent that *any* variety of naturalism is rendered false if it is committed to a purely third-personal and purely observational view of reality:

> The robust first-person perspective is the capacity to conceive of oneself* in the first person. This capacity is directly manifested in I*-thoughts and I*-sentences;[46] it is indirectly manifested in other thoughts and sentences that presuppose that the thinker/speaker has the capacity to conceive of herself as herself* in the first person.[47]
>
> My belief about myself under a first-person description has special behavioural consequences that a similar belief about myself under a third-person description lacks . . . I have a first-person perspective which is irreducible and ineliminable. Consequently, not all the facts are expressible without reference to the first person. Thus, insofar as naturalism provides a conception of the world that has no room for first-person properties, it cannot be true.[48]

For Baker, her specific targets are Dennett (1991) and Metzinger (2003a, 2003b), since both philosophers aim to construct a model of consciousness "from the third-personal point of view since all science is constructed from that perspective".[49] Though she does not reference Hegel at all in her monograph, there is no good reason to suppose that her position would not find some broad support from Hegel; if anything, Hegelian resources can be employed to substantiate a critical remark by Baker that seems somewhat underdeveloped: naturalising the first person "does no justice to the phenomenology or moral significance of I*-thoughts".[50] In what follows, I argue that Hegelian resources offer a more radical and *metaphysical-existential* objection to the third-personal point of view regarding intentionality.

The harm of naturalising the first person involves a radical form of dehumanisation, to the extent that our default self-conception as *Geist* is erased and replaced with a hermeneutically dissonant view of human beings as *unmittelbar natürliche*: what distinguishes *Geist* from mere *Natur* is self-consciousness and the ways in which intentional and goal-driven self-reflexive action renders human beings as thoroughgoingly active in the world. Such a position would be illustrative of Kant's notion of *pragmatic anthropology*, which crucially draws a distinction between *die Welt kennen* and *Welt haben*: "the expressions "to *know* the world" and "to *have* the world" are rather far from each other in their meaning, since one only *understands* the play that one has watched, while the other has *participated* in it".[51] To quote Terry Pinkard: "[o]n Hegel's view, one acts in terms of the nature of that to which one concretely first-personally refers, that is, to oneself and to one's own nature as having practical reason embedded within it".[52] Individuals come to have an understanding of themselves as individuals—their practical relation-to-self, to use Axel Honneth's expression—only through a complex set of *social* interactions.[53]

Crucially, this complex set of social interactions can only play a necessary role in the development and sustaining of a practical relation-to-self if intentional vocabulary is operative at all relevant levels. As Hegel writes:

> A self-consciousness, in being an object, is just as much 'I' as 'object'. With this, we already have before us the Notion of *Spirit*. What still lies ahead for consciousness is the experience of what Spirit is—this absolute substance which is the unity of the different independent self-consciousnesses which, in their opposition, enjoy perfect freedom and independence: the 'I' that is 'We' and the 'We' that is 'I'. It is in self-consciousness, in the Notion of Spirit, that consciousness first finds its turning-point, where it leaves behind it the colourful show of the sensuous here-and-now and the nightlike void of the supersensible beyond and steps out into the spiritual daylight of the present.
> (*PS*, §177: 110–111)

Geist, as mutual recognitive relationships between agents, sees personhood constituted intersubjectively.[54] As Habermas writes:

> individuation is pictured not as the self-realisation of an independently acting subject carried out in isolation and freedom but as a linguistically mediated process of socialisation and the simultaneous constitution of a life-history that is conscious of itself. . . . Individuality forms itself in relations of intersubjective acknowledgement and of intersubjectively mediated self-understanding.[55]

Linguistic socialisation involves not just grasping the Gricean norms of assertion, it also involves knowing how to *move* in the normative space of reasons. Successful navigation in the space of reasons requires grasping the plurality of inferential commitments and entitlements one has in the communicative use of concepts. Emphasis on communication as an intersubjectively constituted performative act transforms the subject from being an *observer/voyeur* to being a *speaker and hearer*. Understood in such a manner, the Intersubjectivist Turn empowers human beings by regarding their communicative practices as *normatively authoritative*, since it is only through successful discourse that one's develops notions of individual identity (as well as establishing the legitimacy and validity of social practices). As such, the following remark from Charles Taylor about the inherently *public* nature of language and the social dimensions of intentionality is relevant to the discussion here:

> The new theory of language that arises at the end of the eighteenth century, most notably in the work of Herder and Humboldt, not only gives a new account of how language is essential to human thought, but also places the capacity to speak not simply in the individual but primarily in the speech community. This totally upsets the outlook of the mainstream epistemological tradition. Now arguments to this effect have formed part of the refutation of atomism that has proceeded through an overturning of standard modern epistemology. Important examples of arguments of this kind are Hegel's in the first chapter of the *Phenomenology of Spirit*, against the position he defines as "sensible certainty," where he shows both the indispensability of language and its holistic character; and Wittgenstein's famous demonstrations of the uselessness of "ostensive definitions," where he makes plain the crucial role played by language in identifying the object and the impossibility of a purely private language. Both are, I believe, excellent examples of arguments that explore the conditions of intentionality and show their conclusions to be inescapable.[56]

One can regard this as one of the huge boosts in cognitive power that Dennett claims language provides.[57] Modern institutions such as the family, civil society, and the state have become indispensable for the development and maintenance of agentive identity. Crucially, however, such communicative practices can only be genuinely communicative *if I*-thoughts, first-personal intentional properties are operative in linguistic interaction*. The norms embedded in the recognitive structures of the family/civil society/the state, for Hegel,

> are not something alien to the subject. On the contrary, his spirit bears witness to them as to its own essence, the essence in which he has a feeling of his selfhood, and in which he lives as in his own element which is not distinguished from himself. The subject is thus

directly linked to the ethical order by a relation which is more like an identity than even the relation of faith or trust

(*PR*: §147).

As with the dissolution of the mind/world dualism, the individual and the social sphere are no longer fundamentally separate from another, *pace* the classical liberal picture. Freedom is understood in terms of a positive capacity to realise oneself by conceiving of individuality as necessarily embedded in a *reflective and social environment*. Social processes and institutions are assessed, therefore, in normative terms with respect to how well they foster communicability and the development of unique subjectivities which help individuals achieve self-realisation.

The intersubjectivist commitment to articulating how a practical-relation-to-self is developed by socialisation nicely supports Baker's argument for how one develops a 'self-concept':

> To have a robust first-person perspective, one must be able to manifest it. To manifest a robust first-person perspective, one must be able to consciously conceive of oneself as oneself*, to be aware that it is oneself qua oneself that one is conceiving of. That is, one must have a self-concept.[58]

> (1) Necessarily, one has a robust first-person perspective only if one has a self-concept.
> (2) Necessarily, one has a self-concept only if one has a battery of empirical concepts.
> (3) Necessarily, one has a battery of empirical concepts only if one has a public language.
> (4) Necessarily, one has a public language only if one has social and linguistic relations.
> (5) Therefore, necessarily, one has a robust first-person perspective only if one has social and linguistic relations.[59]

Understood in this Hegelian way, arguably the most pressing problem with the framework of nomothetic reason as *exhaustive* of enquiry is that the erasure of both the first-person intentional perspective and the intersubjective dimension of rational agency leaves humanity in the grip of a voyeuristic picture: the attempt to translate the vocabulary of the manifest image into the vocabulary of the pure and ideal scientific image[60] amounts to a debilitating variety of alienation in which humanity is estranged from its *Geistig* and therefore necessarily pluralist matrix of sense-making practices.[61] I take this to bear some similarity with Windelband's critique of positivist attitudes towards *historical* enquiry:

> History produces images of men and human life in the total wealth and profusion of their uniquely peculiar forms and with their full

and vital individuality preserved intact. Past languages and nations, their beliefs and their forms, their struggle for power and freedom, their literature and their thought speak to us through the voice of history—resurrecting what is forgotten into a new form of life. The world which the natural sciences construct is completely different. . . . [Natural scientific theories] strive to acquire knowledge of the nomological necessities whose timeless immutability governs all events. From the colourful world of the senses, the natural sciences construct a system of abstract concepts . . . a silent and colourless world of atoms in which the earthy aura of perceptual qualities has disappeared completely.[62]

However, one Hegelian way of re-enchanting enquiry is possible through effecting resistance by labelling scientism as *one-sided* and *one-dimensional*. Such a move is *dialectical* and aims to supplant the perspective of *Verstand* with the perspective of *Vernunft* in *discourse about sense-making*. If one is to resist and eventually overcome scientistic forms of naturalism, one must develop *speculative* sense-making practices, in which hermeneutic power can be rooted in the communicative power of *discourse about sense-making*. Such second-order modes of reflection necessarily presuppose the kind of self-conscious attitudes and intentional vocabulary of *Geist*. Baker makes a similar point here despite not using a Hegelian *tournure de phrase*: "rational agency requires second-order attitudes and second-order attitudes require a self-concept; anyone who has a second-order attitude has a robust first-person perspective. So, no being can be a rational agent in this strong sense without having a robust first-person perspective".[63]

Returning now to the Placement Problem, I earlier claimed that the Placement Problem problematises where 'odd' phenomena, such as norms and intentionality, might 'fit' within the world described by physics, chemistry, and biology. Price skips lightly over this part of the argument, but it is as though he is thinking of reality like a giant container into which scientists 'place' blocks corresponding to scientific facts as they discover them. It is then envisaged that once science has finished its work, and described all the facts, the container is 'full'—there is no room to place any more blocks in it.[64] Such a way of thinking about reality goes some way to explain why exactly the Placement Problem grips the philosophic imagination with such force: rational activity is *exclusively* articulated in terms of the kind of inferential patterns definitive of analytical thinking, namely the kind of thinking symptomatic of *Verstand*. This, in turn, leads to conceiving of the space of reasons and the space of nature as *fundamentally* in tension with another, and to regarding the manifest image and scientific image as metaphilosophical *antagonists*.[65]

Conceived in this way, the vocabulary of the ideal scientific image becomes epistemically authoritarian and imperialistic by forcing other forms of enquiry to adopt the discursive recourses and grammars of *formal* disciplines that are different in various ways to the manifest image's web of meanings.[66] What is central to this Hegelian project is diagnosing scientism as having made the following error described by Windelband:

> [T]he failure to recognise the autonomy of individual provinces of knowledge.[67]

Recognising the autonomy and heterogeneity of the normative space of reasons in no way entails conceiving of intentionality, et al. as "imaginary skyhooks".[68] On the contrary, it *deepens* our way of viewing reality as intelligible by doing justice to our *geistige Einstellung*, our status as *self-interpreting amphibians engaging in multifaceted modes of sense-making*. Though Hegel does not obviously suggest his amphibian analogy applies to shifting between space-of-reason-discourse and space-of-nature-discourse, I think there is sufficient reason to believe the analogy also holds in this context:

> Taken quite abstractly, it is the opposition of universal and particular, when each is fixed over against the other on its own account in the same way; more concretely, it appears in nature as the opposition of the abstract law to the abundance of individual phenomena, each explicitly with its own character; in the spirit it appears as the contrast between the sensuous and the spiritual in man, as the battle of spirit against flesh, of duty for duty's sake, of the cold command against particular interest, warmth of heart, sensuous inclinations and impulses, against the individual dispositions in general; as the harsh opposition between inner freedom and the necessity of external nature, further as the contradiction between the dead inherently empty concept, and the full concreteness of life, between theory and subjective thinking, and objective existence and experience. These are oppositions which have not been invented at all by the subtlety of reflection or the pedantry of philosophy; in numerous forms they have always preoccupied and troubled the human consciousness, even if it is modern culture that has first worked them out most sharply and driven them up to the peak of harshest contradiction. Spiritual culture, the modern intellect, produces this opposition in man which makes him an amphibious animal, because he now has to live in two worlds which contradict one another. . . . If general culture has run into such a contradiction, it becomes the task of philosophy to supersede the oppositions, i.e. to show that neither the one alternative in its abstraction, nor the other in the like one-sidedness, possesses truth, but that they are both self-dissolving; that truth lies only in the reconciliation and mediation of both, and that this mediation is no mere demand, but what is absolutely accomplished and

is ever self-accomplishing. This insight coincides immediately with the ingenuous faith and will which does have precisely this dissolved opposition steadily present to its view, and in action makes it its end and achieves it. Philosophy affords a reflective insight into the essence of the opposition only in so far as it shows how truth is just the dissolving of opposition and, at that, not in the sense, as may be supposed, that the opposition and its two sides *do not exist at all*, but that they exist reconciled.

(Hegel 1975; LA I: 53–55)

Whilst Hegel notes that a positive feature of modernity is the development of individual autonomy and an unwillingness to defer to external authorities, at the same time, one should acknowledge that Hegel deems inflexibility as *defective* in cases when it morphs into *one-dimensionality* and is used to crowd out dialectical means of making sense of things (*SL*: 21.5–6; 7–8). Given the difference between natural science and philosophy in terms of how they respectively make sense of things, I think it would be incorrect to suppose that natural science and philosophy should be understood in terms of a *Geistig* hierarchy. This is because the way in which natural science makes sense of things is so *different* to the way in which philosophy makes sense of things: conceived in this way, one ought not to regard natural science and philosophy as *rival* forms of intelligibility competing with one another to best satisfy our desire for understanding our world.[69] On the contrary, they should be seen as *complementary* reflective practices, practices which are *jointly* indispensable for adequately and holistically engaging with our environment:[70] reflection on our discursivity illuminates the particular kind of amphibian epistemic architecture we have for experiencing the world from our *Geistig* perspective.[71] To quote Bernard Williams here, who elegantly expresses a similar claim: "I take philosophy to be, part of a more general attempt to make the best sense of our life, and so of our intellectual activities, in the situation in which we find ourselves".[72]

Coming to terms with and embracing our amphibious intellectual situation and its complex vocabularies enables us to realise that, for Hegel, "[t]he final end of the world . . . is that of life assuming the position of *Geistigkeit* (our own mindful agency) and coming to a full self-consciousness, that is, our full awareness of our status as self-interpreting animals".[73] Such an achievement is unattainable so long as one remains locked in the framework of the Placement Problem and cognitive voyeurism. From the Hegelian perspective I have aimed to articulate and defend, the world to which we direct our sense-making practices is "capacious. . . —more English garden than desert landscape".[74] For Hegel, then, one must go beyond a *narrow* naturalism that views nature as "self-alienated spirit"[75] and that alienates us from ourselves. By doing so, this "provides material for serious reflection and makes it appear doubtful that the most recently projected mathematical-scientific conception of elementary psychological processes will make a significant contribution to our understanding of real human life".[76]

Notes

1. Cf. Moore (2012).
2. I think Ralph Wedgwood's articulation of reductive naturalism is helpful here, as reduction can be *either explanatory or ontological*: "Roughly, for normative properties to be reducible is for it to be possible, at least in principle, to give a constitutive account of what it is for something to have each normative property in wholly non-normative, non-evaluative terms" (Wedgwood 2007: 145).
3. Habermas 2002: 9.
   See the following by Frederick Olafson as well:

   > Religious and social orthodoxies . . . were identified with constraints that in one way or another block a full development of natural human powers and potentialities for self-realisation. As a result, naturalism came to be understood as a liberation from the dogmas of supernaturalism and the conservative social order for which they served as an ideology, as well as a declaration of independence for scientific inquiry into the nature of the world and also into human nature.
   >
   > (Olafson 2001: 3)

4. Breen 2013: 9.
5. Karlberg 1980: 1176.
6. *PE*: 124.
7. Ibid., p. 123.
   'Iron cage' is Talcott Parsons's translation of Weber's term. However, arguments have been made that 'a shell as hard as steel' is in fact a better rendering. For further on this debate, see Baehr (2001) and Chalcraft (1994).
8. By this, I mean those activities that are not directed at consumption/sexual reproduction/shelter, etc.
9. Breen 2013: 10–11.
10. *SPWR*: 281.
11. Enlightenment as "the dissolution of myths and the substitution of knowledge for fancy" (*DoE*: 3).
12. See the following by Olafson as well:

    > All of our efforts to make ourselves masters of our situation in the natural world have proceeded under the auspices of what is still commonly referred to as the Enlightenment. This was the movement of critical thought in the eighteenth century that, on the basis of the scientific revolution of the preceding century, undertook a searching critique of the religious and metaphysical underpinnings of the Christian civilization of Europe. The great natural philosophers of the seventeenth century had shown that nature can be conceived in mathematical terms that altogether bypass the teleological ordering envisaged by Aristotle. The idea of the Enlightenment *philosophes* was that scientific methods of comparable exactitude could be brought to bear on human life and on human institutions and practices that had traditionally been protected against critical scrutiny by the veil of Christian myth.
    >
    > (Olafson 2001: 3)

13. *SV*: 139.
14. As Descartes concisely expresses the essence of mechanism: "I should like you to consider that these functions (including passion, memory, and imagination) follow from the mere arrangement of the machine's organs every bit as naturally as the movements of a clock or other automaton follow from the arrangement of its counter-weights and wheels" (*Treatise on Man*: 108).

    Such a conception of nature was also shared by figures such as the Baron d' Holbach, le Sage, Gren, and la Mettrie.
15. For further on this subject, see Beiser (2014), Friedman (2013), and Wilson (1998).
16. To quote Adorno and Horkheimer here: "Mathematical procedure became . . . the ritual of thinking. . .; it turns thought into a thing, an instrument . . ." (*DoE*: 25).
17. Cf. "The programme of the Enlightenment was the disenchantment of the world" (*DoE*: 3).
18. Beiser 2014: 99.
19. Friedman 2013: 82. Importantly, one should note that "this principle, for Helmholtz, has more a regulative than a constitutive character: as the 'condition for the complete conceptualisability of nature', it sets up what Kant would call a regulative ideal akin to the ideal of complete systematic unity" (Friedman 2013: 89).
20. See the following from Friedman here:

    > a new experimental science of psycho-physics had been founded by Gustav Fechner and developed, among others, by Helmholtz's teacher Johannes Müller, and the practitioners of this new science understood themselves, quite understandably, to be standing on the threshold of a profound intellectual breakthrough in which the physical sciences, the life sciences and the emerging new science of the mind were all to be comprehended within a single unified scientific framework. Helmholtz himself was one of the greatest of these practitioners, and his epistemological doctrines—including both his overriding emphasis on the principle of causality and his conception of space as a form of external intuition—were entirely framed, as we have seen, by his characteristic 'empiricist' viewpoint in the psychophysiology of sense perception.
    >
    > (Friedman 2013: 90)

    Cf. Peter Atkins's claim that "science, with its currently successful pursuit of universal competency . . . should be acknowledged king" (Atkins 1995: 132). See also Wilson (1998).
21. As Robert Richards phrases it: "Idealism and Romanticism might seem the very antitheses of the kind of empirical biology of the early period, especially the evolutionary theories of Charles Darwin, who, it is usually assumed, banished ideas of purpose and finality from nature, the kind of ideas cultivated by the Idealists and Romantics" (Richards 2013: 105–106).

    For Alex Rosenberg, blind variation and natural selection are just

    > the foresightless play of fermions and bosons producing in us conspiracy theorists, the *illusion* of purpose. . . . The thermodynamic noise among the molecules present on the Earth about three billion years ago every so often randomly produced molecules that combined stability with replication, the first sliver of an adaptation, produced from zero adaptation. . . . The process of piling on adaptations upon adaptations is temporally asymmetrical, driven by the second law of thermodynamics—the law that entropy increases almost everywhere almost all the time. Repeat the process of

thermodynamically random variations enough times and the rest is history—natural history. That's how physics fakes design.

(Rosenberg 2011: 4)

See also Wilson (1998).

22. Windelband 1980: 171.

23. The totalising aspirations of nomothetic disciplines, to use Bernard Williams's expression, involve construing an 'absolute conception of the world'.

24. Price's Placement Problem owes much to Jackson (1998), where it is dubbed 'The Location Problem', although Price endeavours to distinguish them (Price 2013: 27n).

25. Lynne Baker also provides a helpful explication of the naturalisation strategy of the Placement Problem: "A common strategy for naturalists who find some apparent phenomenon that seems resistant to being naturalised . . . is to give a naturalistic account of a closely related phenomenon . . . that leaves the original (putative) phenomenon out in the cold as something that has no purchase on actual reality". (Baker 2013: xviii–xix).

"If nature is exhausted by science, as scientific naturalism claims, then 'no place in science' implies 'no place in nature', which it turn implies 'no place in reality' " (Baker 2017: 339).

26. Cf. Rosenberg 2014: 19; and the following by Hilary Putnam: "I believed that the best metaphysics is what the positivists called 'unified science', science pictured as based on and unified by the application of the laws of fundamental physics" (Putnam 1992: 2); "physics as giving us the ultimate metaphysical truth" (Putnam 1992: 108).

27. See the following respective comments by Jaegwon Kim, and by Mario De Caro and David Macarthur: "If current analytic philosophy can be said to have a philosophical ideology, it is unquestionably, naturalism". (Kim 2003: 84); "[Scientific naturalism is] the current orthodoxy, at least within Anglo-American philosophy" (De Caro and Macarthur 2004: 1).

Additionally, one may argue that reductive varieties of naturalism are committed to the view that ontology is determined by physics and that the condition for being a science here is that a discipline be reducible to microphysics.

28. Sellars puts this philosophical problem nicely:

I want to highlight from the very beginning what might be called the paradox of man's encounter with himself, the paradox consisting of the fact that man couldn't be man until he encountered himself. It is this paradox which supports the last stand of Special Creation. Its central theme is the idea that anything which can properly be called conceptual thinking can occur only within a framework of conceptual thinking in terms of which it can be criticised, supported, refuted, in short, evaluated. To be able to think is to be able to measure one's thoughts by standards of correctness, of relevance, of evidence. In this sense a diversified conceptual framework is a whole which, however sketchy, is prior to its parts, and cannot be construed as a coming together or parts which are already conceptual in character. The conclusion is difficult to avoid that the transition from pre-conceptual patterns of behaviour to conceptual thinking was a holistic one, a jump to a level of awareness which is irreducibly new, a jump which was the coming into being of man. There is a profound truth in this conception of a radical difference in level between man and his precursors. The attempt to understand this difference turns out to be part and parcel of the attempt to encompass in one view the two images of man-in-the-world which I have set out to describe. For, as we shall see, this difference in level appears an irreducible discontinuity in the *manifest* image, but as, in a sense requiring careful analysis, a reducible difference in the *scientific* image.

(Sellars 1963b: 6)

29. Price also invites us to imagine the relationship between our linguistic practices and the world as a child's puzzle sticker book, where the right-hand side of each page holds a picture of a complex scene, and the left-hand side a column of peel-off stickers. For each sticker, Price states, the child needs to find the corresponding object in the picture (Price 2013: 23). He suggests that we think of the right-hand side as the world, and the stickers as the set of sentences true of it. Within this model, issues of 'fit' (or placement) arise insofar as: "We seem to have . . . more stickers than places to put them" (Price 2013: 26). For, he claims, ordinary discourse is 'rich' and the world described by natural science is 'sparse' (Price 2011: 4).

30. Sellars 1958: 283.

31. The following passage from the introduction to the *Treatise of Human Nature* is particularly useful, especially considering how Hume is often (and mistakenly) heralded as the inaugurator of scientific naturalism:

> When I am at a loss to know the effects of one body upon another in any situation, I need only put them in that situation and observe what results from it. But should I endeavour to clear up after the same manner any doubt in moral philosophy, by placing myself in the same case with that which I consider, 'tis evident this reflection and premeditation would so disturb the operation of my natural principles, as must render it impossible to form any just conclusion from the phenomenon. We must therefore glean up our experiments in this science from a cautious observation of human life, and take them as they appear in the common course of the world, by men's behaviour in company, in affairs, and in their pleasures.

(*THN*: xix)

See Mounce (1999) for an excellent discussion of Hume's naturalism.

32. Rosenberg 2014: 19.

33. Parallels can be drawn between this expression and Stanley Cavell's critique of empiricism, cf. Cavell (1979).

34. Beiser 2005: 164.

35. Ibid., p. 165.

36. Baker 2013: 101.

37. As Sellars writes: "in the dimension of describing and explaining the world, science is the measure of all things, of what is that it is, and of what is not that it is not" (Sellars 1997: 83).

38. Cf. the following by Rosenberg: "we'll call the worldview that all us atheists . . . share 'scientism'. This is the conviction that the methods of science are the only reliable ways to secure knowledge of anything; that science's description of the world is correct in its fundamentals; and that when 'complete', what science tells us will not be surprisingly different from what it tells us today" (Rosenberg 2011: 6–7). See also Wilson (1998). However, it is important to note that one can be an atheist without being committed to scientism.

The 'scientism wars' are frustrating, principally because on one side, there are hermeneutic humanists who think that naturalists *tout court* are denying discourse-pluralism; and on the other, there are scientistic naturalists who think hermeneutic humanists are denying that, *in the dimension of describing and explaining the world*, science is the measure of all things.

39. Ferrini 2009: 92–93.
40. Stern 2013: 123.
41. Rescher 2017: 40.
42. In conversation with me.
43. Hanna 2014: 756
44. Baker 2013: xviii.
45. As Sellars puts it: "The task of the philosopher cannot be to show how, in principle, what is said by normative discourse can be said without normative discourse, for the simple reason that this cannot be done" (Sellars 1980: 82).
46. "[A] complex first-person sentence with a psychological or linguistic main verb—for example, "I doubt that I* will live to be ninety," or "I whispered that I* am sorry."" (Baker 2013: 35)
    For further on this subject, see Matthews (1992).
47. Baker 2013: 35.
48. Ibid., p. xv.
49. Dennett 1991: 71.
50. Baker 2013: 121.
51. *APPV*: [120], 4.
52. Pinkard 2012: 184. For further on this subject, see Rödl (2007).
53. To quote G. H. Mead here: "Mentality on our approach simply comes in when the organism is able to point out meanings to others and to himself. This is the point at which mind appears, or if you like, emerges. . . . It is absurd to look at the mind simply from the standpoint of the individual human organism; for, although it has its focus there, it is essentially a social phenomenon; even its biological functions are primarily social" (*MSS*: 132–33).
54. Cf.

    Now this movement of self-consciousness in relation to another self-consciousness has in this way been represented as the action of *one* self-consciousness, but this action of the one has itself the double significance of being both its own action and the action of the other as well. For the other is equally independent and self-contained, and there is nothing in it of which it is not itself the origin. The first does not have the object before it merely as it exists primarily for desire, but as something that has an independent existence of its own, which, therefore, it cannot utilize for its own purposes, if that object does not of its own accord do what the first does to it. Thus the movement is simply the double movement of the two self-consciousnesses. Each sees the *other* do the same as it does; each does itself what it demands of the other, and therefore also does what it does only in so far as the other does the same. Action by one-side only would be useless because what is to happen can only be brought about by both.
    (*PS*: §182: 111–112)

55. Habermas 1992: 152–153.
56. Taylor 1987: 13.
57. Cf. Dennett 2009: 28.
58. Baker 2013: 135.
59. Ibid., p. 135.
60. E.g. what Dennett calls 'heterophenomenology'. I regard heterophenomenology as a sophisticated right-wing Sellarsian position, which would involve, as James O'Shea puts it:

    [a] causal explanation of the motivational efficacy of 'shall' intentions as socially acquired linguistic and psychological dispositions to follow up one's 'I shall do A' intentions and volitions, other things being equal,

with the doing of A. Such a social-behavioural account of the origin, the content, and the motivational force of individual intentions, community intentions, and on that basis, of normative 'ought' statements, would not itself . . . involve the assertion of any 'ought statements'.

(O'Shea 2009: 199)

61. I think this creates space for an engaging area of constructive disagreement between Hegel and Sellars on the subject of personhood: for Sellars, persons are irreducible to ideal scientific image entities, not because they are 'emergent' ontological properties, over and above the descriptive-explanatory categories of science, but because our concept of personhood is not in the business of describing and explaining in the first place: as Dionysis Christias helpfully raised in conversation with me, persons are different kinds of 'things', 'normatively individuated' ones.
62. Windelband 1980: 179.
63. Baker 2013: 192.
64. See Price 2004: 74–75; Macarthur and Price 2007: 93–94.

    Price distinguishes object naturalism, which claims that the proper concern of philosophy is "with something in the natural world, or with nothing at all. For there simply is nothing else" from subject naturalism, which claims that philosophy "needs to begin with what science tells us about ourselves" (Price 2013: 5). Price argues that subject naturalism should 'come first' philosophically in an important sense, for object naturalism depends on "validation from a subject naturalism perspective". This simply means that if certain presuppositions of object naturalism are incompatible with "the recognition that we humans are natural creatures" (Price 2013: 6), then they should be rejected.

    Price can claim that subject naturalism avoids the threat of voyeurism, since the charge of voyeurism only sticks to *object* naturalism. However, subject naturalism assumes that 'the subject' can be divorced from its broader context of surrounding objects (the experienced world) and studied separately—which assumes the subject to be a discrete individual, rather than, for instance, a node in a web of internal relations. For a critical treatment of Price's views here, see Legg and Giladi (2018).
65. Price also argues that a key presupposition of The Placement Problem is what he calls 'the Semantic Ladder', which derives from representationalism. This is "the assumption that the linguistic items in question 'stand for' or 'represent' something non-linguistic. . . . This assumption grounds our shift in focus from the term 'X' or concept X, to its assumed object, X" (Price 2013: 9). This assumption is required for the Placement Problem, for without it we cannot transition from merely studying human linguistic practices (such as ethics talk), to considering their implications for the world. So, one may evade the Problem by refusing to climb the Ladder.
66. As Carl Sachs helpfully raised in conversation with me, in response to the concerns about imperialism and encroachment, a pragmatist may argue the following: because the unity of science thesis, whether reductionist or eliminativist, is not grounded in a careful examination of scientific practice, it risks opening the door to the charge of scientism. However, if one considers those philosophers of science who are looking at science in terms of practices, such as John Dupré, Nancy Cartwright, Steven Horst, and Joseph Rouse, careful explication of how scientific practices yield a pragmatically efficacious grip on reality, there is reason to reject any top-down commitments to the unity of science (as for example driven by some *a priori* commitment to mechanistic physics as the epistemic ideal of empirical inquiry). But, once we see that pragmatic realism in philosophy of science does not entail—and

in fact, strictly speaking, undermines—the unity of science thesis, 'scientism' just becomes a chimera.

67. Windelband 1980: 171.
68. Baker 2013: xxii.
    Cf.

> It can easily seem that there is no space to move here. Setting our faces against bald naturalism, we are committed to holding that the idea of knowing one's way about in the space of reasons, the idea of responsiveness to rational relationships, cannot be reconstructed out of materials that are naturalistic in the sense that we are trying to supersede. This can easily seem to commit us to a rampant platonism. It can seem that we must be picturing the space of reasons as an autonomous structure—autonomous in that it is constituted independently of anything specifically human, since what is specifically human is surely natural . . . and we are refusing to naturalise the requirements of reason. . . . But there is a way out. We get this threat of supernaturalism if we interpret the claim that space of reasons is *sui generis* as a refusal to naturalise the requirements of reason. But what became available at the time of the modern scientific revolution is a clear-cut understanding of the realm of law, and we can refuse to equate that with a new clarity *about nature*. This makes room for us to insist that spontaneity is *sui generis*, in comparison with the realm of law, without falling into the supernaturalism of rampant platonism.
>
> (McDowell 1994: 77–78)

69. Cf. the following passage from the *Encyclopaedia Logic*: "It is only an ill-minded prejudice to assume that philosophy stands antithetically opposed to any sensible appreciation of experience. . . . These shapes [of consciousness, such as science] are recognised by philosophy, and even justified by it. Rather than opposing them, the thinking mind steeps itself in their basic import; it learns from them and strengthens itself" (*EL*: 5).
70. Cf. the following passage from the *Philosophy of Nature*: "Physics must therefore work together with philosophy so that the universalised understanding which it provides may be translated into the Notion by showing how this universal, as an intrinsically necessary whole, proceeds out of the Notion". (*PN*: Z§246, 201)
71. What I have argued here bears some similarity to what Roger Scruton has argued concerning scientism and its 'invasion' of the humanities:

> Just as there is an understanding of art, which forms the domain of criticism, and which is a rational exercise with its own standards of validity, so there is an understanding of people, which forms the domain of interpersonal relations, and which is a rational exercise obedient to norms of its own. And just as it is an error to think you can replace art criticism with the neuroscience that allegedly explains the phenomena with which it deals, so too is it an error to think that you can replace interpersonal understanding with the neuroscience that allegedly explains our behaviour. If you try to do this, you end up describing the behaviour in terms that remove it from the context that gives it sense—you become a reductionist, in other words, someone who fails to see that the most important features of the human condition are emergent features, which inhabit the surface of the world, but are invisible to those whose eyes are fixed on the depths. Human cultures are reflections on and in the surface of life, ways in which we understand the world of persons, and the moral framework within which persons live.
>
> (Scruton 2015: 141–142)

72. Williams 2006: 182.
73. Pinkard 2012: 190.
74. Baker 2013: 234.
75. *PN*: Z§247, 206.
76. Windelband 1980: 183.

References

Adorno, T. W., and Horkheimer, M. 2002. *Dialectic of Enlightenment: Philosophical Fragments*. G. Schmid Noerr (ed.) and E. Jephcott (trans.). Stanford, CA: Stanford University Press.

Atkins, P. W. 1995. 'The Limitless Power of Science'. In J. Cornwell (ed.) *Nature's Imagination: The Frontiers of Scientific Vision*. Oxford: Oxford University Press.

Baehr, P. 2001. 'The "Iron Cage" and the "Shell as Hard as Steel"': Parsons, Weber, and the *stahlhartes Gehäuse* Metaphor in *The Protestant Ethic and the Spirit of Capitalism*'. *History and Theory* 40: 153–169.

Baker, L. R. 2013. *Naturalism and the First-Person Perspective*. Oxford: Oxford University Press.

———. 2017. 'Naturalism and the Idea of Nature'. *Philosophy* 92: 333–349.

Beiser, F. C. 2005. *Hegel*. London and New York: Routledge.

——— 2014. *After Hegel: German Philosophy 1840–1900*. Princeton, NJ and Woodstock, NJ: Princeton University Press.

Breen, K. 2013. *Under Weber's Shadow: Modernity, Subjectivity and Politics in Habermas, Arendt and MacIntyre*. London and New York: Routledge.

Cavell, S. 1979. 'Thinking of Emerson'. *New Literary History* 11: 167–176.

Chalcraft, D. 1994. 'Bringing the Text Back In: On Ways of Reading the Iron Cage Metaphor in the Two Editions of *The Protestant Ethic*'. In L. J. Ray and M. Reed (eds.) *Organising Modernity: New Weberian Perspectives on Work, Organisation and Society*. London and New York: Routledge.

De Caro, M., and Macarthur, D. 2004. 'Introduction: The Nature of Naturalism'. In M. De Caro and D. Macarthur (eds.) *Naturalism in Question*. Cambridge, MA: Harvard University Press.

Dennett, D. C. 1991. *Consciousness Explained*. Boston: Little, Brown.

———. 2009. 'Daniel Dennett'. In P. Grim (ed.) *Mind and Consciousness: 5 Questions*. Copenhagen: Automatic Press, VIP.

Descartes, R. 1984–91. *Philosophical Writings of Descartes*, 3 vols., J. Cottingham, R. Stoothoff, D. Murdoch and A. Kenny (trans.). Cambridge: Cambridge University Press.

Ferrini, C. 2009. 'Reason Observing Nature'. In K. R. Westphal (ed.) *The Blackwell Guide to Hegel's Phenomenology of Spirit*. Oxford: Blackwell.

Friedman, M. 2013. 'Philosophy of Natural Science in Idealism and Neo-Kantianism'. In K. Ameriks, N. Boyle and L. Disley (eds.) *The Impact of Idealism: The Legacy of Post-Kantian German Thought. Volume 1: Philosophy and Natural Sciences*. Cambridge: Cambridge University Press.

Habermas, J. 1992. *Postmetaphysical Thinking*. W. M. Hohengarten (trans.). Cambridge, MA: MIT Press.

———. 2002. 'Modernity—An Incomplete Project'. In H. Foster (ed.) *The Anti-Aesthetic: Essays on Postmodern Culture*. New York: The New Press.

Hanna, R. 2014. 'Husserl's Crisis and Our Crisis'. *International Journal of Philosophical Studies* 22: 752–770.

Hegel, G. W. F. 1970. *Philosophy of Nature (Part Two of the Encyclopaedia of Philosophical Sciences)*. M. J. Petry (trans.) 3 vols. London: George Allen and Unwin.

———. 1975. *Aesthetics: Lectures on Fine Art*. T. M. Knox (trans.), 2 vols. Oxford: Oxford University Press.

———. 1977. *Phenomenology of Spirit*. A. V. Miller (trans.). Oxford: Oxford University Press.

———. 1991a. *Elements of the Philosophy of Right*. A. W. Wood (ed.) and H. B. Nisbet (trans.). Cambridge: Cambridge University Press.

———. 1991b. *The Encyclopaedia Logic: Part 1 of the Encyclopaedia of Philosophical Sciences*. T. F. Geraets, W. A. Suchting and H. S. Harris (trans.). Indianapolis, IN: Hackett.

———. 2010. *Science of Logic*. G. di Giovanni (trans. and ed.). Cambridge: Cambridge University Press.

Hume, D. 1975. *Treatise of Human Nature*. L. A. Selby-Biggs and P. H. Nidditch (eds.). Oxford: Clarendon Press.

Jackson, F. C. 1998. *From Metaphysics to Ethics: A Defence of Conceptual Analysis*. Oxford: Oxford University Press.

Kant, I. 2006. *Anthropology from a Pragmatic Point of View*. R. B. Louden (ed. and trans.). Cambridge: Cambridge University Press.

Karlberg, S. 1980. 'Max Weber's Types of Rationality: Cornerstones for the Analysis of Rationalisation Processes in History'. *American Journal of Sociology* 85: 1145–1179.

Kim, J. 2003. 'The American Origins of Philosophical Naturalism'. *Journal of Philosophical Research, APA Centennial Volume*: 83–98.

Legg, C., and Giladi, P. 2018. 'Metaphysics—Low in Price, High in Value: A Critique of Global Expressivism'. *Transactions of the Charles S. Peirce Society* 54: 64–83.

Macarthur, D., and Price, H. 2007. 'Pragmatism, Quasi-Realism and the Global Challenge'. In C. Misak (ed.) *The New Pragmatists*. Oxford: Oxford University Press.

Matthews, G. B. 1992. *Thought's Ego in Augustine and Descartes*. Ithaca, NY: Cornell University Press.

McDowell, J. 1994. *Mind and World*. Cambridge, MA: Harvard University Press.

Mead, G. H. 1934. *Mind, Self, and Society: From the Standpoint of a Social Behaviourist*. C. W. Morris (ed.). Chicago, IL: University of Chicago Press.

Metzinger, T. 2003a. *Being No One: The Self-Model of Subjectivity*. Cambridge, MA: MIT Press.

———. 2003b. 'Phenomenal Transparency and Cognitive Self-Reference'. *Phenomenology and the Cognitive Sciences* 2: 353–393.

Moore, A. W. 2012. *The Evolution of Modern Metaphysics: Making Sense of Things*. Cambridge: Cambridge University Press.

Mounce, H. O. 1999. *Hume's Naturalism*. London and New York: Routledge.

Olafson, F. A. 2001. *Naturalism and the Human Condition: Against Scientism*. London and New York: Routledge.

O'Shea, J. 2009. 'On the Structure of Sellars's Naturalism with a Normative Turn'. In W. A. deVries (ed.) *Empiricism, Perceptual Knowledge, Normativity, and Realism: Essays on Wilfrid Sellars*. Oxford: Oxford University Press.

Pinkard, T. 2012. *Hegel's Naturalism: Mind, Nature, and the Final Ends of Life.* Oxford: Oxford University Press.

Price, H. 2004. 'Naturalism without Representationalism'. In M. De Caro and D. Macarthur (eds.) *Naturalism in Question.* Cambridge, MA: Harvard University Press.

———. 2011. *Naturalism without Mirrors.* Oxford: Oxford University Press.

———. 2013. *Expressivism, Pragmatism, and Representationalism.* Cambridge: Cambridge University Press.

Putnam, H. 1992. *Renewing Philosophy.* Cambridge, MA: Harvard University Press.

Quine, W. V. 1997. 'On What There Is'. In D. H. Mellor and A. Oliver (eds.) *Properties.* Oxford: Oxford University Press.

Rechter, N. 2017. 'Philosophy as Rational Systematisation'. In G. D'Oro and S. Overgaard (eds.) *The Cambridge Companion to Philosophical Methodology.* Cambridge: Cambridge University Press.

Richards, R. L. 2013. 'The Impact of German Idealism and Romanticism on Biology'. In K. Ameriks, N. Boyle and L. Disley (eds.) *The Impact of Idealism: The Legacy of Post-Kantian German Thought. Volume 1: Philosophy and Natural Sciences.* Cambridge: Cambridge University Press.

Rödl, S. 2007. *Self-Consciousness.* Cambridge, MA: Harvard University Press.

Rosenberg, A. 2011. *The Atheist's Guide to Reality: Enjoying Life without Illusions.* New York and London: W. W. Norton & Co.

———. 2014. 'Disenchanted Naturalism'. In B. Bashour and H. D. Muller (eds.) *Contemporary Philosophical Naturalism and Its Implications.* New York and London: Routledge.

Scruton, R. 2015. 'Scientism and the Humanities'. In R. N. Williams and D. N. Robinson (eds.) *Scientism: The New Orthodoxy.* London: Bloomsbury.

Sellars, W. 1958. 'Counterfactuals, Dispositions, and the Causal Modalities'. In H. Feigl, M. Scriven and G. Maxwell (eds.) *Concepts, Theories, and the Mind-Body Problem.* Minneapolis, MN: University of Minnesota Press.

———. 1963a. 'Philosophy and the Scientific Image of Man'. In R. Colodny (ed.) *Frontiers of Science and Philosophy.* Pittsburgh, PA: University of Pittsburgh Press.

———. 1963b. *Science, Perception and Reality.* London and New York: Routledge.

———. 1997. *Empiricism and the Philosophy of Mind: With an Introduction by Richard Rorty and a Study Guide by Robert Brandom.* R. Brandom (ed.). Cambridge, MA: Harvard University Press.

———. 1980. *Pure Pragmatics and Possible Worlds: The Early Essays of Wilfrid Sellars.* Atascadero, CA: Ridgeview Publishing.

Stern, R. 2013. *Routledge Philosophy Guidebook to Hegel and the "Phenomenology of Spirit",* 2nd ed. London and New York: Routledge.

Taylor, C. 1987. 'Overcoming Epistemology'. In K. Baynes, J. Bonham and T. McCarthy (eds.) *After Philosophy: End or Transformation?* Cambridge, MA: MIT Press.

Weber, M. 1948a. 'The Social Psychology of the World Religions'. In H. H. Gerth and C. W. Mills (eds.) *From Max Weber: Essays in Sociology.* London and New York: Routledge.

————. 1948b. 'Science as a Vocation'. In H. H. Gerth and C. W. Mills (eds.) *From Max Weber: Essays in Sociology*. London and New York: Routledge.

————. 1992. *The Protestant Ethic and the Spirit of Capitalism*. T. Parsons (trans.). London and New York: Routledge.

Wedgwood, R. 2007. *The Nature of Normativity*. Oxford: Oxford University Press.

Williams, B. 2006. *Philosophy as a Humanistic Discipline*. A. W. Moore (ed.). Princeton, NJ: Princeton University Press.

Wilson, E. O. 1998. *Consilience: The Unity of Knowledge*. New York: Vintage Books.

Windelband, W. 1980. 'Rectorial Address: History and Natural Science'. *History and Theory* 19: 169–185.

4   The Idealist Challenge
to Naturalism

Alexis Papazoglou

If you want to know and explain what takes place within reality, the natural sciences are the place to go. Any genuine explanation, even if not obvious at first, ultimately has its foundation in the natural sciences. These are some of the claims of scientific naturalism, a philosophical outlook that has been dominant in much of 20th-century Anglo-American philosophy. Its lesson for philosophy was that if the latter wanted to offer an account of reality or of ourselves as subjects, then it must *at least* start with the results of natural science. This was also understood as the claim that philosophy should be *continuous* with the natural sciences, with the claims of the latter enjoying a priority over any philosophical claims.

Scientific naturalism has come under a lot of criticism, primarily because of the *placement problems* it creates.[1] The placement problems amount to the inability, under the scientific naturalist framework, to find a place within the bounds of nature for phenomena like values, reasons, and norms more broadly, phenomena that seem essential to the human sphere. This has led influential philosophers, amongst them John McDowell and Huw Price, to propose alternatives to scientific naturalism, without, however, veering off to the supernatural[2] or undermining the priority of the natural sciences.[3] Their strategy is to find an underlying assumption of scientific naturalism's position, expose it as problematic, and proceed to reject it, thus leaving behind only the good parts of naturalism, without any of the bad parts. Admirable as these attempts at redefining naturalism are, they seem to fall short of the job. McDowell struggles to show in what sense his position should count as naturalism, since he lacks a clear picture of what is to count as nature, and Price struggles to convince that his position is *really* all that different from scientific naturalism.

If the aim is to overcome the pitfalls of scientific naturalism, however, we have available a tradition of idealist thought, starting with Kant, which offers a very different, and more appealing, approach. This tradition also looks at the underlying assumptions behind scientific naturalism, but unlike Price and McDowell, it focuses on the background assumptions of the *practice* of science itself. Where scientific naturalism suggests we take the results of natural science as the starting point of our inquiries into the world and ourselves, this tradition asks what the philosophical presuppositions of scientific enquiry are in the first place. In this effort, it highlights the fact that the explanatory framework of natural science seems to already presuppose, and depend on, a different explanatory framework, one associated with the human subject. This observation then explains why the human sphere cannot be given a complete account by natural science, as scientific naturalism would have it. It explains, in other words, why scientific naturalism inevitably faces the placement problems that it does.

Two important points can be made about this line of thought: Firstly, this is a transcendental argument against scientific naturalism. It argues that if the conditions for the possibility of natural science cannot themselves be given a scientific account, then scientific naturalism's claim about the priority of scientific accounts cannot hold. Secondly, it is an idealist argument against scientific naturalism. This is because it gives a priority to the explanatory framework of the human subject and subjectivity.

In the first part of this chapter, I will offer a brief account of scientific naturalism and the placement problems it gives rise to, as well as give some reasons for why McDowell's and Price's versions of liberal naturalism remain problematic. In the second part, I will proceed to give an account of the Kantian origins of the idealist argument against scientific naturalism I wish to rearticulate, and then move on to show how it echoes in Hegel's as well as in Husserl's respective accounts of the relationship between *geistige* and natural scientific explanations. For Kant, the explanatory framework that enjoys priority over the framework of the natural science is that of *reason*, conditioning the ways in which nature can be found intelligible. For Hegel, that framework becomes broader, understood through his concept of *spirit*, which Hegel claims is prior to nature. For Husserl, the framework that natural science presupposes is that of the *lifeworld* (the everyday world), filled with meaning, norms, and accounts of ourselves as *persons*. What all three philosophers have in common is an adherence to idealism in a *broad* sense, namely the belief that the explanatory framework of the human subject is that which takes priority over other explanatory frameworks, including, crucially, that of nature and natural science. Ultimately, this idealist tradition makes available a conception of philosophy that is decidedly contrary to the one of the naturalist platform, namely one according to which it is philosophy that enjoys an explanatory priority over natural science, not the other way around.

I

Naturalisms: Scientific and Liberal

Scientific Naturalism and the Priority of Science over Philosophy

Scientific naturalism became the dominant ideology in 20th-century Anglo-American philosophy,[4] perhaps most famously espoused by

Quine.[5] One of the key claims of scientific naturalism, as formulated by Quine, is that there is no such thing as 'first philosophy', and that philosophy must be continuous with the natural sciences. In Quine's own words, naturalism is "the recognition that it is within science itself, and not in some prior philosophy, that reality is to be identified and described".[6] Naturalism therefore "means banishing the dream of a first philosophy and pursuing philosophy rather as a part of one's system of the world, continuous with the rest of science".[7] The first claim amounts to the belief that philosophy does not have a foundational role to play, as, say, Descartes had envisaged, with respect to knowledge and especially with respect to scientific knowledge. This view also implies that science does not presuppose any truths that can be revealed by philosophy, truths at which science itself cannot arrive. The second claim of Quine's naturalism, regarding the relation of science to philosophy, amounts to the belief that philosophy is not an autonomous practice, distinct in kind from that of science, and that philosophical questions might ultimately have their answers provided by the sciences. In fact, even the very questions of philosophy might be best understood and formulated as scientific questions.[8]

These views might seem dogmatic as they stand, after all, what justification is there for believing them? But, they are really a consequence of a more central claim at the heart of scientific naturalism, which is that scientific explanations offer a universal and exhaustive scope of what can be explained: "scientific theory provides a complete understanding of everything that there is in the world. All genuine understanding, on such a view, is scientific understanding".[9] As it stands, scientific naturalism seems tantamount to scientism, the claim that scientific knowledge, scientific understanding, scientific explanations are all the knowledge, understanding and explanations that there are. But, there is a second component to scientific naturalism, which makes reference to nature as the exhaustive ontology of reality. According to David Papineau, scientific naturalism defends the view that: "Reality is exhausted by nature, containing nothing 'supernatural'" and "the scientific method should be used to investigate all areas of reality, including the 'human spirit'" (Papineau 2015).[10] So, scientific naturalism makes not only epistemological and methodological claims about what can be known and how it can be known, but adds to that an ontological claim. The methodological claim is that the way to acquire knowledge about *all* aspects of reality is the scientific method. The ontological claim is that the domain of reality is equivalent to the domain of nature, and that the ontology of nature is dictated by the natural sciences.

Scientific naturalism, then, makes powerful *global* claims as it attempts to offer a complete account of the world and a prescription of how to gain knowledge of reality. The main critique of this philosophical orientation is that, despite its totalizing and unifying aspirations, it appears to be unfeasibly narrow, both ontologically and epistemologically/methodologically, leaving no place within nature for key aspects of human reality, and no plausible method for getting to know them. Huw Price has neatly coined the problems that scientific naturalism creates as *placement problems*.[11] Placement problems stem from the inability to see where things like, values, reasons and norms more broadly, fit within the image of reality that scientific naturalism espouses, namely nature as described by the natural sciences.

A good example of a placement problem, made famous by John McDowell, is the following: The difficulty of locating our ability as human being to provide reasons-based explanations about our beliefs actions, explanations located in, what Wilfrid Sellars dubbed, *the logical space of reasons*,[12] within the realm of nature. According to McDowell, the issue arises because modern natural science understands nature solely through one form of explanation, that of natural law, therefore seemingly leaving no room within nature for the form of explanation that belongs to us as rational creatures, reasons-based explanations, that is, explanations whose elements can stand in a relation of justification to one another. McDowell thinks scientific naturalism promotes the idea that the space of reasons (or at least parts of it) can be re-described in terms of the conceptual apparatus of the natural sciences (the rest should be discarded). However, McDowell persuasively argues that given the way that the natural sciences organise their material, it seems impossible to naturalise the space of reasons, if one accepts that nature is fully described by the natural sciences[13] (McDowell 1996: 70–71).

McDowell's argument hinges on arguing that the natural scientific language fails to do justice to the *sui generis* aspect of the space of reasons. In *Mind and World*, McDowell understands the natural sciences as organising their material in terms of laws of nature. Given that, McDowell sees it as impossible to re-describe the space of reasons through the language of the natural sciences.[14] This is because he thinks that the logical space of the natural sciences is such that it cannot "include relations such as one thing's being warranted—or for the general case, correct—in the light of another" (McDowell 1996: xv),[15] whereas these are exactly the sort of relations that live in the space of reasons. Something being justified in light of something else is something that we cannot imagine showing up anywhere else but in the logical space of reasons.

Philosophy and Liberal Naturalism

McDowell is a major representative of a current trend to offer a solution to the placement problems created by scientific naturalism, by arguing for a broader, more liberal version of naturalism. McDowell's flavour of liberal naturalism is premised on arguing for a broader, more liberal conception of nature than that offered by scientific naturalism. In that effort, McDowell is reclaiming some space for philosophy to have a say in what might constitute nature, rather than leaving the job to the natural sciences alone. McDowell does that by reminding us of the Aristotelian notion of *second nature*, a nature that we acquire as part of the training we receive by our linguistic community. It refers to behaviours that are so habitual, they become completely absorbed into our lives, like, for example, the ability to think and act on the basis of reasons. Even though I believe that the general direction of McDowell's move is correct, namely refusing to uncritically accept the image of nature as that is presented to us by the natural sciences, and digging a little deeper by questioning science's monopoly of acceptable forms of intelligibility, I ultimately think that McDowell's liberal naturalism is problematic. Others have already highlighted what I take to be the main problem: McDowell's inability to convincingly explain in what way second nature counts as nature, and how we are to understand its relationship to 'first' nature, the image of nature that we are offered by the natural sciences.[16]

Another notable case of an attempt to liberalise naturalism, so that it avoids the pitfall of the placement problems narrowness, is that of Huw Price. Price, like McDowell, attempts to undermine what he sees as the problematic presupposition of scientific naturalism. Price argues that the placement problems arise out of a representationalist assumption, namely, the idea that our vocabularies, of science as well as every-day speech, philosophy etc., aim to represent how things are in the world. According to the representationalist thesis there is a word-object relationship that our language, both scientific and non-scientific, aims to get right.[17] Price calls the kind of naturalism that is guilty of the representationalist assumption *object naturalism*, and it essentially amounts what was identified above as scientific naturalism.[18]

Price argues that if we think instead of the statements of science, ethics, aesthetics etc. as parts of different vocabularies, as different tools with different purposes (often non-representational)[19] the placement problems that scientific naturalism faces disappear. Once we drop the idea that our language's primary function is to represent how things are out there in the world, we are no longer puzzled by how terms like 'good' or 'valid argument' or 'beautiful' are supposed to pick out things (objects) in nature as that is described by the natural sciences. Price believes that this leads to different version of naturalism, one free from the tacit representationalist thesis, what he calls *subject naturalism*:

> According to this second view, philosophy needs to begin with what science tells us about ourselves. Science tells us that we humans are natural creatures, and if the claims and ambitions of philosophy conflict with this view, then philosophy needs to give way. This is naturalism in the sense of Hume . . . and arguably Nietzsche.
>
> (Price 2004: 73)

Price sees subject naturalism—unlike object naturalism—as not committed to scientism, the idea that only science reveals true knowledge about the world. As he writes: "[o]bject naturalism gives science not just central stage but the whole stage. . . . Subject naturalism suggests that science might properly take a more modest view of its own importance".[20] However, subject naturalism still gives priority to science and its claims about nature and about human beings, namely that they are natural creatures. Can recognising that scientific vocabulary has a priority over other vocabularies avoid slipping back into scientific naturalism? Another prominent proponent of the movement to liberalise naturalism, David Macarthur, has convincingly argued that it cannot, and that Price's subject naturalism ends up being tantamount to scientism.[21]

Despite the fact that the alternative naturalisms offered by McDowell and Price seem to remain under the shadow of scientific naturalism, the direction of travel is correct. Both philosophers successfully identify some unspoken presupposition of scientific naturalism and attempt to show how those presuppositions are unwarranted, and responsible for the pernicious effects of scientific naturalism. Identifying and questioning the validity of the presuppositions of problematic positions or practices is part of the core of philosophical practice. In the next section, I will look at how a different philosophical tradition, namely German idealism, offers an argument against scientific naturalism by questioning the presuppositions not of scientific naturalism, but of the practice of science itself.

II

Idealism's Alternative to Naturalism

Kantian Origins

As discussed earlier, scientific naturalism is a philosophical position that suggests that all philosophical enquiry should start with the results of the natural sciences, and the conception of nature that the latter offer us. For a philosophical tradition that takes its cue from Kant, taking the results of the natural sciences as the starting point of enquiry, and accepting 'nature' as equivalent to 'reality', seems bizarre. The reason behind this has to do with an insight originally found in Kant's *Critique of Pure Reason:* our scientific knowledge of nature is conditioned by a background of presuppositions that science itself does not think of, and for which it cannot account. It is rather the job of philosophy to do both those things, and in doing so to show what the limits of scientific knowledge are. Hence, a philosophy which prioritises scientific knowledge and explanations over other kinds of knowledge and explanations, is untenable.

Kant's fundamental insight regarding the relationship between mind and world, namely that the mind's relationship to the world cannot be understood as merely passive and that in experiencing reality we are taking an active stance towards the world, has a profound effect on how we think about nature. It implies that we cannot simply take nature as a mere 'given', as something that simply presents itself to us passively through experience, and neither can we think of the natural sciences as simple mirrors, reflecting how nature really is. Instead, nature is something that is mediated through the concepts and first principles we approach it with. We are, in that sense, to some degree *responsible* for what we take nature to be:

> Reason, in order to be taught by nature, must approach nature with its principles in one hand, according to which alone the agreement among appearances can count as laws, and, in the other hand, the experiments thought out in accordance with these principles—yet in order to be instructed by nature not like a pupil, who has recited to him whatever the teacher wants to say, but like an appointed judge who compels witnesses to answer the questions he puts to them. Thus, even physics owes the advantageous revolution in its way of thinking to the inspiration that what reason would not be able to know of itself and has to learn from nature, it has to seek in the latter (though not merely ascribe to it) in accordance with what reason itself puts into nature.
>
> (CPR: Bxiii—Bxiv)

So, according to Kant, nature itself does not, so to speak, instruct us to categorise it in certain ways, e.g. as governed by causality, or to subsume it under laws. In fact, we only see the world as nature *when* we approach it through the schema of universal laws. As he writes: "[n]ature is the existence of things, insofar as that existence is determined according to universal laws" (*PFM*: 46). Kant's remarks show why scientific naturalism jumps the gun by claiming that enquiry should start with the results of the sciences: it entirely forgets to acknowledge the background presuppositions to science's claims. Instead of starting with a conception of nature as that given to us by the natural sciences, Kant shows that the image of nature we arrive at through our empirical and scientific approaches is dependent on a set of background concepts, principles, and questions, not themselves derived from experience or scientific enquiry, but exactly presupposed by them. By showing that experience and scientific investigation are conditioned in this way, Kant is able to undermine scientific naturalism's attempt to place the results of scientific investigation at the start of philosophical enquiry. A corollary of this position is that there are parts of reality, (in Kant's case to do with the structure of the human mind), that are not amenable to scientific investigation, or at least cannot be given an exhaustive account by scientific accounts.

The shape of the argument against naturalism that emerges from this line of thought is one that has come to be understood as characteristically Kantian: it is a transcendental argument. Ralph Walker describes transcendental arguments as "arguments of the form 'There is experience; it is a condition for the possibility of experience that P; therefore P' ".[22] (The argument that can be deduced from Kant's remarks on the preconditions of scientific enquiry aims to validate those preconditions, to show that they must be real, since without them scientific enquiry, which is actual, would not be possible.

With this Kantian insight in mind, we can revisit the placement problems that naturalism creates, and especially the placement problem that McDowell focuses on, namely the difficulty of locating the human, reasoning mind, within nature, and therefore reality, as naturalism equates the two. What Kant's argument shows is that the discursive human mind, which scientific naturalism threatens to expunge from reality, *has* to be part of reality as it is a necessary condition for the possibility of natural science, the very thing which scientific naturalism accepts without question.

Of course, there are well-rehearsed complications with Kant's position. The discursive human mind which conditions scientific knowledge may be a part of reality for Kant, but as it turns out, it is a part of a reality that is beyond the realm of nature and beyond the bounds of experience, part of the *noumenal* world rather than the *phenomenal* world, to use the Kantian jargon. The problems that ensue from this separation have to do with the ways in which the two 'worlds' relate to one another, and specifically with the way in which the *transcendental ego* as the condition for the possibility of experience, which lies outside of space and time, according to Kant, relates to the empirical self that *is* spatio-temporal. I do not intend to get lost in the complications of this issue here, let alone attempt to resolve them. Suffice it to say that the post-Kantian tradition that follows grapples with this issue and tries to offer different solutions to it. These philosophers however, including Hegel and Husserl, also have something deeply in common with Kant when it comes to thinking about science: they do not take the results of science as a given, as a starting point of any philosophical enquiry. Instead, following Kant's project, they expose what the preconditions of science are. In this effort, they highlight the fact that the explanatory framework of science seems to already presuppose and depend on a different explanatory framework, one associated with the subject, albeit an embodied subject in their case.

The details of this story are wildly different in Hegel and in Husserl, but ultimately they both attempt to situate science within a wider context of human activity, a framework of meaning and normativity, one that eludes the explanations of which science is capable. Consequently, Kant's, Hegel's and Husserl's ways of showing that scientific naturalism cannot be true share the same basic structure. The result is reversing the explanatory order of naturalism, giving an explanatory priority to the human domain over the domain of nature and to philosophy over the natural sciences.

Hegel and the Priority of Spirit Over Nature

Already in the *Phenomenology of Spirit*, Hegel can be seen to be arguing against a naïve, pre-Kantian account of science that is characteristic of scientific naturalism. In the chapter *Observing Reason*, Hegel criticises an understanding of science as the 'matching up' of our representations of the natural world, with the world itself as a kind of 'metaphysical relation' between the two. It is Francis Bacon's account of science as neutrally observing and describing the natural world as it reveals itself to us, that Hegel finds faulty. Instead, Hegel aims to show that science is a human activity, the human mind playing an active and not merely a passive role in attempting to offer an account of nature: we are the ones who construe theories, that postulate theoretical entities, that take certain observations to mean something significant or not for the fate of our theories. Hegel develops Kant's idea that what a subject takes to be authoritative when it comes to knowledge claims is that which is rational, the latter being autonomously determined by the subject itself. But, Hegel also develops the conception of rationality from isolated, eternal and universal into, a "developing historically situated rationality . . . consisting of those standards of evaluation that we have come to take as authoritative for ourselves because of the historical insufficiencies of earlier accounts".[23]

Hegel's position on science is further elaborated, of course, in his *Philosophy of Nature*. One of the key lessons of that book is that for Hegel, the answer to the question 'What is nature?' is not the business of science, but of a *philosophy* of nature. In fact, according to Hegel, the question regarding what nature is, acts as the originator of philosophy.[24] As part of his attempt to answer the question of what nature is, Hegel is concerned with understanding the relationship between nature and mind, or *spirit*, in his language. Ultimately, Hegel's aim is to show that *spirit* and nature condition one another, and that *spirit*, in some sense, is already contained in nature:

> This, now, is the specific character and the goal of the Philosophy of Nature, that spirit finds its counterpart in her. The study of Nature is thus the liberation of Spirit in her, for Spirit is present in her in so far as it is in relation, not with an Other, but with itself. This is also the liberation of Nature; implicitly she is Reason, but it is through Spirit that Reason as such first emerges from Nature into existence.
>
> (PN: 13)

In order to understand in what way Hegel thinks nature contains *spirit*, and how nature is implicitly reason, I want to focus on a key passage that can be found in the Introduction of the next book of his *Encyclopedia*, the *Philosophy of Spirit*. This is the place where the transition, between the *Philosophy of Nature* and the *Philosophy of Spirit* takes place. There

Hegel makes the following statement regarding the relationship between nature and *spirit*: "For us mind has nature as its presupposition, though mind is the truth of nature and is the absolute first with respect to it" (*PoS*: § 381–9).

Decoding Hegel's language is never a straightforward feat, but what is clear is that Hegel is here offering two perspectives: from one perspective, nature is prior to *spirit*, but from another, *spirit* is prior to nature. One interpretation of what the two perspectives are could be the following: our human-centred point of view could be identified with the everyday, pre-philosophical, realist point of view, according to which nature exists independently of us, and is the causal origin of everything, including *spirit*. Hegel can then be seen as suggesting that despite this common-sense view, *spirit* is in fact the origin of everything, including nature; *spirit* is that which is prior, not nature. The elucidation that follows makes the statement a bit clearer but even bolder:

> the emergence of mind from nature must not be conceived as if nature were the absolute immediate, the first, the original positing agent, while mind, by contrast, were only something posited by nature; it is rather nature that is posited by mind, and mind is what is absolutely first.
>
> (*PoS*: §381Z—14)

One of the central questions then when attempting to understand Hegel's thought on the relationship between spirit and nature is, in what *sense* does Hegel think that *spirit* is prior to nature, and what does that mean for naturalism?[25] I have argued elsewhere[26] that one way of interpreting the priority of *spirit* over nature is as the priority of the intelligibility of the *logical space* of *spirit* over the *logical space* of nature, that is, as the priority of the kinds of explanations that belong to the framework of *spirit* over the kinds of explanations offered by the natural sciences. Hegel's analysis of the way that mechanical and chemical forms of explanation are dependent for their explanatory force on teleological explanations,[27] offer a route into understanding how the forms of explanation of the natural sciences are dependent on the explanatory framework of *spirit*. The reason for that is that the explanatory force of scientific accounts *depend* for their validation on the normative framework of *spirit*. In order for any of the explanations that natural science offers to *count as* explanations, there have to be criteria for *why* they are to count as appropriate explanations of certain phenomena. In other words, *reasons* have to be given for why a particular explanation is appropriate in accounting for a particular natural phenomenon. These *reasons* belong to the normative explanatory framework that is identified in Hegel with the explanatory framework of *spirit*. If Hegel is right that the explanatory framework of nature is dependent on that of *spirit*, Hegel has shown how scientific naturalism is self-defeating, since scientific naturalism claims that the only valid explanatory framework is that of the natural sciences, ignoring the fact that this framework derives its explanatory force from that of *spirit*.[28] According to this reading, Hegel's argument is an elaboration on Kant's account of scientific knowledge as conditioned by our own cognitive structures. The difference is that for Hegel, these cognitive structures are not static, like Kant's categories, but dynamic, social and historical: they are *spirit*.

The preceding interpretation also allows us to make sense of Hegel's claim that it is *spirit* which posits nature, rather than the other way around, as Hegel believes we might be tempted to think pre-philosophically. Again, if the common-sense view is that nature *posits* everything in the sense of causing everything that develops out of it, it is tempting to think that Hegel's reversal would mean that it is in fact *spirit* that causes nature to come into existence. If we follow this line of interpretation we end up with a quasi-theological picture of Hegel's philosophy. This could, conceivably, be made to cohere with the text.[29] Hegel indeed portrays *spirit* as self-creating, and even though he admits that it presupposes nature, he says that *spirit* itself makes these presuppositions for itself, which could mean that it is *spirit* which creates nature in the first place. However, the term 'posits' should not be read as 'creates' or "causes" in this context. The way I propose we should read the term is along the lines I have been suggesting we read the relationship between spirit and nature. *Spirit* 'posits' nature in that *spirit* is what makes nature intelligible, that which offers the explanations about nature, and which has to see nature as a presupposition of itself. Nature confronts us as a problem, as we saw Hegel saying in the introduction to the *Philosophy of Nature*. It is *spirit* which has to solve that riddle, to see nature as intelligible. This is not to say that *spirit imposes* an intelligibility onto an unintelligible, raw nature. Nature is in itself intelligible and *spirit* comes to recognise that through its own development of different norms and criteria for explaining nature. But, this intelligibility is also not simply read-off of nature either, it is not *given* to *spirit* passively by nature, but is worked out, *posited*, by *spirit* itself.

This argument, has, once again, the recognisable shape of a transcendental argument against scientific naturalism: it shows that the conditions for the possibility of natural scientific explanations are to be found in *spirit*, a normative framework that scientific naturalism allows no room for. The very thing that scientific naturalism finds difficult to accommodate within its picture of reality, the mind and its rational, normative structures, is shown to be exactly that which scientific explanations depend on for their force and validity in the first place.

There is a debate in the literature as to whether Hegel can correctly be understood as a transcendental philosopher, along the lines of Kant.[30] This debate is sometimes about whether a specific argument in Hegel can be understood as transcendental, and sometimes about whether Hegel's overall project, especially in the *Phenomenology*, can be characterised as transcendental.[31] I am not going to enter this debate here. What I want to suggest instead is that Hegel's argument about the priority of *spirit* over nature manages to avoid some of the complications that are found in Kant's equivalent argument about the priority of the *transcendental ego* over nature.

As already mentioned, one of the conundrums that arise in Kant's way of undermining scientific naturalism has to do with fact that the transcendental ego which provides the conditions for the possibility of scientific knowledge, lies beyond the bounds of the empirical world. Unlike Kant's transcendental ego, however, Hegel's *spirit* can be understood as being part of the empirical world, a socially embodied, collective mindedness that evolves through history. Furthermore, it should be understood as a kind of *activity* rather than as a thing or an entity, which can be within or outside the empirical realm. Hegel explicitly draws a connection between *spirit* and Aristotle's conception of the soul as activity, rather than as a thing. Aristotle famously criticised philosophers before him for having conceived of the soul as a thing, as an entity that is separate from material entities and, by some means, connects and interacts with the material world (the human body). He criticises both Plato and the Pythagoreans for attempting to separate the soul from the body, treating both of them as separate substances. For Aristotle, on the contrary, the correct way of understanding the soul is as essentially embodied and as a function of the body. Aristotle reconceived of the soul as the *form* of the living body. Aristotle tries to explain in more detail what a soul is by the use of analogies, the most famous one being that *if an eye were an animal, seeing would have been its soul*. The form, then, of something is like its *function*, its exemplary activity, or its purpose.[32]

Hegel, like Aristotle, also criticises past philosophers for misconstruing the soul as a thing, and in particular as an immaterial entity:

> The soul is no separate immaterial entity. . . . The question of the Immateriality of the soul has no interest, except where, on the one hand, matter is regarded as something *true* and mind conceived as a *thing*, on the other. . . . But in modern times even the physicists have found matters grow thinner in their hands: they have come upon *imponderable* matters, like heat, light, etc, to which they might perhaps add space and time. These imponderables, which have lost the property (peculiar to matter) of gravity and, in a sense, even the capacity of offering resistance, have still, however, a sensible existence
> (PN: §389)

Hegel here might be talking of the soul, which in his system is only the early stage of one of the three levels of *spirit* (namely subjective *spirit*), but the points that Hegel makes about the soul apply equally to *spirit* as a whole. As Willem deVries puts it:

> '[S]pirit' has a much broader use than 'soul', for it denotes the underlying activity informing and accounting for not only the mental activity of the individual but also the social and historical activity of a community. Hegel's shift from 'soul' to 'spirit' emphasises the non-thingishness, the active nature of the human essence as well as its communal or social nature.[33]

Hegel's way of conceiving the dependence of nature on *spirit* then both mirrors Kant's way of understanding the dependence of nature on the *transcendental ego*, namely by the former being conditioned by the latter, but at the same time avoids the problematic aspects of Kant's transcendental story. *Spirit* is separate from nature, in the sense that it cannot be understood as just another part of nature, but it is not *beyond* nature in the way that Kant's transcendental ego is. Another way of putting this is by seeing *spirit* as having an explanatory priority to nature, but not an ontological priority to it. This insight allows Hegel to undermine naturalism's claim regarding the priority of natural scientific explanations, or in other words, the explanatory priority of nature over *spirit*.

Husserl, the Mathematisation of Nature and the Lifeworld

In his *Crisis of the European Sciences*, Husserl diagnoses a host of problems that the mathematisation of the world by natural science has created, much like Price and McDowell diagnose scientific naturalism as causing placement problems. Admittedly, Husserl sees the problems caused by the mathematising of the world as much deeper than merely philosophical, so much so as to identify them as the source of a broader European cultural malaise. Husserl's proposed solution to these problems is in tune with the post-Kantian direction I have been exploring so far: once again, there is a reminder of the presuppositions of scientific activity, this time in the form of the broader context of human activity within which science takes place: the lifeworld. Husserl saw the positivism of the 19th century, which took science as the only valid source of knowledge, just as scientific naturalism does, as leading to the disenchantment of nature, i.e. the loss of meaning within the confines of natural reality. Positivism seemed unable to offer an account of human values, since there was no room left for values within a mechanistic, mathematically structured universe. This, Husserl thought, was bad not only for philosophy, leaving important questions related to the human sphere seemingly unanswerable, or, worse, meaningless, but bad for our understanding of science itself. Positivism, like scientific naturalism, offers an inadequate account of science, since it identifies science merely with its results, and is unable to offer an account of the process of scientific discovery, and the preconditions on which science's success relies. Positivism, according to Husserl, reduces the "idea of science to mere factual science" (*CES*: 6). This "leads to a 'crisis' of science as the loss of its meaning for life" (*CES*: 6). Despite the undisputed success of science, the blind belief in its results, that positivism and scientific naturalism bestow on it, leads to the inability to make sense of value more broadly, and more specifically to fully appreciate the value of science itself:

> The exclusiveness with which the total world-view of modern man, in the second half of the nineteenth century, let itself be determined by the positive sciences and be blinded by the "prosperity" they produced, meant an indifferent turning-away from the questions which are decisive for a genuine humanity. Merely fact-minded sciences make merely fact-minded people.
>
> (CES: 5–6)

Husserl locates the origins of positivism and scientific naturalism already in Galileo's conception of nature. According to Husserl, Galileo sought to explicitly abstract any subjective features from nature, anything relating to a subjective point of view, leaving behind only the objective, formal, mathematical features of objects. Galileo can therefore be seen as the originator of the Lockean distinction between primary and secondary qualities, with the latter being banished from the domain of nature. Galileo, then, 'formalises' nature, by seeing it in terms of an abstract grid of mathematical quantities:

> through Galileo's mathematisation of nature, nature itself is idealized under the guidance of the new mathematics; nature itself becomes— to express it in a modern way—a mathematical manifold.
>
> (CES: 23)

This mathematisation of nature, according to Husserl, is the defining feature of modern science, rather than, say, its reliance on the experimental method, inductive reasoning etc. Science is defined by this *a priori* structure with which we approach nature: mathematics. Husserl sees this formalisation as a projection of an idealised version of nature onto nature as we experience it, and so not as an uncovering of what nature is 'really' like, underneath all of its appearances. And yet, it was this idealised, mathematical nature that came to be identified with the 'real' immutable nature, behind the steam of stream of experience. Galileo was therefore a kind of Platonist who saw mathematics as revealing an eternal reality over and above any subjective experiences of the world. Husserl's strategy in the *Crisis* is to show that this abstraction from subjectivity that Galileo's metaphysics initiated, leads us to a misunderstanding of the very nature of science itself, as it erases the entire context within which science takes place. This is what the concept of the *lifeworld* aims to achieve: to offer an account of the background against which science takes place and thus to highlight, along the lines of Kant, that there are preconditions for the possibility of science. The key point that Husserl wants to make is that science itself is deeply unsuited for offering an account of those preconditions, of the *lifeworld*, as the latter's inherently subjective character is something that cannot be captured by the objectifying tools of science. There are several definitions of the *lifeworld* provided by Husserl,[34] but the aspects of it that concern us here have to do with the fact that the *lifeworld* is the background against which any human activity takes place. Husserl describes the lifeworld as that which

> belongs to what is taken for granted, prior to all scientific thought and all philosophical questioning, that the world is—always is in advance—and that every correction of an opinion, whether an experiential or other opinion, presupposes the already existing world, namely, as a horizon of what in the given case is indubitably valid as existing, and presupposes within this horizon something familiar and doubtlessly certain with which that which is perhaps canceled out as invalid came into conflict. Objective science, too, asks questions only on the ground of this world's existing in advance through prescientific life. Like all praxis, objective science presupposes the being of this world.
>
> (*CES*: 110)

Husserl is here 'reminding' us that we misunderstand the project of science if we only look at its results, its theories, overlooking the fact that science also has a practical aspect to it, the 'doing' of science, and that cannot itself be captured by science. Scientists, Husserl reminds us, are persons with daily, worldly concerns and aims that are unique to each person, that is, subjective, shaped by how each person experiences the world. They live in the world, they have breakfast, drive a car, drop off their kids at school, walk up the stairs. They are embodied individuals, who live in the world, a world that the activity of science presupposes. What is more, the scientist is not an isolated subject working alone, but a part of a community of scientists. These peers are the ones with which one cooperates, learns from, negotiates new findings. They are colleagues, peer reviewers, conference delegates etc. The embodied subject, then, and its relationships to other subjects, is a key part of what the project of science presupposes and depends on, and the subject is an inhabitant of the lifeworld. As Husserl writes:

> The knowledge of the objective-scientific world is "grounded" in the self-evidence of the life-world. The latter is pre-given to the scientific worker, or the working community, as ground; yet, as they build

upon this, what is built is something new, something different. If we cease being immersed in our scientific thinking, we become aware that we scientists are, after all, human beings and as such are among the components of the life-world which always exists for us, ever pre-given; and thus all of science is pulled, along with us, into the— merely "subjective-relative"—life-world.

(*CES*: 130–131)

Reminding us of this relatively obvious fact allows Husserl to challenge scientific naturalism and demonstrate why the placement problems that arise from it are a result of understanding science as merely its final product: mathematical theories about the laws that govern nature. Science, however, is better understood, according to Husserl, as the activity of science, which takes place within a network of meaningful exchanges between embodied subjects, living in the lifeworld.

Husserl's remarks in the *Crisis* then amount to a version of the argument against naturalism we already find in Kant: Naturalism forgets the preconditions of science and its explanations, and in so doing cannot see its limitations. The originality of Husserl's argument is to be found in his bringing our attention to preconditions previously ignored, namely those of the life-world:

> Naturalism is charged with being ignorant not merely of some *feature* of the world, but of *the world*. The world of everyday experience, it is maintained, is not incorporated into the scientifically described world, even though the latter's intelligibility tacitly depends on the former.[35]

So for Husserl, scientific naturalism does not simply create placement problems, finding hard to place certain aspects of the human world within the bounds of reality, it creates a much greater problem: it forgets the human world altogether, the world that science is a product of. In doing this, naturalism also gets science wrong. As Dermot Moran puts it:

> Naturalism betrays the very essence of science. It misunderstands the world because it misunderstands the subject's necessary role in the project of knowledge, and in the very constitution of objectivity. One cannot subtract the knowing subject from the process of knowledge, and treat the desiccated product as if it were the real world.[36]

Husserl's argument against naturalism has a transcendental structure, much like Kant's and Hegel's. Husserl's argument, however, seems to have two transcendental moments. The first one is aims to show the simple truth that science takes place within a broader context of experience, the 'natural attitude' we have towards the world. As Moran puts it

> The natural attitude is 'the attitude of experience'. It has the character of 'pre-giveness' or 'pre-found'. It is always 'on' in the background

as the primary attitude of natural human existence. All activities of consciousness, including all scientific activity, indeed all knowledge, initially take place within the natural attitude. Other attitudes, such as the objective scientific attitude and the formal mathematical attitude are one-sided abstractions from the natural attitude and presuppose it.[37]

This is the argument I have previously highlighted, the one emphasising the background conditions for the possibility of scientific activity, which science is incapable of capturing itself. That alone is enough to counter naturalism, in my view. In this transcendental argument, Husserl is in no need of an appeal to a transcendental ego, for the subject that he is reminding us of is the subject of the lifeworld, embodied and social.

Husserl, however, thinks that this still leaves us with a kind of naturalism, the naturalism of the 'natural attitude', the everyday, pre-philosophical attitude we have towards the world. Philosophy, however, for Husserl goes a step further, breaking with this everyday approach to things, and looking for an even deeper background to everything, a subjectivity that goes beyond that of the lifeworld, a transcendental subjectivity that is the foundation and the condition of the world of phenomena, much like Kant's transcendental idealism aimed to demonstrate:

> Husserl always speaks of the transcendental attitude as 'primary' and 'absolute' as opposed to the 'relative' nature of the natural attitude. Rather than seeing human consciousness as rooted in the world, we must now see the world itself as 'rooted' in transcendental subjectivity.[38]

Negotiating Husserl's pull towards this more fundamental transcendental attitude with the ever-present natural attitude of the *lifeworld*, from which everything, including transcendental reflections, starts, is a tension at the core of the *Crisis* that Husserl negotiates. Ultimately, Husserl thinks philosophy should leave the natural attitude behind, and see things from the standpoint of the transcendental attitude. However, it is important to note that Husserl does not want to envisage the transcendental ego as separate to the ego of the natural attitude, but rather as the ego that arises out of a different attitude towards experience. According to some commentators, Husserl is attempting a renewal of Kant's notion of the transcendental that carries fewer of the conundrums we find in the latter regarding the relationship between the transcendental and the empirical. Husserl, for example, unlike Kant, seems to want to preserve the social and embodied aspects of the natural self in the transcendental ego.[39] According to Dan Zahavi, in doing this, Husserl allows for a broader conception of the transcendental, one that has an advantage over that of Kant's, as it doesn't see the relationship between the empirical and the transcendental perspective as paradoxical and incompatible, but as "as intertwined and complementary perspectives".[40]

Whether Husserl's notion of the transcendental is more convincing that Kant's, is a question beyond the theme of this chapter. What I would like to emphasise here is that already within the bounds of the natural attitude, Husserl allows for a transcendental argument that is sufficient to undermine scientific naturalism. The *lifeworld* as Husserl reminds us is already there, before science and its 'objective' mathematical attitude take off. It is a precondition to the very practice and existence of the scientific enterprise, a part of reality of which science has deprived itself. Recognising this simple truth is enough to render the claim that we should start our philosophical investigations with the results of the natural sciences, as even the liberal naturalist Price suggests, forgetful and naïve.

Conclusion

Kant and the post-Kantian tradition to which Hegel and Husserl both belong, then, offer a critique of naturalism that has been forgotten in the more recent attempts by philosophers to escape the inevitable problems of scientific naturalism. Instead of seeing the results of science as the starting point of philosophical enquiry, they shed light on what has to already be in place for scientific enquiry to even take place. Following Kant's transcendental turn, they highlight the fact that science presupposes and is conditioned by a framework associated with the subject, its mind and the normative structures associated with it. For Kant, the explanatory framework that takes priority over that of science is that of the reason, conditioning the ways in which nature can be understood by us. For Hegel, that framework of human intelligibility becomes much broader, understood through his concept of *spirit* to include all aspects of human mindedness, and to account for the fact that the latter is dynamic, developing over history into ever more sophisticated forms. For Husserl, the framework that science presupposes is the lifeworld, our everyday world, filled with meaning and norms and accounts of ourselves as persons, something to which only a phenomenological account could do justice.

These moves by Kant, Hegel, and Husserl allows us to understand science as a project for which *we* are responsible for, one which we shape, according to our own standards of rationality, rather than as the unquestionable starting point of all further reflection. What these philosophers have in common, also, is an adherence to idealism in a *broad* sense, the belief the explanatory framework of the human mind is that which takes priority over all other explanatory frameworks, including that of nature. Given that a consequence of this position is that science is not capable of offering an account of the explanatory framework of human mindedness, the latter being something that science already presupposes, an important consequence follows regarding the relationship between philosophy and science. Instead of science and philosophy being continuous with one other, as naturalism would have it, philosophy is given its rightful first place in the order of human enquiry.

Notes

1. See Price (2004).
2. See McDowell 1999: 99.
3. See Price 2004: 73.
4. See Kim (2003).
5. Macarthur 2008: 2.
6. Quine 1981: 21.
7. Quine 1986: 430–431.
8. Ibid., p. 7.
9. Ibid., p. 8.
10. Papineau 2015: https://plato.stanford.edu/archives/win2016/entries/naturalism.
11. Cf. Price (2004)
12. Cf. Sellars (1997).
13. Cf. McDowell 1996: 70–71.
14. Of course it has been pointed out in the literature that understanding the natural sciences in this way is a narrow way of representing the type of explanations that the natural sciences provide, focusing almost exclusively on the science of physics. McDowell concedes to this objection in his response to Macdonald's article 'The Two Natures: Another Dogma?' (MacDonald 2006: 222–239)—which brings up this point about the inability of the law-like model to accommodate types of explanations that we undoubtedly consider part of the ones natural sciences offer:

    > I try to isolate relations in natural science to capture "a special space-of-reasons kind of intelligibility—a kind of intelligibility we find in phenomena when we explain them in a way that turns on the idea of responsiveness to reasons as such—partly by contrasting it with a different kind of intelligibility. I should not have suggested, as I did in *Mind and World*, that the image of the realm of law fits the whole extent of the kind of intelligibility I want to contrast with space-of-reasons intelligibility.
    > (McDowell 2006: 235–239)

15. McDowell 1996: xv.
16. See MacDonald (2006) and Gubeljic et al. (1999).
17. "The view implies that insofar as philosophy is concerned with the nature of objects and properties of various kinds, its concern is with something in the natural world, or with nothing at all. . . . The difficulties [then] stem from the fact that in many interesting cases it is hard to see what natural facts we could be talking about." (Price 2004: 73)
18. "The popular kind of naturalism . . . exists in both ontological and epistemological keys. As an ontological doctrine, it is the view that in some important sense, all there *is* is the world studied by science. As an epistemological doctrine it is the view that all genuine knowledge is scientific knowledge." (Price 2004: 73)
19. In Price (2013), Price allows that some vocabularies do indeed have a representational purposes, but that can only be revealed if we first treat language's function as being broader than just representational.
20. Price 2004: 88.

21. See Macarthur (2014).
22. Walker 2006: 238.
23. Pinkard 1994: 131.
24. Cf. *PN*: 3.
25. Paul Giladi (2014) argues that this priority should be understood as the priority of teleological explanations over mechanical explanations. Hegel indeed argues for the priority of teleological explanations over those of mechanism and chemism in his *Science of Logic*. However, given that according to Hegel nature itself exhibits teleological structures, especially at the biological level, the priority of spirit over nature could not be understood merely in terms of the priority of teleology over mechanism and chemism, the other two explanatory structures found in nature.
26. Viz., Papazoglou (2012).
27. See Kreines (2004).
28. Pinkard seems to be offering a similar argument in the context of the *Logic*:

    > Having supposedly committed ourselves . . . to a conception of naturalistic, causal explanations as necessarily being brought into normative play in all our other judgments about the world—we find that such a naturalistic conception of the world itself can legitimate itself only by invoking a non-naturalistic sense of normativity and truth. To keep the naturalistic view of the world intact, we must bring into play (or realise that we have always, already brought into play) a more complex picture of the relation of judgments to the world, namely, that the distinction itself between 'showing forth', 'seeming-to-be' and essence . . . is itself a unitary complex thought that can only be redeemed by understanding its role as part of a more comprehensive pattern of inferences. 'Reflective' judgments, that is, can themselves be redeemed only by being understood as part of a more comprehensive *practice* of judging that is itself to be construed as a *normative* matter of judgment and inference, not as part of the naturalistically construed world. Such judgments are moves in a logical space, not causal relationships.
    >
    > (Pinkard 2002: 257)

29. Charles Taylor's interpretation of Hegel comes close to this reading, see Taylor (1975).
30. See Williams 1985.
31. See Stern (2013) on this, where he argues against Stephen Houlgate's objections to Charles Taylor, and defends the idea that some of Hegel's arguments can indeed be understood as transcendental. See also Giladi (2016) for a similar argument.
32. For more on Aristotle on the soul, see Everson (1995).
33. deVries 1988: 25.
34. See (Moran 2012)
35. Ratcliffe 2013: 71.
36. Moran 2013: 92–93.
37. Moran 2008: 414.
38. Ibid., p. 418.
39. According to Zahavi, "Husserl ultimately argued that transcendental subjectivity must necessarily conceive of itself as a worldly being if it is to constitute an objective world, since objectivity can only be constituted by a subject which is both embodied and socialised" (Zahavi 2015: 239).
40. Zahavi 2015: 241.

References

deVries, W. A. 1988. *Hegel's Theory of Mental Activity: An Introduction to Theoretical Spirit*. New York: Cornell University Press.

Everson, S. 1995. 'Psychology'. In J. Barnes (ed.) *The Cambridge Companion to Aristotle*. Cambridge: Cambridge University Press.

Giladi, P. 2014. 'Liberal Naturalism: The Curious Case of Hegel'. *International Journal of Philosophical Studies* 22: 248–270.

———. 2016. 'New Directions for Transcendental Claims'. *Grazer Philosophische Studien* 93: 212–223.

Gubeljic, M., Link, S., Muller, P., and Osburg, G. 1999. 'Nature and Second Nature in McDowell's *Mind and World*'. In M. Willaschek (ed.) *John McDowell: Reason and Nature, Lecture and Colloquium in Münster*. Munster: LIT—Verlag. Available at: http://web.uni-frankfurt.de/fb08/PHIL/willaschek/mcdowellkolloq.pdf

Hegel, G. W. F. 1969. *Science of Logic*. A. V. Miller (trans.). Amherst, NY: Humanity Books.

———. 1970. *Philosophy of Nature (Part Two of the Encyclopaedia of Philosophical Sciences)*. M. J. Petry (trans.), 3 vols. London: George Allen and Unwin.

———. 1977. *Phenomenology of Spirit*. A. V. Miller (trans.). Oxford: Oxford University Press.

———. 2007. *Philosophy of Mind: Part Three of the Encyclopaedia of the Philosophical Sciences* (together with the Zusatze). W. Wallace (trans.) and M. Inwood (revised). Oxford: Oxford University Press.

Husserl, E. 1970. *The Crisis of the European Sciences and Transcendental Philosophy*. D. Carr (trans.). Evanston, IL: Northwestern University Press.

Kant, I. 1998. *Critique of Pure Reason*. P. Guyer and A. W. Wood (eds. and trans.). Cambridge: Cambridge University Press.

———. 2004. *Prolegomena to Any Future Metaphysics*. G. Hatfield (ed. and trans.). Cambridge: Cambridge University Press.

Kim, J. 2003. 'The American Origins of Philosophical Naturalism'. *Journal of Philosophical Research, APA Centennial Volume*: 83–98.

Kreines, J. 2004. 'Hegel's Critique of Pure Mechanism and the Philosophical Appeal of the *Logic* Project'. *European Journal of Philosophy* 12: 38–74.

Macarthur, D. 2008. 'Quinean Naturalism in Question'. *PHILO* 11: 5–18.

———. 2014. 'Subject Naturalism and the Problem of Linguistic Meaning: Critical Remarks on Price's "Naturalism Without Representationalism"'. *Análisis: Revista de investigación filosófica* 1: 69–85.

Macdonald, G. 2006. 'The Two Natures: Another Dogma?' In C. Macdonald and G. Macdonald (eds.) *McDowell and His Critics*. Oxford: Blackwell.

McDowell, J. 1996. *Mind and World*. Cambridge, MA: Harvard University Press.

———. 1999. 'Responses'. In M. Willaschek (ed.) *John McDowell: Reason and Nature, Lecture and Colloquium in Münster*. Munster: LIT Verlag. Available at: http://web.uni-frankfurt.de/fb08/PHIL/willaschek/mcdowellkolloq.pdf

———. 2006. 'Response to Graham Macdonald'. In C. Macdonald and G. Macdonald (eds.) *McDowell and His Critics*. Oxford: Blackwell.

Moran, D. 2008. 'Husserl's Transcendental Philosophy and the Critique of Naturalism'. *Continental Philosophy Review* 41: 401–425.

———. 2012. *Husserl's Crisis of the European Sciences and Transcendental Phenomenology: An Introduction*. Cambridge: Cambridge University Press.

————. 2013. ' "Let's Look at It Objectively': Why Phenomenology Cannot Be Naturalised". *Royal Institute of Philosophy Supplement* 72: 89–115.

Papazoglou, A. 2012. 'Hegel and Naturalism'. *Hegel Bulletin* 33: 74–90.

Papineau, D. 2015. 'Naturalism'. In E. N. Zalta (ed.) *The Stanford Encyclopaedia of Philosophy*, Winter 2016. Available at: https://plato.stanford.edu/archives/win2016/entries/naturalism

Pinkard, T. 1994. *Hegel's Phenomenology: The Sociality of Reason*. Cambridge: Cambridge University Press.

————. 2002. *German Philosophy 1760–1860: The Legacy of Idealism*. Cambridge: Cambridge University Press.

Price, H. 2004. 'Naturalism without Representationalism'. In M. De Caro and D. Macarthur (eds.) *Naturalism in Question*. Cambridge, MA: Harvard University Press.

————. 2013. *Expressivism, Pragmatism and Representationalism*. Cambridge: Cambridge University Press.

Quine, W. V. 1981. *Theories and Things*. Cambridge, MA: Harvard University Press.

————. 1986. 'Reply to Putnam'. In L. E. Hahn and P. A. Schillp (eds.) *The Philosophy of W. V. Quine*. Chicago, IL: Open Court Press.

Ratcliffe, M. 2013. 'Phenomenology, Naturalism and the Sense of Reality'. *Royal Institute of Philosophy Supplement* 72: 67–88.

Sellars, W. 1997. 'Empiricism and the Philosophy of Mind: With an Introduction by Richard Rorty and a Study Guide by Robert Brandom'. In R. Brandom (ed.). Cambridge, MA: Harvard University Press.

Stern, R. 2013. 'Taylor, Transcendental Arguments, and Hegel on Consciousness'. *Hegel Bulletin* 34: 79–97.

Taylor, C. 1975. *Hegel*. Cambridge: Cambridge University Press.

Walker, R. C. S. 2006. 'Kant and Transcendental Arguments'. In P. Guyer (ed.) *The Cambridge Companion to Kant and Modern Philosophy*. Cambridge: Cambridge University Press.

Williams, R. R. 1985. 'Hegel and Transcendental Philosophy'. *The Journal of Philosophy* 82: 595–606.

Zahavi, D. 2015. 'Husserl and the Transcendental'. In S. Gardner and M. Grist (eds.) *The Transcendental Turn*. Oxford: Oxford University Press.

5   An Hegelian *Actualist* Alternative to Naturalism

Paul Redding

The reasons why philosophers with a this-worldly bent reject idealism are obvious enough. Idealism is typically understood as a philosophical outlook that gives a necessary place to mind in reality, and this seems to suggest traditional theological views like that which sees the material world as a creation of a transcendent mind. Naturalism has seemed the obvious alternative: why should the natural sciences stop at explaining our minds as the products of natural processes? Did not Darwin make plausible this general idea of the mind as something that has appeared in an essentially mind-less world?

Hegel's idealism, however, never fitted this picture of idealism against which naturalism reacts, as Hegel, like Spinoza, was critical of the metaphysics allowing an other-worldly God. But while many naturalists have felt an affinity with Spinoza, extending such good will to Hegel seems blocked at the point at which Hegel was critical of Spinoza's naturalism. For Hegel, although mind ("spirit") is in the world, it cannot be treated as a face of that which nature is another.

In this chapter, I defend Hegel's alternative to Spinozist naturalism, focussing on his approach to modality. Critical of Spinoza's necessitarianism, Hegel insisted on finding a place for possibility in the actual, and with this, he might be compared to some contemporary "actualists" who, affirming the reality of possibility, oppose David Lewis's commitment to other possible worlds. As the actual is all there is, alternate possibilities must be, somehow, internal to it—unrealised states or properties of the actual.

Drawing on this parallel, I interpret Hegel's idealism as consequential to his actualism. If, as some argue (and as is suggested by the phrase "this-worldly"), "actual" functions as a type of indexical, must not the actualist be committed to minds and their subjective points of view in some sense that escapes our conception of nature? If so, actualism seems to presuppose a type of idealism. This position would be toxic only if the necessity of mindedness in reality were meant in a stronger sense—for example, were the mind thought of as necessary *per se*—i.e. as present in every possible state of the world. But this is just what Hegel opposes in Spinoza.

Naturalism is often said to be the default philosophical outlook within analytic philosophy, and from a broader intellectual perspective this might be expected. Very crudely, the development of modernity in the West since the seventeenth century has witnessed the gradual acceptance of the authority of the natural sciences concerning claims about the world.[1] Of course, this has not happened without a struggle. In medieval times, the authority holder in relation to almost all epistemic claims had been the church, and the trial of Galileo in 1610 might serve as an image of the constraints from which an autonomous scientific approach to the world had to break free. This particular struggle was, of course, one in which the views of Galileo were ultimately successful, although it was not until 1992 that the church actually came to concede defeat. Clearly, resistance to science on the basis of traditional religious teaching still exists in the most developed parts of the world. Surely philosophy might then be expected to be on the side of Galileo in aligning itself with the authority of a fallible but self-correcting approach to belief in contrast to any that, seeking reassuring absolutes, is willing to locate those absolutes in cultural forms handed down from earlier pre-scientific times.

As the familiar but simplified story of the birth of analytic philosophy goes, two young philosophers at Cambridge in the closing years of the nineteenth century—G. E. Moore and Bertrand Russell—pitted themselves and their conception of philosophy against a *status quo* that had come to dominate philosophy at British universities for a number of decades—British idealism. Idealism in this British form had effectively recycled the idealistic form of philosophy that had started in Germany about a century earlier with Kant's transcendental idealism and that had concluded with Hegel's "absolute" idealism (Förster 2012). On Hegel's death, his followers famously had split on the issue of the nature of his philosophy, the 'left faction' arguing for it as an expression of the modern aspiration to freedom and taking it in a *materialist* and 'scientific' direction, while the 'right' saw in it metaphysical grounds of a defence of religion that had been coming under attack from such approaches.

The form of idealism reanimated in Britain half a century *after* the death of Hegel would seem to have had much in common with the right-wing within Hegel's successors, and it is plausible to assume that at least part of the motivation for the revival of idealism had been the challenge to religion provided by developments such as Darwin's naturalistic account of the origins of the human species. In the case of Darwin, not all supporters of religion were ready to dismiss his theories, and in Britain some liberal theologians were happy to try to reconcile Darwin's naturalistic picture with God's underlying plan. An idealistic theory like Hegel's might have been seen as appropriate here, promising a form of metaphysics that was meant to provide a way of reconciling science with the underlying truths of religion, now understood as presenting a picture of the world in a somewhat metaphorical way. A place for God, perhaps one unrecognizable from the perspective of the pious *non-philosophical* believer, could thus be rescued within the baroque complexities of Hegel's logically based metaphysics upon which the diverse claims of the natural sciences and the creeds of religion could be both grounded.

To critics, however, this would look more like a redundant attempt to save religious culture in a world of science. Moreover, Hegel's idiosyncratic claims about *logic* seemed to have been bypassed by the growth of a genuine *science* of logic in the nineteenth century, the type of mathematical or symbolic approach to logic developed by Bolzano, Boole, de Morgan and others and that, towards the end of the century resulted in the influential views of Gottlob Frege which broke with the tradition of Aristotelian logic that had dominated for over two millennia. Russell, introduced to neo-Hegelianism by his idealist teachers, had been converted to Frege's powerful logic in 1900, and would dismiss Hegel's metaphysics as based upon an outdated logic. It would be easy, then, to assume that the revolt of Russell and Moore, an atheist and an agnostic respectively, had reacted against the late nineteenth-century idealist compromise with religion, and had launched their attack on idealism from a fundamentally naturalistic world-view. Such a way of construing things here is easy but wrong, however, given that the early analytic views of Russell and Moore were positively antithetical to naturalism. Having been originally established on explicitly *anti-naturalistic* assumptions, analytic philosophy would pose problems for later attempts to naturalize it. Here I want to argue that, paradoxical as it may sound, a version of the idealism against which the early analysts had revolted may provide the best route to the achievement of the ends that have been sought in the naturalistic turn.

I

The Anti-Naturalistic Origins of Analytic Philosophy

Moore's revolt against the views of the idealists had been expressed in his paper from 1899, "The Nature of Judgement", but the first fruits of his new philosophical approach to gain a wide readership were those of his 1903 *Principia Ethica*, at the centre of which was a critique of what he called the "naturalistic fallacy" in ethics. It would hardly be likely, then, that naturalism would be the attitude underlying his famous paper, "The Refutation of Idealism" published in the same year. Moore's naturalistic fallacy concerned any naturalistic analysis of an evaluative concept such as "good", as found, say, in the utilitarian tradition. His position, then, concerned the irreducibility of normative concepts to naturalistic ones in the context of practical philosophy. For Russell, a like-minded break from idealism had resulted from his having taken up the equally explicit *anti-naturalistic* approach to *logic* as developed by Frege, and with this

his thought converged with Moore's. What Moore's criticism had been directed to in 'The Nature of Judgment' was the failure of idealism, as he understood it, to acknowledge the *independence* of the objects known by the mind from the psychological processes at work in a knower's coming to know them. In this sense, for much of the first decade of the new philosophy both Russell and Moore developed ideas about the contents of judgments that were more Platonist than naturalist, and close to the views of the earlier Bernard Bolzano or the contemporary Alexius Meinong (Sundholm 2009: 280–284). Russell's turn away from this early form of Platonic realism towards an attitude closer to empiricism is usually said to have commenced with the 1905 paper 'On Denoting'; while Moore's adherence to a more Platonic type of realism is usually said to have lasted up to the years 1911–1912. Certainly they changed, but the question must be asked as to how systematic and successful such a change could hope to be, given the peculiar point from which they commenced. Stepping back to consider the role played by philosophy in modern culture *vis-a-vis* other areas might be helpful to bring issues into perspective.

It might be said that from the seventeenth century philosophy had been intimately involved in the need to provide the emerging natural sciences with epistemic justification given events such as Galileo's trial. The philosophical attempt to ground scientific knowledge was also close to Russell's motivations, but one explanation for the specifically anti-naturalism of his early form of analysis would surely lie in the *particular* science for which he was keen to establish epistemic credentials—mathematics—a science in relation to which Platonism rather than naturalism had been the dominant interpretative stance.

Since Euclid, the conception of mathematical proof had been the deduction of theorems by logically transparent steps from self-evident axioms, but in the late 19th century, radical progress in mathematics transformed the discipline to such a degree that the search for foundations arose with a new urgency (Mehrtens 1990). One response to this had been that of Frege's program of "logicism"—the attempt to find the certain foundations for mathematics in logic itself. In the ancient context Aristotle's syllogistic had been regarded as a means of establishing deductive inferences within geometric proofs, but in the 17th century, Leibniz had brought mathematics and logic together in a different way by introducing *algebra* into logic. Assertions could now be conceived effectively on the model of equations, and Leibniz had even introduced the idea of a binary arithmetic in which the numbers 1 and 0 could represent "true" and "false" respectively so as to link equations to truth-bearing propositions. This move had been effectively rediscovered in the nineteenth century by George Boole, giving rise to the explicit doctrine of "mathematical" or "symbolic" logic to contrast with the traditional syllogistic, and in this way, mathematical operations like addition and multiplication could be conceived as being applied to the project of calculating the logical consequences of sets of premises. While for Boole this pointed in the direction of treating the contents of logic itself as a *branch* of mathematics, this move was denied by Frege for whom the claims of mathematics were meant to be proven *by logic*, specifically by their being able to be expressed in a "concept script"—a *"Begriffschrift"*—(Frege 1879), the logic of which could be understood as reflecting the basic structure of the world itself.

All this required logic itself to be independent of, and more basic than, the truths of mathematical assertions themselves, and if the truths of mathematics were thought to be independent of and prior to the truths of the natural world, then surely this must be even more so for the case for logic. Hence Frege's opposition to the movement of 'psychologism' that had been gathering momentum during the 19th century, in which logic was effectively conceived as a branch of the empirical and naturalistically conceived science of psychology. This had put Frege and, by implication, Russell, in odd company, as the first critic of *Psychologizmus* as such had been the Hegelian, Johann Eduard Erdmann, who had critically characterized the philosophical position of Friedrich Eduard Beneke with this term (Kusch 2015).[2]

In short, "naturalism" was far from being an obvious self-conception of analytic philosophy at the time of its origins, and the route to a naturalistic version of it might not be expected to have been either straight or smooth. To pick up the story of the structural problems involved here from a more contemporary point of view, I want to consider the way in which Huw Price, an advocate of philosophical naturalism, has identified problems facing conventional ways of articulating it, as his diagnosis brings out, I believe, ways in which the legacy of Russell's original anti-naturalism has compromised standard analytic ways of conceiving of itself in a naturalistic way.

II

Price's Critique of the "Object Naturalism" of Mainstream Analytic Philosophy

Let us commence by considering an observation made by Price concerning what he has taken to be the *wrong* path for a naturalistic philosophy— what he calls "object naturalism" and for which he suggests an alternative of "subject naturalism". "Object naturalism" broadly refers to a type of empirical realist conception of philosophy of the sort that Russell came to accept after his turn from his early Platonism, and that came to be challenged in the 1930s by the more radical forms of empiricism advocated by Carnap and other members of the "Vienna Circle".

Price (1992, 1997, 2004) sets up the problem in the following way. Hitherto, orthodox naturalistic conceptions of philosophy have regarded philosophy as taking as *its* object the world as contemporary science describes it. For some, this had effectively ablated the distinction between science and philosophy, but others who resisted this had seen their own tasks as that of finding a place *in* the world as scientifically described, for certain things that do not appear there but nevertheless seem fundamental to our everyday conception of ourselves, and to the world as containing ourselves. Price considers, for example, the interrelated conceptions we have about the mind, morality or modality. We conceive ourselves as having minds, the capacities of which seem of a very different kind to those belonging to things belonging to the world of science. Thus we conceive of ourselves *qua minded* as able to experience and know the world, and act freely within it. This links mind and morality, as we see ourselves as morally accountable for such free actions, and it links both to modality, in that we think of ourselves as being able to freely bring about situations that would not have occurred without *our* intervention. And yet these phenomena are not easily reconcilable with a naturalistic starting point. In short, the problem here confronting these three 'M' realms is effectively a version of that of reconciling freedom in a deterministic world.

From the perspective of this dilemma, the task of philosophy becomes that of addressing a variety of 'placement problems': "[A] typical placement problem" Price notes, "seeks to understand how some object, property, or fact can be a *natural* object, property, or fact" (Price 2004: 75). But Price thinks that contemporary analytic philosophy is caught in a bind in that it addresses these questions in a way that assumes, at a methodological level, an *implicit* conception of ourselves and our epistemic powers that seems incompatible with the naturalistic world it assumes as its base in the task of "placing" talk of mind, morals or modality. We need something more comprehensively naturalistic than 'object naturalism'—a type of naturalistic conception of the objective world. Thus he advocates what he calls 'subject naturalism', in which we try to root out and counter the types of *non*-naturalistic assumptions about ourselves that stand in contrast with the purportedly naturalistic orientation of 'object naturalists'. Price aligns his own subject naturalism with historical forebears such as Hume, Carnap, and, especially, the later Wittgenstein. Transposed into the framework of philosophy of language with Wittgenstein, Price is thus critical of the assumptions that language can unproblematically represent the world as it is in itself. Rather, we must look at our linguistic usages—our language games—in the same way that we look at natural phenomena, in order to understand what is really at issue in the relation of language to the world.

In contrast to Price's self-classification as being in the Humean tradition, I have argued elsewhere that it seems to presuppose a type of logical self-consciousness that resembles more a type of naturalised Kantianism (Redding 2010). That is, there are elements of the Fries-Beneke position against which both Frege and the neo-Hegelian Erdmann reacted. Further, I have urged an Hegelian alternative to naturalized Kantianism—a form of idealism that, I've argued, is not premised on any 'supernatural' ontology. More recently I have advocated a reading of idealism in modal terms, interpreting idealism as a type of 'modal actualism' (Redding 2017, 2018), and here want to explore this further as an alternative to both orthodox analytic naturalism (object naturalism) and its Pricean alternative (subject naturalism). In particular, I want to do it by exploring conceptions of *logic* that have attempted to break with the problems that Price identifies as generated by object naturalism—conceptions here understood as stemming from the platonistic dimensions of the Frege-Russell tradition in logic. This will involve a strengthening of the idealist position against which Moore pitted his early platonic aspirations.

III

Idealism and Non-Classical Logics in the 20th Century

The placement problem as described by Price not only applies to objects of everyday experience, it also applies to finding a place in the natural world for objects we normally think as objects of scientific inquiry, albeit, not the inquiries of the *natural* sciences. This knowledge in question is mathematics—another of Price's 'M worlds'. We might ask, however, as to whether it might not also apply to an '*L*' world that for Frege and Russell was conceived as coming before Price's M worlds—Logic. The logic with which Russell denounced that of Hegel and that was introduced by Frege was, of course, subject to a specific problem that was to challenge Frege's logicist program from the very start—the problem communicated in a letter by Russell to Frege in 1902 (van Heijenoort 1967), pointing to a paradox entailed by the 'naïve' conception of sets originating in Cantor and presupposed within Frege's *Begriffschrift* of 1879. This allowed *any* definable collection to be a set, and so effectively equated collections *intensionally* understood, to be equivalent to ones *extensionally* understood. As Russell showed, this allowed the formation of a set defined as the collection of all sets that are not members of themselves, and this could be shown to involve a contradiction. Russell's proposed solution was his ramified theory of *types*, which he built into *Principia Mathematica* (1910–13), co-authored with Alfred North Whitehead.

The subsequent history of logic in the 20th and 21st centuries is complex and controversial, but one might point to developments in it that have emerged at least *partly* motivated by concerns that are similar to those expressed by Price in relation to the conventional way of attempting to naturalize analytic philosophy. These concerns are directed to the *non-finitistic* assumptions about the nature of rational thinking that seem presupposed by classical conceptions of logic. After a brief summary of a few of these directions taken within logic I will turn to Hegel and suggest that premonitions of such conceptions of logic are already to be found there, motivated by similar metaphysical concerns. While Hegel is often associated with ideas of some divine "infinite thought", it should not be forgotten that for him such thought only exists as distributed over an evolving community of finite thinkers (Redding 2012).

C. I. Lewis and Early 20th-century Modal Logic

Within a few years of the publication of the first volume of *Principia Mathematica*, C. I. Lewis published the first of a string of articles critical of Russell's conception of "material implication" that was based on his extensionalist reduction of the form of Aristotelian judgments (e.g. C. I. Lewis 1912, 1914). Russell's reduction had entailed the elimination of Aristotle's *modal* distinctions, and Lewis complained that this move left him incapable of conveying the idea of the necessity implicit in the logical conception of valid inference itself. Moreover, Russell's material implication resulted in a problematic conception of implication that put it at variance with both the everyday and scientific understandings of the notion, as according to Russell, counter-intuitively, a false proposition implied *any other* proposition, and a true proposition was implied *by* any other proposition. To rectify these problems Lewis then set about developing a formal logic with modal propositional operators ("it is necessary that . . ." and "it is possible that . . .") to provide a model of modal judgment adequate to capture the necessary character of implication, and thus opposed his "strict implication" to Russell's "material implication" (C. I. Lewis 1918; Lewis and Langford 1932).

In fact Lewis's logical move had an Hegelian genealogy in that he had been deeply influenced by his teacher, the American 'absolute idealist', Josiah Royce, from whom he had derived much of the logical formalizations used for his systems of modal logic (C. I. Lewis 1918: vi). In turn Royce himself had been influenced in his logic by C. S. Peirce, who was deeply influenced by Kant and whose thought was close to the German idealists in many respects. Lewis was to make explicit this link to idealism of his own *intensional* approach to logic (Lewis 1930), describing it as a mathematical, or "logistical", development of the type of intensional logic that had been typical of "continental" thinkers since the time of Leibniz (Lewis 1930: 33). In contrast to Russell's attempt to reduce the mind-related intensional reading of logical relations to the extensional, Lewis claimed that the intensional implication relation was the more inclusive: "when the extensional relations are introduced by definition, it includes the calculus of propositions, as previously developed, as a subsystem" (Lewis 1930: 36).

Further, while Lewis may not have been aware (although his teacher Royce would surely have been), his criticism of Russell closely paralleled features of Hegel's criticism in his *Science of Logic* of Leibniz's "characteristica universalis"—in many ways a precursor to Frege's *Begriffschrift*. Hegel had been familiar with Leibniz's extensionalistically conceived project with its link to an algebraically based "calculus", because as a student at Tübingen he had been taught the logic of Gottfried Ploucquet, a staunch supporter of Leibniz's project (Pozzo 2010). In his treatment of syllogisms in the "subjective logic" of Book 3, Hegel argues that the form of the "mathematical syllogism" pursued by Leibniz and Ploucquet actually *undermines* the very inferential relations that this syllogism is meant to formalize (Hegel 2010: 602–608, XII 104–110; Redding 2014).

From his earliest criticisms of Russell, Lewis had proceeded to develop his systems of propositional modal logic, the fruits of which were contained in the 1932 work co-authored with C. H. Langford, *Symbolic Logic*. Constrained within the framework of Lewis's somewhat awkward logical systems, S1 to S5, modal logic remained something of a logical backwater until the 1950s and 1960s when it underwent a revolution with the extension to modal logic of the type of semantics that had been developed by Tarski and others for *non*-modal logic in the style of Russell. This led to the creation of *quantified modal predicate* logic and so-called "possible-world semantics". Considered as a development *internal* to the program of formal logic, these developments have generally been regarded within analytic philosophy as amounting to an eventual triumph of Russell's *extensional* approach over C. I. Lewis's early intensionalist revolt. From a broader philosophical perspective, however, many have found problematic the very counter-intuitive metaphysical consequences that David Lewis came to derive from possible world semantics.

The roots of David Lewis's approach to philosophy lead back through his teacher Quine to Russell, and we might see Lewis here as having recovered an implicit metaphysics in the analytic approach closer to Russell's original Platonistic anti-naturalism rather than the "official" naturalistic self-understanding of analytic philosophy endorsed by most of its practitioners.[3] One type of challenge to Lewis's metaphysics has come to be made in the name of 'actualism' rather than 'naturalism', and this approach, I suggest, has connections to earlier idealist conceptions of logic, as revealed in the work of Arthur Prior.

Arthur Prior and the Development of Modal Logic

Saul Kripke is usually credited as the first theorist to work out a way of smoothly extending the type of semantic program Alfred Tarski and others had developed for the earlier non-modal classical logic to C. I. Lewis's systems of propositional modal logic (Kripke 1959, 1963). In using Tarski's mathematical models in relation to quantified modal logic, Kripke had invoked Leibniz's idea of "possible worlds" for the purpose of making sense of truth conditions for necessary and possible propositions. One can think of a proposition that is necessarily true as one that is true in all possible worlds, and one that is possibly true as one that is true in some possible worlds (Kripke 1959: 2). But a common response has here been that surely *merely* possible worlds don't exist: they are worlds made up of things that we think might have existed but, in fact, do not. What sense then is one to make of the idea of 'quantifying' over such domains of non-existent entities? This is the claim in relation to which David Lewis famously bit the bullet, defending the extensionalist program by treating thoughts about merely possible objects as being made true or false by objects existing in such alternate worlds—that is, concrete worlds considered as just as 'real' as the actual world (D. Lewis 1973, 1986). Among those who found the metaphysical costs of this solution too high, was the New Zealand logician Arthur Prior, whose early work on tense logic had played a pivotal role in Kripke's achievements (Copeland 2002, 2008).

Early in the reception of David Lewis's work, Prior signalled his resistance to this metaphysics and provided an early instantiation of an 'actualist' alternative. In his work on tense logic, Prior resisted attempts to reduce the logic of tensed sentences to an extensionally conceived logic of untensed, or 'eternal,' ones—sentences that were conceived as rendered true or false by being 'indexed' to states of the world at *discrete points in time*. In the early 1970s, David Lewis had argued that it is just as irrational to deny the reality of non-actual possible worlds as it is to deny the reality of times other than the present (Lewis 1973: 86). We don't think of the inhabitants of ancient Rome, for example, as unreal simply because they do not belong to the *present* world, and similarly we shouldn't think of the inhabitants and the goings-on of non-actual *possible* worlds as unreal, simply because they don't occur in the *actual* world. Here Lewis exploited various parallels between the structures of tense logic and the 'alethic' modal logic of possible and necessary truths that had figured in Prior's own work, but Prior had already rejected Lewis's way of thinking of the *temporal* vehicle of the analogy. Thus Prior was suspicious of the desire to try to speak meaningfully about other times in ways that purported to completely free the meanings of a speaker's sentences from the temporal context of their utterance, and he did this because of metaphysical consequences involving what he thought to be an illegitimate appeal to 'Platonic' entities such as "instants of time".[4] That is, Prior's response to Lewis can be thought of as applying to Moore's original critique of idealism in 'The Nature of Judgment', and as in the case of C. I. Lewis, we might discern here the hidden hand of an Hegelian, in the form of the influence of his teacher, John N. Findlay.

Findlay was later to be well known for his attempts to revive Hegel's philosophy in an analytic context in the 1950s (Findlay 1955–1956, 1958), but had spent the years 1934–1944 teaching in New Zealand where he had introduced Prior to logic. In his first book, Prior had attributed to Findlay "almost all that I know of either Logic or Ethics" (Prior

1957: xi), and in his later work on tense logic, Prior acknowledged the influence of a paper on time first published in 1941 (Findlay 1941), referring to Findlay as the "founding father of modern tense logic." (Prior 1967: 1).

Earlier in his career Findlay had embraced a Fichtean form of idealism, and although it is not clear when exactly he returned to idealism, he had done so after a flirtation with the type of Platonism found in early Russell and Meinong. Thus his PhD thesis written on Meinong written in the early 1930s (Findlay 1933) strongly suggests a reattraction back to an idealism, now with a more Hegelian 'objective' form, as way of avoiding the strongly counter-intuitive nature of Meinong's metaphysics.[5] Consistent with this, papers published in the 1940s express underlying Hegelian themes that are not overtly referred to as such, possibly because of his own concern with the impact of this interest on his career prospects.[6] Prior himself seems not to have thought of his own work as in any way idealist, but the Findlay-Prior 'actualist' line of opposition to what they both took to be the objectionable metaphysics accompanying the way logic had been standardly conceived suggests a connection with Hegel that was subsequently made explicit in Findlay's own work.

Intuitionistic Logic from Brouwer to Theoretical Computer Science

Both C. I. Lewis and Arthur Prior had resisted aspects of modern 'classical logic' on the basis of its inability to encompass modal claims without counterintuitive metaphysical implications that seemed to be in themselves *anathema* to any modern point of view that, like a naturalistic one, did not rely on some transcendent realm of objects. Around the time of the original publication of *Principia Mathematica*, another line of critique of classical mathematics and the logic associated with it had been expressed in the 'intuitionist' mathematics of the Dutch mathematician L. E. J. Brouwer. Brouwer's approach to mathematics had clear idealist origins in Kant's understanding of mathematics as based on the "pure intuitions" of time and space, Brouwer reducing these, however, to the intuition of time alone. Rejecting any Platonist understanding of mathematical objects, Brouwer had insisted that they were constructions in the mind of the mathematical thinker, and linking *concepts* to linguistic communication, had considered the communication of mathematical truths as entirely external to the truths themselves as well as to their proofs, which consisted of the mathematician retracing the steps involved in her own construction of such objects. Thus, adopting the other extreme to Frege's logicist position, Brouwer took logic to be largely irrelevant to mathematics rather than its 'foundation'.

This stark opposition was softened, however, by his student Arend Heyting, who reconceived the logic relevant for mathematical proofs in a decidedly *non*-classical way (Moschovakis 2015). Using algebraic models for inferences between judgments, Heyting produced an algebraic logic that was *weaker* than the Boolean algebra presupposed by classical logic, in that in excluded the universality of the law of excluded middle.[7] An intuitionistic approach to logical proofs was also developed by Gerhart Gentzen in the 1930s, and in the 1940s Kurt Gödel was to show that Heyting algebra was equivalent to the modal logic of C. I. Lewis's system S4, a system weaker than S5 which reproduced the logical behaviour found in classical logic and encoded the system of "logical possibility" as standardly conceived.[8] While making any systematic case for connection of these developments with the idealist tradition is well beyond the scope of this chapter, nevertheless, when taken in conjunction with the developments we have witnessed the history of intuitionism in mathematics and logic is suggestive.

The "ramified theory of types" introduced by Russell to avoid the contradictions into which "naïve" set theory had led continued to be developed after Russell (Kammareddine et al. 2002). Important for the future computationalist turn in mathematics was the introduction of the "typed lambda calculus" by Alonzo Church in the 1930s (Church 1940), which was given an intuitionist interpretation by his student Stephen Kleene, while later, this intuitionistic construal of type theory was developed in the work of Per Martin-Löf (1996). At least one important figure connected with this tradition, the American "categorical logician" F. William Lawvere, has claimed Hegel as the ancestor of so-called "category theory" which has developed in relation to this tradition and which has come to challenge set theory as the foundational framework of logic itself (e.g. Lawvere 1992).[9]

Central to these approaches has been the idea that intuitionistic logic is more suited to an understanding of the mathematical idea of function that is relevant to the way logic is applied in modern computer science. In short, from such a perspective, functions are better understood as instructions for the production of determinate outputs by finitistically conceived processes applied to determinate inputs, contrasting with the way that they are understood in set theory as abstractly conceived mapping relations holding between members of two different sets. Striking parallels here with the convergence between idealism and a pragmatist direction in philosophy are apparent.

Such issues, I suggest, bear on the relation of logic to the project of naturalism in ways that might be thought to be broadly parallel to the issues raised by Price's critique of "object naturalism" in that both are critiques of the non-finitistic assumptions behind classical logic. Some intuitionists, for example, argue that the problem with classical logic and its truth-functional definition of logical operators is that it presupposes an omniscient mind, for whom all propositions can be known to be either true or false. However, we finite thinkers have to reason in contexts, such as those involving reference to counterfactual situations, in which it is not the case that all the relevant facts are decidable.[10] Thus intuitionists take issue with the practice of defining logical axioms in truth-functional ways, and have adopted the idea of introducing rules of deduction conceived in more 'natural' ways, a technique pioneered by Gerhard Genzen in the 1930s. This results in weaker logical systems than those used by classical logicians, such as those encoded in Heyting algebra rather than Boolean algebra. But these weaker logics are better suited to finitistic thinkers who must reason against a background of general assumptions or 'ceteris paribus' clauses. That is, such non-Boolean algebras allows rational processes to be conceived in ways more akin to finitistic computational processes.[11]

For their part, modal logics are associated with similarly finitistic conceptions of the thinking subject. As currently understood (e.g. Blackburn et al. 2001), modal logics include a variety of logics linked by the idea that the thought processes being modelled are contextually indexed in different ways: the truth or falsity of sentences in tense logic, for example, are indexed to particular times, those of 'alethic' modal logic to a particular possible world (the actual world), those of doxastic logic (the logic of belief) to the beliefs of a particular believer, and so on. While such sentences can be translated into non-indexical equivalents of non-modal classical logic, those who advocate an 'actualist' approach here see these non-modal equivalences as constructions from the more basic modal claims. From this perspective, the more commonplace way of understanding the relation of modal to classical logic, such that the latter is regarded as the explanatory 'metalanguage' of the former, is rejected as presupposing an unacceptable Platonic metaphysics and a 'theological'—that is, non-finitistic conception of thought—that accompanies it. Thus again we see at work here a critique of assumptions a little like Price's critique of the assumptions of 'object naturalism', but on the idealist-related line of criticism pursued here, this is made not in the name of another 'deeper' form of naturalism, 'subject naturalism', but more in the name of an 'actualism', that, can be understood as another way of designating what used to be labelled 'idealism'.

IV

Hegel's Idealism as Actualism

Regarding idealism as an alternative to naturalism that is motivated by considerations similar to those of naturalism will seem bizarre if idealism is here understood as based on the metaphysical commitments that are traditionally ascribed to it. However, interpreting idealism as a type of 'actualism' is a counter to this. Understood as a variety of actualism, idealism involves a re-articulation of metaphysics along the lines of that first introduced by Kant: it is thus is a 'meta-metaphysical' thesis rather than a first-order metaphysical one. Thus we should not be too surprised then if, as I have suggested previously, we encounter the influence of idealists such as Kant and Hegel in some of those who have played central roles in the development of non-classical logic in the twentieth century, or at least in those who have influenced such players.

As conceived as a systematic investigation of the *actual* world, Hegel's project can be considered as akin to that of Aristotle who, as it were, having brought Platonic forms *into* the world, used them as a means of modally enriching our everyday notion of the actual. Thus for Aristotle, a platonic idea of a thing had, especially in the case of the thinking soul, effectively become a potential, *dynamis*, capable of actualizing itself in the world *qua energeia*. But the thinking soul, *nous*, Aristotle tells us, "is, before it thinks, not actually any real thing", but a "potentiality which precedes the acquisition of knowledge by learning or discovery" (*De Anima*, Book III, ch 4).[12] While Hegel's account of modality is often understood in this Aristotelian way, it is importantly different, as Hegel is critical of remnants of other-worldly platonism in Aristotle's attempted actualist metaphysics.[13]

Preserving the links to Plato's ideas as the original objects of metaphysics, but denying them an otherworldly status, Aristotle's metaphysics can be understood as directed to what is *necessary* in the actual. However, while maintaining Aristotle's this-worldly metaphysical focus, Hegel, in contrast, had incorporated contingency—for example, the sphere of history—into the domain of logic and metaphysics. This transformation, I suggest, reflects Hegel's 'modernity' in that subjectivity plays a crucial role in relation to the actualization of possibility that is not obvious in Aristotle.[14] Here, the way the notion of possibility had been transformed in modern thought played an essential part of the background in understanding Hegel's complex approach.

Leibniz had introduced a logical way of treating possibility and necessity such that these notions were now to be understood primarily as qualifying *judgments* rather than *objects*—modality was now "de dicto" rather than "de re" concern. This move allows the conception of a realm of actual truths as a subset of a larger realm of possible ones, as *p*'s being actually true implies its being possibly true but not vice-versa, and hence to that of the actual world as one of a larger set of *possible* worlds. Considered in this context, Hegel's conception of the relation of the actual and the possible now becomes more like a reversal of that of Leibniz, and results in a picture closer to the contemporary modal actualist opponent of Lewis than to Aristotle's 'ontological' approach. In this way Hegel preserves the modern link between modality and subjectivity not apparent in Aristotle. Aristotle's 'potential' loses some of its Platonic shape, and comes to be understood as a totality of conditions existing in the actual world, a totality that a subject can grasp together in thought and act upon so as to bring about a new situation that would not have come about without its intervention.

With these modal distinctions presupposing subjectivity in this way, Hegel's actualism is, unlike Aristotle's, a form of 'idealism', but this need not have the type of counter-intuitive connotations usually attributed to it. It is not counter-intuitive, for example, to think of the actual world as containing *minds* in the sense of containing *ourselves* as minded beings, as long as it is not conceived as *necessarily* containing minds, as if we humans were the realization of some cosmic plan. There is a *sense* in which Hegel's actualism has the actual world as necessarily containing us, but on the reading suggested here, this becomes deprived of metaphysical weight in that it only presupposes what is now referred to as an "indexical" account of the meaning of actuality itself.[15] That is, the actual world is effectively defined as having us in it, with this being no more an affront to common sense or science than the similar 'presentist' position in which we grasp the past as necessarily leading to the present, simply because the present provides the perspective from which we cognize the past. Features of such an 'actualist' metaphysics are in turn reflected in—might be understood as having their ground in—Hegel's logic,[16] and in the remainder of this essay I wish to sketch how those features of 20th-century non-classical logic as surveyed above and reflected in Hegel's treatment of judgment might serve such a metaphysics.

V

Hegel's Logic of Recognitive Relations

Among the interpretations of Hegel over the last decades seeking to defuse Hegel's philosophy of counter-intuitive metaphysical claims have been those portraying Hegel as having extended Kant's earlier critique of traditional metaphysics, and indeed, of turning this critique to remnants of traditional metaphysics in Kant himself. Within this more general field, one approach has been to place considerable weight upon Hegel's notion of "*Anerkennung*" or "recognition", *qua* condition of self-consciousness.

Kant had insisted on *self*-consciousness as a condition of a mind's capacity to be conscious in a more general sense—that is, its capacity to be conscious of anything grasped as *other to itself*. To such a general account of consciousness and self-consciousness, Hegel had added the complex requirement of any individual mind's recognition of *other* minds—specifically its recognition of those other minds' acts of recognition *of it*. This theory of 'mutual recognition' now stood at the centre of his ontological concept of *Geist*, or spirit. With this, *Geist*'s contrast with nature is no longer dependent on any mysterious added spiritual substance. Rather, while making the existence of *Geist* dependent on nature, *Geist* represents a discontinuity with it in terms of the complexity of its structures and processes. Hegel's peculiar logic, with its similarities to recent non-classical logics and its concomitant contrast with Kant's transcendental logic *qua* logic of "*der Verstand*", might now be understood as providing the logical infrastructure for these constitutive relations of objective spirit, and so providing *his* account of the conditions of self-consciousness.

Kant's notion of the transcendental unity of apperception had been meant to express a conception of a logically unified world conceived as the objective correlate of a unified subject *for whom* that world exists as so unified. On the subjective side, we are presumably to think of the unity of the logical architecture of the world of conscious experience and judgment as something like that of a consistent set of propositions, and in this sense, Kant's transcendental logic is distinctly 'modern' rather than Aristotelian. But Hegel's account of the recognitive preconditions of self-consciousness suggests something more complex: there must be within the framework of the world as it so appears to a consciousness, places for *other* centres of consciousness or perspectives onto the same world, and this, presumably, should be reflected in his logic. That there *are* meant to be such places is apparent, I suggest, from his treatment of judgment in the Subjective Logic of the *Science of Logic*.

There Hegel generates a sequence of judgment forms that provide increasingly adequate instantiations of the very *concept* of judgment, a sequence leading from simple 'positive' judgments of immediate ego-reflexive appearances (judgments or *Dasein* [existence]) to, finally, the 'syllogism' which he declares to be the 'truth' of the judgment. Driving the development of these judgment forms (and then the subsequent development of the forms of syllogism) is a process involving 'negation' that effectively makes judgment forms oscillate between two distinct patterns in a circular but cumulative fashion. These two judgment forms are marked by differences in how predication is conceived in each (predication as the "inherence" of the predicate in the subject, and as the "subsumption" of the subject under the predicate) expressed as differences in the way *negation* is treated in each (as predicate or internal negation in the former and as external negation in the latter) (Redding 2014). Judgments of 'inherence' thus have a 'de re' structure, in which properties 'inhere' in some concrete 'res' designated by the subject term conceived as an instance of some kind. For example, in a judgment of *Dasein*, about a particular *rose*, that rose is determined as an instance of the kind *rose*, and its inhering predicates, for example its being *red*, are understood as instances of certain kinds of property, in this case the kind *colour*, that are appropriate to the kind to which the subject belongs. In short, they are conceived something like the way *Aristotle* had conceived of singular judgments.

The other, contrasting, form of judgment, as in the 'reflective', or quantitative, judgment that succeeds the judgment of *Dasein*, is one in which the predicate term 'subsumes' the subject, these being familiar 'de dicto' judgments, with properly 'propositional' contents. While inherence judgments stand in relation to other inherence judgments in terms of the relation of contrariety (as when a rose's being blue provides a contrary property to its being red), subsumptive judgments are opposed in terms of the *contradictory* relations holding between them. Here subjects have been stripped of their 'kind' determinations and are determined solely by whether they instantiate or fail to instantiate the abstract predicates under which they are subsumed. In contrast to the Aristotelian logic reflected in inherence judgments, subsumptive judgments represent a more modern conception of judgment, such as are found in Leibniz or Gottfried Ploucquet, or indeed Kant's transcendental logic. These are what Hegel describes as judgments of the understanding, *"der Verstand"*.

Elsewhere I have suggested that Hegel's first variety of "inherence" judgments, the simple positive judgments of *Dasein* or existence—clearly meant to be immediate perceptual judgments—have logical features similar to the logically weak context-sensitive sentences of Prior's tense logic (Redding 2018). In contrast, Hegel's subsumptive judgments are closer to the non-modal properly 'propositional' judgments of classical logic. As in contemporary conceptions of the relations between modal and non-modal judgments, Hegel conceives of ways of "translating" judgments of each kind into the form of the other, a process enabled by a logical device that he had taken from Leibniz via Ploucquet.

Ploucquet had distinguished two ways in which determinate reference to individual entities can be established—an individual subject can be conceptually determined as either a case of "exclusive" or "comprehensive" particularity (Ploucquet 2006: §§14–15)—in Hegel's terminology, a distinction according to whether the subject term expresses the logical determinations of "singularity" or "particularity". This distinction had come from Leibniz's dual way of solving the problem of assimilating singular judgments into the Aristotelian syllogism. Following the practice of medieval nominalists, he had construed singular judgments on the model of universal judgments, but had added to this the alternative of construing them as manifesting the form of *particular* judgments, and had now treated these two forms as equivalent and intersubstitutable. Hegel regards such a capacity to transition between these different conceptual determinations— the "process of passing over into an other" (Hegel 1991a: §84)—as a central feature of his "dialectical" approach to logic that differentiates it from the static logic of *"Verstand"* in which such a distinction is treated as the dichotomous opposition of concept and intuition.

This circular process enabled by these transitions, in which one judgment form is translated into its opposite and then back again, is conceived as driven by a series of negations, but here double negation does *not* return one to the original judgment, but rather to a more logically complex analogue of it. Thus when judgments of *Dasein* are translated through the (subsumptive) judgments of reflection to a new form of de re judgment, the resulting "judgments of necessity" are no longer about individual instances of kinds (individual roses, for example), but the kinds themselves ("the rose as such").

Just as the *objects* of these judgments become progressively more complex with the successive "cycles of determination" (Hegel 2010: 95 [21.110]), so too do the cognitive *subjects* of such judgings, but here a word of caution is needed concerning the role of subjectivity in the *Logic*. While in contrast to the *Phenomenology of Spirit*, Hegel's *Logic* is not meant to reflect the experience *of a subject*, nevertheless one finds encoded within the structures of the Subjective Logic *places* for finite subjects. For example, the simple positive judgments of *Dasein* can be thought to encode in their structures a place for a simple sensuously affected corporeal subject that is *co-located* with the object about which the judgment is made. Furthermore, the subject of an explicit *kind* judgment is also 'located', but in a different and more abstract way—we may say that she is located in a world in which instances of the kind in question are known to behave in particular ways rather than others, and are subject to certain *laws* rather than others, and so on. It is only against such a background of expectation that the notion of 'kinds' makes sense.

In the development of judgment forms the "judgment of necessity" with its new concrete referent ("the rose as such") is similarly rendered more complex in the following cycle, resulting in a new object, an individual instance of a new and more complex and evaluatively judgable kind—the judgment of the concept. Hegel's examples include a judgment about a house, that, built in such-and-such a way, can be judged *good*. In turn this judgment form will be shown to be an implicit syllogism (Hegel 2010: 593 [12.95]), whose triadic logical structure of singular-particular-universal gives expression to the fully *unpacked* logical structure implicit in the original binary subject-predicate judgment.[17]

It is clear that with this syllogistic structure the original judgment is now represented as located *within* a more encompassing logical space that relates it to other judgments—to opposing ones, such as contraries and contradictories, as well as to judgments to which it is inferentially connected. Thus this broader structure will now not only provide a 'place' for the original judge, but analogous places for other judges with whom the first judge is dialectically engaged.[18] Hegel's recurring "modal" or contextual (inherence) judgments are appropriate for the provision of such places, in the way, for example, that modern modal logics include "doxastic logics" in which the truth claims of assertions are indexed to the belief states of particular believers in a similar way to that in which tensed judgments are indexed to particular times or alethic modal judgments to other "possible worlds".

That Hegel *does* have something like this in mind is clear from his application of such judgment and inference structures to relations of "recognition" [*Anerkennung*] such as those found in the discussion of property and contract in *Elements of the Philosophy of Right* (Hegel 1991b). Thus, at §71, Hegel notes that that an existence [*Dasein*]—that is, something determined as the subject term of a positive judgment of inherence (*Urteil des Dasein*)—is "as determinate being . . . essentially being for another". The '*Dasein*' at issue here is of course an object of practical rather than theoretical intentionality, something *desired* by rather than simply *perceived* by a particular subject, and *as* an 'external' object of a particular will it can equally become a desired *Dasein* "for the will of another person". It is this relation of will to will that is the true ground of *freedom*, describing this linking of wills via their external objects as one of *recognition* (§71, Rem).

As in the *Logic*, this 'syllogistic' structure of recognition has made explicit the structures inhering in the earlier 'judgments' constituting the relations of possession and property, thus coming to represent the 'truth' of these simpler structures. The particular form of subjectivity involved, 'personality', in its immediate determination, had earlier been described as that of a corporeal agent related to immediately qualified things via its "subjective ends" (Hegel 1991b: §43). Our immediate, biologically determined desires thus relating us to worldly external things, such a structure exemplifies in practical form the "positive judgment of Dasein" subject to its two negations—the first involving the *use* of the thing, the second its *alienation*—resulting in the "infinite judgment". These three abstractions (positive, negative, and infinite judgments) from that which is immediate and concrete now allow "the reflection of the will from the thing back into itself" (§53): the intentional *subject* (the will) has been redetermined from mere possessor to a proprietor, while the intentional object (originally the object desired) has been redetermined from something merely possessed to an instance of *property*. And the *truth* of this judgment will turn out to be a 'syllogism' in which the recognitive will-to-will relation of contracting subjects determines the possessions of each as their *property*.

Thus the passage from the judgment of *Dasein* to that of reflection has allowed the originally opposed arbitrary desires of the distinct desiring subjects to be redetermined as united by a common content. We might think of two contracting subjects as entering into the contract with opposed wills: one wants what the other has and is willing to alienate what he has in exchange for it, while the indexical will of the other has exactly the opposite determinations. The processes of abstraction, however, enable these opposed contents to be logically redetermined so that the two contracting parties now want *the same thing*: "*that the exchange takes place*". This is akin, for example, to different perceptual judges disagreeing over the exact *shade* of a rose's colour but agreeing, nevertheless, that it is *red*. In such cases, abstraction results in a common intentional content in which the originally *opposed* cognitive stances are "*aufgehoben*"—negated but preserved, and it is this *preservation* of the logically weaker *modal* judgments that mark Hegel's opposition to Kant for whom the singularity belonging to intentional states is *simply* negated.

VI

Conclusion

In his critique of the object naturalism of contemporary analytic philosophy, Huw Price has revealed the contradictions in the object naturalist's position: there naturalism stops short of applying to the object naturalists' own cognitive capacities. Price's response is a more extensive application of naturalistic thought, but unless the placement problem is not to recur, this must surely involve a quite systematic disruption to the conception of 'the natural' and it far from clear what positive alternative Price has to offer here. We already have first-order ways of thinking about those things that resist placement in natural world—the forms of thought broadly exploited by the humanities or "*Geisteswissenschaften*" that invoke some kind of "interpretative" or "hermeneutic" alternatives to the "explanations" of the natural sciences—but it is unclear how Price's philosophical stance relates to such already existing resources.

In contrast, I have suggested that a more promising way forward is to reconsider the idealistic framework against which early analytic philosophy first rebelled, a framework more ready to articulate with the content of the humanities than Price's extended naturalism. Moore's original complaint against idealism was that it could not fully free the constitution of objects known from the working of those minds doing the knowing: it could not assure us that what we know is what the world is like 'anyway'. But the epistemic assumptions in play here seem deeply at variance with an understanding of ourselves as finite or non-supernatural creatures, and naturalism is not the only alternative to non-supernaturalism. Moore's original target, idealism—but now understood in the right way, as a variety of actualism—is available. Idealism as actualism redetermines the object of metaphysics as the actual world, and the actual world, rather than the natural world, already has minds within it, thus circumventing worries about "the placement problem". And treating philosophy as *about* the actual understood as containing the possible, rather than as what is *necessary* in the actual, actualism is not burdened with the crypto-supernaturalism of Moore's original platonic realism. For his part, Russell's original revolt against idealism was a revolt against its logic, but *contra* Russell, idealism's logic has reestablished an important place for itself over the last half century. It is surely time to reconsider idealism as a serious alternative to a much-troubled naturalistic metaphysics of analytic philosophy.[19]

Notes

1. C.f. Timothy Williamson: "Many contemporary philosophers describe them-selves as naturalists. They mean that they believe something like this. There is only the natural world, and the best way to find out about it is the scientific method" (Williamson 2011).
2. Beneke had in turn been influenced by Jacob Fries, an opponent to Hegel, who pursued a psychologistically construed version of Kant's transcendental idealism.
3. See, for example, Linsky and Zalta (1991) on the relation of Lewis to Meinong.
4. In reducing tensed sentences to tenseless ones that are "indexed" to a point of time, Prior argued, one effectively treats the original propositions as a propositional *function* that, applying to that point of time yields a complete proposition.
5. Especially significant in this regard was Findlay's use of a predicative distinc-tion used by his supervisor, Ernst Mally, to avoid Meinong's ontology. See Redding 2018, sect. II.
6. Not long after he had secured a job back in the UK, Findlay was open in his advocacy of Hegel's philosophy.
7. Technically, a Heyting algebra is a "bounded lattice", as in a Boolean algebra, with least element 0 (false) and greatest element 1 (true). Unlike a Boolean algebra, however, it is not "complemented", and the negation operator, $\neg a$, rather than being defined, is introduced by the rule that the least element (0 or false) implies any proposition a. Algebraic lattices were first applied to logic by George Boole, and later developed by Ernst Schröder. For details of the mathematics of lattices, see, for example, Donnellan 1968.
8. In modal terms, Lewis's S5 captures the type of necessity found in *logical* necessity, while S4 is a modal system closer to that found, for example, in the logically weaker tense logic as invented by Prior.
9. On Lawvere's Hegelianism see Patterson 1997.
10. For a classic statement, see Michael Dummett 1993: 45–46.
11. Seen from this perspective, computer science may have very different conse-quences for naturalism within the philosophy of mind than expected. Since the second half of the twentieth century, computational models have been widely invoked in the effort to understand how the brain might be thought to implement forms of reasoning traditionally associated with thought. Super-ficially this looks like a "materialist" or "naturalist" approach to the mind traditionally opposed to "idealism", however the idealist approach to *logic* that has appeared within the very science at the heart this work tends to being this assumption into question.
12. In Book II, the soul is described as as the "first actuality" of the body, a potential that becomes the final actuality, using again the model of a *hexis* or capacity that precedes its activity.
13. For a recent critique of Aristotle's actualism, see Bechler 1995.
14. This point is made by Ferrarin in his criticism of Hegel's tendency to read this into Aristotle (Ferrarin 2001).
15. As noted above, intuitionistic logic reconceives the relation between truth and falsity as found in Boolean logic. Algebraically, truth and falsity are no longer treated as "complements" so that laws such as those of excluded mid-dle and double negation no longer automatically apply. Analogously, the relations between necessity and possibility are altered in similar ways.
16. It is easy to misunderstand this point in that it is often urged that, in con-trast to, say, Hegel's *Phenomenology of Spirit*, there is no "consciousness"

within his Logic, nor is the presentation of the Logic's content in the form of *"Vorstellungen"*. This is true, but this is not to say that there is no place for conscious subjects in the Logic, since, as I will try to show, Hegel's logic can only be understood as inscribing within its structures *places* for conscious subjects, indeed, embodied and located subjects.

17. Such a structure emerges as the final form of the final type of judgment, the judgment of the Concept.

18. We can also understand it as representing changes in the constitution of the subject as its intentional contents expand in this way.

19. Research for this chapter was carried out with the help of a Discovery Grant from the Australian Research Council, DP130102346. I'd like to thank Paul Giladi for helpful comments on an earlier draft of this chapter.

References

Bechler, Z. 1995. *Aristotle's Theory of Actuality*. Albany: State University of New York Press.

Blackburn, P., di Rijke, M., and Venema, Y. 2001. *Modal Logic*. Cambridge: Cambridge University Press.

Church, A. 1940. 'A Formulation of a Simple Theory of Types'. *Journal of Symbolic Logic* 5: 52–68.

Copeland, J. B. 2002. 'The Genesis of Possible Worlds Semantics'. *Journal of Philosophical Logic* 3: 99–137.

———. 2008. 'Arthur Prior'. In E. N. Zalta (ed.) *The Stanford Encyclopaedia of Philosophy*. Available at: http://plato.stanford.edu/archives/fall2008/entries/prior/

Donnellan, T. 1968. *Lattice Theory*. Oxford: Pergamon Press.

Dummett, M. 1993. 'What Is a Theory of Meaning? (II)'. In M. Dummett (ed.) *The Seas of Language*. Oxford: Clarendon Press.

Ferrarin, A. 2001. *Hegel and Aristotle*. Cambridge: Cambridge University Press.

Findlay, J. N. 1933. *Meinong's Theory of Objects*. Oxford: Oxford University Press. Expanded in 2nd ed. as, *Meinong's Theory of Objects and Values*, 1963.

——— 1941. 'Time: A Treatment of Some Puzzles'. *Australasian Journal of Philosophy*, reprinted in Flew, A. G. N. 1951. *Logic and Language, first series*. Oxford: Blackwell.

———. 1955–1956. 'Some Merits of Hegelianism: The Presidential Address'. *Proceedings of the Aristotelian Society New Series* 56: 1–24.

———. 1958. *Hegel: A Re-Examination*. London: Allen and Unwin.

Frege, G. 1897. *Begriffsschrift, eine der arithmetischen nachgebildete Formelsprache des reinen Denkens*. Halle: Louis Nebert. English translation by S. Bauer-Mengelberg. In J. van Heijenoort (ed.) *From Frege to Gödel: A Source Book in Mathematical Logic, 1879–1931*. Cambridge, MA: Harvard University Press, 1967.

Hegel, G. W. F. 1968. *Gesammelte Werke*. Hamburg: Felix Meiner.

———. 1991a. *The Encyclopaedia Logic: Part I of the Encyclopaedia of Philosophical Sciences with the Zusätze*. T. F. Geraets, W. A. Sutching and H. S. Harris (trans.). Indianapolis, IN: Hackett.

———. 1991b. *Elements of the Philosophy of Right*. A. W. Wood (ed.) and H. B. Nisbet (trans.). Cambridge: Cambridge University Press.

———. 2010. *Science of Logic*. G. di Giovanni (ed. and trans.). Cambridge: Cambridge University Press.

Kammareddine, F., Laan, T., and Nederpelt, R. 2002. 'Types in Logic and Mathematics Before 1940'. *Bulletin for Symbolic Logic* 8: 185–245.

Kripke, S. 1959. 'A Completeness Theory in Modal Logic'. *Journal of Symbolic Logic* 24: 1–14.

———. 1963. 'Semantical Considerations on Modal Logic'. *Acta Philosophica Fennica* 16: 83–94.

Kusch, M. 2015. 'Psychologism'. In E. N. Zalta (ed.) *The Stanford Encyclopaedia of Philosophy*. Available at: https://plato.stanford.edu/archives/win2015/entries/psychologism/

Lawvere, W. F. 1992. 'Categories of Space and of Quantity'. In A. Ibarra, J. Echeverria and T. Mormann (eds.) *The Space of Mathematics: Philosophical, Epistemological and Historical Explorations*. Berlin: De Gruyter.

Lewis, C. I. 1912. 'Implication and the Algebra of Logic'. *Mind* 21: 522–531.

———. 1914. 'Review of A. N. Whitehead and Bertrand Russell, *Principia Mathematica*'. *Journal of Philosophy* 11: 497–502.

———. 1918. *A Survey of Symbolic Logic*. Berkeley, CA: University of California Press.

———. 1930. 'Logic and Pragmatism'. In G. P. Adams and W. P. Montague (eds.) *Contemporary American Philosophy*, vol. 2. New York: Palgrave Macmillan, 31–51.

Lewis, C. I., and Langford, C. H. 1931. *Symbolic Logic*. New York: Century Books.

Lewis, D. K. 1973. *Counterfactuals*. Oxford: Blackwell.

———. 1986. *On the Plurality of Worlds*. Oxford: Blackwell.

Linsky, B., and Zalta, E. N. 1991. 'Is Lewis a Meinongian?' *Australasian Journal of Philosophy* 69: 438–453.

Martin-Löf, P. 1996. 'On the Meaning of the Logical Constants and the Justification of Logical Laws'. *Nordic Journal of Philosophical Logic* 1: 11–60.

Mehrtens, H. 1990. *Moderne—Sprache—Mathematik: Eine Geschichte des Streits um die Grundlagen der Disziplin und des Sujekts formaler Systeme*. Frankfurt: Suhrkamp.

Moore, G. E. 1899. 'The Nature of Judgement'. *Mind* 8: 176–193.

———. 1903a. 'The Refutation of Idealism'. *Mind* 12: 433–453.

———. 1903b. *Principia Ethica*. Cambridge: Cambridge University Press.

Moschovakis, J. 'Intuitionistic Logic'. In E. N. Zalta (ed.) *The Stanford Encyclopaedia of Philosophy*. Available at: https://plato.stanford.edu/archives/spr2015/entries/logic-intuitionistic/

Patterson, A. L. T. 1997. 'Towards a Hegelian Philosophy of Mathematics'. *Idealistic Studies* 27: 1–10.

Ploucquet, G. 2006. *Logik*. Hildesheim: Georg Olms Verlag.

Pozzo, R. 2010. 'Gottfried Ploucquet'. In H. F. Klemme and M. Kuehn (eds.) *The Dictionary of Eighteenth-Century German Philosophy*, 3 vols., vol. 2. London and New York: Continuum Press.

Price, H. 1992. 'Metaphysical Pluralism'. *The Journal of Philosophy* 89: 387–409.

———. 1997. 'Naturalism and the Fate of the M-Worlds'. *Proceedings of the Aristotelian Society* supp. 7: 247–267.

————. 2004. 'Naturalism Without Representationalism'. In M. De Caro and D. Macarthur (eds.) *Naturalism in Question*. Cambridge, MA: Harvard University Press.

Prior, A. N. 1957. *Time and Modality: The John Locke Lectures for 1955–56*. Oxford: Clarendon Press.

————. 1967. *Past, Present and Future*. Oxford: Clarendon Press.

Redding, P. 2010. 'Two Directions for Analytic Kantianism: Naturalism and Idealism'. In M. De Caro and D. Macarthur (eds.) *Naturalism and Normativity*. New York: Columbia University Press.

————. 2012. 'Some Metaphysical Implications of Hegel's Theology'. *European Journal for Philosophy of Religion* 4: 139–150.

————. 2014. 'The Role of Logic "Commonly So Called" in Hegel's *Science of Logic*'. *British Journal for the History of Philosophy* 22: 281–301.

————. 2017. 'Findlay's Hegel: Idealism as Modal Actualism'. *Critical Horizons* 18: 359–377.

————. 2018. 'Hegel's Subjective Logic as a Logic for (Hegel's) Philosophy of Mind'. *Hegel Bulletin* 39: 1–22.

————. 2019. 'Hegel's Treatment of Predication Considered in the Light of a Logic for the *Actual* World'. *Hegel Bulletin* 40: 51–73.

Sundholm, G. 2009. 'A Century of Judgment and Inference, 1837–1936: Some Strands in the Development of Logic'. In L. Haaparanta (ed.) *The Development of Modern Logic*. Oxford: Oxford University Press.

van Heijenoort, J. (ed.). 1967. *From Frege to Gödel: A Source Book in Mathematical Logic, 1879–1931*. Cambridge, MA: Harvard University Press.

Whitehead, A. N., and Russell, B. 1910–1913. *Principia Mathematica*. Cambridge: Cambridge University Press.

Williamson, T. 2011. 'What Is Naturalism?' *The Stone*, September 4.

6 How to (and Not to) Defend the Manifest Image

Giuseppina D'Oro

There are more things in heaven and earth, Horatio,
Than are dreamt of in your philosophy.
—*Hamlet* (1.5.167–8), Hamlet to Horatio

Claims such as 'there are no tables and chairs' have become increasingly common in the philosophical context, and eliminativism is now a fairly well-established position in contemporary debates in analytic metaphysics.[1] This outbreak of eliminativism has prompted a number of responses aimed at saving the manifest image of reality.[2] Prominent amongst the attempts to save the manifest image is a view, powerfully articulated by Frank Jackson in *From Metaphysics to Ethics*,[3] according to which the manifest properties of objects, properties such as solidity or fragility, can be spared from the eliminativist's guillotine if it can be shown that they are entailed (through the relation of supervenience) by scientific properties. Jackson's strategy for saving the manifest image rests on a modest conception of the role of conceptual analysis in metaphysics. On this view, the role of conceptual analysis is modest because it is not the task of philosophy to establish *a priori* what there is, but rather to determine *which features of the manifest image can be located within the scientific image*: the manifest properties which cannot be so located are shown to be rogue concepts that have no place in serious metaphysics.

This chapter argues against the attempt to save the manifest image by invoking the relation of entailment (whether that implied by the notion of supervenience or by the more traditional notion of analytic entailment) on the grounds that the manifest image is *sui generis*. The defence of the manifest image that I propose as an alternative here rests on the idealist assumption that knowledge makes a difference to what is known,[4] and that since the manifest and the scientific image are the correlative of two different ways of knowing they do not compete with one another. I call the idealist view that knowledge makes a difference to what is known as the Reciprocity Thesis. Rather than seeking to determine what kind of manifest image one is entitled to have in order to comply with the scientific image, the Reciprocity Thesis limits the claims of science to its own *explanandum* and therefore sees no need to legitimise the manifest image by invoking the relation of entailment. The need to legitimise the manifest image in the light of the scientific image arises because the relation between the scientific and the manifest image has not been properly conceptualised. Once the scientific and the manifest image are understood as the correlative of different ways of knowing, the problem which the location strategy seeks to solve is shown to rest on a misconception of the relationship holding between different kinds of knowledge.

Section I outlines Jackson's strategy for saving the manifest image from elimination. Jackson's strategy relies on a modest conception of the role of conceptual analysis in metaphysics which presupposes a hierarchical view of the relation between the sciences, with physics as the most basic science. I contrast the strategy for saving the manifest image which relies on a modest conception of the role of philosophical analysis with a strategy that relies on a metaphilosophical commitment to the Reciprocity Thesis. According to the Reciprocity Thesis, the role of conceptual analysis in metaphysics is not modest: conceptual analysis establishes what the subject matter of different kinds of knowledge is by making explicit the inferences or judgments which they deploy to generate their own distinctive kinds of knowledge claims. I argue that although the Reciprocity Thesis rests on a more robust conception of the role of conceptual analysis in metaphysics, it does not pit philosophy against science. There is therefore no need to espouse the location strategy advocated by the modest conception in order to save the manifest image from the eliminativist's guillotine *and* avoid conflict between philosophy and science. Sections II and III show how the Reciprocity Thesis is at work in Heidegger's argument for the irreducibility of the ready-to-hand to the present-at-hand and in Collingwood's claim for the irreducibility of actions to events. I conclude by clarifying the specific target of the claims of this paper. The claims of this paper are not directed against science or scientists themselves, but against certain philosophers or certain philosophical claims. For the key assumption which is responsible for problematising the manifest image (the layered/hierarchical view of the sciences with physics at the base) is not essentially a *scientific* one; it is a *philosophical* assumption concerning *how to conceptualise the relation between different forms of knowledge.*

I

The Reciprocity Thesis and the Metaphilosophical Constraint That Philosophy Should Not Undermine Science

In his influential *From Metaphysics to Ethics*, Frank Jackson outlines an account of what he takes the role of conceptual analysis in "serious" metaphysics to be.[5] Serious metaphysics is not concerned with very long shopping lists, baked beans, cat food, mustard, rock salt etc., or with what goes under the name of dry middle-sized goods.[6] Serious metaphysicians seek to comprehend what there is in terms of a limited number of more basic notions. For this very reason, Jackson says, serious metaphysics inevitably faces the "location" problem.[7] Since the ingredients on the ontological list of the serious metaphysician are very limited, "some features of the world are not going to appear explicitly in the more basic account".[8] The task of conceptual analysis is to establish "when and whether a story told in one vocabulary is made true by one told in some allegedly more fundamental vocabulary"[9] thus showing which ingredients on the long list are implicitly contained in the short list. The role of conceptual analysis in metaphysics, so envisaged, is a modest one because philosophers do not, for example, uncover any (deep) ontological truths while simply sitting in the proverbial armchair. Rather, the role of conceptual analysis is to establish *which* putative features of the manifest image have a place in the serious metaphysician's account of what the world is like and to establish which do not: those features of the manifest image which cannot be located on the serious metaphysician's shortlist then face the ontological guillotine.

Locating manifest properties requires us to demonstrate that they are entailed (in an unorthodox sense of "entail" that needs to be carefully unpacked) by the items on the shortlist of the serious metaphysician. Consider, for example, the macroscopic property of 'solidity': one need not deny that objects such as tables and chairs are solid if it is possible to account for their solidity in terms of the lattice-like arrays of molecules. Thus, whether or not we are justified in employing ordinary notions such as 'solidity' depends on whether such notions are entailed, in a very specific sense of 'entailed', by the ingredients on the more basic list. The notion of entailment that Jackson invokes is *not* the traditional notion of entailment according to which *a* entails *b* if *b* can be deduced *a priori* from *a*.[10] It is rather the notion of 'necessary determination' or "fixing"[11] that is captured by the relation of supervenience according which the features of the manifest image are fixed or determined by those of the scientific image. The avowed advantage of this account is that it retains philosophy's traditional role as an *a priori* activity whilst crucially also avoiding conflict with the claims of science. Since philosophical reflection, so understood, does not lead to conclusions that clash with those of science, philosophical analysis respects the desideratum that philosophical views should *not* be at odds with science.[12] On the modest conception, the desideratum that philosophical views should not contradict those of science is taken to imply that the direction of metaphilosophical travel should be from metaphysics to the philosophy of mind, or from metaphysics to the philosophy of perception or from metaphysics to ethics etc. On this approach, therefore, the question one should ask is 'What kind of philosophy of x can one have, given the ontological starting point inherited from science'?

But there is no need to accept the modest conception of the role of conceptual analysis in metaphysics which is presupposed by the asking of the Location Question in order to meet this metaphilosophical constraint. If what motivates the modest conception is the assumption that in order not to breach the constraint that philosophical views should not be at odds with science one should seek to locate the manifest in the context of the scientific image, then one is operating under *false* assumptions. For in fact there are metaphilosophical alternatives which are not in breach of that constraint. The alternative metaphilosophical starting point that I will outline in this chapter is committed to the idealist view that there is a reciprocal relation between *how* we know and *what* we know. On this view, the reality that is disclosed by the method of a science is the correlative of a certain kind of explanation. This means that what is explained by different sciences[13] is brought under a particular categorial description that is linked to the method through which that particular category of thing is known (the Reciprocity Thesis). The Reciprocity Thesis embraces the virtuous circularity holding between knowledge and what is known in the idealist tradition and shows that the attempt to deny the view that knowledge makes a difference to what is known rests on a failure to acknowledge the range of presuppositions that science brings to the investigation of reality. From this metaphilosophical perspective, the view that physics replaces metaphysics as the science of pure being merely replaces one dogmatism (metaphysical dogmatism) with another (scientific dogmatism).[14] According to the Reciprocity Thesis, therefore, philosophy does not begin 'modestly' with ontological truths which are handed over to the philosopher from the physicist, and subsequently tries to establish what other truths are 'entailed' (through the relation of supervenience) by these more fundamental truths. Rather, philosophy seeks to uncover the *forms of inference or judgment which are implicit in the categorial descriptions of reality*. The kind of entailments philosophical analysis is concerned with are those holding between method and subject matter, the form of an explanation (with its characteristic *explanans*) and its corresponding *explanandum*.

The Reciprocity Thesis goes back to Kant, who understood ontological categories to be embedded in forms of judgment. The category of causality, for example, does not denote an extensional relation, but an inference of the kind 'if x, then y'. Just as the categories of Kantian metaphysics are embedded in forms of judgment, so the metaphilosophical position defended here takes the category of the sort of thing one describes to be the correlative of a specific form of inference. Philosophical analysis exposes this correlation by showing *which category of thing is entailed by which form of inference*. But while the ancestry of the view defended here is Kantian, the Reciprocity Thesis also goes beyond Kant in some important respects. Kant left the door open for the possibility that being might be known *qua* being (at least to the extent that he did not deny that things could be knowable as they are in themselves if only by God); the Reciprocity Thesis closes off that option: it denies both that pure being as such is accessible to physics, as the modest conception allows, *and* that it is accessible to an intuitive intellect, as it is allowed by transcendental idealism. The Reciprocity Thesis, therefore, closes off the epistemic gap that Kant left open and which led to the charge of subjective idealism that was levelled against him by much post-Kantian idealism.[15]

A selective application of the Reciprocity Thesis may be deemed to be reasonably unproblematic, since many would concede that the special sciences bring reality under a description that is characteristic of their own way of knowing and tailored to their own investigative interests. What is more problematic, or at least *perceived* to be problematic, on the other hand, is the view that the Reciprocity Thesis applies across the board. As an across-the-board claim, the Reciprocity Thesis is controversial because endorsing it entails forsaking the hierarchical model of the sciences that is presupposed by the modest conception. Since, on the modest conception physics displaces metaphysics as the first science, the modest conception goes hand-in-hand with a particular view of the relation between the sciences according to which

1.   The sciences are hierarchically arranged.
2.   The explanations of physics are complete and ontologically basic.
3.   The claims of the special sciences supervene upon those of physics.

The Reciprocity Thesis abandons this layered/hierarchical model of the sciences. Thus the question it addresses is not (like the modest conception) 'how can we locate the manifest within the scientific image?' but rather 'what is the distinctive *explanandum* of the natural sciences and how does it differ from that of other forms of knowing'? The direction of metaphilosophical travel is not from the scientific to the manifest image or, as in the title of Jackson's book, *from metaphysics to ethics*, but the other way around. Rather than altering the manifest image so as to make it compliant with the scientific image, the Reciprocity Thesis limits the claims of science to its own domain of inquiry.

The Reciprocity Thesis rejects the hierarchical view of the sciences with physics as its basis that is presupposed by the modest conception. Yet its defence of the autonomy of the manifest image does not breach the desideratum that philosophical claims should not contradict those of science. For to claim that nature is the correlative of scientific method, or is the distinctive *explanandum* of natural science rather than the *Ding-an-sich*, is not tantamount to denying science authority over its own domain of inquiry. The view that the manifest image cannot be located within the scientific image because it is the correlative of a distinctive way of knowing does not therefore breach the constraint under which the modest conception of the role of conceptual analysis in metaphysics operates, i.e. that philosophical claims should not contradict those of science and thereby undermine its emancipatory potential. Defending the autonomy of the manifest image by denying that it can be derived by entailment from the scientific image does not, therefore, require one to advocate a return to the conception of reality that was decisively disenchanted through the success of a mechanistic conception of causality.

The strategy for saving the manifest image from the jaws of physics, to borrow an expression from Raymond Tallis (2017), is neither one that tries to establish what features of the manifest image are compatible with those of the scientific image (as in the modest conception), nor one that harks back nostalgically to a re-enchanted conception of nature of the kind one finds in Greek mythology, but rather to *limit the claims of physics to its own explanandum*. Nature, as the scientist conceives it, remains exactly the same. It is made up of molecules (or whatever other ontology turns out to be the correlative of scientific explanation), not of ordinary macroscopic goods such as baked beans, and it is explained mechanistically. The Reciprocity Thesis does not change anything within or about the scientific image.[16] The flip side of the claim that commitment to the reciprocity thesis does not change anything about the scientific conception of nature is that, conversely, the scientific image changes nothing about the manifest image because the criteria by which the objects of the manifest image are identified, and the kind of explanations which are at work in the manifest image, do not respond to the norms and expectations of scientific enquiry, but to different ones.[17]

In sum: although the role of conceptual analysis in metaphysics that emerges from a commitment to the Reciprocity Thesis differs from the modest conception advocated by Jackson, it does not violate the metaphilosophical constraint under which the modest conception operates, namely that philosophy should not contradict the claims of science and undermine its emancipatory potential. If it is indeed the case, as it is argued here, that commitment to the Reciprocity Thesis does not breach that constraint, then there is a metaphilosophical alternative that cannot be ruled out on that account. If the modest conception of the role of conceptual analysis is recommended on the grounds of its ability to abide by the constraint that philosophy should not undermine science, the same recommendation also holds for the metaphilosophical view that the role of conceptual analysis in metaphysics is to uncover the explanatory norms that govern different forms of knowing. For one is not entitled to invoke an argument simply when it suits one's own philosophical agenda.

The next two sections show how the idealist insight that knowledge makes a difference to what is known is at work in two philosophers who have denied that the manifest image can be legitimised by entailment from the scientific image.

II

Actions Are Not Events: Collingwood

The modest conception of the role of conceptual analysis in metaphysics that is offered by Jackson as a solution to the problem of elimination has been hugely influential in shaping the kind of questions that have been occupying 20th century philosophers of mind who have tended almost unanimously to assume that the problem which the philosophy of mind should address is that of the place of mind in nature, or the so-called Placement Problem. The Placement problem is another manifestation of the Location Problem: it arises within a metaphilosophical framework that operates with a modest conception of the role of conceptual analysis in metaphysics and assumes a layered/hierarchical view of the sciences.

The question of the place of mind in nature has been formulated in different ways. For some, the placement problem is *ontological*: can mental states be accommodated within the material universe? For some, it is *epistemological*: can the distinctive first-person perspective of the mental find a place in the third person perspective of science?[18] And for others, the Location Question is *causal*: can explanations in the special sciences be reconciled with the causal explanations of physics or is there a problem of causal overdermination?[19] However, whether the placement question raises its head in an ontological, epistemological or causal context, it is generated by the *same* set of metaphilosophical assumptions, namely the hierarchical relations between forms of knowledge with physics at the base, the metaphysical priority of the explanations of physics, and a metaphilosophical commitment to a modest conception of the role of conceptual analysis in metaphysics.[20] In the philosophy of mind, this metaphilosophical consensus concerning the nature and purpose of philosophical analysis has been so pervasive as to enjoy cross-party consensus, uniting non-reductivists *and* reductivists alike. In fact, while it has been a matter of on-going debate whether the supervenience relation (which Jackson invokes to legitimise the manifest image) can be mobilised in support of a reductivist or a non-reductivist agenda,[21] both reductivists and non-reductivists agree at a metaphilosophical level that the question which the philosophy of mind should address is, in the title of one of Kim's books, the question of *The Place of Mind in a Physical World*.[22]

A powerful challenge to the modest conception of the role of conceptual analysis in metaphysics (and its concomitant view of the relation between the sciences) can be found in the work of the British idealist R. G. Collingwood. Collingwood was concerned not with vindicating our right to use concepts of ordinary objects such as table and chairs, but with vindicating our right to use the term 'action' in a way that fundamentally differs from the concept of 'event'. As a *sui generis* concept 'action' does not denote a subset of events, events whose efficient causes are internal (e.g. brain processes) rather than external, but the correlative of a distinctive form of explanation which invokes a teleological notion of cause. Collingwood refers to this as the *causa ut* as opposed to the *causa quod*.[23]

He invokes the Reciprocity Thesis to deny that humanistic and scientific explanations have the same *explanandum* and thus that explanations which invoke an efficient concept of cause compete with explanations which invoke a teleological notion of cause. They do not compete because scientific explanations explain events, whereas humanistic explanations explain actions. Actions and events, however, are not ontological categories of traditional metaphysics; they are the correlative of humanistic and scientific explanations respectively. They belong to what Collingwood calls a metaphysics of *absolute presuppositions*, a metaphysics aimed at uncovering the fundamental assumptions that govern the methods at work in different contexts of inquiry. Actions, therefore, are not transcendent metaphysical entities; nor are events what 'really' exists independently of certain methodological assumptions concerning how they can be explained. Actions cannot be distinguished from events by invoking any visible empirical differences between the two. Rather, actions are identified by invoking a purpose. The action of opening a garage door, for example, is not individuated through a description of the bodily movements performed (since these might range from the manual lifting of the doors to the pressing of a button on a remote control without leaving the driving seat) but by bringing it under a teleological description. Since actions are the correlative of a distinct form of explanation (one which invokes a notion of teleological rather than efficient causality), they are not a subset of events (in the way in which the extension of the concept 'goat' is a subset of the extension of the more general concept 'mammal') but their own genus. The category 'action' is *sui generis* and conceptually independent of the category 'event' because actions and events are the correlatives of different kinds of judgments, judgments which invoke different senses of the term "cause".

Collingwood mobilises the Reciprocity Thesis to argue that the privileged place that scientific knowledge occupies in the layered/hierarchical arrangement of the sciences rests on a form of dogmatism, i.e. on the failure to acknowledge that the objects of scientific investigation are the correlative of scientific method, and to deny that what (natural) science seeks to know, nature, replaces the object of traditional metaphysical inquiry: the thing-in-itself. He denies that there is any such thing as a science of pure being, whether this be metaphysics or physics. His challenge to the layered view of the sciences presupposed by the modest conception is therefore not motivated by a desire to reinstate metaphysics as the science of pure being. For, so he argued, there is no such science. Being can only be known under certain categorial descriptions that are in turn determined by the relevant methodological assumptions which are made.

Conceptual analysis uncovers the presuppositions through which Being is known *qua* event (the correlative of scientific explanation) or *qua* action (the correlative of humanistic explanation). Given the reciprocal relation between method and subject matter it is not possible to individuate and explain an action through the methods of science; this is not because actions are transcendent metaphysical entities, but because they have to be explained in a different way in order to be understood as actions.[24]

The privileged status accorded to scientific knowledge in the layered/hierarchical conception of the sciences, Collingwood argues, is sedimented in language where the term 'science' has come to mean 'natural science' (just as the term 'drink' has become slang for 'alcoholic drink').[25] Similarly, the term 'cause' has become synonymous with 'efficient cause'. His rejection of the layered view of knowledge with its privileging of the inferential patterns established in natural science gives rise to a distinctive defence of the autonomy of the mental. There is, for Collingwood, no problem of causal overdetermination because causation is an intensional/explanatory relation which holds between the explanans and explananda of a particular type of inquiry, and the choice between one sense of causation and another is dictated by the explanatory needs served by a particular form of knowing. Rather than claiming that there is no problem of causal overdetermination because mental states are token identical with physical states and thus causally efficacious only qua physical states (as non-reductive physicalists argue), Collingwood denies that the concept of efficient causation has any application in the context of action explanation. Nor does Collingwood seek to save the mental from the threat of epiphenomenalism by arguing, in the manner of functionalists such as Ned Block,[26] that mental states are causally efficacious *qua* mental.

Instead, his solution to the problem of causal overdetermination is to reject the metaphilosophical picture that privileges the sense of (efficient) causation that responds to the explanatory goals of natural science; he argues that the sense of causation one invokes when providing an explanation must be sensitive to the nature of the questions one is answering. The role of conceptual analysis in metaphysics is to disambiguate the different senses of the term 'cause' to avoid any illegitimate trespass beyond the proper domain of application of each sense of causation. Thus, rather than seeking to answer the question of the place of mind in nature Collingwood rejects the metaphilosophical picture which gives rise to the problem in the first place. Humanistic explanations are not causal explanations (in the sense of efficient causes) which invoke macroscopic entities (human beings) as their *explanans* rather than microscopic ones (brain cells). They are explanations of a different kind which invoke an altogether different sense of causation and which serve different explanatory needs.

Collingwood mobilises the Reciprocity Thesis in the service of an argument for the disunity of science in the Latin sense of the word *scientia* (meaning a body of knowledge with a distinctive method and subject matter) rather than (as he puts it) in the 'slang' sense in which the term science is used in the context of the layered/hierarchical model, where the term is assumed to be synonymous with natural science. He became posthumously famous when his claim for the disunity of *scientia* was revitalised by W. H. Dray[27] in his response to Hempel's claim for methodological unity.[28] The methodological disagreement between Hempel and Dray over the logical structure of explanation, however, never made explicit that the metaphilosophical platform from which Collingwood articulated his argument for the disunity of knowledge stemmed from a commitment to the idealist claim that knowledge makes a difference to what is known. It is a commitment to the Reciprocity Thesis that lies behind the claim that actions have to be understood in a different way, if they are to be understood at all. The concept of action eludes the scientific image because it is the correlative of a different kind of judgment, one which invokes a teleological notion of causation; its *sui generis* nature means that it cannot be accommodated. The modest conception of the role of conceptual analysis in metaphysics not only relegates the philosopher to the role underlabourer of science; it also fosters the illusion that one can have one's cake and eat it, i.e. accept a metaphilosophical commitment to the priority of the scientific image *and* save the manifest image. Collingwood dispels that myth, for a robust conception of action has no place within the inferential framework of science.

Collingwood denies that actions can be located, but he does not infer from this that, since they cannot be located, they should be eliminated. His view is rather that the choice between location and elimination is one that must be made by those who operate with a conception of the role of conceptual analysis (the modest conception) which gives rise to the location/placement problem in the first place. Whether one accepts or rejects the Reciprocity Thesis, it is at the very least important to be metaphilosophically aware of the stranglehold that the modest conception has exercised over the kind of questions that are deemed to be important within the philosophy of mind, and of the kind of moves that philosophers of mind are allowed to make.

III

A Table Is Not a Table-wise Arrangement of Molecules: Heidegger

Another philosopher who rejected the metaphilosophical commitment to the hierarchical view of the sciences that informs the location strategy is Heidegger. This section presents Heidegger's claim that the ready-to-hand is not a category derivative from the present-at-hand, but its own genus, as based on an underlying commitment to the Reciprocity Thesis, according to which manifest and scientific judgments have their own distinctive and *sui generis explananda*.

The association of Heidegger with the idealist tradition is not unproblematic, for while in *Being and Time* he flirted with idealism, and held it in greater esteem than realism, he stopped short of giving it full-hearted endorsement.[29] My argument here is not that Heidegger is a card-carrying idealist, but that his defence of the autonomy of the manifest image in *Being and Time* can be presented as arising from a commitment to the idealist insight contained in the Reciprocity Thesis. When his defence of the autonomy of the manifest image is presented in this way, it is shown to be much more radical than contemporary attempts to rescue the manifest image by showing that it is entailed (either by the relation or supervenience or the more traditional notion of analytic entailment) by the scientific image.

In *Being and Time*, Heidegger distinguished the category of the ready-to-hand from the category of the present-at-hand. The former comprises objects viewed from the perspective of the specific function they fulfil within a practice (the needle is for sowing; the desk for writing on, etc.). The latter, on the other hand, capture their purely scientific properties. For Heidegger, the ready-to-hand is *sui generis* because it is not accessible from the purely scientific perspective of the present-at-hand. Understanding an object as ready-to-hand requires understanding it in a completely different way, namely by grasping its function or purpose, or what Heidegger calls its "in-order-to".[30] This function or purpose cannot be gleaned from the object's present-at-hand properties: for example, knowing the molecular structure of an object will tell us nothing about its purpose. The *purpose* of the desk, the *function* of the needle, is understood in the context of the *practices of writing and sowing*, and this functionality is not covertly entailed by the molecular constitution of the table top or the needle's head, any more than it is possible to glean from the chemical composition of a piece of clay that it was the fragment of a pot once used as a vessel for transporting oil. To understand the needle *qua* needle, the desk *qua* desk, the piece of clay *qua* fragment of a pot, is to understand them as ready-to-hand from the inception because there is no covert relation of entailment that leads from the molecular structure of the wooden top, the needle's head and the pot's fragment to their function as tools or use objects. This is why, Heidegger argues, it is not possible to understand an object as ready-to-hand through an *operation of addition*, by starting from present-at-hand properties and then adding something on to them (the value of the object to *Dasein*). To understand the object as ready-to-hand, one must shift to a different way of knowing, one which brings the purpose of the object into view by subsuming it under a *teleological judgment*. It is because the object can be understood as ready-to-hand only when it is understood teleologically (in terms of its role or purpose) that the category of the ready-to-hand is conceptually independent of the category of the present-at-hand, and inaccessible from the perspective of science.

The picture of the manifest image that is presented in *Being and Time* is considerably richer than the one allowed by the modest conception of the role of conceptual analysis in metaphysics. For Heidegger, the nature of the table as a ready-to-hand object found in kitchens and restaurants is not exhausted by the solidity of the table-top against which we rest our elbows and crockery at meal times: solidity may be inferred from the lattice-like arrangement of molecules, but 'table-ness' cannot. The modest conception of the role of conceptual analysis in metaphysics presents ordinary objects as a conglomerate of the kind of secondary qualities that would be allowed by Locke and then legitimises them by locating them on the 'serious' metaphysician's list of primary properties by invoking the relation of supervenience. But if Heidegger is right, the manifest image is much richer than the Lockean conception of an object's nominal essence. This richer conception of ordinary objects, unlike the impoverished version that is captured by Locke's list of secondary qualities, is not amenable to being located on the serious metaphysician's short list. For in describing an object as ready-to-hand, one necessarily invokes a teleological judgment that presents the object not merely as having a colour, a smell, and as emitting a noise when tapped, but as having a role or function. If one presents a candle as a piece of wax, as Descartes did in the *Second Meditation*,[31] one will also find it easier to think that the essence of the candle can be described through the vocabulary and explanations of mathematical physics.

According to Heidegger the table, qua ready-to-hand, eludes the scientific perspective because its "in-order-to" does not supervene upon the arrangement of molecules accounting for the solidity of its surface. Molecules are not arranged table-wise, for they do not configure themselves with a view to making convivial dinners possible; to speak of them as being arranged table-wise is to import a way of grasping the relation between them which is completely alien to the scientific description of the object as present-at-hand. Strictly speaking, we cannot say that the table is an arrangement of molecules, for molecules do not arrange themselves in tables and chairs. From the scientific perspective, "everything must go"—to use the title of James Ladyman and Don Ross's book.[32] Talk of molecules arranged table-wise and chair-wise, illegitimately smuggles in features of the manifest image into the scientific one thereby creating the misleading impression that the ways in which we speak in non-scientific contexts can be accommodated by the scientific image. Once one accepts, as the modest conception does, the primacy of the scientific image, it may be harder than one might have originally envisioned to resist the eliminativist's conclusions. This is a problem that Heidegger does not face because, unlike the modest conception, he denies the primacy of the scientific image. As a result, his suggestion for saving the manifest image is not to locate manifest properties in terms of the scientific properties by arguing that the former are entailed by the latter. Rather, Heidegger's argument is that 'tableness' is *sui generis* because *purposiveness does not belong to the description of reality in terms of its molecular structure.* While molecules may be arranged in such a way as to account for the solidity of the materials out of which the table is made, they are not arranged in such a way as to account for the table's use in the context of, say, the practices of writing and dining. The table's "in-order-to" is grasped through a different kind of judgment, one that is teleological in nature. Heidegger's defence of the distinction between the ready-to-hand and the present-at-hand, and his defence of the *sui generis* nature of the ready-to hand, therefore, rests on what we have called the Reciprocity Thesis. For, it is only through the application of a certain kind of purposive judgment that the object can be described as ready-to-hand.

Now one may try to undermine this strategy for defending the *sui generis* nature of the manifest image by arguing that we often infer manifest properties from scientific ones: an archaeologist, one might object, could infer that a piece of clay found on a site could not have been a fragment of a pot used for storing oil or water. This is because its chemical composition, as tested in the laboratory, indicates that the material out of which it is made is porous, thus making it unsuitable for the purpose of storing liquids. Clearly there are causal conditions which determine whether a certain material can be used to build, for example, a suitably impermeable vessel for the storage of liquids, or a suitably impenetrable surface on which to rest one's crockery when eating. But this observation does not show that one can thereby derive the manifest image by entailment from the scientific image. For the unsuitability of a given material for a certain purpose (its unreadiness-to-hand, as Heidegger might put it) can only be grasped in relation to a goal, albeit one whose fulfilment it fails to promote. This would-be objection to the *sui generis* and irreducible nature of the manifest image actually reinforces rather than undermine the point that to understand an object as ready-to-hand is to grasp its role or function, *even in cases where it fails to fulfil it.* The table with a broken leg and the broken pot are not present-at-hand objects; they are ready-to-hand objects which have lost what Heidegger calls their "serviceability",[33] their ability to fulfil their 'in-order-to' or serve a goal.

There are no such things as broken tables and uncomfortable chairs from the perspective of the scientific image, which at best can inform us about the molecular constitution of the wood but can say nothing about the function that the table fulfils in the practices of dining and writing. It is only from a perspective that allows for purposive judgment that an object can be described as either succeeding or failing by those teleological standards. A table is broken, or a chair is uncomfortable, *only* to the extent that it is brought under the category of the ready-to-hand. This richer conception of the manifest image will forever remain beyond the ken of science because molecules do not arrange themselves table-wise, needle-wise or pot-wise. To speak of them as arranged pot-wise, table-wise and needle-wise is to import the *very teleology which the scientific image seeks to excise*. While the scientific image can inform us about the *molecular structure* of wood, metal and clay, it cannot tell us about the *function* of the table, the needle and the pot. The scientific image, crucially, can describe them neither as ready-to-hand nor as unready-to hand, neither as fit nor as unfit for a given purpose.

This way of saving the manifest image from elimination also differs from another recent attempt to defend the manifest image, one which seeks to deflate the conflict by invoking the more traditional notion of analytic entailment.[34] Amie Thomasson recently argued that just as anyone who knows that there is a left-hand glove and a right-hand glove also knows (by analytic entailment) that there is a pair of gloves, so anyone who knows 'that there are molecules arranged baseball-wise' knows (by analytic entailment) 'that there is a baseball'. And just as anyone who grasps the analytic entailments between the claims 'there is a left-hand glove and a right-hand glove' and 'there is a pair of gloves' would not say 'there is a right-hand glove, a left-hand glove *and* a pair of gloves', anyone who grasps the analytic entailments between the claims 'there are molecules arranged baseball-wise' and 'there is a baseball' should not say 'there are molecules arranged baseball-wise *and* there is a baseball'. These conversational prohibitions undermine the idea that it is necessary to eliminate ordinary macroscopic objects in order to avoid causal rivalry between scientific and ordinary explanations. For if it is illegitimate to conjoin the claims 'there is a baseball *and* there are atoms arranged baseball-wise', it is also illegitimate to conjoin the claims 'the shattering of the window was caused by the baseball *and* by the atoms arranged baseball-wise'. The moral of this story is that the view that scientific and common-sense explanations are mutually exclusive is the result of a failure to grasp the analytic entailments holding between scientific and manifest properties. Making such analytic entailments explicit defuses the problem of explanatory exclusion and eases the pressures that have driven contemporary metaphysicians to advocate eliminativism. Once we correctly grasp the grammar of certain expressions, the apparent conflict between scientific and manifest explanations simply evaporates and there is no longer any need to resort to the extreme measures proposed by some eliminativists in order to avoid the problem of explanatory exclusion. Thomasson's strategy for saving the manifest image differs from Jackson's because it deflates the tension between the manifest and the scientific image by appealing to a more traditional notion of entailment. Jackson argues that the manifest image can be saved from elimination because properties such as solidity can be derived through the relation of supervenience from the scientific image. By appealing to a more traditional notion of entailment, on the other hand, Thomasson aims to show that the tension between the scientific and the manifest image rests on a failure to grasp that e.g. 'baseball' is (analytically) entailed by 'molecules arranged baseball-wise'.

Heidegger's strategy for saving the manifest image is quite different from Thomasson's. On the strategy pursued by Thomasson, one should always expect to find a table where there are molecules arranged in a certain way. As a result, she denies that it makes any sense to conjoin scientific and manifest judgments. Just as someone who thinks that there are washing machines and electrical appliances alongside one another as in 'in my kitchen there are two things: a washing machine *and* an electrical appliance' has failed to understand that the concept 'washing machine' is a species of the genus 'electrical appliance' so someone who says 'there is a table *and* molecules arranged table-wise' has failed to understand the analytic entailments holding between 'molecules arranged table-wise' and 'table'. On Heidegger's strategy by contrast, a present-at-hand arrangement does not entail a ready-to-hand one. Because the category of things which are captured by present-at-hand and ready-to-hand descriptions are conceptually distinct, it does not follow that where one finds one, one should expect to find the other too: there may be wood molecules arranged in a particular lattice-like way that account for the macroscopic secondary quality of solidity and yet no table-top. And there may be a table-top but no wood-like arrangement of molecules. In other words, for Heidegger the classification of items according to their manifest properties is tangential to the classification of objects according to their scientific properties.[35]

In Heidegger's account of the relation between the ready-to-hand and the present-at-hand the conflict between the scientific and the manifest image is eased in a very different way. For Thomasson there is no problem of causal overdetermination or explanatory exclusion because there is only one kind of causal judgment that is simply made twice: firstly, at the microscopic level of the molecular arrangement; and secondly, at the macroscopic level, captured by the secondary qualities that can be derived from entailment from the scientific image. It is the failure to discern that 'there is a baseball' is entailed by 'there are molecules arranged baseball-wise' which creates the *misleading* impression that there are two competing causal explanations: (i) that the window broke because it was hit by the baseball; and (ii) that it broke because it was hit by the molecules arranged baseball-wise. For Heidegger, by contrast, the tension between the manifest and the scientific image is eased by denying that the distinction between manifest and scientific judgments is ontologically deep whilst at the same time acknowledging the *sui generis* nature of manifest judgments.[36]

Rather than explain away[37] the conflict between scientific and manifest descriptions by arguing that they denote the same thing at different levels of generality, Heidegger denies the existence of any relation of entailment between the present-at-hand and the ready-to-hand and defends the autonomy of the manifest from the scientific image. He does so by suggesting that manifest judgments are purposive/teleological judgments that conceptualise the relation between objects with reference to their in-order-to (the chair *is for* sitting at the table; the needle *is for* weaving with the thread; the pot *is for* storing oil; the hammer *is for* banging the nail in the wall). These judgments differ in kind from scientific judgments about the spatial arrangements of and causal relations between molecules. Since Heidegger denies that the ready-to-hand is analytically entailed by the present-at-hand, he would not deem someone who, in the presence of a building, asked 'but where is the home?' to be conceptually confused. For this question is unlike that of the person who, in the presence of a washing machine asks, 'but where is the electrical appliance?' The washing machine is a species of electrical appliance, and the person who wonders where the electrical appliance is, is simply ignorant of the relation of entailment holding between the species (washing machine) and the genus (electrical appliance). A building, on the other hand, is not a species of a home. For one concept belongs to the category of the present-at-hand, and the other belongs to the *sui generis* category of the ready-to-hand. Contrary to what Ryle claimed,[38] there is no category mistake in asking 'but where is the university?' while standing on its campus with its student accommodation, lecture theatres etc. intact: many academics under the pressures of the REF and TEF may ask themselves precisely *that* question when they start feeling they are no longer in the same job as the one they applied for. For Heidegger we may therefore continue to speak about tables and chairs, not because such manifest descriptions are entailed by more fundamental descriptions of properties that the objects 'really' have, but because since the scientific image is not about tables and chairs it does not affect, nor is it affected by, judgments about tables and chairs. There is no conflict between the scientific and the manifest image not because the manifest image is entailed by the scientific image but because manifest judgments bring objects under a categorial description that is *sui generis*.

A distinctive advantage of the modest conception of the role of conceptual analysis in metaphysics (so its supporters argue) is that since it privileges the inferential system of the scientific image it allows for no entities which are beyond the ken of scientific explanation. Its disadvantage is that it accommodates only a very anaemic version of the objects of the manifest image, namely those which are allowed entry by entailment. As we have seen, the modest conception can accommodate, for example, solidity and impenetrability but not tableness, for the latter requires employing purposive judgments that are extraneous to the scientific perspective; the modest conception can accommodate actions understood merely in terms of bodily movement and thus as species of events, but it cannot accommodate the concept of action as a *sui generis* category.

According to Jackson's modest conception of the role of conceptual analysis in metaphysics, the richer conception of the manifest image must be excised precisely because the functional objects that belong to the category of the ready-to-hand and the teleological descriptions of action cannot be accounted for within the inferential system of science. As Heidegger and Collingwood show, they can only be understood by switching to a different way of knowing. The Reciprocity Thesis, by contrast, acknowledges a conception of the manifest image that is much richer than the one allowed by recent attempts to legitimise the manifest properties of objects by invoking the relation of entailment, whether this be the relation of supervenience or the more traditional relation of analytic entailment. It does so by showing that manifest objects are the correlative of a different kind of inference and belong to a category of objects that is *sui generis*.

This chapter has sought to fend off the objection that the philosophical attempt to defend a richer conception of the manifest image informed by the Reciprocity Thesis is in breach of the desideratum that philosophy should not contradict the claims of science. The Reciprocity Thesis defends a notion of the manifest image that is *sui generis* and considerably more robust than the one allowed by the modest conception, one that *cannot* be accommodated, but, I have argued, it does not breach the constraint that philosophical claims should not contradict those of science. To say that there are such things as tables/chairs (or actions), and that such concepts belong to *sui generis* categories that are not reducible either to molecular arrangements (or to events), is not to contradict the claims of science, for tables and chairs (or actions) are not the *explananda* of scientific inquiry. It is, on the other hand, to contradict the claims of a philosophical standpoint (naturalism) which argues for the all-pervasiveness of the perspective of science. The Reciprocity Thesis is therefore in conflict not with science, but with scientism. There are indeed more things on heaven and earth than the naturalistic metaphilosophy which governs debates in contemporary analytic metaphysics and philosophy of mind allows one to say there are; but the Reciprocity Thesis allows one to say *this* without committing us to some form of supernaturalism precisely because it understands tables and chairs (or actions) to be the correlative of teleological/purposive inferences, and molecules (or whatever ontological claims science commits us to) to be the correlative of scientific judgments. Rather than accepting the primacy of the scientific image, the Reciprocity Thesis confines the claims of science to its own *explanandum* by denying that there is a categorial description of reality that is ontologically basic.

Supernaturalism is the shadow cast by naturalism, a shadow which naturalism struggles to shrug off. The objects of manifest judgments are problematic from the naturalistic standpoint because if they cannot be explained scientifically then they must be not-natural in character. And if they are not-natural, then they must be supernatural, and they must therefore be excised. No such conclusion, however, needs to be drawn if one does not assume that physics has displaced metaphysics as the science of pure being and that nature has taken the place of the traditional object of metaphysical reflection: the thing-in-itself. So, to repeat, the argument of this paper is not directed against science but against the metaphilosophical view that physics has replaced metaphysics as the science of Being. The problem does not lie with our reluctance to part with a robust conception of the manifest image, nor does the problem lie with the scientific image; it lies rather with the ways in which the relation between the two has been conceptualised by philosophers. The conclusion that one should draw from this is not that we should stop philosophising, but rather that we should philosophise in a different way.

Notes

1. Cf. Merricks (2000), Unger (1979a, 1979b), Inwagen (1990).
2. The term "manifest image" was coined by Sellars (1963). It is used in a different way in this paper.
3. Cf. Jackson (1998).
4. For the claim that idealism is committed to the metaphilosophical view that knowledge makes a difference to what is known and that this is what is at stake between idealists and realists, see Prichard 1909: 115–119.
5. Jackson 1998: 4.
6. Austin 1962: 8.
7. In the philosophy of mind, where the question many philosophers address concerns the place of mind in nature, the location problem tends to be referred to as the "placement problem". This is essentially the same problem that arises in two contexts: that of contemporary analytic metaphysics, where the major concern has been that of how to accommodate ordinary objects in the scientific world view, and in contemporary philosophy of mind, where the major concern has been that of how to accommodate the mind in the scientific world view.
8. Jackson 1998: 5.
9. Ibid., p. 28.
10. Ibid., p. 25.
11. Ibid.
12. De Caro and Voltolini 2010: 71.
13. I am here using the term 'science' in the Latin sense (*Scientia*) to mean simply a form or way of knowing.
14. Cf. Tse (2019).
15. For further on this, see D'Oro (2018).
16. In this respect, the defence of the *sui generis* nature of the manifest image canvassed here is not the same as that advocated by liberal naturalists such as John McDowell (1996). The latter advocates a softening of the scientific image which is not required by the view I defend for which there is only one sort of naturalism, not two. Cf. McDowell (1998).
17. Cf. Smithson (2019).
18. Cf. Levine (1983).
19. Cf. Block (1997a, 1997b).

20. For an account of how this conception of the role of conceptual analysis in metaphysics informs debates in the philosophy of mind, see D'Oro et al. (2019).
21. The relation of supervenience has been used in service of a non-reductivist agenda by Davidson (1980); while others, such as Kim (1995, 2000) have denied that the relation of supervenience can support non-reductivism.
22. Kim (2000).
23. Collingwood [1940] 1998, Ch. XXX.
24. I discuss this further in D'Oro (2018a).
25. Collingwood [1940] 1998: 4.
26. Cf. 1997a, 1997b.
27. Dray (1957, 1958, 1963).
28. Hempel (1942).
29. Cf. Heidegger [1927] 1962: § 43.
30. Ibid., §15, 32.
31. Descartes [1641] 2008: 22.
32. Ladyman and Ross (2007).
33. Heidegger [1927] 1962: § 17.
34. Cf. Thomasson (2007).
35. This is why, for example, a retailer's marketing policy would not be improved by reclassifying its stock according to scientific descriptions (the molecular structure of wood or iron) rather than manifest descriptions (dining room furniture, office furniture) for scientific classifications would be of little use to the person searching for an office chair or a dining table.
36. While Thomasson's attempt to defend ordinary object by invoking the relation of entailment differs in some important respects from Heidegger, her argument for making ontology easy (Thomasson 2015) has more in common with the idealist/pragmatist approach defended here than this disagreement suggests.
37. For a similar claim, see Smithson (2019).
38. Viz., Ryle 1949, Ch. 1.

References

Austin, J. L. 1962. *Sense and Sensibilia*. London: Oxford University Press.
Block, N. 1997a. 'Can the Mind Change the World?' In G. Boolos (ed.) *Meaning and Method: Essays in Honour of Hilary Putnam*. Cambridge: Cambridge University Press.
———. 1997b. 'Anti-Reductionism Slaps Back'. *Philosophical Perspectives* 11: 107–132.
Collingwood, R. G. 1940/1998. *An Essay on Metaphysics*. R. Martin (rev. ed. with an introduction). Oxford: Oxford University Press.
Davidson, D. 1980. 'Mental Events'. In D. Davidson (ed.) *Essays on Actions and Events*. Oxford and New York: Oxford University Press.
De Caro, M., and Voltolini, A. 2010. 'Is Liberal Naturalism Possible?' In M. De Caro and D. Macarthur (eds.) *Naturalism and Normativity*. New York: Columbia University Press.
Descartes, R. 1641/2008. *Meditations on First Philosophy*. Oxford: Oxford University Press.
D'Oro, G. 2018. 'The Touch of King Midas: Collingwood on Why Actions Are Not Events'. *Philosophical Explorations* 21: 1–10.

———. 2019. 'Between Ontological Hubris and Epistemic Humility: Collingwood, Kant and Transcendental Arguments'. *British Journal of the History of Philosophy* 27: 336–357.

D'Oro, G., Giladi, P., and Papazoglou, A. 2019. 'Non-Reductivism and the Metaphilosophy of Mind'. *Inquiry* 62: 477–503.

Dray, W. H. 1957. *Laws and Explanation in History*. London: Oxford University Press.

———. 1958. 'Historical Understanding as Rethinking'. *University of Toronto Quarterly* 27: 200–215.

———. 1963. 'The Historical Explanation of Actions Reconsidered'. In S. Hook (ed.) *Philosophy and History*. New York: New York University Press.

Heidegger, M. 1962. *Being and Time*. J. Macquarrie and E. Robinson (trans.) New York: Harper & Row.

Hempel, C. 1942. 'The Function of General Laws in History'. *Journal of Philosophy* 39: 35–48.

Jackson, F. 1998. *From Metaphysics to Ethics*. Oxford: Oxford University Press.

Kim, J. 1995a. 'The Myth of Nonreductive Materialism'. In J. Kim (ed.) *Supervenience and the Mind*. Cambridge: Cambridge University Press.

———. 1995b. 'The Nonreductivist's Troubles with Mental Causation'. In J. Kim. *Supervenience and the Mind*. Cambridge: Cambridge University Press.

———. 2000. *Mind in a Physical World*. Cambridge, MA: MIT Press.

Ladyman, J., and Ross, D. 2007. *Everything Must Go: Metaphysics Naturalised*. Oxford: Oxford University Press.

Levine, J. 1983. 'Materialism and Qualia: The Explanatory Gap'. *Pacific Philosophical Quarterly* 64: 354–361.

Locke, J. 1690/2014. *An Essay Concerning Human Understanding*. Ware: Wordsworth Editions Limited.

McDowell, J. 1996. *Mind and World*. Cambridge, MA: Harvard University Press.

———. 1998. 'Two Sorts of Naturalism'. In J. McDowell (ed.) *Mind, Value and Reality*. Cambridge, MA: Harvard University Press.

Merricks, T. 2000. 'No Statues'. *Australasian Journal of Philosophy* 78: 47–52.

Prichard, H. A. 1909. *Kant's Theory of Knowledge*. Oxford: Clarendon Press.

Ryle, G. 1949. *The Concept of Mind*. Chicago: University of Chicago Press.

Sellars, W. 1963. 'Philosophy and the Scientific Image of Man'. In R. Colodny (ed.) *Science, Perception and Reality*. Pittsburgh, PA: University of Pittsburgh Press.

Smithson, R. 2019. 'An Idealist Critique of Naturalism'. *Inquiry* 62: 504–526.

Tallis, R. 2017. *Of Time and Lamentation: Reflections on Transience*. Newcastle upon Tyne: Agenda Publishing.

Thomasson, A. L. 2007. *Ordinary Objects*. New York: Oxford University Press.

———. 2015. *Ontology Made Easy*. New York: Oxford University Press.

Tse, P. 2019. 'Fichte's Critique of Physicalism'. *Inquiry* 62: 527–545.

Unger, P. 1979a. 'There Are No Ordinary Things'. *Synthese* 41: 117–154.

———. 1979b. 'Why There Are No People'. *Midwest Studies in Philosophy* 4: 177–222.

van Inwagen, P. 1990. *Material Beings*. Ithaca, NY: Cornell University Press.

7 From the Experimentalist Disposition to the Absolute

Peirce's Pragmatic Naturalism

Shannon Dea and Nathan Haydon

Naturalism has as many meanings as it has proponents. For about a century, starting with such figures as John Dewey, Ernest Nagel, Sidney Hook and Roy Wood Sellars (Papineau 2015: n.p.), and steadily proceeding such that today the *Philosopher's Index* lists nearly 6000 works with the keyword 'naturalism', it has been *de rigueur* for philosophers in the Anglo-American tradition to embrace naturalism. For most of them, this has meant (among other things) rejecting supernatural explanations in favour of scientific ones, modelling philosophical inquiry on science, and adopting a sceptical stance toward idealism. However, beyond these commonalities, individual philosophers precisify naturalism in various ways, or not at all.

In this chapter, we examine the *avant-la-lettre* naturalism of the American pragmatist Charles Sanders Peirce. We argue that Peirce was both a methodological and a metaphysical naturalist. Strikingly, he was also a theological naturalist and a naturalistic idealist. That Peirce's naturalism is at once realist and idealist, lends support to Dunham et al.'s view that idealism need not be anti-realist or anti-science.[1]

In Section I, prefatory to our elaboration of Peirce's naturalism, we trace the development of naturalism through two scientific revolutions—the 17th-century revolution in physics and the 19th-century revolution in biology. By the second half of the 19th century, these revolutions eventuated in a philosophical naturalism organised around three tenets: (i) that all of reality is in-principle commensurable; (ii) that all that exists is natural; (iii) and that the same methods apply to all modes of inquiry.

In Section II, we characterise the pragmatic maxim as an attempt to formalise what Peirce called *the experimentalist disposition*; as such, we argue, it exemplifies Peirce's commitment to the third tenet. In Section III, we sketch Peirce's metaphysical naturalism, and trace connections between his famous injunction against blocking the path of inquiry, and the second tenet of 19th-century naturalism—that all of reality is in-principle commensurable. In Section IV, we link Peirce's idealism and theological naturalism, noting that the latter violates, but in a deflationary way, the anti-supernatural tenet of 19th-century naturalism.

While Peirce preceded the 20th-century baptism of naturalism, attending to the historical precursors of Peirce's naturalistic thought and to Peirce himself helps us to understand the sources of the philosophical naturalism of the last century.

I

Two Scientific Revolutions and the Evolution of Naturalism

One way to sharpen our conception of philosophical naturalism is to look at the historical movements that led to it. In particular, naturalism as it was developed in the first half of the twentieth century is (*inter alia*) an attempt to model philosophy on the natural sciences—an effort, as it were, to realise Kant's hoped-for 'Copernican revolution'.[2] Kant's ambition was inspired by the first great scientific revolution of modernity—the 17th-century shift from Aristotelian to Newtonian physics. That first revolution, supplemented by the 18th-century development of statistics and probability theory led in to a second modern scientific revolution in the 19th century—namely, the rise of evolutionary theory. Each of these revolutions had echoes in philosophy broadly conceived. The revolution in physics forced philosophers to reconsider the relationship between nature/matter and grace/mind, whereas the biological revolution raised new questions about determinism. Each of these historical shifts helped to establish and refine the key tenets of the Copernican revolution in philosophy, and its ultimate realization in early 20th-century naturalism. In this section, we examine in turn each of these shifts and their respective contributions to naturalism. While it was Kant who ultimately heralded the naturalistic turn in philosophy, it was Descartes and the thinkers he most directly influenced who, in the century leading up to Kant, worked through the implications for philosophy of the 'New Science'. We begin our account there.

Modernity's first scientific revolution had both a metaphysical aspect and a methodological one. Metaphysically, the shift from Aristotle to Newton was a shift from understanding objects in the universe as having proper places and proper motions—earth's proper place is on the ground and its proper motion is rectilinear, whereas fire's proper place is in the heavens and its proper motion is circular—with corresponding distinctions between place and space, to the Newtonian model in which all bodies are subject to the same laws of nature. Metaphysically, the 17th century in Europe began with a conception of the universe as fundamentally heterogeneous and ended with a conception of the universe as fundamentally homogeneous.[3]

This metaphysical shift was accompanied by a methodological and epistemological shift. If everything in the universe follows the same laws, the new view went, then they are all discoverable and understandable using the same methods—the methods of the sciences.

This double-revolution provoked considerable theological anxiety. If everything follows the same laws and is explicable in the same way, then what role is there for divine intervention and, more broadly, for theology? This anxiety is perhaps most palpable in Berkeley's worry that materialism leads inevitably to atheism, and in his consequent championing of idealism. In any event, a great deal of 17th- and 18th-century European philosophy in one way or another seeks to adjudicate the question *What role is there for faith in the context of the New Science?*

The attempt in that period to answer the question that is best known and, in some ways, most influential today is Descartes's. Descartes's dualism is the articulation of a radical heterogeneity between material and thinking substance. With his metaphysical dualism, Descartes sought to build a firewall between the study of nature and the study of both infinite and finite minds. For Descartes, the material world is subject to and understandable via simple, universal, deterministic laws of nature. By contrast, minds are completely unlike matter and hence neither deterministic nor mechanistic. Thus, on the Cartesian account, the New Science in no way disproves the freedom of the will or the immortality of the soul, nor indeed the existence or puissance of God. (It is easy to trace a line from the Cartesian 'firewall' to the space that, late in the next century Kant—another philosopher deeply committed to the New Science—sought to clear for God, freedom and immortality).[4]

Arguably, the strongest expression of the Cartesian intervention was developed by a figure who was hugely influential in the period, but who has since then been largely forgotten by philosophers—Pierre-Sylvain Régis, the so-called "prince of the Cartesians".[5] Régis's 1704 *L'usage de la raison et de la foy ou l'accord de la foy et de la raison* (*The usage of reason and faith or the agreement between faith and reason*) was his response to the Paris Formulary's 1691 *de facto* prohibition against teaching Cartesian philosophy on the grounds that Cartesianism subordinates faith to reason. In *L'usage*, Régis advanced the view that faith and reason are never in conflict. According to Régis, God is the author of both faith and reason, and both means of understanding the world are, in themselves, reliable. It is only human misuse that renders either faculty defective. The greatest source of such misuse, argued Régis, resides in the human tendency to confuse the proper provinces of the two faculties. Where reason is the proper faculty for knowledge of the natural world, faith is the faculty that we must use in order to know the divine.

We said above that Régis wrote *l'Usage* in response to the Paris Formulary, but he also had a second purpose—to distance himself from Spinoza. Régis's earlier (1691) *Cours entier de philosophie, ou systeme general selon les principes de M. Descartes, contenant la logique, la metaphysique, la physique, et la morale* (*Complete course in philosophy, or general system according to the principles of Monsieur Descartes, containing logic, metaphysics, physics, and ethics*), and in particular his discussion therein of the nature of substance, had exposed him to charges of Spinozism, a view from which he was keen to distance himself.

For, unlike Descartes and Régis, Spinoza's response to the New Science was to naturalise God, freedom, and immortality, and in so doing, to dilute them of any theological content. Spinoza was one of the prominent early philosophical figures to take on board the conceit at the heart of the New Science that all phenomena are governed by the same laws and understandable using the same scientific methods. In his preface to Part 3 of his *Ethics*, Spinoza draws a sharp distinction between his own approach and that of 'the illustrious Descartes' in a passage that is worth quoting from at length:

> Most of those who have written about the affects, and men's way of living, seem to treat, not of natural things, which follow the common laws of Nature, but of things which are outside Nature. Indeed they seem to conceive man within nature as a dominion within a dominion. For they believe that man disturbs, rather than follows, the order of Nature, that he has absolute power over his actions, and that he is determined only by himself. . . . Nature is always the same, and its virtue and power of acting are everywhere one and the same, that is, the laws and rules of Nature, according to which all things happen, and change from one form to another, are always and everywhere the same. So the way of understanding the nature of anything, of whatever kind, must also be the same, namely, through the universal laws and rules of Nature. . . . Therefore, I shall treat the nature and powers of the affects, and the power of the mind over them, by the same method which, in the preceding parts, I treated God and the mind, and I shall consider human actions and appetites just as if it were a question of lines, planes, and bodies.
>
> (E3Pref.)

By the 18th century, Spinozism was synonymous with materialism and atheism. However, we might rather think of it as the prototype for the naturalism that emerged in the 19th century. By contrasting Spinoza with Descartes and Régis, we can see three central commitments of that proto-naturalism:

- The homogeneity of all that exists.
- The view that all that is, is natural; correspondingly, a denial of the supernatural.
- A single set of scientific methods for all modes of inquiry.

By the 19th century, however, the rise of evolutionary biology led to a less mechanistic, deterministic naturalism. Where the 17th-century revolution in physics had led philosophers of a naturalist bent to assert homogeneity across nature, and in particular across laws of nature, the 19th-century biological revolution created the possibility for an understanding of nature as varied and changing, and for a naturalism that was itself tychistic and evolutionary. Thus, 19th-century naturalism retained unchanged the last two of the preceding three commitments, but adapted the first commitment. Rather than assuming that reality is homogeneous, 19th-century evolutionary naturalists regarded reality as varied, but not to the point of incommensurability. Thus, by the second half of the 19th century, when American pragmatism emerged, naturalism might be said to have had three tenets:

- The in-principle commensurability of all that exists (metaphysical naturalism).
- The view that all that is, is natural, and correspondingly, a denial of the supernatural (metaphysical/theological naturalism).
- A single set of scientific methods for all modes of inquiry (methodological naturalism).

This new biology-inspired naturalism was embraced in various ways by the classical pragmatists.[6] However, while they all more or less agreed on the in-principle commensurability of all that exists, and on the single set of scientific methods for all modes of inquiry, they disagreed on the denial of the supernatural. Both Peirce and James admitted the possibility of God's existence, but they approached it differently. James favoured a finite, accessible God or gods, and scoffed at the notion of a transcendent Absolute (James 1909). Peirce, in part owing to a mystical experience later in life,[7] and in part owing to his well-known injunction not to block the path of inquiry (EP 2.48),[8] inclined toward a kind of panentheism, in which God is both immanent and transcendent. By contrast, Dewey was himself an atheist, but advocated for retaining the concept of God and the religious impulse, but naturalising 'God' to mean "the unity of all ideal ends arousing us to desire and action" (Dewey 1934: 42).

While Peirce's panentheism might seem to disqualify him from naturalism, his synechism saves him. Peirce was committed to the notion that all of reality is fundamentally continuous. On his account, there is no sharp line between consciousness and unconsciousness, between mind and matter, between life and death, or between the natural and the divine. Thus, unlike Descartes and Régis, who sought a clean demarcation between the realms of nature and Grace, for Peirce there is no such distinction. Thus, he was not only a philosophical naturalist in both the methodological and metaphysical senses; he was also a theological naturalist. In the next three sections, we sketch each of these aspects of Peirce's naturalism, and conclude by tracing connections between Peirce's theological naturalism and his idealism.

II

Peirce's Methodological Naturalism: The Experimentalist Disposition and the Pragmatic Maxim

"Philosophy," Peirce wrote in 1868, "ought to imitate the successful sciences in its methods" (EP 1:29). Peirce spent a great deal of time studying the methods of natural scientific inquiry and characterising its practice. As the quote suggests, he also spent a great deal of time developing a philosophical method modelled on these scientific methods. The pragmatic maxim, Peirce's formulation of a method for making our ideas clear (EP1.132), is in many ways at the heart of both projects. It is Peirce's attempt to characterize scientific practice—and in particular, the experimentalist disposition that lies behind the practice—in order to generalise it to philosophical inquiry more broadly.

Let us consider one of Peirce's important characterisations of scientific practice. According to Peirce, what is essential to scientific practice is what he calls *the experimentalist's disposition*. This is detailed in the following passage:

> to think of everything just as everything is thought of in the laboratory, that is, as a question of experimentation . . . when you have found, or ideally constructed upon a basis of observation, the typical experimentalist, you will find that whatever assertion you may make to him, he will either understand as meaning that if a given prescription for an experiment ever can be and ever is carried out in act, an experience of a given description will result, or else he will see no sense at all in what you say.
>
> (CP 5:411)[9]

The typical scientist, according to Peirce, thinks of everything broadly as a matter of experimentation. Peirce offers another example of the experimentalist's disposition when he discusses the commitments of the practicing chemist:

> We must dismiss the idea that the occult state of things (be it a relation among atoms or something else), which constitutes the reality of a diamond's hardness can possibly consist in anything but in the truth of a general conditional proposition. For to what else does the entire teaching of chemistry relate except to the behavior of different possible kinds of material substance? And in what does that behavior consist except that if a substance of a certain kind should be exposed to an agency of a certain kind, a certain kind of sensible result would ensue, according to our experiences hitherto.
>
> (CP 5:457)

The chemist rejects an occult explanation that might be attributed to an object or its behaviour. Instead, the chemist assumes that a material substance is best characterised by how it would behave under experimental conditions. In both cases, the characteristic feature of Peirce's practicing scientist is to think of everything as a question of experimentation, where a better understanding of an object comes from understanding how it would behave under various conditions.

Peirce's focus on the dispositions of the scientist rather than specific experimental methods or specific experimental results demonstrates his commitment to epistemic fallibilism as well as the importance he places on recognising the changing and evolving nature of science itself.

While scientific practice can be partly be characterised by its methods and its results, what is more essential, according to Peirce, is an underlying scientific disposition or spirit. Elaborating on this point, Peirce writes:

> That which constitutes science, then, is not so much correct conclusions, as it is a correct method. But the method of science is itself a scientific result. It did not spring out of the brain of a beginner: it was a historic attainment and a scientific achievement. So that not even this method ought to be regarded as essential to the beginnings of science. That which is essential, however, is the scientific spirit, which is determined not to rest satisfied with existing opinions, but to press on to the real truth of nature.
>
> (CP 6:428)

Because the results and methods of science are both susceptible to change and revision, what best characterises the behaviour of a practicing scientist cannot be participation in a *particular* method or result, but is rather an openness to what the future methods and results would (or at least could) be. Peirce argues that science and its practitioners are best typified by this regulative disposition, and indeed that it is responsible for the historical development of science.

Peirce takes the experimentalist disposition to regulate the behaviour of the practicing scientist and to best exemplify the practice. The practising scientist will not know at the start of scientific inquiry all the ways that an object might behave and under what conditions, but they nonetheless assume that some general claim could be made about an object's behaviour.

This regulative commitment is indefinite at the start of inquiry. The indefiniteness captures Peirce's fallibilism, his commitment that our ideas and beliefs be open to revision and updating in light of inquiry. For Peirce, science is self-correcting. Any process that is not susceptible to correction is not scientific. In terms of the experimentalist disposition, the practicing scientist does not know, or at least does not yet know, all the ways that an object would behave, and therefore, must be open to learning more. The indefiniteness also captures Peirce's commitment to evolutionary processes and to the evolving nature of scientific practice. The experimentalist disposition is itself in a stage of growth and development with respect to any inquiry. Inquiry begins as a "vague, special and meagre" belief-habit, and "becomes more precise, general, and full, without limit" (CP 3:160). Peirce's twin conceptions of science as adaptive and evolving echoes the 19th-century biological thought.

Peirce's focus on the experimentalist disposition is his attempt to characterise what is distinctive about science and scientists. The pragmatic maxim is Peirce's attempt to extend this characterization to philosophical inquiry more broadly.

Over the course of his career, Peirce offered various formulations of the maxim. The most familiar version of the maxim reads: "Consider what effects, which might conceivably have practical bearings, we conceive the object of our conception to have. Then the whole of our conception of those effects is the whole of our conception of the object" (EP 1.132). However, an earlier version of the maxim found in 'Questions Concerning Certain Faculties Claimed for Man' (1868) makes more explicit the connection between the maxim and the experimentalist disposition: "Admit no statement concerning what passes within us except as a hypothesis necessary to explain what takes place in what we commonly call the external world" (EP 1:30). This maxim suggests that every opinion be entertained as a potential hypothesis accountable to further scientific testing. Just as an experimentalist is disposed to view an object in the laboratory in terms of its expected behaviour, the pragmatic maxim asks that we take our opinions more broadly to likewise be subject to testing and experimentation.

Put differently, the pragmatic maxim, and Peircean pragmatism more generally, follows from applying a demand for scientific accountability to inquiry more broadly. Robert Burch agrees with the characterization of the maxim as a more general demand for holding opinions accountable to scientific practice. He writes that when Peirce gave his original formulation of the pragmatic maxim in 'How to Make Our Ideas Clear' (1878), "[Peirce] had in mind that a meaningful conception must have some sort of experiential 'cash value,' must somehow be capable of being related to some sort of collection of possible empirical observations under specifiable conditions" (Burch 2017: 6). Nathan Houser supports this characterization as well: "The pragmatic maxim may thus be taken as a test for whether our conceptions, our theories, are indexed to experience" (EP 1:xxxiv). On both Burch's and Houser's accounts, the pragmatic maxim is motivated by a *general demand for scientific accountability*.

The pragmatic maxim construes scientific practice (at least as Peirce sees it) in terms of the adoption of the experimentalist's disposition and applies this disposition to the practice of (philosophical) inquiry more broadly. Peirce makes this point explicitly in the following passage:

> All pragmatists will . . . agree that their method of ascertaining the meanings of words and concepts is no other than that experimental

method by which all the successful sciences . . . have reached the degrees of certainty that are severally proper to them today.

(CP 5:465)

Notice in the foregoing passage is Peirce's explicit commitment to what we have characterised as the third tenet of 19th-century naturalism, namely the endorsement of a single set of scientific methods for all modes of inquiry. For Peirce, not only do all scientific domains owe their success to the experimentalist disposition, but that very disposition—formalised as the pragmatic maxim—is the *right* way to engage in philosophical inquiry, and indeed inquiry more generally. Peirce holds that philosophical inquiry should model itself on scientific inquiry because of the connection he discerns science, logic and philosophy. For Peirce, logic and science go hand in hand. Insofar as philosophy is interested in correct reasoning, it needs to learn and adopt those lessons of applied logic found in science. One cannot engage in inquiry and better reasoning in general without taking science and its lessons seriously—indeed without modelling one's method of inquiry, as Peirce argues, on logic and science.

III

Peirce's Metaphysical Naturalism

We earlier portrayed 19th-century metaphysical naturalism as largely comprising the claim that all phenomena are, at least in principle, commensurable, even across wide natural variation. We are now in a position to observe how closely this principle aligns with the experimentalist disposition. On Peirce's account, the experimentalist—and the philosopher who models themself on the experimentalist—assumes the explicability of phenomena, and commits to inquire into those phenomena in a way that is evolving and fallibilist. The experimentalist, then, on encountering something novel and in need of explanation, thinks that explanation is possible, and that an adaptive, non-dogmatic process is the best way to pursue that explanation. Put simply, for the Peircean experimentalist, there is a world, and that world is within our cognitive reach.

Let us take a moment to contrast this approach to John Locke's cautions about the limits of human inquiry. In his introduction to the *Essay Concerning Human Understanding*, Locke tells us that the purpose of understanding is to help us survive and flourish in this life and the next, not to understand the whole of the universe. Accordingly, he cautions that when we launch our little boats (which were only meant for nearby inlets) on the "vast Ocean of Being", the effect is an increase of doubts leading to "a perfect Scepticism" (Locke 2014: 5).

For Peirce, to assume that the vast ocean beyond our own inlet is unattainable is itself a perfect scepticism, and blocks inquiry before it can even begin. He most famously expresses this view in his well-known

1898 discussion of the so-called "first rule of reason" (EP 2:48–56). This discussion occurs in the context of a broader discussion contrasting "miserably insignificant" American universities with European universities.[10] For Peirce, the former are organised around teaching—roughly, the retention and transmission of established knowledge—and the latter are organised around learning—the expansion of knowledge. Peirce tells us that to learn, we must desire to learn. The true test of whether we desire to learn, Peirce says, is whether we block the path of inquiry.

In the discussion that follows, Peirce identifies four broad ways in which scholars block inquiry (and thereby, one assumes, align themselves with seminary rather than laboratory philosophy): (i) by making absolute assertions (i.e. reasoning from axioms instead of postulates); (ii) by asserting something's unknowability; (iii) by asserting something's fundamentality; and (iv) by holding that we have reached the final formulation. The second of these is particularly germane as a response to Locke. Locke tells us: *do not try to understand more than you are able; it will only frustrate you and make you sceptical.* Peirce replies:

> It is easy enough to mention a question the answer to which is not known to me today. But to aver that that answer will not be known tomorrow is somewhat risky; for oftentimes it is precisely the least expected truth which is turned up under the ploughshare of research.
>
> (EP 2:49)

What Peirce here discusses in methodological and epistemological terms is easily translated into a *regulative* assumption of pragmatist metaphysics. If we genuinely desire to expand our knowledge, and not merely to rest with what we already think we know, we must not adopt the *prima facie* assumption that some portions of the universe are beyond our ken. While Peirce famously rejects axiomatic, foundationalist thinking, he is cognisant that the regulative assumption of knowability starts from the premise that the world is real. On Peirce's view, we ought to treat the assumption that the world is real as just that—an assumption—and not as an *a priori* truth. Peirce rejects anti-metaphysical stances that would have us say nothing about reality, on the grounds that it is better to recognise our background assumptions and expose them to critique rather than to pretend that we do not have them. Elsewhere, he writes:

> Find a scientific man who proposes to get along without any metaphysics . . . and you have found one whose doctrines are thoroughly vitiated by the crude and uncriticized metaphysics with which they are packed. We must philosophize, said the great naturalist Aristotle—if only to avoid philosophizing. Every man of us has a metaphysics, and has to have one; and it will influence his life greatly. Far better, then, that that metaphysics should be criticized and not be allowed to run loose.
>
> (CP 1.129)

For Peirce, metaphysics is licit when we approach it with the experimentalist mindset—treating the hypotheses of metaphysics as hypotheses susceptible of updating in light of further inquiry in a long-term, fallible, evolving process. For Peirce, the truths of any meaningful metaphysics will be revealed at the end of inquiry, not asserted at the outset. Peirce's metaphysics is naturalistic, then, in two senses. First, he accepts the 19th-century naturalistic tenet of the in-principle commensurability of all that exists. Second, though, he treats this tenet—and other metaphysical assumptions that we bring to inquiry—as themselves subject to naturalistic inquiry and hence to revision and falsification. Among these other metaphysical assumptions are the reality of mind(s) and ideas and the existence of God. It is to these that we now turn.

IV

Peirce's Theological Naturalism and Naturalistic Idealism

In Section I, we characterised three historical idealists—Descartes,[11] Berkeley, and Kant—as engaged in various ways in securing God, freedom, and immortality against the determinism of the New Science. Other historical idealists, from Malebranche to Fichte, were likewise arrayed against naturalism. It is tempting to suggest that idealists and naturalists are always opposed to each other, like the gods and giants in Plato's *Sophist*—the former "maintaining forcibly that real existence consists of certain ideas which are only conceived by the mind and have no body" (*Sophist*: 246b) while the latter "lay their hands on all such things [as rocks and trees] and maintain stoutly that that alone exists which can be touched and handled" (*Sophist*: 246a).[12]

We should be cautious, though, about concluding too quickly that idealism and naturalism are always opposed to each other. In their *Idealism: the History of a Philosophy*, Dunham, Grant, and Watson offer a capacious account of idealism and a forceful challenge to the twin notions that idealism is anti-realist and anti-science. They observe that contemporary accounts of idealism often focus on certain figures and approaches to the neglect of others, thereby generating a skewed perception of the scope of idealism: "Most contemporary idealism . . . has been preoccupied with constructing a metaphysics on the basis of a normativity posed as an alternative to naturalism. While this has of course been one theme in the history of idealism, it does not exhaust it".[13] Dunham et al. point to evidence that idealism has often engaged with and influenced, rather than opposed, the natural sciences.

Dunham et al. charge that the too-frequent reduction of idealism writ large to Berkeleyan subjective idealism has led to the common view that idealism is anti-realist. Against this stereotype, they offer a characterisation of idealism not as denying the reality of physical things, but rather as admitting the reality of some things—specifically minds and ideas—that are excluded from *purely* materialist ontologies:

> An idealism that is a realism concerning Ideas is not therefore committed *only* to the existence of Ideas, but rather to the claim that any adequate ontology must include *all* existence, including the existence of the Ideas and the becomings they cause. Idealism, that is, is not anti-realist, but realist precisely about the existence of Ideas.[14]

Peirce is a striking exemplar of an idealist who is neither anti-realist nor anti-science. For, while he was a philosophical naturalist, he was also a self-described idealist—at once laying hands on rocks and trees and maintaining the real existence of ideas. In an 1891 article for the *Monist*, Peirce tells us that "the one intelligible theory of the universe is that of objective idealism, that matter is effete mind, inveterate habits becoming physical laws" (CP 6.25).

In the foregoing quote, we see two central elements of Peirce's thought: synechism and evolutionism. Joseph Esposito (Esposito, n.p.) lists ten interconnected ideas that make up Peirce's synechism:

1. "the doctrine that all that exists is continuous" (CP 1.172).
2. the rejection of atomism and the existence of ultimate elements
3. the view that continuity of being is a condition for communication (CP 7.572)
4. the view that to exist in some respect is also to not exist in that respect (CP 7.569)
5. the view that "all phenomena are of one character" consisting of a mixture of freedom and constraint that tends in a teleological manner to increase the reasonableness in the universe (CP 7.570)
6. the view that consciousness has a bodily and social dimension, the latter originating outside the individual self (CP 7.575)
7. "the doctrine . . . that elements of Thirdness cannot entirely be escaped" (CP7.653)
8. a theoretical synthesis of pragmatism and tychism (the doctrine that chance events occur)
9. the fallibilist view that our scientific facts are continually subject to revision
10. "a purely scientific philosophy [that] may play a part in the onement of religion and Science" (CP 7.578).

Let us briefly focus on (5) and (10) from this list, both of which play important roles in Peirce's distinctive brand of idealism.

In the claim that " 'all phenomena are of one character' consisting of a mixture of freedom and constraint that tends in a teleological manner to increase the reasonableness in the universe", we see the homogeneity claim of seventeenth century naturalism tempered by nineteenth century evolutionary theory. Inspired by evolutionary theory in biology, Peirce worked in the 1890s to develop an evolutionary cosmology—that is, a theory of the evolution of the universe. In fact, he developed several cosmological models, but the one that he thought likeliest to be proven true characterises the universe as beginning in pure spontaneity that, over time, firms up into ever-tightening laws of nature.

In the reference to freedom and constraint, we see echoes of Cartesian dualism in which minds are free and bodies are constrained. For Peirce though, unlike Descartes, the properties of freedom and constraint do not individuate between types of substances, or indeed between worlds.[15] The very same universe—and the very same types of things—are capable of being either free or constrained. When something is free or lively, we term it *mind* and when something is constrained we term it *matter*. However, mind and matter do not make up separate realms. On Peirce's view, the universe begins as pure mind and becomes material as habits take hold. However, Peirce denies that matter, no matter how effete, is ever not-mind; matter always maintains some weak liveliness. This synechistic denial that "physical and psychical phenomena are entirely distinct,—whether as belonging to different categories of substance, or as entirely separate sides of one shield" (EP 2:2) is the heart of Peirce's objective idealism.

As we noted previously, Peirce also describes synechism as "a purely scientific philosophy [that] may play a part in the onement of religion and Science" (CP 7.578). The reference here to science and to its "onement" with religion is both an assertion of the methodological naturalism that emerged in the 17th century and a hint about the role of the supernatural in Peirce's ontology.

We mentioned in Section I that Peirce disagreed with James's opposition to the notions of the Absolute and of an infinite, transcendent deity. In a 1903 introduction to 'The Fixation of Belief' (1877), Peirce acknowledged James as an important pragmatist, but claimed that James had pressed pragmatism

> further than the tether of [its] author would reach, who continues to acknowledge, not indeed the Existence, but yet the Reality, of the Absolute, nearly as it has been set forth, for example, by Royce in his *The World and the Individual*, a work not free from faults of logic, yet valid in the main.
>
> (CP 5.358n.1)

James's pragmatism and his radical empiricism inclined him to what he termed 'pluralistic pantheism' (James 1909: 50 *et passim*) and to a conception of God as finite and accessible to human beings. This is because he was unwilling to contemplate an ontology in principle beyond the scope of human understanding. Peirce's longstanding complaint was that James lacked the patience and the facility with logic to understand the infinite and the infinitesimal. Peirce wished to leave open the possibility an Absolute, infinite deity precisely because he found it unscientific and self-defeating to draw a line and say *beyond this, human understanding cannot pass*. Just as, on Peirce's account, Berkeley's no-abstraction rule blocked the progress of mathematics by ruling out "negative quantities, the square root of minus, and infinitesimals" (CP 8.33), James's impatience with logic placed obstacles in the way of the philosophical consideration of the Absolute. Philosophers, Peirce cautions, ought not to mistake "an impotence of thought, really due to their own insufficient study, for an impossibility of human thought universal" (CP 6.179).

Peirce, then, was an idealist, both in the sense that he regarded mind as real and immanent in the universe, and in the sense that his commitment to the potential of scientific inquiry made him optimistic about human beings' long-run capacity to grasp the divine as infinite and absolute. Whereas philosophers from Descartes to Kant had constructed firewalls between nature and Grace in order to protect God, freedom and immortality from the New Science and determinism, Peirce's optimism about science made him likewise optimistic about the prospects for understanding God, freedom and immortality.

In Section I, we characterised metaphysical naturalism not merely as the assertion that all that is, is natural, but also as the denial of the supernatural. In truth, Peirce cannot really be said to deny the reality of the supernatural. On the other hand, he would deny that the assertion that all that is, is natural is equivalent to the denial of the supernatural. For Peirce, as for Spinoza, nature is all that is the case. However, just as mind, as it becomes habituated and effete, is also matter, so for Peirce nature, as it approaches infinity, is also supernatural. We noted earlier that Peirce's synechism led him to deny clean distinctions between consciousness and unconsciousness, mind and matter, and life and death, seeing each of these pairs instead as origins and termini of continua. Likewise for the natural and the divine. Thus, in the end, Peirce is at once a philosophical naturalist of both methodological/epistemological and metaphysical stripes, an objective idealist, and a possible absolute idealist. He is also a natural theologian.

Naturalism as a philosophical movement had its official debut in the first half of the 20th century. However, it did not emerge in a vacuum. Rather, it was the culmination of two modern scientific revolutions and philosophers' responses to those revolutions. In Descartes and the rationalistic philosophers who followed him, that response first took the form of a dualistic 'firewall' between Nature and Grace, and ultimately the dissolution of that firewall in Spinoza's naturalistic monism. Concurrent with this movement, we see in epistemology a shift from the view that different domains of reality are knowable by different faculties or methods to the view that all of reality is knowable in the same way.

In the 19th century, the emergence of evolutionary theory led to the readmission of diversity and contingency to naturalistic metaphysics. Peirce's pragmatism and synechism were responses to this second scientific revolution. The main lines of Peirce's response were (i) his development of an epistemology modelled on the experimentalist's disposition—that is, on a willingness to answer questions experimentally, to hold one's views on probation, and to update those views in light of new evidence—(ii) his optimism that the world is knowable by us; and (iii) his dissolution of hard distinctions between mind and matter, and between the natural and the supernatural. In the decades that followed, the framers of 20th-century naturalism were to varying degrees influenced by (i) and (ii), but (iii) received less uptake. In Peirce, then, we see both the source and outline of philosophical naturalism, and one of modern philosophy's boldest applications of the commensurability thesis.

Notes

1. See also Giladi (2014), Stern (2008), Stone (2013) and Westphal (2008).
2. Viz., *CPR*: Bxvii.
3. On this transition, see, for example, Drake (1989, 1999), Reitan (1996) and Heidegger (1977).
4. See Kant 1960.
5. Schmaltz 2017: 145.
6. See, for instance, James 1891; Dewey 1925.
7. Brent 1998: 18.
8. EP 2.48 denotes Vol. 2, page 48 of *The Essential Peirce*. We follow this convention throughout.
9. CP 5:411 denotes Vol. 5, paragraph 411 of *The Collected Papers of Charles Sanders Peirce*. We follow this convention throughout.
10. Peirce calls German universities "the light of the whole world" (EP 2:47).
11. On Descartes's idealism, see Lennon (1988).
12. We follow Thomas Lennon in applying Plato's useful metaphor to philosophers who came much later than Plato. It is worth noting that while he have here characterised Descartes and Locke as undertaking somewhat similar efforts to delimit the scope of human understanding, Lennon sees the two philosophers as thoroughgoing foes, and Locke's *Essay* as "an anti-Cartesian polemic from beginning to end" (Lennon 1993: x *et passim*).
13. Dunham et al. 2011: 1.
14. Ibid., p. 4.
15. Notice here the echoes of Spinoza, who, like Peirce, denies that mind and matter comprise two kingdoms. However, on the standard account, Spinoza's monism lacks the evolutionary aspect of Peirce's.

References

Brent, J. 1998. *C. S. Peirce: A Life*, rev. ed. Bloomington: Indiana University Press.
Burch, R. 2017. 'Charles Sanders Peirce'. In E. N. Zalta (ed.) *The Stanford Encyclopedia of Philosophy*. Available at: https://plato.stanford.edu/archives/fall2017/entries/peirce/

Dewey, J. 1925. *Experience and Nature*. London: Allen and Unwin.

———. 1934. *A Common Faith*. New Haven: Yale University Press.

Drake, S. 1989. *History of Free Fall: Aristotle to Galileo*. Toronto: Wall and Thompson.

———. 1999. 'Galileo and the Law of Inertia'. In N. M. Swerdlow and T. H. Levere (eds.) *Stillman Drake's Essays on Galileo and the History and Philosophy of Science, Vol. 2*. Toronto: University of Toronto Press.

Dunham, J., Grant, I. H., and Watson, S. 2011. *Idealism: The History of a Philosophy*. Durham: Acumen.

Esposito, J. 2005. 'Synechism: The Keystone of Peirce's Metaphysics'. In *The Commens Encyclopedia: The Digital Encyclopedia of Peirce Studies*. Available at: www.commens.org/encyclopedia/article/esposito-joseph-synechism-keystone-peirce%E2%80%99s-metaphysics

Giladi, P. 2014. 'Ostrich Nominalism and Peacock Realism: A Hegelian Critique of Quine'. *International Journal of Philosophical Studies* 22: 734–751.

Heidegger, M. 1977. 'Modern Science, Metaphysics, and Mathematics'. In D. F. Krell (ed.) and W. B. Barton, Jr. and V. Deutsch (trans.) *Martin Heidegger: Basic Writings*. New York: Harper and Row.

James, W. 1891. 'The Moral Philosopher and the Moral Life'. *International Journal of Ethics* 1.3: 330–354.

———. 1909. *A Pluralistic Universe*. London: Longman, Green.

Kant, I. 1960. *Religion within the Limits of Reason Alone*. T. M. Greene and H. H. Hudson (trans.). New York: Harper and Row.

———. 1998. *Critique of Pure Reason*. P. Guyer and A. W. Wood (eds. and trans.). Cambridge: Cambridge University Press.

Lennon, T. M. 1988. 'Descartes's Idealism'. *Philosophie Et Culture: Actes du XVIIe Congrès Mondial de Philosophie* 4: 53–56.

———. 1993. *The Battle of the Gods and Giants: The Legacies of Descartes and Gassendi, 1655–1715*. Princeton: Princeton University Press.

Locke, J. 2014. *An Essay Concerning Human Understanding*. Ware: Wordsworth Editions Limited.

Papineau, D. 'Naturalism'. In E. N. Zalta (ed.) *The Stanford Encyclopedia of Philosophy*, Winter 2016 ed. Available at: https://plato.stanford.edu/archives/win2016/entries/naturalism/

Peirce, C. S. 1931–58. *Collected Papers of Charles Sanders Peirce*. C. Hartshorne, P. Weiss and A. Burks (eds.), 8 vols. Cambridge, MA: Harvard University Press.

———. 1992–98. *The Essential Peirce: Selected Philosophical Writings*. N. Houser, C. Kloesel, and the Peirce Edition Project (eds.), 2 vols. Bloomington, IN: Indiana University Press.

Plato. 1921. *Plato in Twelve Volumes*. H. N. Fowler (trans.), vol. 12. Cambridge, MA: Harvard University Press.

Régis, P. S. 1691/1970. *Cours entier de philosophie, ou systeme general selon les principes de M. Descartes, contenant la logique, la metaphysique, la physique, et la morale*. Amsterdam: Huguetan, reprinted New York and London: Johnson.

———. 1704/1996. *L'usage de la raison et de la foy ou l'accord de la foy et de la raison*. Jean-Robert Armogathe (ed.). Paris: Fayard.

Reitan, E. A. 1996. 'Nature, Place, and Space: Albert the Great and the Origins of Modern Science.' *American Catholic Philosophical Quarterly* 70.1: 83–101.

Schmaltz, T. 2017. *Early Modern Cartesianisms: Dutch and French Construc-tions*. Oxford: Oxford University Press.

Spinoza, B. 1994. *A Spinoza Reader: The "Ethics" and Other Works*. E. Curley (ed. and trans.). Princeton: Princeton University Press.

Stern, R. 2008. 'Hegel's Idealism'. In F. C. Beiser (ed.) *The Cambridge Com-panion to Hegel and Nineteenth-Century Philosophy*. Cambridge: Cambridge University Press.

Stone, A. 2013. 'Hegel, Naturalism, and the Philosophy of Nature'. *Hegel Bul-letin* 34: 59–78.

Westphal, K. R. 2008. 'Philosophising About Nature: Hegel's Philosophical Pro-ject'. In F. C. Beiser (ed.) *The Cambridge Companion to Hegel and Nineteenth-Century Philosophy*. Cambridge: Cambridge University Press.

8 Common-sense and Naturalism

Mario De Caro

To disavow the very core of common sense, to require evidence for that which both the physicist the man in the street accept as platitudinous, is no laudable perfectionism; it is a pompous confusion, a failure to observe the nice distinction between the baby and the bath water.[1]

Traditionally, some of the main intellectual enemies of the strictest naturalists are the philosophers who assume that (i) barring special conditions, perception gives us access to the external world as it really is; (ii) middle-size objects have properties that are not identical to whatever microphysical properties constitute them; and (iii) empirically adequate scientific theories that appeal to unobservable entities may be useful heuristic tools, but are not true descriptions of the world. Among those philosophers (and barring some obvious differences between them) are most of the Aristotelians, Reid, James, Duhem, Austin, van Fraassen, and, in some relevant aspects of their thinking, Husserl, Moore, Bergson, and Wittgenstein. In this chapter, I will argue that common-sense realists have excellent reasons for arguing against the reductive or eliminativist views of the strict naturalists regarding the common-sense view of the world, but they are unjustified in defending antiscientific realism. In this light, I will contend that the most reasonable view is a form of liberal or pluralistic naturalism that is realist in regard to both the common-sense and the scientific views of the world.

I

Against the Common-sense Worldview

In her last book, the late philosopher Lynne Rudder Baker wrote "[w]e should not embrace a metaphysics that makes mundane but significant phenomena unintelligible".[2] These phenomena include what we common-sensically conceive as fundamental for conceptualising the world: the reality of material objects, free will and moral responsibility, consciousness, the objectivity of mathematics, the difference between the first-person and the third-person point of view, the objective correctness/incorrectness of some moral judgments and actions, and so on.

Baker's statement may seem obvious, but in some contemporary philosophical quarters it is not accepted—and some philosophers may even scoff at it. A good example of this anti-common-sense attitude is offered by Alex Rosenberg, who writes:

> What is the world really like? It's fermions and bosons, and everything that can be made up of them, and nothing that can't be made up of them. All the facts about fermions and bosons determine or 'fix' all the other facts about reality and what exists in this universe or any other if, as physics may end up showing, there are other ones. In effect, scientism's metaphysics is, to more than a first approximation, given by what physics tell us about the universe. The reason we trust physics to be scientism's metaphysics is its track record of fantastically powerful explanation, prediction and technological application. If what physics says about reality doesn't go, that track record would be a totally inexplicable mystery or coincidence.[3]

In Rosenberg's world, there is no space for the 'mundane but significant phenomena' to which Baker referred. According to him, the realm of existence strictly coincides with the world of physics—and the mundane but significant phenomena, which do not belong to it, are mere *illusions*:

> Science forces upon us a very disillusioned 'take' on reality. It forces us to say 'No' in response to many questions to which most everyone hopes the answers are 'Yes.' These are the questions about purpose in nature, the meaning of life, the grounds of morality, the significance of consciousness, the character of thought, the freedom of the will, the limits of human self-understanding, and the trajectory of human history.[4]

This eliminativist attitude about the features of the common-sense view of the world is nothing radically new in some respects, as the birth of modernity was typically characterised by the opening of a big gap between common sense and science, one whose consequences soon became relevant for philosophy as well. Galileo, in particular, refused to attribute genuine epistemic value to testimony of the senses. In doing so, he connected himself to the classic atomistic tradition, which had always been a minority view, and made it one of the dominant trends of modern philosophy.[5] Against the Aristotelians of his time, in particular, he defended a rigorous mathematical realism that relegated secondary properties in the context of subjectivity (which science cannot study) and credited as real only primary properties:

> I say that whenever I conceive any material or corporeal substance, I immediately feel the need to think of it as bounded, and as having

this or that shape; as being large or small in relation to other things, and in some specific place at any given time; as being in motion or at rest; as touching or not touching some other body; and as being one in number, or few, or many. From these conditions I cannot separate such a substance by any stretch of my imagination. But that it must be white or red, bitter or sweet, noisy or silent, and of sweet or foul odour, my mind does not feel compelled to bring in as necessary accompaniments. Without the senses as our guides, reason or imagination unaided would probably never arrive qualities like these. . . . I think that tastes, odours, colours, and so on are no more than mere names so far as the object in which we place them is concerned, and that they reside only in his consciousness. Hence if the living creature were removed, all these qualities would be wiped away and annihilated.[6]

Galileo was very aware that this view was very detrimental of the epistemic legitimacy of common sense. For him, common sense is often responsible for taking as astray, and we should praise the great thinkers who abandon any trust in it:

I cannot sufficiently admire the eminence of those men's wits, that have received and held it to be true, and with the sprightliness of their judgments offered such violence to their own senses, as that they have been able to prefer that which their reason dictated to them, to that which sensible experiments represented most manifestly to the contrary. . . . I cannot find any bounds for my admiration, how that reason was able in Aristarchus and Copernicus, to commit such a rape on their senses, as in despite thereof to make herself mistress of their credulity. . . . [There is] a sense more sublime and excellent than those common and vulgar.[7]

After Galileo, the legitimacy of common-sense decreased progressively in the view of most philosophers. In this respect, one can think of David Hume's sceptical attitude towards fundamental metaphysical beliefs such as personal identity, libertarian free will, or the existence of external things; and of Kant's third antinomy in the *Critique of Pure Reason*, in which the possibility of human freedom is said to be incompatible with the nomological structure of the natural world.

In the last couple of decades, however, the attack on the philosophical reliability of common-sense has become particularly pervasive. This phenomenon has many causes, but two are, in my view, the most relevant. First, many philosophers have recently taken a sceptical attitude toward the so-called 'Placement Problem', to use Huw Price's term:

If all reality is ultimately natural reality, how are we to 'place' moral facts, mathematical facts, meaning facts, and so on? How are we to locate topics of these kinds within a naturalistic framework, thus conceived?[8]

That is to say that many philosophers have become convinced that the traditional attempts to reduce the features of common-sense to those of the coverage domain of a natural science-based ontology were, and had to be, unsuccessful. According to this view, there is no way of 'placing' the common-sense features into the natural world, and consequently they do not have any reality. This attitude has been reinforced by a second prevalent intellectual phenomenon. In recent years, a growing number of scientists and (more surprisingly) philosophers has come to believe that the questions that traditionally were considered as part of the purview of philosophy, such as 'What exists?' or 'What can we know?', should be answered in *purely* scientific terms. Stephen Hawking and Leonard Mlodinow, for example, expressed such attitude when they wrote that today philosophy is dead because it 'has not kept up with modern developments in science, particularly physics.'[9] In this light, all the concepts that do not belong to the natural sciences have to be disposed, *pace* our common-sense intuitions. Rosenberg is only one of the most vocal advocates of the movement that proposes the elimination of the common-sense features from our ontology. Today, one can find many prominent examples of such a philosophical tendency.

A kind of belief that looks unshakeable to common-sense concerns arithmetical propositions: how could the statement '2 + 2 = 4' ever be doubted? Well, it can, at least for stern physicalist philosophers such as Harty Field,[10] Mark Balaguer,[11] and Stephen Yablo.[12] According to Field, in particular, if mathematical kinds (such as numbers or sets) were abstract, and consequently unable to participate in any causal interaction, it would be mysterious how one could know anything about such kinds. Consequently, we should treat mathematical entities as *mere fictions*, as we do with fictional characters in literature. As Field writes, '[w]hat my anti-realism involves . . . is a disbelief in mathematics. Or at least, it involves a disbelief in mathematics if mathematics is taken at face value'.[13] The consequences of this view are striking, but Field is happy to bite the bullet:

> The sense in which 2 + 2 = 4 is true is pretty much the same as the sense in which 'Oliver Twist lived in London' is true: the latter is true only in the sense that it is true according to a certain well-known story, and the former is true only in that it is true according to standard mathematics.[14]

A similar attack has been articulated by Paul Churchland and Patricia Churchland and concerns the fundamental features of intentional psychology.[15] According to the Churchlands, when it will be mature enough, the (neuro-)science of human thought and action will not contain any reference to the common-sense features proper of intentional psychology, since these features are only pseudoscientific relics. Exactly as had happened with the concepts of ether, witchcraft, and epicycle, concepts such as those of *belief* and *desire* do not correspond to anything in neurophysiological reality; consequently the alleged features that should correspond to them do not have any ontological legitimacy. In this light, for Paul Churchland, intentional psychology is

> a false and radically misleading conception of the causes of human behaviour and the nature of cognitive activity. On this view, folk psychology is not just an incomplete representation of our inner natures; it is an outright misrepresentation of our internal states and activities.[16]

Other philosophers have proposed some more 'local' eliminativist interpretations of common-sense psychological terms such as emotion,[17] concept,[18] belief,[19] mental illness,[20] mental representation,[21] consciousness,[22] and (the ordinary concept of) pain.[23]

Another fundamental pillar of common-sense is the reality of the ordinary objects. A few philosophers (including Cian Dorr and Gideon Rosen)[24] refuse to accept the reality of those objects—a view that has its authoritative inspirer in Wilfrid Sellars, who famously wrote:

> Speaking as a philosopher, I am quite prepared to say that the common sense world of physical objects in Space and Time is unreal—that is, that there are no such things.[25]

As argued by Terence Horgan and Matjaž Potrč,[26] the reality of ordinary objects is denied on the basis of several arguments: (i) ordinary objects do not have any *distinctive causal* work to do, besides that done by the subatomic entities of physics that compose them; (ii) they violate the general principle of composition that 'several objects compose another object when and only when each is in contact with one of the others'—i.e. when two people touch one another, they do not become a composite object); (iii) the same parts cannot compose two distinct objects at the same level of composition—the classic example being a statue such Michelangelo's David, which cannot exist besides the marble that composes it; (iv) if they existed, ordinary objects would be vague about their own spatiotemporal boundaries.

The first of these strategies is arguably the most common and has been very clearly presented by Peter van Inwagen (1990: 122):

> All activities apparently carried out by shelves and stars and other artifacts and natural bodies can be understood as disguised cooperative activities [of the simplest components of reality, properly arranged]. And, therefore, we are not forced to grant existence to any artifacts or natural bodies.[27]

Another bold attack against the common-sense worldview concerns morality. Boldly, John Mackie denied any ontological legitimacy to moral features. His argument was that, if these features were real, they would be very 'queer' entities, outside of the causal structure of the world; so we do not have reason to accept them:

> If there were objective values, then they would be entities or qualities or relations of a *very strange sort, utterly different from anything else in the universe.*[28]

Consequently, according to Mackie, moral statements—since they refer to non-existing entities—are hopelessly false.[29] It has to be added that today most moral philosophers deny Mackie's thesis that moral statements are false; many of them, however, espouse and defend views such expressivism, sentimentalism, quasi-realism, etc., rather than defend moral objectivism or varieties of moral realism.

The critique of the common-sense features of the world does not end here, since it also includes eliminativism about secondary qualities,[30] and moral responsibility,[31] abstract musical structures (such as Beethoven's Seventh symphony),[32] and so on.[33]

Considering all this, it appears, *pace* Baker, that the views denying any legitimacy to the 'mundane but significant phenomena' of the common-sense view of the world are becoming more and more common.

II

Common-sense Philosophy

The first attempts to defend common sense against more naturalised philosophy were not very solid. Arguably, the most prominent of such attempts were the criticisms that Aristotelians levelled against Galileo mathematisation of physics. In the *Dialogue on the Two Chief Systems of the World*, Galileo puts this objection in the mouth of Simplicio, the representative of the Aristotelians:

> Mathematicians may prove well enough in theory that *sphaera tangit planum in puncto* . . .; but when it comes to matter, things happen otherwise. What I mean about these angles of contact and ratios is that they all go by the board for material and sensible things.

Galileo offered a brilliant response to this objection. If a physical sphere does not touch the plane just in one point, Galileo says, this simply means that it is not a sphere, but another solid body, with its peculiar geometrical properties ("whatever form this rock has, [. . . it has] this perfectly").[34] Since these geometrical properties are the objective properties of the physical bodies, geometry is not a mere tool for saving phenomena, but serves for describing and explaining physical reality. Do physical laws concern perfect spheres? Well, scientists 'must deduct the material hindrances', i.e. must calculate the (geometrical) differences between a perfect sphere and this specific body. "The errors, then, lie not in the abstractness or concreteness, not in geometry or physics, but in a calculator who does not know how to make a true account".[35] For Galileo, physical laws apply also to material hindrances, since everything in the natural world can be mathematically evaluated.

As is well-known, Galileo won his battle, and physics became a mathematical science. For the advocates of common sense another, less ambitious front was opened: to show that mathematised natural science, if legitimate in itself, could not account for *everything*. But this is exactly how many have interpreted the success of physics: this science can *potentially explain everything*—and if something in principle cannot be explained in the terms and language of physics, then it is illusory. In *The Crisis of European Sciences and Transcendental Phenomenology*, Husserl famously wrote in this regard:

> [Galileo performed a] surreptitious substitution of the mathematically substructured world of idealities *for the only real world*, which is actually given through perception, which is ever experienced and experienceable—*our everyday life-world*. This substitution was promptly passed on to his successors, the physicists of all succeeding centuries.[36]

Husserl probably did not imagine that in the next decades the view that only science can account for the world would also be adopted by many philosophers. However, one minority tradition should be mentioned here that made the defence of common sense its main purpose. According to Noah Lemos,[37] the protagonists of the pro-common sense philosophical movement have been Thomas Reid, G. E. Moore, and Roderick Chisholm. If Lemos is right in claiming that these three thinkers are the most important exponent of 'commonsensism' (as Chisholm named it), one could also mention other philosophers that in their reflections have tried to give relevance to the instances of common sense, including Peirce, James, Husserl, Bergson, Dewey, Wittgenstein, Strawson, and Austin. Moreover, nowadays many Continental philosophers—at least those who come from the hermeneutic tradition, such as Gadamer—see in common sense the horizon within which the effort of clarification of philosophy has necessarily to be located. Moreover, as argued by Claudio Ciancio, these philosophers also see common sense a bulwark against the rationalistic and philo-scientific attitudes of other philosophical orientations (including, one can safely assume, analytic philosophy and pragmatism):

> There is no doubt that the topic of common sense plays an important role for the thinkers of a hermeneutic orientation, or at least for some of them, although in their writings there is a fairly limited mention of it. What attracts hermeneutics to the issue of common sense is its

antirationalistic and antiscientistic orientation aimed at developing a notion of the concrete universal.[38]

There is not much doubt, however, that it was Thomas Reid who established the agenda of commonsensism:

> Philosophy . . . has no other root that the principles of Common Sense; it grows out of them, and grows its nourishment from them. Severed from this root, his honour wither, its sap is dried out, it dies and rots.[39]

According to Reid, philosophers who deny the philosophical legitimacy of the appeal to common sense and, even more, those who reach conclusions that are incompatible with our most entrenched beliefs (such as Hume's denials of objective causality) are just wrongheaded. In this sense, philosophy should have a status similar to that of the other human activities, which tend to shy away from absurdities:

> A traveller of good judgment may mistake his way, and be unawares led into a wrong track; and while the road is fair before him, he may go on without suspicion and be followed by others but, when it ends in coal pit, it requires no great judgments to know he hath gone wrong, nor perhaps to find out what misled him.[40]

The other two members of the commonsensism triad expressed similar views. G. E. Moore, in particular, defended the correctness of our most basic beliefs against the sceptic who denies them. What can be more basic, Moore argued, that the perceptual judgment 'this is my finger'? What kind of evidence could one offer in order to deny such obvious belief?

> It seems to me a sufficient refutation of such views as these [the sceptical ones], simply to point to cases in which do know such things. This, after all, is a finger; there is no doubt about it: I know it, and you all know it. And I think we may safely challenge any philosopher to bring forward any argument in favour either of the proposition that we do not know it, or of the proposition that is not true, which does not at some point rest upon some premises which is beyond comparison, less certain, than the proposition which it is designed to attack.[41]

Finally, Chisholm drew the moral of Reid's attitude: respecting what common-sense strongly suggests to us is the best way of doing philosophy (even if this does not mean, of course, that common sense is *always* correct, and the wrong common-sense belief that the Earth does not move is a classic example here):

> It is characteristic of 'commonsensism,' as an alternative philosophical tradition, to assume that we do know, pretty much, those things

we think we know, and then having identified this knowledge, to trace it back to its sources and formulate criteria that will set it off from those things we do not know.[42]

These authors (and the others who have respected common sense as a legitimate source of philosophical inspiration) share two important ideas—which can function as good antidotes against the scientistic attitude of a good part of contemporary Anglophone philosophy that tend to deny the reality of Baker's 'mundane but significant' phenomena. The first idea is that, barring special conditions—such as optical illusions or the cases in which perceptual conditions are not optimal—perception tends to give us access to the (mesoscopic) world as it really is; and this means that we can assume that the observable objects that we perceive really exist and they have the properties that, on the basis of perception, we typically tend to attribute to them (which include both primary qualities and secondary qualities). The second idea is that the properties of the ordinary objects that we perceive are not identical to the microphysical properties that constitute those objects. Consider the case of a table in front of me: its functional characteristics and aesthetic value are neither identical nor can be reducible to its constitutive microphysical properties. Consequently, no description of the table that only mentions its physical properties could account, even in principle, for its functional or aesthetic characteristics.

However, commonsensism may run into a philosophical problem. This is generated when common sense is taken as a parameter of *all* philosophical investigations—that is, when common sense is considered the *only* legitimate parameter to which philosophers can appeal. To put it simply: the world of common sense is real, but not all aspects of the world can be interpreted through the categories of common sense. Some defenders of common sense, however, tend to overburden it with philosophical responsibilities: for example, when they appeal to it in order to devaluate what science tells us about the natural world or to rule out the possibility that abstract entities exist. One way of putting this commonsensical bias can be stated by saying that only what we can experience directly, with our senses or by using instruments that extend our senses (such as microscopes or telescopes), is ontologically legitimate.[43]

In fact, we have excellent reasons to think, in fact, that both some abstract entities (numbers, set, musical structures, propositions, etc.)[44] are real; and so do some microphysical entities, which are in principle unobservable, should figure in our ontological inventory.[45] This is not the place to defend these views, which are versions of platonism, in detail. However, with regard to abstract entities, it will be enough to remember that even some physicalists (such as Quine), who would love to reject all abstract entities as *entia non grata*, had to accept to the existence of mathematical entities, since this is part of the ontology that one has to admit when one accepts the explanatory and predictive accuracy of our best current science. Platonism is well-regarded also in other fields besides philosophy of mathematics, such as in philosophy of music where, by appealing to the existence of abstract musical structures, it arguably offers the best explanation of what it means that the same piece of music can be played an indefinite number of times, in different places and ages.[46]

As to realism about microphysical entities, which is now a majority view in philosophy of science, it will be enough here to say that this view is justified both by some convincing replies that have been offered to the traditional antirealist arguments (such as pessimistic induction, under-determination of theories by empirical data, social constructivism, epistemic relativism) and by some positive arguments, such as the so-called 'no-miracles argument'.

In this way, the challenge is how to reconcile realism about common-sense, about unobservable entities, and about abstract entities. In one world, the challenge is how to be a good ontological pluralist. In the next section, I will consider the answer that has been offered in his last years by Hilary Putnam.

III

Putnam's Liberal Naturalism

In the early years of his academic career, together with Paul Oppenheim, Putnam advocated a form of physicalist monism, which articulated the logical-positivist thesis of the 'Unity of Science' by claiming the principled reducibility of the concepts and laws of higher-level sciences to the concepts and laws of the lower-level sciences, with microphysics representing the most basic level:

> Every phenomenon that can be explained by 'higher-level' sciences such as psychology and sociology could in principle be explained by 'lower-level' sciences, and ultimately by physics.[47]

Interestingly, however, Putnam also claimed that such thesis was not justified *a priori*, since it was inspired by 'a pervasive trend within scientific enquiry . . . notwithstanding the simultaneous existence (and, of course, legitimacy) of other, even *incompatible* trends' (emphasis in original).[48] Thus, even in his initial physicalist years, Putnam put the concrete scientific practice at the centre of his philosophical project—an early sign of his dedication to the spirit and themes of the pragmatist tradition.

Afterwards, beginning in in the 1960s and until his death in 2016, Putnam defended various versions of pluralistic realism that simultaneously accepted the approximate and revisable truth of both the view of the world offered by the natural science and that offered by common sense. In this light, Putnam rejected all philosophical conceptions that were unable (or, even worse, were not supposed to) do full justice, in a realistic spirit, to both science and common sense. More specifically, in his mature philosophical career, Putnam went through four different versions of conceptual, epistemological, and ontological pluralistic realism.

In the 1960s, he developed 'Computational Functionalism', an extremely influential conception of the mind-body problem, which was pluralist in ontology, since he accepted the existence of irreducible mentalistic properties. According to that view, mental functions (that is, mental properties) are 'hardwired' in the brains of the speakers so that the relation between the mind and the brain is analogous to the relation between the software and the hardware. In this framework, mental properties depend for their existence on physical properties, but could not be reduced to them; consequently one cannot investigate mental properties by only appealing to the conceptual tools offered by physics—or by any of the natural sciences. Expanding on this doctrine, during this period Putnam explicitly rejected the Unity of Science and developed (contemporaneously with Jerry Fodor,[49] but independently from him) a pluralistic view that later Ned Block called the 'Many Levels Doctrine'.[50] According to that view, 'nature has joints at many different levels, so at each level there can be genuine sciences with their own conceptual apparatus, laws and explanations'.[51] An example that clarified that view was offered by Putnam in the influential article 'Reductionism and the Nature of Psychology':[52] Why does a solid rigid round peg a little less than 1 inch in diameter fit through a round square of 1 inch in diameter but does not fit in a square hole with a diagonal of 1 inch? The correct answer to this question, according to Putnam, cannot be given by appealing to the physical (lower-level) properties of the peg and holes, but only to their the geometrical (high-level) properties: and this shows that different levels of reality are composed by different and mutually irreducible properties. At this stage of his career, therefore, Putnam began to believe in the irreducibility of the mental to the physical—a cornerstone of the common-sense view of the world—and, more generally, saw several reasons for thinking that physics does not delimit the boundary of reality and knowledge, and that a conceptual, epistemological, and ontological pluralism recommends itself.

In a similar pluralistic spirit, Putnam also developed the famous 'no-miracles argument', aimed at showing that the unobservable entities of our best physical theories, such as subatomic particles, should not be taken as useful heuristic tools, but as real entities.[53] According to this argument, the only way of explicating the extraordinary explanatory and predictive success of the theories of modern science is to acknowledge that they are true (or approximately true) and that their theoretical terms refer to real entities, even when those entities are in principle unobservable. The critical target of this argument was represented by the antirealist views in philosophy of science, such as instrumentalism, operationalism, and nominalism, for which—Putnam claimed—the fact that science works so well in offering comprehensive explanations and extremely precise predictions of observable phenomena is an inexplicable mystery, if not a sheer miracle. At that stage of his career, then, Putnam had already articulated some sophisticated arguments that advocated realistic interpretations of both the common-sense and the scientific views of the world.

In 1976, under the influence of Kant's transcendental idealism, Peirce's epistemic theory of truth, and Michael Dummett's semantic conception (which was in turn inspired by intuitionism),[54] Putnam started to articulate 'Internal Realism', a view that he later considered as too weighted in favour of the idealist side.[55] The core of that view was the identification of truth with 'justification in idealised epistemic conditions':

> If I say 'There is a chair in my study', an ideal epistemic situation would be to be in my study with the lights on or with daylight streaming through the window, with nothing wrong with my eye-sight, with an unfocused mind, without having taken drugs or been subjected to hypnosis, and so forth, and to look and see if there is a chair there.[56]

The main target of this view was 'metaphysical realism', the conception according to which there is only one true and complete description of the world—which according to many is offered by the natural sciences, if not by physics alone. For Putnam, metaphysical realism was a dogmatic and philosophically pernicious conception; thus, he developed several arguments against it. For our purposes, however, what is important to notice is that, in this period, Putnam saw his internal realism as the best way of articulating the idea that the language of physics cannot account for everything there is since there are real features of the world that cannot be described, even less explained, with the conceptual tools of that science—and the latter was an idea that he did not abandon anymore. As Putnam later wrote:

> The world cannot be completely described in the language game of theoretical physics, not because there are regions in which physics is false, but because, to use Aristotelian language, the world has many levels of forms, and there is no realistic possibility of reducing them all to the level of fundamental physics.[57]

From this perspective, a plurality of mutually irreducible but not incompatible conceptual systems is indispensable for dealing with reality and, *pace* Quine, there is no first-grade conceptual system. This, in turn, generates a pluralistic ontology and a pluralistic epistemology.

In this regard, Putnam stressed a couple of points. First, he described a phenomenon that he called 'conceptual relativity', for which some theories can be cognitively equivalent, even if *prima facie* they appear incompatible. (It would have been better if this phenomenon had been called 'cognitive equivalence', since Putnam's original term may suggest a connection with relativism and antirealism that is entirely inappropriate.) As Putnam convincingly argued, in some scientific fields, such as mathematical physics, that phenomenon is ubiquitous:

> To take an example from a paper with the title 'Bosonization as Duality' that appeared in Nuclear Physics B some years ago, there are quantum mechanical schemes some of whose representations depict the particles in a system as bosons while others depict them as fermions. As their use of the term 'representations' indicates, real live physicists—not philosophers with any particular philosophical axe to grind—do not regard this as a case of ignorance. In their view, the 'bosons' and 'fermions' are simple artifacts of the representation used. But the system is mind-independently real, for all that, and each of its states is a mind independently real condition, that can be represented in each of these different ways. And that is exactly the conclusion I advocate. . . . [These] descriptions are both answerable to the very same aspect of reality . . . they are 'equivalent descriptions'.[58]

The second point stressed then by Putnam was more familiar, but in this period he articulated it with greater clarity. It concerned the phenomenon of 'conceptual pluralism', that is, the fact that for dealing with the different levels of reality we need a plurality of mutually irreducible but not incompatible conceptual systems.

A favourite example by Putnam was that, depending on our interests, we can correctly and usefully describe a chair in the alternative languages of carpentry, furniture design, geometry, or etiquette. Each of those descriptions is useful in its specific way, without being reducible to any of the others. There is no fundamental and unifying theory of what being a chair is, so to speak. And this is true of a vast amount of entities (possibly all of them, with the exception of the entities of microphysics), since they can be described in different ways not just because of conceptual relativity, but also because things have different properties that belong to different ontological regions.

At the beginning of the 1990s, Putnam abandoned internal realism. The main reason of that change was that he realised the inadequacy of the foundation of that view, that is, epistemic conception of truth, which he now saw as too inclined toward anti-realism—or, more specifically, toward idealism. A clear example offered by Putnam of why, contrary to internal realism, truth should be not conceived of as epistemically constrained was a conjecture such as 'There is no life in the universe outside

Earth'—which may well be true but, if it is so, it would be unverifiable even in ideal epistemic conditions. In abandoning the epistemic view of truth, however, Putnam also realised that he did not need to go anti-realist in order to reject the dogmatic view that he had called 'metaphysical realism'. His new aim was in fact to develop 'a modest non-metaphysical realism squarely in touch with the results of science'.[59]

In articulating this new conception, Putnam was inspired by Wittgenstein's quietist attitude toward metaphysical problems (which should be 'dissolved' more than 'solved', since they are based on conceptual confusions), Austin's direct realism, and McDowell's insistence on the conceptual independence of the 'realm of reason' from the 'realm of law'. However, as usual, also other pragmatists themes worked in the background of this phase of Putnam's philosophical development as well. Let us now consider some of them.

The first pragmatist theme that inspired Putnam during that phase (and also later) was the idea that causality is an essentially intentional notion, since it is inextricably connected with our explanatory practices. In this respect, after approving John Haldane's saying that there are as many kinds of causes as there are senses of 'because',"[60] Putnam wrote that "[c]ausality depends on the interests at stake when one asks the question: 'What is the cause of that?' ".[61] It should be noted that with the term 'senses of 'because'', Putnam means, in the spirit of pragmatism, 'our ever expanding repertoire of explanatory practices'. Therefore, the combination of pluralism about explanation, on the one hand, and the conceptual link between explanation and causation, on the other hand, generate pluralism about causation.

In line with this thesis, Putnam claimed that the so-called 'principle of the physical causal closure of the world' should be rejected, as long as one takes it in one of its classic formulations: 'If x is a physical event and y us a cause or effect of x, then y, too, must be a physical event'.[62] Given Putnam's pluralist and non-reductionist ontology, physical event can indeed be caused by non-physical events that are irreducible to physical events—which is a form of downward causation. (It should be noted, however, that this does not mean that event cannot have physical causes as well). The crucial point, for Putnam, is that different causal explanations generalise to different classes of cases: and whether we are interested in an event as a member of one or another class is a completely context-relative question. For example, we can be interested in the physiological chain of events that ended in the movement of my hand; but can be interested also in the reasons for which I intentionally moved it. Neither of these causal chains have priority on the other since their respective interests are context-relative.

An entire section of Putnam's 1994 collection *Words and Life* was titled *The Inheritance of Pragmatism*; in 1995 his book *Pragmatism. An Open Question* was published, which translated a collection of lectures that had first been published in Italian in 1992; and finally, in 2017, shortly after Putnam's death, a book of essays titled *Pragmatism as a Way of Life. The Lasting Legacy of William James and John Dewey*, written with his wife Ruth Putnam, was also published. In one of the essays of Putnam, he wrote '[w]hat I find attractive in pragmatism is not a systematic theory in the usual sense. It rather a certain group of theses . . . which became the basis of the philosophies of Peirce, and above all of James and Dewey'.[63] These were the thesis about which Putnam was thinking was at that point:

1. *Anti-scepticism*: pragmatists hold that *doubt* requires justification as much as belief.
2. *Fallibilism*: pragmatists hold that there is never a metaphysical guarantee to be had that such-and-such belief will never need revision (that one can be both fallibilistic *and* anti-sceptical is perhaps *the* unique insight of American pragmatism.
3. The thesis that there is no *fundamental* dichotomy between 'facts' and 'values'.
4. The thesis that, in a certain sense, practice is primary in philosophy.[64]

Putnam defended these theses for most of his career, especially in the last three decades of activity. Indeed, he did not like to use '-isms' in order to define his own views very much, but in his later years, which I will shortly discuss, he made two exceptions: he described himself as an advocate of pragmatism and of liberal naturalism.

In the 2000s and 2010s, until his death in 2016, Putnam rejected the Wittgensteinian quietism he had defended in the previous decade and went back to metaphysics, even if he still rejected metaphysical realism in all its forms. Rather, he developed the Aristotelian view mentioned previously, based on the idea of different mutually irreducible levels of reality, and endorsed the Aristotelian principle of on the multivocality of being.[65] However, even in this Aristotelian context, the influence of James and Dewey was still very clear.[66]

In this period, for example, Putnam explored in depth his old idea that between factual and evaluative statements there is no conceptual *dichotomy*, since between them there is only a (sometimes useful) *distinction*.[67] This is because, according to Putnam, values and normativity are ubiquitous: even scientists appeal to values—which can be epistemic or even aesthetic—in order to choose between cognitively equivalent theories. Going back to Galileo, for example, it should be remembered that his main reason for accepting the Copernican system was an *aesthetic* one. While that system was very simple and harmonic, the alternative Ptolemaic system (with all its epicycles, deferents, and huge number of glassy spheres supporting the orbits of the planets) was unbearably complicated and ugly:

> [The Ptolemaic system was] a monstrous chimera composed of mutually disproportionate members, incompatible as a whole. Thus

however well the astronomer might be satisfied merely as a ***calculator*** [whose only role is to predict the future positions of planets], there was no satisfaction and peace for the astronomer as a ***scientist*** [the scientist-philosopher, who searches for the real laws of the universe]. And since he very well understood that although the appearances might be saved by means of assumptions essentially false in nature [because disproportionate and adverse to geometrical simplicity], it would be very much better if he could derive them from true suppositions.[68]

It is interesting to notice that in light of Putnam's dismissal of the fact-value dichotomy, Hume's famous principle "One cannot infer an 'ought' from an 'is' "[69] should be rejected, since it would be false. It, however, would not be false for the reason that many physicalists use to criticize it. They contend that values and normativity are not real phenomena, so (depending on which semantic theories the different philosophers adopt) the statements that refer to these alleged phenomena alternatively are taken as (i) referring only to descriptive facts; (ii) devoid of a truth-value; or (iii) plainly false. Putnam instead thinks that Hume's principle is false since the 'oughts' are everywhere, even in connections with science. For Putnam, 'facts and values cannot be disentangled'[70]—i.e. in particular contexts we may able to distinguish between fact and values, but there is no metaphysically grounded dichotomy.

Another important idea with a pragmatist flavour that Putnam developed in the last decades of his life was 'long-armed functionalism'. This is a view of the mind as a system of object-involving abilities that involve, from the start, the natural and social environment in which a speaker is located. Several things have to be noted in this respect. First, this view is different from his old 'computational functionalism', according to which mental functions were hardwired in the brain of a speaker. In fact, the fundamental reason for why Putnam abandoned computational functionalism was that he realised it was incompatible with his own 'semantic externalism' (the view that the relation between the thinkers and the environment they inhabit is necessary for constituting the content of at least some of their thoughts). In this regard, Putnam wrote:

I had to give up 'functionalism,' . . . that is, the doctrine that our mental states are just our *computational* states (as implicitly defined by a 'program' that our brains are hard-wired to 'run'), because that view is incompatible with the semantic externalism that years of thinking about the topic of reference had eventually led me to develop. If, as I said in 'The Meaning of 'Meaning',' our intentional mental states aren't in our heads, but are rather to be thought of *as world-involving abilities*, abilities identified by the sorts of transactions with our environment that they facilitate, then they aren't identified simply by the 'software' of the brain.[71]

200 Mario De Caro

Then, with regard to long-armed functionalism, he wrote:

> [it] is an antireductionist but naturalist successor to the original, reductionist, functionalist program. For a liberalized functionalist, there is no difficult in conceiving of ourselves as organisms whose functions are, as Dewey might have put it, 'transactional', that is environment-involving, from the start.[72]

The last of Putnam's later views that we can mention here is *liberal naturalism*, which he saw as the general framework of most of the ideas he had held in his last years.[73] Liberal naturalism is a metaphilosophy that advocates a pluralistic attitude both in ontology and epistemology, because not all the real features of the world can be reduced to the scientifically describable features, and the natural sciences are not the only genuine source of knowledge to which all the other apparent sources should hand over their epistemic pretensions. Still, a liberal naturalist cannot accept any entity in her ontology or any view in her epistemology that would contradict the current scientific worldview.[74]

Putnam's liberal naturalism appears a very promising perspective. As with any serious philosophical view, however, it faces several problems, the most important of which can be called 'The Reconciliation Problem': what kind of relation is there between the accounts of the world offered by the natural sciences and those offered by the social sciences, common-sense, the arts, and spirituality? In particular, what is the relationship between the ontological realm studied by the natural sciences and the other ontological regions? Is that a relation of *supervenience* (and in case, of which kind?), *emergence*, *grounding*, *incommensurability*, or something else? Putnam was happy with global supervenience, but this is a controversial issue. And connected with this difficulty, another one immediately raises: what about the traditional problems of causal over-determination and the violation of the closure of the physical world?

It should be noted that while the Placement Problem—which, as we have seen, troubles the philosophers who try to reduce the common-sense features to the scientific ones—, the Reconciliation Problem has to be addressed by the philosophers who want to legitimise the common-sense features of the world. In fact, they have the unavoidable task of showing how the common-sensical and the scientific images of the world can co-exist when they are both taken as fully legitimate and non-hierarchically related.[75]

The Reconciliation Problem is not an easy one. Despite this, Putnam thought that liberal naturalism was the preferable view since, without appealing to any supernatural feature, it is much less revisionist than the scientistic views mentioned at the beginning of this chapter regarding the common-sense feature of the world. For, the attempt to reduce the ordinary view of the world to the scientific one, besides being unattainable, is very impoverishing—and even more so are the various eliminativist projects. At the same time, Putnam was extremely critical towards the attempts of delegitimising the fundamental function played by science in our knowledge and in our lives. And one thing I am certain about is that his constant insistence on the fundamental inspirational role that common sense and science play in philosophy is one of the most precious intellectual gifts that this eminent philosopher has left us.[76]

Notes

1. Quine 1957: 229–230.
2. Baker 2013: 73.
3. Rosenberg 2014: 19.
    Interestingly, Rosenberg uses the term 'scientism' to label his view—a term that is *normally* used with derogatory connotations.
4. Rosenberg 2014: 17.
5. On the return of atomism in the Western tradition, see Clericuzio (2000), Chalmers (2009), Palmer (2014).
6. Galilei 1623/1957: 274
7. Galilei 1967: 103. Galileo's dismissal of common sense was motivated by his convinced commitment to a Platonist view according to which the only real properties where those geometrical in character: see De Caro (2017).
8. Price 2004: 74.
9. Hawking and Mlodinow 2010: 5.
10. See Field (1980, 1989).
11. See Balaguer (1998, 2018).
12. See Yablo (2002).
13. Field 1989: 227.
14. Ibid., p. 3.
15. See Churchland (1986), Churchland (2002).
    For a discussion of the recent developments of eliminativism about intentional psychology, see Ramsey (2016).
16. Churchland 1988: 43.
17. See Griffiths (1997).
18. See Machery (2008).
19. See Stich (1983).
20. See Murphy and Stich (1999).
21. See Hutto and Myin (2012).
22. See Dennett (1991), Frankish (2005, 2016, 2017). See also Ramsey (2016).
23. See Dennett (1978), Hardcastle (1999).
24. See Dorr and Rosen (2002).
25. Sellars, 1956/1997:§83.
    On Sellars's distinction between the two images of the world, see deVries (2005), and O'Shea (2007).
26. Horgan and Potrč (2008).
27. van Inwagen 1990: 122. For independent reasons, besides the simplest components of reality, van Inwagen accepts *persons* as real. The category of 'person' therefore, is an exception to his general ontological ban against the entities that commonsense tends to accept.
28. Mackie 1977: 38.
29. See also Nolan et al. (2005).
30. See Maund (2011).

31. See Smilansky (2002), Strawson (2010), Pereboom (2001, 2014), Harris (2012), and Caruso (2013).
32. See Goodman (1968), Predelli (2001), Killin (2018).
33. For a general presentation of fictionalism, see Caddick Bourne (2013).
34. Galilei (1632/1967): 210.
35. Ibid., p. 207.
36. CES: 48.
37. See Lemos (2004).
38. Ciancio 2004: 156.
    See also Bunge (2006, especially ch. 3).
39. Reid 1983: 7.
40. Ibid., p. 11.
41. Moore 1960: 228.
42. Chisholm 1977: 16.
43. This attitude can be found in the phenomenological, existentialist and hermeneutic traditions, and is often taken without much knowledge of the debates concerning the epistemic status of the natural sciences (see De Caro 2015).
    An exception to this simplistic attitude is offered by Bas van Fraassen, who offers a sophisticated version of scientific antirealism ('constructive empiricism') that, according to him "is set squarely within . . . common sense realism". The common basis on that view, he states "is language in which reference is unproblematic to trees and mountains, people and book" (van Fraassen 2003: 479; see also his 2007).
44. See Rosen (2017).
45. See Chakravartty (2007), Psillos (2009).
46. See Levinson (1990), Kania (2013).
47. See Oppenheim and Putnam (1958).
48. Putnam 1959: 4.
49. See Fodor (1965).
50. See the essays collected in Putnam (1975a).
51. Block 1996: 108.
52. See Putnam (1973).
53. See Putnam (1975a) and (2012b).
54. See Dummett (1978).
55. The most complete presentation of internal realism is in Putnam (1981).
56. Putnam 1990: vii.
57. Putnam 2005/2012: 65.
58. Putnam 2012a: 63–64.
59. Putnam 2004: 286, n.1.
60. Putnam 1999: 201, n. 17, writes that neither him nor Haldane could remember where the latter wrote the quoted phrases.
61. Quoted in Putnam 1999: 77; also 137, 149–150.
62. Putnam 1999: 215; Kim 1996: 147.
63. Putnam 1994: 152.
64. Ibid.
65. See Putnam (2004, part I).
66. See De Caro and Macarthur (2012).
67. See Putnam (1979/1990, 2002), and (2011/2012).
68. Galilei 1632/1967: 341; emphasis added.
69. THN: 3.1.1.27.
70. Putnam 1981: 141.
71. Putnam 2005/2012: 58.
72. See Putnam (2012a).

73. Putnam contributed to both De Caro and Macarthur (2004) and (2010), which advocated liberal naturalism.
74. On Putnam's liberal naturalism, see Putnam (2015, 2016b, forthcoming), and De Caro (2015) and (2016).
75. See De Caro (2015).
76. My gratitude goes to Hilary Putnam for the innumerable conversations on the issues discussed in this chapter. I also thank Robert Audi, David Macarthur, and Ruth Anna Putnam for their help in thinking on those issues. Finally, I am grateful to Paul Giladi for his useful comments on a previous version of this chapter.

References

Baker, L. R. 2013. *Naturalism and the First-Person Perspective*. Oxford: Oxford University Press.
Balaguer, M. 1998. *Platonism and Anti-Platonism in Mathematics*. Oxford: Oxford University Press.
———. 2018. 'Fictionalism in the Philosophy of Mathematics'. In E. N. Zalta (ed.) *The Stanford Encyclopaedia of Philosophy*. Available at: https://plato.stanford.edu/entries/fictionalism-mathematics/
Block, N. 1996. 'Anti-Reductionism Slaps Back'. *Philosophical Perspectives* 11: 107–133.
Bunge, M. 2006. *Chasing Reality: Strife Over Reality*. Toronto: University of Toronto Press.
Caddick Bourne, E. 2013. 'Fictionalism'. *Analysis* 73: 147–162.
Caruso, G. 2013. *Exploring the Illusions of Free Will and Moral Responsibility*. Lanham, MD: Lexington Books.
Chakravartty, A. 2007. *A Metaphysics for Scientific Realism: Knowing the Unobservable*. Cambridge: Cambridge University Press.
Chalmers, A. 2009. *The Scientist's Atom and the Philosopher's Stone: How Science Succeeded and Philosophy Failed to Gain Knowledge of Atoms*. Dordrecht: Springer.
Chisholm, R. M. 1977. *Theory of Knowledge*. Englewood Cliffs: Prentice Hall.
Churchland, P. M. 1988. *Matter and Consciousness*, Revised Edition. Cambridge, MA: MIT Press.
———. 1996. *The Engine of Reason, the Seat of the Soul*. Cambridge, MA: MIT Press.
Churchland, P. S. 1986. *Neurophilosophy: Toward a Unified Science of the Mind-Brain*. Cambridge, MA: MIT Press.
———. 2002. *Brain-Wise: Studies in Neurophilosophy*. Cambridge, MA: MIT Press.
Ciancio, C. 2004. 'Il senso comune nel pensiero ermeneutico'. In E. Agazzi (ed.) *Valore e limiti del senso commune*. Milano: Franco Angeli.
Clericuzio, A. 2000. *Elements, Principles and Corpuscles: A Study of Atomism and Chemistry in the Seventeenth Century*. Dordrecht: Kluwer.
De Caro, M. 2015. 'Realism, Common Sense, and Science'. *The Monist* 98: 197–214.
———. 2016. 'Introduction: Putnam's Philosophy and Metaphilosophy'. In Putnam 2016a.

———. 2017. 'On Galileo's Platonism, Again'. In R. Pisano, J. Agassi and D. Drozdova (eds.) *Hypotheses and Perspectives Within History and Philosophy of Science: Hommage to Alexandre Koyré 1964–2014*. Dordrecht: Springer.

De Caro, M., and Macarthur, D. (eds.). 2004. *Naturalism in Question*. Cambridge, MA: Harvard University Press.

———. (eds.). 2010. *Normativity and Naturalism*. New York: Columbia University Press.

———. 2012. 'Hilary Putnam: Artisanal Polymath of Philosophy', in Putnam 2012c.

Dennett, D. 1978. 'Why You Can't Make a Computer that Feels Pain'. In D. Dennett (ed.) *Brainstorms*. Cambridge, MA: MIT Press.

———. 1991. *Consciousness Explained*. New York: Little, Brown.

deVries, W. A. 2005. *Wilfrid Sellars*. Montreal and Kingston: McGill-Queen's University Press.

Dodd, J. 2007. *Works of Music: An Essay in Ontology*. Oxford: Oxford University Press.

Dummett, M. 1978. *Truth and Other Enigmas*. Cambridge, MA: Harvard University Press.

Field, H. 1980. *Science Without Numbers*. Oxford: Blackwell.

———. 1989. *Realism, Mathematics, and Modality*. New York: Blackwell.

Fodor, J. 1965. 'Explanation in Psychology'. In M. Black (ed.) *Philosophy in America*. Ithaca, NY: Cornell University Press.

Frankish, K. 2005. *Consciousness*. Milton Keynes: Open University.

———. 2016. 'Illusionism as a Theory of Consciousness'. *Journal of Consciousness Studies* 23: 11–39.

———. (ed.). 2017. *Illusionism as a Theory of Consciousness*. Exeter: Imprint Academic.

Galilei, G. 1623/1957. 'The Assayer'. In S. Drake (trans.) *The Controversy of the Comets of 1618*. Philadelphia: University of Pennsylvania Press.

———. 1632/1967. *Dialogue Concerning the Two Chief World Systems*. S. Drake (trans.). Berkeley and Los Angeles: University of California Press.

Goodman, N. 1968. *Languages of Art: An Approach to a Theory of Symbols*. Indianapolis, IN: Bobbs-Merrill.

Griffiths, P. E. 1997. *What Emotions Really Are: The Problem of Psychological Categories*. Chicago: University of Chicago Press.

Hardcastle, V. G. 1999. *The Myth of Pain*. Cambridge, MA: MIT Press.

Harris, S. 2012. *Free Will*. New York: Free Press.

Hawking, S., and Mlodinow, L. 2010. *The Grand Design*. New York: Bantam Books.

Horgan, T., and Potrč, M. 2008. *Contextual Semantics Meets Minimal Ontology*. Cambridge, MA: MIT Press.

Hume, D. 2007. *A Treatise of Human Nature: A Critical Edition*. D. F. Norton and M. J. Norton (eds.). Oxford: Clarendon Press.

Husserl, E. 1970. *The Crisis of the European Sciences and Transcendental Philosophy*. D. Carr (trans.) Evanston, IL: Northwestern University Press.

Hutto, D., and Myin, E. 2012. *Radicalising Enactivism: Basic Minds without Content*. Cambridge, MA: MIT Press.

Kania, A. (ed.). 2013. 'Platonism vs. Nominalism in Contemporary Musical Ontology'. In C. M. Uidhir (ed.) *Art and Abstract Objects*. Oxford: Oxford University Press.

Killin, A. 2018. 'Fictionalism About Musical Works'. *Canadian Journal of Philosophy* 48: 266–291.

Kim, J. 1996. *Philosophy of Mind*. Boulder, CO: Westview.

Lemos, N. 2004. *Common Sense: A Contemporary Defense*. Cambridge: Cambridge University Press.

Levinson, J. 1990. 'What a Musical Work Is, Again'. In J. Levinson (ed.) *Music, Art, and Metaphysics*. Ithaca, NY: Cornell University Press.

Machery, E. 2008. 'The Folk Concept of Intentional Action: Philosophical and Experimental Issues'. *Mind & Language* 23: 165–189.

Mackie, J. 1977. *Ethics: Inventing Right and Wrong*. New York: Penguin.

Maund, L. 2011. 'Colour Eliminativism'. In L. Nolan (ed.) *Primary and Secondary Qualities: The Historical and Ongoing Debate*. Oxford: Oxford University Press.

Moore, G. E. 1960. 'Some Judgements of Perceptions'. In G. E. Moore (ed.) *Philosophical Studies*. London: Routledge and Kegan Paul.

Murphy, D., and Stich, S. 1999. 'Griffiths, Elimination and Psychopathology'. *Metascience* 8: 13–25.

Nolan, D., Restall, G., and West, C. 2005. 'Moral Fictionalism Versus the Rest'. *Australasian Journal of Philosophy* 83: 307–330.

Oppenheim, P., and Putnam, H. 1958. 'Unity of Science as a Working Hypothesis'. In H. Feigl, M. Scriven and G. Maxwell (eds.) *Minnesota Studies in the Philosophy of Science. Vol. 2*. Minneapolis, MN: University of Minnesota Press.

O'Shea, J. 2007. *Wilfrid Sellars: Naturalism with a Normative Turn*. Cambridge: Polity Press.

Palmer, A. 2014. *Reading Lucretius in the Renaissance*. Cambridge, MA: Harvard University Press.

Pereboom, D. 2001. *Living Without Free Will*. Cambridge: Cambridge University Press.

———. 2014. *Free Will, Agency, and the Meaning of Life*. Oxford: Oxford University Press.

Predelli, S. 2001. 'Musical Ontology and the Argument from Creation'. *British Journal of Aesthetics* 41: 279–292.

Price, H. 2004. 'Naturalism without Representationalism'. In M. De Caro and D. Macarthur (eds.) *Naturalism in Question*. Cambridge, MA: Harvard University Press.

Psillos, S. 2009. *Knowing the Structure of Nature: Essays on Realism and Explanation*. London: Palgrave Macmillan.

Putnam, H. 1973. 'Reductionism and the Nature of Psychology'. *Cognition* 2: 131–146.

———. 1975a. *Mind, Language, and Reality. Philosophical Papers*, vol. 2. Cambridge: Cambridge University Press.

———. 1975b. 'The Meaning of "Meaning"', in Putnam 1975a.

———. 1975c. 'What Is Mathematical Truth?' In his *Mathematics, Matter and Method. Philosophical Papers*, vol. 1. Cambridge: Cambridge University Press.

———. 1979/1990. 'The Place of Facts in a World of Values', reprinted in Putnam, *Realism with a Human Face*. J. Conant (ed.) Cambridge, MA: Harvard University Press.

———. 1981. *Reason, Truth, and History*. Cambridge: Cambridge University Press.

———. 1990. *Realism with a Human Face*. Cambridge, MA: Harvard University Press.

———. 1994. *Words and Life*. Cambridge, MA: Harvard University Press.

———. 1995. *Pragmatism: An Open Question*. Oxford: Blackwell.

———. 1999. *The Threefold Cord. Mind, Body, and World*. New York: Columbia University Press.

———. 2002. *The Collapse of the Fact/Value Dichotomy and Other Essays*. Cambridge, MA: Harvard University Press.

———. 2004. *Ethics Without Ontology*. Cambridge, MA: Harvard University Press.

———. 2005/2012. 'A Philosopher Looks at Quantum Mechanics (Again)', reprinted in Putnam 2012c.

———. 2011/2012. 'The Fact/Value Dichotomy and Its Critics', reprinted in Putnam 2012c.

———. 2012a. 'Corresponding to Reality', in Putnam 2012c.

———. 2012b. 'On Not Writing Off Scientific Realism', reprinted in Putnam 2012c.

———. 2012c. *Philosophy in an Age of Science: Physics, Mathematics, and Scepticism*. M. De Caro and D. Macarthur (eds.) Cambridge, MA: Harvard University Press.

———. 2015. 'Naturalism, Realism, and Normativity'. *Journal of the American Philosophical Association* 1: 312–328.

———. 2016a. *Naturalism, Realism, and Normativity*. M. De Caro (ed.). Cambridge, MA: Harvard University Press.

———. 2016b. 'Realism'. *Philosophy and Social Criticism* 42: 117–131.

———. 2016c. 'The Development of Externalist Semantics', in Putnam 2016a.

———. forthcoming. *In Dialogue*. M. De Caro and D. Macarthur (eds.). Cambridge, MA: Harvard University Press.

Putnam, H., and Putnam, R. A. 2017. *Pragmatism as a Way of Life: The Lasting Legacy of William James and John Dewey*. Cambridge, MA: Harvard University Press.

Quine, W. V. 1957. The Scope and Language of Science', reprinted in his *Ways of Paradox and Other Essays*. New York: Random House.

Ramsey, W. 2016. 'Eliminative Materialism'. In E. N. Zalta (ed.) *The Stanford Encyclopaedia of Philosophy*. Available at: https://plato.stanford.edu/archives/win2016/entries/materialism-eliminative/

Reid, T. 1983. *Inquiries and Essays*. R. E. Beanblossom and K. Lehrer (eds.). Indianapolis, IN: Hackett.

Rosen, G. 2017. 'Abstract Objects'. In E. N. Zalta (ed.) *Stanford Encyclopaedia of Philosophy*. Available at: https://plato.stanford.edu/entries/abstract-objects/

Rosen, G., and Dorr, C. 2002. 'Composition as Fiction'. In R. Gale (ed.) *The Blackwell Companion to Metaphysics*. Oxford: Blackwell.

Rosenberg, A. 2014. 'Disenchanted Naturalism'. In B. Bashour and H. D. Muller (eds.) *Contemporary Philosophical Naturalism and Its Implications*. New York and London: Routledge.

Sellars, W. 1997. *Empiricism and the Philosophy of Mind: With an Introduction by Richard Rorty and a Study Guide by Robert Brandom*. R. Brandom (ed.). Cambridge, MA: Harvard University Press.

Smilansky, S. 2002. *Free Will and Illusion*. Oxford: Oxford University Press.

Stich, S. 1983. *From Folk Psychology to Cognitive Science: The Case Against Belief.* Cambridge, MA: MIT Press.

Strawson, G. 2010. *Freedom and Belief,* rev. ed. Oxford: Oxford University Press.

van Fraassen, B. 2003. 'McMullin's Appreciation of Realism Concerning the Sciences'. *Philosophy of Science* 70: 479–492.

———. 2007. 'From a View of Science to a New Empiricism'. In B. Monton (ed.) *Images of Empiricism: Essays on Science and Stances, with a Reply from Bas C. van Fraassen.* Oxford: Oxford University Press.

van Inwagen, P. 1990. *Material Beings.* Ithaca, NY: Cornell University Press.

Yablo, S. 2002. 'Abstract Objects: A Case Study'. *Noûs* 36 (Supplementary Volume 1): 220–240.

9 Peirce and Methodological Naturalism

Gabriele Gava

Was Charles S. Peirce a 'naturalist'? If one has a look at the literature on Peirce, it seems that there is not a straightforward answer to this question. Some interpreters argue that he clearly is a naturalist,[1] but perhaps of a very original sort. Some others instead claim that there are elements in his thought that are incompatible with a naturalist perspective.[2] Of course, it is not surprising that scholars disagree on how to interpret a particular philosopher. However, as far as the disagreement about Peirce's naturalism is concerned, this is partly dependent on the ambiguity of the term naturalism itself. For when interpreters ask whether Peirce is a naturalist or not, they often do not have the same question in mind. The question is alternatively taken to ask: whether Peirce regarded the method of the natural sciences as the only one able to deliver genuine knowledge;[3] whether Peirce envisioned the need for a 'first philosophy' in his system;[4] whether his rejection of psychologism was compatible with naturalism;[5] whether his account of mind and intentionality implies that these phenomena are part of or in continuity with nature;[6] whether he saw knowledge as a natural process;[7] whether he could be considered an anti-metaphysical philosopher.[8] The list could probably be much longer. For my purposes, it is sufficient to emphasise how a positive answer to one of these questions need not necessarily imply a positive answer to *all* of them. Therefore, when one interpreter is stressing that Peirce is a naturalist with respect to one of these questions, she is not necessarily contradicting another interpreter who says the opposite, but with respect to a *different* question in the list.

Furthermore, there is a second way in which the term naturalism is ambiguous. For when an interpreter identifies a position that is apparently at odds with a naturalist perspective, in some cases, two seemingly contrasting options are available. One could either argue that that position is evidence that a philosopher is *not* a naturalist, or that, given other commitments that are broadly in agreement with naturalism, that position is what makes her naturalism *original*. These different options are available because there is not only one 'naturalism' with which the philosopher to be interpreted can be compared. Therefore, it is not always straightforward what a 'naturalist' should say on a particular issue. Take the question concerning the existence of modal properties. While a more 'standard' naturalist would see these properties as derivative and try to reduce them to natural properties, a more 'liberal' naturalist could instead say that modal properties exist and are irreducible.[9] In interpreting the mature Peirce, who clearly is a realist about modal properties, we could either say that he is not a naturalist or that his naturalism is original, depending on whether we use the 'standard' or 'liberal' understanding of naturalism.

These two ambiguities in the term naturalism have consequences for how we should approach the question whether Peirce (or any other philosopher who did not clearly take a stand on the issue of naturalism, for that matter) is a naturalist or not. As far as the first ambiguity is concerned, asking *in general* whether Peirce is a naturalist seems unhelpful and potentially misleading. The risk is that the issue simply becomes that of putting a general label on Peirce, in a way that obfuscates his *specific* position on each of the questions I have listed above. As far as the second ambiguity is concerned, even when we focus on one or a set of the issues that the question might involve, it seems that the question cannot be taken as having a clear 'yes' or 'no' answer. Since the *same* position on a particular issue might be categorised as naturalist or anti-naturalist depending on the understanding of 'naturalism' that is at stake, the relevant task is *not* to pick *one* understanding of naturalism and say if Peirce is a naturalist according to that. Rather, the task is to clearly represent Peirce's position on one topic and place it within (or without) the spectrum of positions that can plausibly be described as naturalist. When this task is adequately achieved, one could leave to the reader to decide whether Peirce 'is' a naturalist or 'not' on a particular issue, depending on the kind of naturalism that she finds more appealing.

Given these considerations, in this chapter I will not try to determine whether Peirce is a naturalist in general. Rather, I will try to establish where Peirce's views should be placed with respect to different forms of *methodological* naturalism, broadly understood as the view that all genuine knowledge is at least informed by the application of the method of the empirical sciences. The chapter has the following structure. In Section I, I will present two different forms of methodological naturalism and show their respective implications for the human sciences in general, and for philosophy in particular. This analysis will constitute the background for determining where Peirce's views are to be placed on the issue of methodological naturalism. Section II will take into consideration Peirce's 'The Fixation of Belief' (1877), where Peirce seems to endorse a strong version of methodological naturalism. Section III will instead introduce the classification of the sciences Peirce developed between the end of the 19th and the beginning of the 20th century. As we will see, Peirce's later position is more difficult to categorise with respect to methodological naturalism and appears to advance views that are clearly *anti*-naturalist. Sections IV and V will then have a closer look at Peirce's account of the methods of ancient history and philosophy respectively. In particular, Section V will mitigate those aspects of Peirce's mature position that suggests a decidedly *anti*-naturalist view of philosophy.

I

What Methodological Naturalism Is

Methodological naturalism is a claim regarding what method of inquiry is able to deliver genuine knowledge of reality. In this section, I will identify two forms of methodological naturalism, which we can respectively call 'extreme' and 'moderate' methodological naturalism.[10] I will then consider the consequences of these two forms of naturalism for the human sciences, on the one hand, and for philosophy, on the other.

Both 'extreme' and 'moderate' forms of methodological naturalism comprise two claims: one *general* claim regarding the proper method for obtaining genuine knowledge of reality; and one *metaphilosophical* claim which makes explicit the implications of the general claim for our understanding of the tasks and nature of philosophy.[11] Let me start with 'extreme' methodological naturalism. In this case, the general claim can be put as follows: the experimental method of the natural sciences is the only genuine source of knowledge of reality. Since the experimental method is regarded as the only genuine source of knowledge, traditional methods used in philosophy, like introspection, the appeal to 'intuitions', *a priori* reasoning etc., are deemed to be inadequate for obtaining genuine knowledge. But, if philosophical knowledge is not obtained by using a privileged method, it seems that philosophy cannot claim any foundational role on the natural sciences. Given these considerations, the following metaphilosophical claim can be derived here: philosophy must apply the same empirical method of the natural sciences and cannot offer a foundation of those sciences. Quine's famous verdict that there should not be any 'first philosophy' exemplifies this approach well.[12]

'Moderate' methodological naturalism tempers the general claim of 'extreme' methodological naturalism in two respects. First, the 'moderate' form is more inclusive regarding what counts as 'proper scientific method'. Crucially, what counts is not *only* the experimental method of the natural sciences that provides the model of knowledge acquisition. Empirical methods used in the human sciences are seen as equally legitimate.[13] Second, the general claim will not be that it is *only* by following one of the empirical methods of the sciences that we can obtain genuine knowledge. The claim will be that we can only obtain genuine knowledge if our method of investigation is at least informed by the application of the methods of the empirical sciences. Of course, 'informed' might mean many things here. I take it to mean that genuine knowledge can in principle be obtained by methods (e.g. introspection, the appeal to 'intuitions', *a priori* reasoning, etc.) that are different from those of the empirical sciences, broadly construed. However, these methods cannot *ignore* the results of inquiries in the empirical sciences. Moreover, the results of the investigations carried out by non-scientific methods must be considered *defeasible* by empirical inquiries in the sciences, while, by contrast, the results of the empirical inquiries are not defeasible by non-scientific methods. We can then put the general claim of 'moderate' methodological naturalism as follows: genuine knowledge can be obtained either by following the empirical method of the sciences, broadly construed, or by using methods that differ from those of the empirical sciences but are informed by them in a way that makes results obtained through non-scientific methods always defeasible by results obtained by empirical scientific methods. As far as the metaphilosophical claim of 'moderate' methodological naturalism is concerned, it agrees with 'extreme' methodological naturalism that philosophy cannot have a foundational role on the sciences, but it concedes that philosophy can use methods that are different from the methods of the empirical sciences. Why is that? Even though philosophy enjoys a partial methodological independence from the sciences, it cannot be considered to be offering a foundation to them because its investigations are defeasible by discoveries obtained by following empirical scientific methods.

What are the consequences of 'extreme' and 'moderate' methodological naturalism for investigations in the human sciences? What are their consequences for how one views philosophy itself? We already know the answer to the second question. While 'extreme' methodological naturalism claims that philosophy must itself become an empirical science and, as such, must give up any foundational role on the other sciences, 'moderate' methodological naturalism only claims that philosophy cannot be foundational for the sciences; however, 'moderate' methodological naturalism grants philosophy some sort of methodological autonomy.

What about the consequences for the human sciences, such as history, anthropology, cultural theory, etc.? As we saw, 'extreme' methodological naturalism claims that genuine knowledge can only be obtained by following the experimental method of the *natural* sciences. Therefore, according to this view, human sciences can only be considered offering genuine knowledge if their investigations adhere to the experimental method of the natural sciences. Now, it is plausible to think that some human sciences—like psychology, sociology, or economics for example—*could* be made to fit this model of scientific explanation. By contrast, disciplines classically belonging to the humanities—like history for example—seems *prima facie* too far away from the procedures of experimental natural sciences to attempt a restructuring of their methods along the lines of those procedures. According to 'extreme' methodological naturalism, these disciplines can of course continue to do what they do. However, they cannot be regarded as providing *genuine knowledge* of reality. In contrast to 'extreme' methodological naturalism, 'moderate' methodological naturalism does not claim that the methods of the human sciences must adhere to the experimental method of the natural sciences in order to be considered capable of genuine knowledge. Empirical methods used in the human sciences that differ from the experimental method of the natural sciences are seen as equally capable of genuine knowledge.[14]

Where should we place Peirce with respect to what I have called 'extreme' and 'moderate' methodological naturalism? I will answer this question in the following sections.

II

The Fixation of Belief

'The Fixation of Belief' is certainly one of Peirce's most famous papers. It is often considered his clearest endorsement of methodological naturalism. First, 'Fixation' seems to imply an *implicit* endorsement of methodological naturalism. Peirce supports methodological considerations concerning what is the best method for fixing our beliefs by appealing to psychological concepts. As is well-known, inquiry is defined as the 'struggle' to attain belief or settle our opinion (W 3:247).[15] As the aim of inquiry, belief is a "calm and satisfactory state" (W 3:247) which indicates that we are prepared to act according to the 'habit' or disposition that the belief expresses. By contrast, doubt, which is the state Peirce opposes to belief, is an "uneasy and dissatisfied state from which we struggle to free ourselves" (W 3:247). Therefore, inquiry is the process through which we try to pass from a state of doubt to a state of belief. Given that Peirce sets the stage for answering the question regarding what the best method of inquiry is by appealing to such psychological concepts, it appears that he endorses a kind of methodological naturalism in epistemology. The question is what the best method to obtain a psychological state (belief) is, where this question is arguably best answered by means of empirical (psychological) research.

Second, 'Fixation' appears to contain an *explicit* argument for methodological naturalism, since it *concludes* that the 'method of science' is the best method for fixing belief. The *implicit* methodological naturalism of 'Fixation' is often discussed in the context of studies of Peirce's anti-psychologism in logic, because it appears to contradict or undermine such anti-psychologism.[16] Even though this issue is relevant for determining Peirce's approach toward methodological naturalism, I will avoid considering it here. I will instead focus on Peirce's *explicit* argument for methodological naturalism because that would comprise a *conscious* and *deliberate* endorsement of that view.

As is well-known, Peirce considers four methods of inquiry in 'Fixation': the method of tenacity, the method of authority, the *a priori* method, and the method of science. The method of tenacity proceeds by holding fast to the view one already has in the face of evidence to the contrary (W 3:249–50). By contrast, the method of authority consists in the imposition of a belief by an institution, like the church for example (W 3:250–1). The *a priori* method instead proceeds by assuming those propositions "which we find ourselves inclined to believe" (W 3:252). This in fact seems to be really close to what Peirce calls tenacity, since, like in tenacity, we end up believing what we are individually driven to accept. The difference is that while in tenacity there is a conscious resolve to ignore all evidence and stick to our view, in the *a priori* method there is at least the illusion of responsiveness to evidence, where this evidence is provided by what appears "agreeable to reason" (W 3:252). Finally, the method of science is the only one that starts from the hypothesis that there is an external reality. Assuming an external reality provides a measure of the adequacy of our beliefs that is independent from individual attitudes and preferences (W 3:253–4). The method thus consists in (empirically) testing our beliefs against this external measure.

Peirce discusses these four methods in the order I presented them. The order is not casual, since each method is described as superior in comparison to the one that precedes it but defective with respect to the method that comes next. Accordingly, the method of authority is superior to tenacity because it provides a ground for social agreement. Peirce describes the human being as an essentially social creature that tends to take seriously the beliefs of her fellows. Realising that other human beings have beliefs different from ours is enough to put into question the beliefs on which we were holding fast (W 3:250). The method of authority, being based on the imposition of a belief on a group of people provides a ground for social agreement, but this agreement is destined to fail, since it cannot prevent some individuals in a group to question at least some of the beliefs imposed on them (W 3:251–2). The *a priori* method is better than authority because it tries to find a ground for the agreement in reason and not in an institutional imposition. However, reason, understood as the *a priori* method characterises it, is inadequate to work as an intersubjectively valid measure of agreement, because what has been called reason is simply what *this* or *that* philosopher was more inclined to think: the intention was good, but the result disappointing (W 3:253). It is then only the method of science, with its hypothesis of an external reality, that can provide an intersubjectively valid measure of agreement (W 3:253–4), which, in turn, is the only one that introduces the distinction between 'right' and 'wrong' reasoning (W 3:254). This is the method one ought to use if "he wishes his opinion to coincide with the facts" (W 3:256).

According to the general claim of 'extreme' methodological naturalism, the experimental method of the natural sciences is the only genuine source of knowledge of reality. Given that Peirce claims that the method of science should be preferred because it is the only one that uses reality as a measure of intersubjective agreement, and given that this method is the only one that guarantees a coincidence of opinions and facts, it is plausible to submit that Peirce endorses a form of 'extreme' methodological naturalism in 'Fixation.' However, there are a couple of issues that should be kept in mind. First, Peirce does not argue that the method of tenacity, the method of authority and the *a priori* method are irrational. They can instead be rational and even *preferable* to the method of science with respect to some purposes (W 3:255–6). True, those purposes cannot be the coincidence of opinions and facts. If *that* is the purpose of inquiry, then the method of science must be privileged.

Second, Peirce's use of the concept of reality to justify the preference for the method of science is problematic. At the time Peirce wrote 'Fixation' he defined reality *through* belief. More specifically, he defined truth as the ultimate opinion or belief which is destined to be believed and reality as the object represented in that final opinion or belief (see for example 'How to Make Our Ideas Clear,' W 3:274). Given this account of reality, it seems illegitimate to say that the method of science is more adequate for obtaining intersubjective agreement because it can refer to reality as an external measure of this agreement. In this account, reality is both *constituted* by agreement and the *source* of agreement, where this seems inconsistent. The presence of this problem only implies that Peirce's 'extreme' methodological naturalism in 'Fixation' might not be supported by a valid argument. It does not constitute a problem for attributing such a view to him.

III

Peirce's Classification of the Sciences

If 'Fixation' appears to commit Peirce to a form of 'extreme' methodological naturalism, we get a completely different picture if we look at the classification of the sciences Peirce developed between the end of the nineteenth- and the beginning of the 20th century. The picture is completely different because Peirce seems to provide an account of philosophy that is at odds with methodological naturalism, both in its 'extreme' and 'moderate' forms. By contrast, a broadly naturalist picture regarding the human sciences (excluding philosophy) is still suggested by the fact that both natural and human sciences are regarded as different divisions of 'idioscopy,' whose particular task is that of providing positive knowledge about the word thanks to the "accumulation of new facts" (EP 2:259). While providing a description of the human sciences that put them under the same heading of the natural sciences suggests a form of methodological naturalism, it is not clear if the latter should be seen as 'extreme' or 'moderate.' It would be an 'extreme' form of methodological naturalism if the human sciences were characterised in a way similar to the natural sciences because they used the *same* experimental method of the latter. It would be a 'moderate' form of methodological naturalism if Peirce endorsed a form of pluralism regarding what counts as 'scientific method.' In this case, the human sciences could be considered sciences as good as the natural sciences, even though they did not used their exact same method.[17] In this section, I will reconstruct what Peirce says on philosophy and the human sciences in the context of the classification of the sciences he provides starting after 1900. The next two sections will instead give a closer look at Peirce's mature account of the method of ancient history and philosophy.

Peirce places philosophy and the human sciences within his classification of the 'sciences of discovery,' which are sometimes also called 'heuretical' or 'theoretical' sciences. Sciences of discovery are sciences that have only the attainment of knowledge as their purpose. These are opposed to the 'practical' sciences where the acquisition of knowledge is subordinated to different aims. Practical science "embraces whatever scientific inquiry is conducted with a view to some ulterior end" (EP 2:458; see also NEM 4:228). I will avoid going into the details of Peirce's classification of the sciences of discovery. For our purposes, it is sufficient to bear in mind its main headings, which can be represented as follows, according to Peirce's 1903 'A Syllabus of Certain Topics of Logic':

1. Mathematics;
2. Philosophy;
3. Idioscopy or special sciences;

    a. Physical sciences;
    b. Psychical or human sciences. (EP 2:258)

Let us start by focusing on philosophy. The important thing to notice is that philosophy is regarded as a discipline that does *not* belong to the special sciences and, in turn, comes *before* these sciences.[18] Now, Peirce submits that the order of the sciences in the classification represents relationships of logical dependences among them. This means that a science that comes before another in the classification should be seen as more fundamental from a logical point of view. The 'principles' identified in a more fundamental science are used in a less fundamental one, while the opposite is not possible. In Peirce's words: "one science depends upon another for fundamental principles, but does not furnish such principles to that other" (EP 2:258). Moreover, "[t]he general rule is that the broader science furnishes the narrower science with principles by which to interpret its observations while the narrower science furnishes the broader science with instances and suggestions" (NEM 4:227). Since philosophy is placed *before* idioscopy, Peirce's classification of the sciences commits him to the view that philosophy offers fundamental principles to the special sciences. In turn, this appears to imply that Peirce accepts the idea of a 'first philosophy' and, in so doing, defends a form of methodological *anti*-naturalism. This would be the case because both 'extreme' and 'moderate' methodological naturalism reject the idea of a 'first philosophy' which is foundational with respect to the sciences. Accordingly, Christopher Hookway has suggested that "the description of him [Peirce, *my note*] as sympathetic to naturalism is bound to sow confusion: in most of his writings, Peirce seeks for a 'first philosophy', a discipline which makes use of no materials derived from the sciences but rather offers an independent justification of science".[19]

What about the human sciences? First of all, since the natural sciences are placed before the human sciences, it means that they provide 'principles' that are fundamental in the latter. However, in this case the relation of logical dependence is not strict, and sometimes human sciences can offer principles to the natural sciences: "psychical sciences borrow principles continually from the physical sciences; the latter very little from the former" (EP 2:259).[20] Now, it is not easy to understand what Peirce has in mind when he speaks of 'principles' in the context of idioscopy. What it seems he means is the idea that a science, in approaching its object of study, takes for granted some general propositions regarding the nature of certain phenomena. This is suggested by what Peirce says regarding the dependence of psychology on biology, for example (EP 2:259). It is even more obscure in which sense, in certain cases, natural sciences can rely on 'principles' of the human sciences.

We can leave aside the question whether the relation of logical dependence within idioscopy goes only in one direction (from natural to human sciences) or is sometimes bidirectional (from natural to human sciences and *vice versa*). Granted, if it were only natural sciences that offered 'principles' to the human sciences, that would grant a more fundamental role to the natural sciences within idioscopy. Doing so would speak in favour of attributing to Peirce an 'extreme' version of methodological naturalism, according to which the human sciences can only be considered sciences (or part of idioscopy) because they incorporate fundamental truths discovered in the natural sciences. Notice, however, that the fact that the human sciences must rest on some truths discovered by the natural sciences does not imply that they must also apply the method of these disciplines. Peirce could coherently hold that, within idioscopy, the natural sciences are more fundamental, while granting that the human sciences have their own specific methods that differ from the experimental method of the natural sciences. This would lean toward a form of 'moderate' methodological naturalism regarding the human sciences.

A convergence between the methods of the natural sciences and the human sciences is suggested by the internal subdivisions of what Peirce calls 'physical' and 'psychical' sciences, respectively. For Peirce use the *same* categories to obtain a threefold subdivision of these sciences. Accordingly, we have *nomological, classificatory*, and *descriptive* physics, on the one hand, and *nomological, classificatory*, and *descriptive* psychics, on the other (EP 2:259). In 'A Syllabus of Certain Topics of Logic,' Peirce lists different subdivisions of physics as examples of nomological physics (EP 2:260), whereas the main sciences within classificatory physics are crystallography, chemistry and biology (EP 2:260). Descriptive physics instead contains 'geognosy' and astronomy (EP 2:261). As far as 'psychics' is concerned, its nomological part is identified with *general* psychology (EP 2:259, 261), whereas classificatory psychics comprises *special* psychology, linguistics, and ethnology. Finally, descriptive psychics is divided into history, biography and criticism (e.g. literary criticisms, art criticisms, etc.).

For my purposes, what is interesting is not where Peirce places the single sciences within idioscopy. Rather, what is more relevant is how Peirce justifies his use of the same categories to obtain an internal subdivision of 'physics' and 'psychics.' Let me quote a passage dating from 1911:

> In each wing alike we find three orders of sciences: first, the Nomological, or *Sciences of Laws*; second, the Classificatory, or *Sciences of Kinds*; third, the Descriptive and Explanatory, or *Sciences of Individual Objects*. There is more or less parallelism in the subdivisions of these Orders in the two wings. As under Nomological Physics, we find the general science of Dynamics and the special branches of Physics. . ., so under Nomological Psychics we find General Psychology as sharply distinguished from General Politics, Economics, the General Science of Law, etc., and these subdivided by similar causes to those of the subdivision of Physics.[21]
>
> (EP 2:458–9)

There are two important things in this passage. First, Peirce postulates a fundamental parallelism between the way in which the internal subdivisions of the natural and the human sciences are obtained. Second, this parallelism is due to the fact that nomological, classificatory and descriptive sciences in both the natural and the human sciences have respectively similar aims. Nomological sciences aim to identify general laws, whereas classificatory sciences focus on providing classifications of different kinds of objects. Finally descriptive sciences aim at obtaining knowledge of individual objects.[22] Now, it seems plausible to assume that since the sciences in each subdivision of the human sciences have aims that are similar to those of its correlate in the natural sciences and *vice versa*, the sciences in each associated subdivision proceed by using similar methods. That is to say, if the aim of nomological sciences is always to establish general laws, it is plausible to think that the methods we use for establishing those laws in nomological physics and nomological psychics should at least converge.

This analysis of Peirce's classification of the sciences provides a paradoxical picture regarding his perspective on methodological naturalism. On the one hand, he seems to defend a clearly *anti*-naturalist account of philosophy, since he appears to accept the idea of a 'first philosophy'. On the other, he leans toward a form of 'extreme' methodological naturalism regarding the human sciences (excluding philosophy), since he submits that the latter have aims (and presumably methods) that are similar to those of the natural sciences. In the following two sections, I will consider whether this diagnosis is correct by having a closer look at Peirce's account of the methods of ancient history and philosophy he developed around the same time of his classification.

IV

Peirce on the Method of Ancient History

In the previous section, I have argued that Peirce's classification of the sciences seems to commit him to a form of 'extreme' methodological naturalism regarding the human sciences (excluding philosophy), since he views the natural and the human sciences as having similar aims. This claim was only based on Peirce's general strategy to obtain an internal subdivision of the natural and the human sciences. In this section, my aim is to determine whether this general claim finds support in Peirce's account of the method of one discipline belonging to the human sciences, that is, ancient history. I will take into consideration a manuscript written in 1901: 'The Logic of Drawing History from Ancient Documents.' This text confirms, with some qualifications, our first impression, since it claims that ancient history had better abandon its traditional method of balancing likelihoods and adopt a procedure that is closer to the method of the natural sciences. After briefly presenting what the method of balancing likelihoods is, I will list Peirce's reservations concerning its suitability for inquiries in ancient history. Then, I will illustrate the method that Peirce proposes as an alternative.

Peirce chooses Hume's proposed method for evaluating testimonies regarding miraculous events as a representative formulation of the method of balancing likelihoods,[23] a method he considered widespread among historians and philologists. Peirce offers a mathematical formalisation of Hume's approach, which we can skip over here.[24] He describes the method as follows:

> When a reputable witness makes, or witnesses make, an assertion which experience renders highly improbable, or when there are other independent arguments in its favor, and independent argument *pro*

or *con* produces a certain impression upon the mind of the wise man, dependent for its quantity upon the frequency with which arguments of those kinds lead to the truth, and the algebraical sum of these impressions is the resultant impression that measures the wise man's state of opinion on the whole.

(CP 7.165)

Roughly put, the method of balancing likelihoods has it that, in evaluating if we should believe that a certain event has happened in ancient history, we should compute together the different probabilities that can be ascribed to the event on the basis of independent factors. For example, we can ascribe a probability to the event with respect to our given experiential knowledge. According to this knowledge, it would be really unlikely, say, that ten soldiers defeated an army of hundred people in a given historical battle. The fact that some witnesses reported the event might however increase its probability. Let us suppose that a reliable witness reported the event and we have no reason (except the improbability of the reported event) to think that she lied or that her belief is false (because, for example, she was hallucinating). This might increase the probability of the event. On the basis of a single testimony, the event would still be really unlikely, though. Let us now suppose that we have several apparently independent testimonies that report the same event, which would further increase its probability.

Peirce believes that the method of balancing likelihoods is for the most part misleading and inappropriate in ancient history. For my purposes, it is not necessary to go into the details of Peirce's argument against this method. What I am more interested in is the method Peirce proposes as a viable approach in ancient history. Still, let me briefly list Peirce's main reasons for the inappropriateness of the method. In general, Peirce maintains that the method of balancing likelihoods, when adequately formulated, can indeed sometimes lead to trustworthy conclusions in inquiries regarding ancient history. However, this can only happen if certain conditions are met. Since it is really difficult that these conditions are met in the evaluation of testimonies, the method is inadequate in the majority of cases. Let us now see why.

First, Peirce notices that in order for the method of balancing likelihoods to work, the different testimonies according to which the probability of the event is calculated must be independent from one another. However, "the different testimonies and other arguments are not commonly even in a rough sense independent, as the only rational basis for the method requires that they should be" (CP 7.176). Moreover, the testimonies would have to be not only independent from one another, but also independent from the previous probability of the event they reported. But even this condition is hardly met in testimonies, since in ancient history the fact that some events gets reported is dependent on the fact that they are *out of the ordinary*: "we may almost say that ancient history is simply the narrative of all the unlikely events that happened during the centuries it covers" (CP 7.176). Second, the theory makes an inadequate use of the notion of probability in the determination of the 'credibility' of a witness. The idea is that the 'credibility' of a witness affects the probability we can ascribe to an event given a testimony of that witness, where her credibility is determined according to the likelihood that what she reports is true. Peirce argues that in order to determine the credibility of a witness through probability one would have to determine the ratio of true statements in a sample of her statements. However, on the one hand, when we have to evaluate a witness, we have normally to do with a *single* statement and so no ratio can be determined. But even if this ratio would be available, there is no reason to suppose that the person in question will report the truth with the same frequency in future cases, since the circumstances in which she makes those future statements and the reasons why she does that might change so greatly that the previous ratio would become useless for the determination of her credibility (see CP 7.178).

Peirce adds two further objections that do not have to do with the extreme difficulty to meet the conditions for an adequate use of the method of balancing likelihoods. The third objection says that the method of balancing likelihoods is insufficient on its own to attain the aim of science, which is an *amplification* of our knowledge. The method of balancing likelihoods is a piece of the doctrine of chances, which, in turn, belongs to mathematical reasoning. According to Peirce, this reasoning is *necessary* reasoning and "consists of tracing out what is virtually asserted in the assumed premises" (CP 7.180). What does it mean that the theory of probability belongs to necessary reasoning? Take the case in which we calculate the probability of a complex event (for example: that a certain combination of numbers is drawn in a lotto game) on the basis of the probability of the single events that form that complex (in our example, the independent probabilities that each number in the combination is drawn from the relevant urn). The result of this calculation can be considered a piece of deductive reasoning for Peirce, since it follows necessarily from the independent probabilities of the single events that form that complex.

But, Peirce argues, mathematical reasoning of this sort cannot be used to "amplify our positive knowledge; although it may render our understanding of our own assumptions more perfect" (CP 7.180). Therefore, the method of balancing likelihoods cannot, by itself, help us in attaining the aim of science, which is to amplify knowledge. Finally, the fourth objection has it that the method of balancing likelihoods has *in fact* been proved inadequate by many archaeological findings. These findings have often totally disproved the theories obtained using the method of balancing likelihoods (see CP 7.182).

These objections are sufficient to show that a different approach in ancient history is needed. What does Peirce propose as an alternative? Briefly put, Peirce suggests that ancient history should follow the method that is typical of the natural sciences and that he considers appropriate for *all* the special sciences (natural and human alike). How should this method be characterised? Peirce first submits that the demand for scientific explanation is caused by the occurrence of a surprising phenomenon:

> the only case in which this method of investigation, namely, by the study of how an explanation can further the purpose of science, leads to the conclusion that an explanation is positively called for, is the case in which a phenomenon presents itself which, without some special explanation, there would be reason to expect would *not* present itself.
>
> (CP 7.194)

Accordingly, the purpose of a scientific explanation is to render the surprising phenomenon 'unsurprising': "what an explanation of a phenomenon does is to supply a proposition which, if it had been known to be true before the phenomenon presented itself, would have rendered that phenomenon predictable" (CP 7.192). Formulating a proposition that would render a surprising phenomenon predictable is however the same as formulating a *hypothesis*. Formulating hypotheses is the task of the inference Peirce calls 'abduction':

> Accepting the conclusion that an explanation is needed when facts contrary to what we should expect emerge, it follows that the explanation must be such a proposition as would lead to the prediction of the observed facts. . . . A hypothesis then, has to be adopted, which is likely in itself, and renders the facts likely. This step of adopting a hypothesis as being suggested by the facts, is what I call *abduction*.
>
> (CP 7.202)

Abduction is the first step for achieving a scientific explanation, but it is not certainly sufficient for that. Abduction provides a hypothesis that would make a certain given fact predictable. The hypothesis however needs to be tested. Two steps are needed for testing. First, we must derive experimental consequences of the hypothesis by *deduction* (see CP 7.203). Second, we must perform the actual testing and see if those consequences obtain or not. We do that by *induction* (see CP 7.206).[25]

Peirce proposes this method of forming hypotheses and putting them to the test as the appropriate method for ancient history. Now, it is perhaps easy to understand what it means to say that historians should develop hypotheses that make a certain testimony 'unsurprising.' But what does it mean to say that historians should draw predictions on the basis of their hypotheses and tests those hypotheses?

> A hypothesis having been adopted on probation, the process of test-ing it will consist, not in examining the facts, in order to see how well they accord with the hypothesis, but on the contrary in examining such of the probable consequences of the hypothesis as would be capable of direct verification, especially those consequences which would be very unlikely or surprising in case the hypothesis were not true. It is not easy to enumerate the different kinds of consequences; but among them may be, that the hypothesis would render the pre-sent existence of a monument probable, or would result in giving a known monument a certain character; that if it were true, certain ancient documents ought to contain some allusion to it; that if it is misstated by some authority not considered in the selection of the hypothesis, that misstatement would be likely to be of a certain kind; that if the hypothesis is true, and an assertion or allusion found in an ancient work is to be explained by the author's knowing it to be true, he must have had certain other knowledge, etc.
>
> (CP 7.231)

According to Peirce, the predictions that ancient history can draw con-cerns further historical evidence that is likely to be found if a certain hypothesis regarding an historical event is true.

The need of predictions is probably the most striking feature of the method Peirce proposes for ancient history, but it is not the only diver-gence from the method of balancing likelihoods. Two additional dif-ferences are contained in first two 'rules' that Peirce derives from the application of his scientific approach to history.[26] First, when we treat a testimony as untrustworthy, it is not sufficient to exclude it (say, on the basis of the unlikeliness of its truth). We must instead offer an *explanation* of the reason why that false testimony has been given. This follows from Peirce's claim that science must offer explanations of surprising events. Saying that a testimony must be disregarded because likely false does not offer any explanation of the fact that that testi-mony has been given. Second, we must start from the assumption that *all* the testimonies we have on a given event are true. Peirce justifies this approach by first saying that, in producing hypotheses, we must select those that "repose[] upon a deep and primary instinct" (CP 7.226). One such instinct is "the instinct to believe testimony" (CP 7.226). The main point seems however to be that, in excluding testimonies because of their supposed untrustworthiness, we exclude possibly important materials for the formulation of our hypotheses, and we do that in a science in which we rely almost exclusively on testimonies as evidence (see CP 7.226).

To conclude, Peirce defends a form of 'extreme' methodological naturalism in ancient history, since he argues that ancient history should proceed by using the same method of the natural sciences. In particular, it should formulate hypotheses that explain the facts, it should draw predictions on the basis of those hypotheses, and it should test those predictions. One might say that it is inadequate to call this approach to ancient history a form of 'extreme' methodological naturalism, since it is based on a very broad characterisation of the scientific method which, say, does not require a quantitative approach. This might be true, but, as I wrote in the introductory section, I am not interested in putting a label on Peirce. Moreover, the fact that he thinks that all the special sciences effectively share the same method seems to justify calling him an 'extreme' methodological naturalist regarding the human sciences. Let me now turn to my analysis of Peirce's account of the method of philosophy.

V

Peirce and the Method of Philosophy

As we saw in Section III, the position that Peirce gives to philosophy in his classification of the sciences suggests that he defends an *anti*-naturalist account of its method and aims. More specifically, it seems that he defends a form of 'first philosophy', which is foundational with respect to the special sciences. In this section, I will first consider how Peirce describes the method of philosophy in *general* (there are of course important differences if one takes into account the main subdivisions of philosophy: phenomenology, the normative sciences and metaphysics). This description seems in fact to confirm the worry that Peirce is an *anti*-naturalist regarding the method of philosophy. I will then argue that this initial impression can be challenged and that Peirce can be viewed as defending a 'moderate' form of methodological naturalism.

Let us see what Peirce has to say on the method of philosophy and its relationship with the special sciences. In the Harvard Lectures of 1903, he addresses the issue as follows:

> Philosophy . . . is distinguished from all the special theoretical sciences, whether they belong to the great Physical wing or to the great Psychical wing of special science, that is, whether they be inquiries into dynamics, physics, chemistry, physiology, anatomy, astronomy, geology, etc., or whether they be inquiries into psychology, anthropology, linguistics, history, etc.—Philosophy, I say, is distinguished from all of these by the circumstance that it does not undertake to make any special observations or to obtain any perceptions of a novel description. Microscopes and telescopes, voyages and exhumations, clairvoyants and witnesses of exceptional experience are substantially superfluous

for the purposes of philosophy. It contents itself with a more attentive scrutiny and comparison of the facts of everyday life, such as present themselves to every adult and sane person, and for the most part in every day and hour of his waking life. The reason why a natural classification so draws a line between Philosophy, as *cenóscopy* (κοινοσκοπία) and Special Sciences, as idioscopy (ἰδιοσκοπία) . . . is that a very widely different bent of genius is required for the analytical work of philosophy and for the observational work of the special science.

(EP2:146)

Peirce here clearly states that philosophy has a method that is essentially different from the method of the special sciences, natural and human alike. While the special sciences rest on *special* observations, philosophy works with a common-sense understanding of the world that can be considered available to and shared by any rational human being.[27] This description of philosophy certainly excludes that Peirce is an 'extreme' methodological naturalist regarding philosophy. But, Peirce seems to also reject 'moderate' methodological naturalism. The latter requires that philosophy, even if it has a different method in comparison with the special sciences, must at least be informed by the special observations of the latter. Peirce seems to deny *exactly* this point. Results obtained in the special sciences by using their experimental method are considered *irrelevant* for philosophical analyses of our common-sense understanding of the world. In another Harvard Lecture, Peirce accordingly stresses that philosophy

does not gather new facts, because *it does not need them* [my emphasis], and also because new general facts cannot be firmly established without the assumption of a metaphysical doctrine; and this, in turn, requires the cooperation of every department of philosophy; so that such new facts, however striking they may be, afford weaker support to philosophy by far than that *common experience* which nobody doubts or can doubt, and which nobody ever even *pretended* to doubt except as a consequence of belief in that experience so entire and perfect that it failed to be conscious of itself.

(EP 2:196)

Peirce makes two important claims here. First, he says that philosophy does not need the kind of facts that are discovered by the special sciences. This suggests that the method and discoveries of the special sciences are *irrelevant* for what philosophy does. Second, even in those cases in which facts gathered by the special sciences have some minimal relevance for philosophical investigation, this is ultimately way less important than the kind of 'evidence' we get from common-sense. As a consequence, philosophy does not need to be informed by experimental investigations in the special sciences as 'moderate' methodological naturalism would still require.

To sum up, there are two main reasons to regard Peirce's position on the method of philosophy after 1900 as *anti*-naturalist. On the one hand, as we saw in Section III, he claims that philosophy must come before the special sciences in the classification because it furnishes principles to these sciences. This appears to commit him to a form of 'first philosophy'. On the other, he contends that facts obtained through the experimental investigations of the special sciences are irrelevant for philosophy. This seems to commit him to the view that philosophy does not need to be informed by the experimental investigations of the special sciences.

I think we can resist attributing to Peirce a form of *anti*-naturalism regarding the method of philosophy. As far as the first point is concerned, the fact that philosophy comes before the special sciences in the classification does not necessarily mean that it is foundational with respect to those sciences. It might simply mean that philosophical propositions have a higher level of abstraction. For example, consider what Peirce says on the law of gravitation and the relationship between general physics and astronomy:

> In much the same way, astronomy borrows from general physics the law of gravitation and applies it to explaining the apparent motions of the planets. It is true that the law of gravitation happens to have been proved by means of astronomical observations, and that there existed no other objects but the celestial bodies which would have been able to furnish so satisfactory of proof of the exactitude of the law of gravitation.
>
> (HP 2:806)

The law of gravitation belongs to general physics. It can be considered a 'principle' on which astronomical research rests. This however does not mean that the formulation of the law was obtained independently of astronomical observation or that astronomical observation cannot be used to defeat a wrong formulation of the law in general physics. Therefore, the fact that general physics comes before astronomy in the classification does not mean that physics is 'foundational' with respect to astronomy.[28] It simply means that its principles are more abstract and are presupposed in astronomical inquiries. The latter can however both contribute to the formulation of principles in general physics and defeat principles that belong to the latter science. There is nothing preventing us to see the precedence of philosophy over the special sciences in the classification in a similar way.

Peirce's claim that philosophy relies on common sense and is not affected by the investigations of the special sciences is more challenging, since it suggests that philosophy can ignore discoveries in the special sciences and, consequently, is not defeasible by such discoveries. But, even here, I think Peirce's contention need not be read in this way. When Peirce later elaborates his 'critical commonsensism' and distinguishes it from the Scottish tradition of common-sense, he emphasises that common-sense beliefs are revisable and evolve in history (see EP 2:349). However, what is more important for our purposes is that discoveries in the special sciences can have an effect on the evolution of common-sense beliefs:

> [A] modern recognition of evolution must distinguish the Critical Common-sensist from the old school. Modern science, with its microscopes and telescopes, with its chemistry and electricity, and with its entirely new appliances of life, has put us into quite another world; almost as much so as if it had transported our race to another planet. Some of the old beliefs have no application except in extended senses, and in such extended senses they are sometimes dubitable and subject to just criticism. It is above all the normative sciences, esthetics, ethics, and logic, that men are in dire need of having severely criticized, in their relation to the new world created by science.
>
> (CP 5.513; see also EP 2:349)

Peirce's point here is that it is a task of philosophy, and of the normative sciences in particular, to inquire whether discoveries in the sciences have consequences for our common-sense beliefs. The idea might be that discovery in the sciences naturally affects our common-sense beliefs. However, the process through which common-sense beliefs evolve on the basis of those discoveries can take really long. Therefore, even though philosophy rests on our common-sense beliefs, since we are aware of the historical nature of those believes, philosophy must put them under critical scrutiny to anticipate if it is likely that those believes will evolve, where the influence of discoveries in the special sciences is *one* way in which common-sense beliefs are subject to changes.

If this is true, philosophical inquiries must indeed be informed and are defeasible by inquiries in the special sciences. This does not mean that philosophy loses its fundamental focus on common sense, since its use of discoveries in the special sciences is essentially connected to foreseeable changes in our common-sense beliefs on the basis of those discoveries. Given what I have written on the position of philosophy within Peirce's classification and on the use in philosophy of discoveries in the special sciences, we can resist attributing to Peirce a form of methodological *anti*-naturalism in philosophy and see him as defending a form of 'moderate' methodological naturalism instead.

VI

Conclusion

In this chapter, I have tried to determine where we should place Peirce with respect to the issue of methodological naturalism. I have distinguished a 'moderate' and an 'extreme' form of methodological naturalism. I have then argued that while Peirce in 1877 defends a form of 'extreme' methodological naturalism, his position gets more complex between the end of the nineteenth- and the beginning of the twentieth-century. He seems to still endorse a form of 'extreme' methodological naturalism regarding the human sciences (excluding philosophy), while he appears to be committed to an *anti*-naturalist view concerning the method of philosophy. Upon further scrutiny, Peirce's mature position regarding the human sciences (excluding philosophy) was confirmed to be a form of 'extreme' methodological naturalism. By contrast, I have argued that Peirce's mature view concerning the method of philosophy is consistent with a 'moderate' form of methodological naturalism.

Notes

1. See, for example, Almeder (1980), Short (2007), Forster (2017).
2. See Goudge (1947), Hookway (1985: 3).
3. See Ketchum (1996).
4. See Hookway (1985: 3), Forster (2017).
5. See Colapietro (2003), Hookway (2012: especially Ch. 4); Chevalier (2014).
6. See Short (2007: particularly 174–175).
7. See Wilson (2016: especially 22).
8. See Goudge (1947).
9. On this issue, see De Caro and Voltolini (2010: 79–82).
10. For similar labels, see Ye (2017). See also De Caro and Macarthur (2004b), De Caro and Macarthur (2010b) for the distinction between scientific and liberal naturalism.
11. Papineau (2016) only emphasises the metaphilosophical aspect of methodological naturalism, whereas De Caro and Macarthur (2004b, 2010b), and Ye (2017) recognise both aspects.
12. Quine 1981: 21, 72.
13. What Macarthur (2010) calls 'broad scientific naturalism' seems to incorporate this first characteristic of what I characterise here as 'moderate' methodological naturalism.
14. See Macarthur (2010).
15. In citing Peirce, I will use the following abbreviations: CP volume.paragraph = Peirce 1931–58; EP volume:page = Peirce 1992–1998; HP volume:page = Peirce 1985; NEM volume:page = Peirce 1976; W volume:page = Peirce 1982.
16. See Colapietro (2003); Hookway (2012, Ch. 4); Chevalier (2014), Cristalli (2017).
17. See Macarthur (2010).
18. See also Forster (2017).
19. Hookway (1985: 3).
20. This is what Peirce claims in 1903. In 1902, however, he placed the human sciences *before* the natural sciences in the classification, which suggests that it is the latter that depend on principles of the former. See NEM 4:17.
21. Notice that, in this classification, nomological psychics contains much more than the 1903 classification, where nomological psychics was identified with general psychology.
22. It is interesting to note here that Peirce's account of the natural and the human sciences is completely different from the one we find in authors like Windelband (1915) and Rickert (1926), who both respectively argued that

the natural sciences and the human sciences could be distinguished in the following manner: the natural sciences aim at formulating general laws, while the human sciences focus on individual events. If Peirce were right, we would find sciences with the former aim and sciences with the latter aim within both the natural and the human sciences.

23. See 'Of Miracles', Section X of Hume (1975).
24. However, see Merrill (1991), Legg (2001), and Jantzen (2009) for useful reconstructions.
25. Peirce then discusses different types of deductions and inductions, as well as economical factors that should guide the choice of hypotheses to put to the test (CP 7.204–223).
26. In addition, Peirce lists other four rules that result from the application of his account of inquiry to the special case of investigations regarding ancient history (see CP 7.227–30). For our purposes, we can avoid discussing these.
27. I will here avoid considering whether Peirce accepts some form of *a priori* reasoning in philosophy. His description of the method of philosophy after 1900 sounds anti-naturalist even if one disregards this issue. For contrasting reading of Peirce on the issue of the *a priori* see Gava (2011a, 2011b, 2011c, 2014, Ch. 5), on the one hand, and Wilson (2015), on the other.
28. For a similar point, see G. Gava (2014: 21–25).

References

Almeder, R. 1980. *The Philosophy of Charles S. Peirce: A Critical Introduction*. Oxford: Blackwell.

Chevalier, J-M. 2014. 'Why Ought We to Be Logical? Peirce's Naturalism on Norms and Rational Requirements'. In J. Dutant, D. Fassio and A. Meyla (eds.) *Liber Amicorum Pascal Engel*. Geneva: Université de Genève.

Colapietro, V. 2003. 'The Space of Sings: C. S. Peirce's Critique of Psychologism'. In D. Jacquette (ed.) *Philosophy, Psychology, and Psychologism*. Boston, MA: Kluwer.

Cristalli, C. 2017. 'Experimental Psychology and the Practice of Logic: Charles S. Peirce and the Charge of Psychologism, 1869–1885'. *European Journal of Pragmatism and American Philosophy 9*. Available at: https://journals.openedition.org/ejpap/1006

De Caro, M., and Macarthur, D. (eds.). 2004a. *Naturalism in Question*. Cambridge, MA: Harvard University Press.

———. 2004b. 'Introduction: The Nature of Naturalism'. In M. De Caro and D. Macarthur 2004a.

———. (eds.). 2010a. *Naturalism and Normativity*. New York: Columbia University Press.

———. 2010b. 'Introduction: Science, Naturalism, and the Problem of Normativity'. In M. De Caro and D. Macarthur 2010a.

De Caro, M., and Voltolini, A. 2010. 'Is Liberal Naturalism Possible?' in M. De Caro and D. Macarthur 2010a.

Forster, M. 2017. 'First Philosophy Naturalised: Peirce's Place in the Analytic Tradition'. *Cognition* 18: 33–44.

Gava, G. 2011a. 'Does Peirce Reject Transcendental Philosophy?' *Archiv für Geschichte der Philosophie* 93: 195–221.

———. 2011b. 'Peirce's "Prescision" as a Transcendental Method'. *International Journal of Philosophical Studies* 19: 231–253.

————. 2011c. 'Can Transcendental Philosophy Endorse Fallibilism?' *Contemporary Pragmatism* 8: 133–151.

————. 2014. *Peirce's Account of Purposefulness: A Kantian Perspective*. London: Routledge.

Goudge, T. 1947. 'The Conflict of Naturalism and Transcendentalism in Peirce'. *The Journal of Philosophy* 44: 365–375.

Hookway, C. 1985. *Peirce*. London: Routledge and Kegan Paul.

————. 2012. *The Pragmatic Maxim: Essays on Peirce and Pragmatism*. Oxford: Oxford University Press.

Hume, D. 1975. 'An Enquiry Concerning Human Understanding'. In L. A. Selby-Bigge (ed.) and P. H. Nidditch (rev.) *Enquiries Concerning Human Understanding and Concerning the Principles of Morals*, 3rd ed. Oxford: Clarendon Press.

Jantzen, B. 2009. 'Peirce on the Method of Balancing "Likelihoods"'. *Transactions of the Charles S. Peirce Society* 45: 668–688.

Ketchum, R. 1996. 'Peirce and Naturalism'. *Philosophia Scientiae* 1: 121–132.

Legg, C. 2001. 'Naturalism and Wonder: Peirce on the Logic of Hume's Argument Against Miracles'. *Philosophia* 28: 297–318.

Macarthur, D. 2010. 'Taking the Human Sciences Seriously', in M. De Caro and D. Macarthur 2010a.

Merrill, K. 1991. 'Hume's "of Miracles", Peirce, and the Balancing of Likelihoods'. *Journal of the History of Philosophy* 29: 85–113.

Papineau, D. 2015. 'Naturalism'. In E. N. Zalta (ed.) *The Stanford Encyclopedia of Philosophy*, Winter 2015 ed. Available at: https://plato.stanford.edu/archives/win2016/entries/naturalism/

Peirce, C. S. 1931–1958. *Collected Papers of Charles Sanders Peirce*. C. Hartshorne and P. Weiss (eds.), vols. 1–6 and A. Burks (ed.), vols. 7–8. Cambridge, MA: Harvard University Press.

————. 1976. *The New Elements of Mathematics*. C. Eisele (ed.), 4 vols. The Hague: Mouton.

————. 1982. *Writings of Charles S. Peirce: A Chronological Edition*. The Peirce Edition Project (ed.), 7 vols. Bloomington, IN: Indiana University Press.

————. 1985. *Historical Perspectives on Peirce's Logic of Science: A History of Science*. C. Eisele (ed.), 2 vols. The Hague: De Gruyter.

————. 1992–1998. *The Essential Peirce*. The Peirce Edition Project (ed.), 2 vols. Bloomington, IN: Indiana University Press.

Quine, W. V. 1981. *Theories and Things*. Cambridge, MA: Harvard University Press.

Rickert, H. 1926. *Kulturwissenschaft und Naturwissenschaft*, 6th and 7th expanded ed. Tübingen: Mohr Siebeck.

Short, T. 2007. *Peirce's Theory of Signs*. Cambridge: Cambridge University Press.

Wilson, A. 2015. 'Peirce and the *A Priori*'. *Transactions of the Charles S. Peirce Society* 51: 201–224.

————. 2016. *Peirce's Empiricism: Its Roots and Its Originality*. Lanham, MD: Lexington Books.

Windelband, W. 1915. *Geschichte und Naturwissenschaft*, in *Präludien. Aufsätze und Reden zur Philosophie und ihrer Geschichte*, vol. 2, 5th expanded ed. Tübingen: Mohr Siebeck.

Ye, F. 2017. 'On Extreme Versus Moderate Methodological Naturalism'. *Philosophia* 45: 371–385.

10 Picturing

Naturalism and the Design of a More Ideal Truth

Willem A. deVries

Naturalism (of some kind) and pragmatism seem likely companions. That one can be a naturalist while retaining important insights from idealism as well is a central claim of Wilfrid Sellars's philosophy. Working this idea out, however, led Sellars into a complex thicket that has not received sufficient attention. In particular, I will argue, Sellars's notion of *picturing*, often complained about,[1] although not often discussed, plays a crucial role in his attempt to find a stable middle ground between crass naturalism[2] and the sophisticated idealism that flourished in the Germanic states between 1781 and 1831.

I do not want to claim that Sellars was in any important sense an idealist. Realism—one of the contrasts that give sense to the notion of idealism—is one of Sellars's fundamental commitments. He describes himself as "always a realist" (NAO, Introduction, ¶3: 9).[3] He is a bit less committed concerning materialism—another of the contrasts that give sense to the notion of idealism. He is clear that, as his philosophy was maturing, "What was needed was a new, nonreductive materialism" (NAO, Introduction, ¶7: 10). But, so many different doctrines have paraded themselves under the banner of materialism that Sellars is wary of calling himself a materialist—a title his father claimed without hesitation. Sellars prefers to call himself a naturalist, even though he recognizes that that term was almost as beset with vagueness, ambiguity, and problematic fellow-travellers as 'materialist'.

However, like his great idealist predecessor Hegel, Sellars believed that every significant philosopher captured some important part of the truth—this is, perhaps, the most significant way in which Sellars differs from most other analytic philosophers of the 20th century. Kant and Hegel, greats even among the great, had insights that all subsequent philosophy ought to preserve, even if their idealisms were, in the end, "radically false" (SM, V, ¶78: 143). Preserving those insights in a nonreductive materialistic naturalism, however, requires a sophisticated and innovative approach.

The plan for this chapter is as follows: first, I will discuss Sellars's conception of naturalism and try to distinguish it from what I have called 'crass naturalism'. In the second section, I will try to isolate those insights of the German Idealists that Sellars thought needed to be permanent parts of the philosophical tradition. In Section III, the topic will be why Sellars thought he needed to introduce a special notion of a picturing relation that holds between (some) intentional representings and the items they represent. In Section IV, I will explore in more detail how Sellars transposed the idealistic analysis of representation and conceptuality into a naturalistic key, leaving both need and room for a further provision: picturing. Then, I suggest we interpret picturing as a design-level provision (à la Dennett) that provides a necessary condition for the existence of properly intentional-level activity.

I

What Is Naturalism?

Sellars counts himself a naturalist, but as I have already remarked, 'naturalism' is a rather protean term: what does Sellars mean by it? Unfortunately, he does not give us a great deal to go on. In the book with 'Naturalism' in the title, the term (including relatives) is used only 11 times, in none of which Sellars bothers to explain what he means by it.

Anglo-American philosophers often distinguish two forms of naturalism: methodological and ontological/metaphysical.[4] Those who think of naturalism as *primarily* a methodological doctrine often identify philosophic methodology with the methodology of natural science. Natural science—particularly physics—becomes the paradigmatic, if not the sole exemplar of knowledge. Those who think of naturalism, in contrast, as *primarily* an ontological doctrine identify the natural with the sensible world, the material world, or at least the spatio-temporal world, and insist that there is no other realm (a 'supersensible', immaterial, or transcendent realm) to our world beyond the natural.[5]

One can triangulate Sellars's own conception of naturalism by noting three important associations to be found in his talk of naturalism. The first is an association between naturalism and empiricism. Despite empiricism's frequent fraternisation with phenomenalism, which identifies physical objects with actual and possible representations, and which puts our normal sense of nature at a remove that can be hard to overcome, empiricists have been steadier in their rejection of the supersensible and the transcendent than rationalists. Importantly, empiricists have also emphasised the causal connections that tie empirical knowledge to empirical objects, even while they have probed profoundly the nature and justification of inductive methods. This association with empiricism, with empiricism's distrust of ontology generally, favours the methodological form of naturalism.

Second, Sellars also systematically associates naturalism with materialism, as we saw previously in discussing the introduction to *Naturalism and Ontology*. Since quantum mechanics has made matter seem much less material than it used to be, 'materialism' is no longer the popular name for the doctrine that takes the world as described by physics to be ontologically fundamental; the slightly less-specific 'physicalism' seems to have taken its place. In Sellars's own view, 'materialism' does not quite hit the right substantive note, not just because he is "surprised by some of the views of the new, new Materialists" (NAO Intro, §7), but also because he thinks the ultimate description of the physical world will be one that employs a process ontology in which *matter* is not fundamental. Sellarsian naturalism, therefore, has an ontological aspect in addition to the methodological, and this is important for Sellars, because he always considered himself a scientific realist. Proper methodology is the way to understanding the true nature of things.

But, it is the third association that provides the spin that makes Sellarsian naturalism fairly distinctive. Sellars was always very interested in the argument between *ethical* naturalism and non-naturalism. He writes,

> 2.3 Traditional moral philosophers, however, Naturalists and Non-naturalists alike, have tended to assume that Ought can be causally reducible to Is only if Ought is logically reducible to Is.
>
> 2.31 Thus, Ethical Naturalists have tended to assume that it can only be possible (which they think it to be) to explain the history of moral agents without making ethical assertions in characteristically ethical language, on condition that Ought is logically reducible to Is.
>
> 2.32 While Ethical Non-naturalists have tended to assume that it is reasonable to deny (as they do) that Ought is logically reducible to Is, only if one is prepared to deny that Ought is causally reducible to Is. This latter, of course, they are prepared to do, since they characteristically insist that the existence of moral concepts and beliefs in the human mind cannot be accounted for in purely descriptive terms. Human thinking on ethical matters is, as they see it, ultimately grounded in and controlled by objective values and obligations.
>
> 2.33 The moral philosophy we have been adumbrating combines a thesis characteristic of Ethical Naturalism with a thesis characteristic of Ethical Nonnaturalism: the causal reducibility of Ought with the logical irreducibility of Ought. Is it a form of Naturalism? Of Non-naturalism?
>
> 2.331 Would we not dodge these alternatives, and point out that the value of a system of classification is threatened when one of its presuppositions is abandoned? . . .
>
> [O]ur rejection of Ethical Naturalism did not entail an acceptance of Ethical Non-naturalism—for we saw that both are complex theses involving a logical claim and a causal claim. We rejected the logical claim of Ethical Naturalism, but accepted its causal claim; we rejected the causal claim of Non-naturalism, but accepted its logical claim.

3.3221 The common presupposition of Naturalist and Non-naturalist is causal reducibility implies logical reducibility. We rejected this presupposition.

(MMB: 85–6, 87)

It is this belief that the normative is causally reducible but not logically reducible to the descriptive vocabulary of the physical that James O'Shea has made much of in his writings on Sellars's naturalism with a normative turn.

What does it mean to say that normative terms are causally reducible but not logically reducible? My interpretation of this claim is that (i) there is a physicalistic description of any situation in which a norm is being obeyed or realised; (ii) such a physicalistic description contains no normative terminology; and (iii) that description—as far as the strict physical chronology of the situation is concerned—*leaves nothing out*. The description is not "gappy" at the level of the fundamental ontology of the natural world. The physical description of the event is complete unto the day, in the sense that no empirically well-established causal principles will be violated. But, the norm-involving description of the situation is logically irreducible to the physical: the physical description of any such norm-involving situation does not *entail* the norm-involving description; they are certainly not synonymous. The norm-involving description describes something that cannot be described in the purely physical language, despite the fact that the physical description is complete on its own terms.

The significance of this for us is that Sellarsian naturalism places ontological priority on the physical, but it does not demand that the physical, descriptive story is the *whole* story. In fact, the rest of Sellars's philosophy requires that the physical, descriptive story *cannot be* the whole story. This is where Sellars's naturalism importantly departs from 'crass' naturalism.

This emerges most clearly in Sellars's lengthy 1957 essay 'Counterfactuals, Dispositions, and the Causal Modalities'. Here is what Sellars tells us there:

79. Now, once it is granted—and the point cannot be argued here—that empiricism in moral philosophy is compatible with the recognition that 'ought' has as distinguished a role in discourse as descriptive and logical terms, in particular that we *reason* rather than "reason" concerning *ought*, and once the tautology 'The world is described by descriptive concepts' is freed from the idea that the business of all nonlogical concepts is to describe, the way is clear to an *ungrudging* recognition that many expressions which empiricists have relegated to second-class citizenship in discourse, are not *inferior*, just *different*.

Clearly, to use the term 'ought' is to prescribe rather than describe. The naturalistic "thesis" that the world, including the verbal behaviour of those who use the term 'ought'—and the mental states involving the concept to which this word gives expression—can, "in principle," be described without using the term 'ought' or any other prescriptive expression, is a logical point about what is to count as a description *in principle* of the world. For, whereas in ordinary discourse to state what something *is*, to describe something as Φ (e.g. a person as a criminal) does not preclude the possibility that an "unpacking" of the description would involve the use of the term 'ought' or some other prescriptive expression, naturalism presents us with the ideal of a *pure* description of the world (in particular of human behaviour), a description which simply says what things *are*, and never, in any respect, what they *ought* or *ought not* to be; and it is clear (as a matter of simple logic) that neither 'ought' nor any other prescriptive expression *could be used* (as opposed to *mentioned*) in such a description.

80. An essentially similar point can be made about modal expressions. To make first hand use of these expressions is to be about the business of *explaining* a state of affairs, or *justifying* an assertion. Thus, even if to state that p entails q is, in a legitimate sense, to state that something is the case, the primary use of 'p entails q' is not to state that something is the case, but to explain *why* q, or justify the assertion that q. The idea that the world can, in principle, be so described that the description contains no modal expression is of a piece with the idea that the world can, in principle, be so described that the description contains no prescriptive expression. For what is being called to mind is the ideal of a statement of "everything that is the case" which, however, serves, *through and through*, *only* the purpose of stating what is the case. And it is a logical truth that such a description, however many modal expressions might properly be used in *arriving at* it, or in *justifying* it, or in showing the *relevance* of one of its components to another, could *contain* no modal expression.

(CDCM §§79–80)

These passages raise some puzzles. For instance, one knows that Sellars considered himself to be not only a naturalist, but also a scientific realist—and from the way he describes them, his commitment to scientific realism seems deeper than his commitment to naturalism.[6] Sellars sums up his scientific realism in his well-known *scientia mensura*: "in the dimension of describing and explaining the world, science is the measure of all things, of what is that it is, and of what is not that it is not" (EPM, IX, §41: in SPR: 173). But, in CDCM, it is clear that describing and explaining are different enough enterprises that their vocabularies differ in non-trivial ways. The *explanatory* enterprise employs a distinctive modal vocabulary in which talk of physical necessities and entailments is indispensable. However, the descriptive enterprise, at least in its *pure* form, need make no use of such vocabulary. Is the naturalism contemplated in CDCM essentially ontologically sparser—because it does not recognise ontologically independent modal properties—than the scientific realism promulgated in EPM?[7]

That question is an interesting attempt to drive a wedge between two fundamental Sellarsian commitments, but I think the answer is relatively straightforward. Sellars spends a great deal of time, both in CDCM and elsewhere, (e.g. NAO) analysing the semantics of the modalities and of predication itself. He does so precisely in order to be able to claim that the verbiage employed in the explanatory enterprise (and also any new vocabulary employed in the prescriptive enterprises of action and deliberation) does not add any new *objects* to the world—the ontology remains unchanged.[8] Sellars tells us that

> although describing and explaining (predicting, retrodicting, understanding) are distinguishable, they are also, in an important sense, inseparable. It is only because the expressions in terms of which we describe objects, even such basic expressions as words for the perceptible characteristics of molar objects[9] locate these objects in a space of implications, that they describe at all, rather than merely label.
>
> (CDCM §108)

One has to recognise that descriptive language is not (and cannot be) entirely self-sufficient and that many other linguistic functions are requisite for description to be *possible*. Then we can see that, as Sellars writes:

> once the tautology 'The world is described by descriptive concepts' is freed from the idea that the business of all nonlogical concepts is to describe, the way is clear to an *ungrudging* recognition that many expressions which empiricists have relegated to second-class citizenship in discourse, are not *inferior*, just *different*.
>
> (CDCM §79)

The important point to take here is that when ontology is done properly, recognition of the different distinctive uses of language is perfectly compatible with naturalism, which, therefore, need not try to force all language into the Procrustean bed of reductive materialism. This is a crucial point to remember in assessing Sellars's naturalism.

II

What Is Worth Saving in Idealism?

Not all idealisms are equally worthy. Sellars found little to preserve in epistemologically motivated idealisms, that is, idealisms that presume that we know our own mental states 'first and best', and that, therefore, everything non-mental has, at best, a second-class status, not just epistemically, but ontologically as well. However, he found something else in German Idealism. It was not any argument for (much less the simple presumption of) the primacy of the mental; it was a more thoroughgoing analysis of the fundamental conditions of the existence of mentality (that is, intentionality) and cognition of the world in which it exists.

Basic to this analysis is the distinction between intuition, or, rather, sensation, and concept that Kant (re)introduced. I think Sellars thought of this distinction as a revival in some degree of the Aristotelian distinction between sensible forms and intellectual forms, which play different roles in Aristotle's understanding of animal and human behaviour.[10] What this means for Sellars is that there are (at least) two different (though interconnected) ways in which intelligent organisms "relate" to their world in cognition, not the one way (with different degrees of clarity and distinctness) contemplated in the *New Way of Ideas*.[11] It turns out a third form of relation will also be necessary, in Sellars's view.

The distinction between sensation and concept breaks any immediate relation between concept and ultimate reality and in its own way solidifies the 'veil of ideas' behind which the non-mental world hides. Only in Kant's hands, the line is not drawn between the mental and the non-mental, for we are appearances to ourselves just as much as physical objects are appearances to us. The veil of sensation, in Kantian perspective, both connects us and separates us from the really real, things as they are in themselves. And, in Kant's view, conceptual relations to the world cannot re-connect us any better with the in-itself—nor does it need to in order to constitute the only kind of cognition available to humanity.

From the point of view of post-Kantian thinkers, the sensation/concept distinction is both a blessing (by enabling a richer conception of experience that is both phenomenologically more faithful and explanatorily more fruitful than those without such a distinction) and a problem (because it apparently cuts concepts off from direct relation to things in themselves). Post-Kantian German Idealists sought to do away with Kant's notion of an unknowable *Ding an sich*. And, here Sellars is with the post-Kantians.

No less important than the sensation/concept distinction is the analysis of conceptuality to be found in the German Idealists. Kant first made clear that representations of objects-in-the-world can only occur as items in a complex representational *system* that includes ways of referring to the subject of thought and experience, ways of marking (and measuring) locations in space and time, a conception of persistence enduring through time, and causal connections among the events that the objects represented are involved in. The content of conceptual episodes is determined by their functional role within the complex representational system.

This is an insight that one can claim the rationalists also had, though nowhere nearly as clearly articulated. However, many empiricists have not understood this, and it led to serious flaws in their views, flaws that Sellars examined, among other places, in his classic 'Empiricism and the Philosophy of Mind'.

The systematicity of representation is joined in Sellars's mind to the sociality of representation. This is where Sellars goes beyond his explicit Kantian orientation towards a more post-Kantian vision of how we engage the world around us. Notice that an important distinction can be drawn between representational systems that are shared across organisms because of their shared evolutionary/genetic history and representational systems that are shared across a group of organisms because of their common cultural (and therefore conventional) history and environment.[12] Both kinds of representational systems become "tuned" to the world around them, but only the latter is subject to explicit, self-conscious, methodical adjustment to its world. Such activity is a crucial factor in lifting us beyond the immediate responses of our sensory systems and into objective, truth-evaluable *conceptual* representations. Language is the primary medium of such shared representations, and it is now a commonplace that language is a shared, communal possession. Though Sellars is not committed to the idea that *all* thought is in language (see the opening paragraph of MEV as well as the more fully elaborated reflections in SK, I, section VI), he is committed to the idea that full-fledged conceptual thought is possible only in those that employ an intersubjectively shared language.

The last of the German Idealist insights I want to cite here is the possibility of not only conceptual change, but categorial change as well. Again, this takes a step beyond the Kantian conception of the categorial, for Kant took his categories to be eternally fixed. The possibility of conceptual and categorial change is deeply significant for Sellars, for it means that *selection* is possible and with it incremental change that can be, over time, both radical and adaptive.

Before moving on to the next section, however, I want to pause to re-emphasise the fact that the analysis of conceptuality Sellars found in the German Idealists is compatible with a phenomenalism of the experienced. This is *not* the kind of phenomenalism familiar from empiricism, whether the empiricism of J. S. Mill or of the early Carnap, which still presume the priority and immediacy of our knowledge of the mental. Rather, the entire conceptual system is at a remove from reality, with no *direct* relations tying concepts, as such, to the fundamental reality of the world. For Kant, our conceptual system, tuned as it is to the human capacities of sensibility, is *in principle* distanced from things as they are in themselves. Others, like Hegel and Sellars, attempt to show that the distance between the conceptual and the real, though initially significant, can (and ought) be made to vanish, and that that is the ultimate goal of properly *wissenschaftlich* methodologies. It is in this understanding of the nature of reality and conceptuality that Sellars's conception of picturing plays its role.

III

The Problem: Synthesising Naturalism and Idealism

We can now see why Sellars seems to have a problem: he is committed to scientific realism and to naturalism, so he takes the methods of natural science to be ontologically decisive and the objects identified in and identifiable by the natural sciences to be fundamental. However, he is also committed to the idealistic conception of concepts, of the content of language and thought generally. This view emphasises the systematic interrelations of conceptual episodes, rather than any purported relation to natural or material objects, as determinative of their content. What, then, is it that guarantees—or even makes possible—that our concepts and the judgments that employ them are about the natural world in which we live and have our being? What reason is there to think that the world is the way we think it is, that our concepts 'carve nature at its joints', as Plato might have put it?

Of course, one also has to recognise that Sellars does not want a too-easy or too-quick answer to that question, for he is convinced that the world is *not* the way we currently commonly think it is: the world of the 'manifest image' is a merely phenomenal world. The world as it is 'in itself' will be the world as it is revealed in an ultimate, ideal scientific image to be achieved in some Peircean culmination of the scientific enterprise. There are obvious implications for Sellars's project. Firstly, he has to be able to point to a difference between the framework to be achieved by Peircean science and all its predecessors. But, secondly, it is important that the manifest image not be pure fiction: it must be an image *of our world* and not some other merely possible world.

Of course, one might think that *truth* and the elements of truth (in traditional conception, reference and meaning), suffice to tie our conceptual framework to our world. However, that is not an option open to Sellars, for he takes truth to be internal to each framework. Truth is *always* a matter of truth-in-some-conceptual-scheme and every sophisticated conceptual scheme will determine some set of truths. Truth alone is not sufficient to sort out the relationships among conceptual frameworks. Sellars does not think truth is a scalar property, so that we can rank some conceptual schemes as 'more true' than others: with respect to what conceptual framework (with its attendant conception of truth) would such a judgment be made?[13] Of course, Sellars sometimes seems to violate this principle by telling us that the manifest image is 'false,'[14] and, indeed, no sooner has he pointed out the bivalence of truth in SM than he moves to try to make sense of claims to greater or lesser 'adequacy' about conceptual frameworks:

> On the other hand, one conceptual framework can be more "adequate" than another, and this fact can be used to define a sense in

which one proposition can be said to be "more true" than another. Once again I find myself in the position of attempting to revitalize central themes in nineteenth-century Idealism.

(SM, V, ¶54: 134)

Sellars cannot simply disavow the ultimate truth of the manifest image and leave it, in John McDowell's words, spinning frictionlessly in the void. Sellars's notion of picturing is his provision for the necessary friction that ties our conceptual frameworks to the world and thereby also enables us to make sense of the notion that one conceptual framework can be 'more true' than another. This is the notion, Sellars thinks, that Peirce lacked:

> Notice that although the concepts of "ideal truth" and "what really exists" are defined in terms of a Peircean conceptual structure they do not require that there ever be a Peirceish community. Peirce himself fell into difficulty because, by not taking into account the dimension of "picturing," he had no Archimedeian point outside the series of actual and possible beliefs in terms of which to define the ideal or limit to which members of this series might approximate.

(SM, V ¶75: 142)

Sellars thinks that his notion of picturing enables us to explain both why Peircean science gives us the *ultimate* truth and why, despite its ultimate falsehood (or better, inadequacy), the manifest image is not mere fiction. Locating the role of picturing in this nexus of ideas is, I think, the best way to see why Sellars felt compelled to develop the idea. We are now ready to dive into more detail. I will first review how the Idealists' coherence theory of concepts is updated and embodied in Sellars's analytic framework. I will then try to make the idea of picturing more intelligible by explicating its place in Sellars's doctrine in terms of Daniel Dennett's well-known distinction between the physical, design, and intentional stances (or levels of description). There simply is not room to get into the details of picturing, but we can do enough to understand how pictures operate to tie together the *ordo essendi* and the *ordo cognoscendi*.

IV

Naturalising Idealistic Insights

Deconstructing Standard Semantics

I have been fairly cavalier so far in the discussion of the relations between words or thoughts and things in the world, assuming the idealist analysis of representationality. It is time now to see how Sellars takes inspiration from the idealists, but develops a coherent, non-traditional conception of semantics that rejects the empiricist and metaphysical assumptions that plague philosophical semantics as traditionally practised.

It is a fundamental tenet of Sellars's philosophy that the semantic vocabulary of *meaning, reference*, and *standing for*, which all seem to be relational terms, are not relation words at all.[15] Sellars's motives for denying that the semantic relations of meaning, signifying, standing for, or reference are really *relations* at all are rooted in his naturalism. One such motive is his radical nominalism.[16] Sellars thinks that treating semantic statements, statements in which we say what some expression means, stands for, or refers to, as relational statements would inevitably lead us to a form of Platonism. Indeed, according to Sellars, being seduced by the superficially relational form of semantic statements is the primary (though not the only) motivation behind Platonism. Platonism as traditionally understood is non-naturalistic, for it recognises objects that exist outside the spatio-temporal, causal order. I will return in a moment to what Sellars thinks is the real form of semantic statements.

Another motive for Sellars's peculiar approach to semantics is that he takes the distinction between object-language and meta-language very seriously. He recognises, of course, that they do not differ as English and French differ, and that natural languages contain their own meta-languages in some perfectly good sense. But disregarding the distinction between object-language level statements in, e.g. English, and meta-language level statements leads to inevitable philosophical confusion. Such confusion contributes significantly to Platonism, for instance, for the Platonist takes metalinguistic, functional classifiers to be object-language names of individuals.[17] Sellars might agree that recognising the distinction between object- and meta-languages is one of the most significant philosophical discoveries of the 20th century, for it is an important tool in developing a naturalistic understanding of language. Semantic statements are all in the meta-language; because of this, there are systematic differences in how they are to be interpreted compared to object-language statements.

Finally, there is a complex of reasons surrounding Sellars's rejection of the Myth of the Given. One way of characterising the doctrine of the given is that there is a fixed and immutable interface between the order of being and the order of cognition or conception. This fixed interface point can be located at the level of propositional cognition, where what is given is knowledge that p, for certain kinds of p. Or it can be located at a sub-propositional level in the givenness of meaning or reference: the 'new way of ideas' and Russellian acquaintance are attempts to locate the given at a sub-propositional level.[18] The general idea of a given is the idea that there is some level at which the cognitive content (by which one can mean either the *semantic* content or the *epistemic* content) of at least some of our concepts or thoughts is determined directly and solely by their relation to an object. Sellars rejects this idea: our interface with the world in perception, intuition, introspection, or even self-consciousness is at no point independent of the holistic, norm-laden conceptual scheme we bring to the situation. This entails rejecting the givenness of meaning and reference as well as the givenness of knowledge. Semantics is no more a foundationalist, linearly structured realm than is knowledge. All of this is crucial for the development of naturalistic theories of knowledge and understanding.

Towards a Naturalistic Semantics

The traditional view of semantics is precisely that it concerns the relation between language and the world. In Sellars's view, it too often attempts to explain that relation either in terms of fundamentally mysterious (or at least non-natural) 'reference' and 'meaning' relations or by positing an intermediate realm of (non-natural) entities, meanings. Sellars rejects that view; what does he put in its place? According to Sellars, semantic statements that appear to be relational in character, statements such as

(A) 'Brother' means *male sibling*
(B) 'Schwartz' (in German) means *black*
(C) 'Dreieckig' (in German) stands for *triangularity*
(D) 'Wien' (in German) refers to Vienna

are all really monadic predications. In each case, on the right-hand side of the verb is an illustrating functional sortal; that is, these statements employ a kind of indexical predication[19] that uses a word of the speaker's language to form a common noun that applies to any word in any language that plays a role in its language relevantly similar to that of the illustrating word. Sellars developed the idea of dot-quotes to capture this notion formally: •Black• is a common noun that is true of any linguistic object that functions in its language system in a manner relevantly similar to the function of 'black' in English. On the left-hand side of the verb in the preceding sentences is a distributive singular term that applies to all relevantly similar tokens of the language in question. The verbs themselves, on his analysis, are just forms of the copula specialized for use in metalinguistic contexts. The full story, of course, is complex, but according to Sellars, in the end, the depth grammars of our sample sentences are:

(A') 'Brother's are •male sibling•s
(B') 'Schwartz's are German •black•s
(C') 'Dreieckig's are German •triangulars•
(D') For some •S•, 'Wien's are German •S•s, and •S• is materially equivalent to •Vienna•[20]

The point is that the semantic characteristics of expressions concern only how those expressions function in the complex linguistic system. There is one important condition on this claim and at least one interesting corollary. (i) The *linguistic system* must be construed broadly; rules governing proper language-entry and language-exit transitions are part of the system (I will call these collectively 'interface rules'), and therefore the linguistic system could not be fully specified without including a description of the environment it is involved in.[21] (ii) The distinctions between syntactic, semantic, and even pragmatic characteristics of expressions are ultimately artificial, that is, practical. Saying that 'brother' is an adjective says something about how that expression functions in the language; saying that 'brother' is a •male sibling• also says something about its functions in the language. The syntactic characterization can usually be spelled out via a limited set of formalisable intralinguistic formation and transformation rules, independently of any interface rules; the semantic characterisation usually, for descriptive terms and names, cannot be spelled out in any such conveniently formalisable, interface-rule independent fashion. Sellars speaks in such cases of *material* rules of formation and transformation. Because the complexities of most descriptive and prescriptive expressions make simple statements of the formation and transformation rules governing them impossible, we have developed 'means'-talk to enable us to convey those complex rules of usage by comparison with another, hopefully already understood expression. Hence, the use of illustrating sortals.

Let me return to an important theme in Sellars's treatment of semantics for greater clarity: what does his denial that either meaning or reference is a *relation* ultimately comprise? There are, of course, many relations between linguistic episodes (which are, of course, items in the world in a perfectly straightforward sense) and the objects in the world in the context of which they occur. An utterance of 'red' may occur nearby and in response to some red object, for instance. Similarly, an utterance of "Tom!" may occur nearby and in response to someone named "Tom." An utterance of 'drink' may precede someone's grabbing a glass, filling it, and drinking. But, none of these relations could be identified as either the meaning or the reference relation. In fact, a complete specification of all the actual relations between a linguistic utterance type and the objects and events surrounding occurrences of that object type could not equate to either the meaning or the reference of that linguistic type. It is easy to see why: the function the term or phrase plays is constituted by the norms of usage in the community, and the actual usage, though necessarily reflective of those norms, never matches them exactly. People sometimes use expressions incorrectly.

One might be tempted, then, to think that the 'relation' between word and world could be characterised along these lines:

> It ought to be the case that English speakers have a propensity to respond to red items in their visual field with the vocable 'red'.

It ought to be the case that English speakers use 'Vienna' to denominate the capital of Austria.

But, there is a fundamental objection: relations that ought to be are not, in general, relations that *are*. 'Ortiz ought to clobber that ball' does not describe a relation between Ortiz and some ball, though it makes sense to say (*ceteris paribus*) only if there is some ball that does stand in one of several relations to Ortiz.

Talk of a meaning relation or a reference relation encourages the thought that there is some one repeatable, actual feature that all cases of reference or meaning have in common. But, this is just not the case. Even if one weakens the claim by including only *successful* meaning or reference, it still would not be true. There are many relations between linguistic events and the world in which they occur, and without such relations, it would be impossible for language to be about that world, indeed, for it to be about *anything*. But, none of those relations is a relation of reference or meaning.

According to Sellars, semantic talk is meta-linguistic speech that classifies linguistic objects by their function within the language community as it interacts with its environment. Because functions are multiply realisable, none of the semantic talk states or describes any *particular* relation our expressions have to the world or to objects in the world. But then, that lack of specific relations to the world might make language, and with it thought, seem separated from and without *any* relation to the world and the objects in it. Speech that *appears* to or that we normally *take* to state the relations between our words and our world in fact simply classifies our words by their function within the language system. We can and, indeed, *have to* give the semantics of a language, that is, say what its descriptive expressions mean and what its terms refer to, without specifying any particular *relation* between those expressions and anything in the world. If one is entranced by the myth that there must be some privileged reference relation if we are to be able to talk about the world at all, the norm-constituted logical space within which language and thought operate seems, then, to float independently of the world. Our efforts to say what the word-world relation is are unsuccessful, it seems. This is the way the idealist notion that thought is a self-contained system is preserved and interpreted in Sellars.

On the one hand, Sellars thinks the objection that language and thought in his system are left floating free of relation to the world is just confusion. There are plenty of relations in the neighbourhood. It is part of the meaning of observation terms that they tend to be evoked by items or events of certain kinds, for instance. All the causal uniformities that reflect and sustain the normative principles of the language are real relations, in Sellars's view, but none of them is itself a *semantic relation*. The worry expressed in the objection is generated by false assumptions about what reference and meaning are as well as being seduced into thinking that anything that seems to be described relationally must be a relation. To put a point to the matter, Sellars thinks that the actual usage of a language/conceptual scheme in the ordinary activities of life is an adequate guarantee of its relation to the world. We need not believe in some magical 'reference relation' to account for it. But on the other hand, Sellars also wants to be able to compare conceptual schemes and make sense out of the notion that one may be "more true" than another. This requires something above and beyond the strict language-relative predicate 'true,' and this is where picturing comes into play.

V

Picturing as a Sub-Intentional Design Feature

Perhaps I should rather have said that making sense of comparative adequacy between conceptual schemes is *one* of the roles that picturing plays in Sellars's philosophy. For there is another role picturing plays that we can discern in Sellars's discussions.

According to Sellars, certain statements that occur in what he calls "first-level matter-of-factual discourse" (SM V §9: 119) have as a distinctive function within the overall language system "constituting a projection [that is, a picture] in the language users of the world in which they live" (TC: 223). The first thing to note is that neither the syntax nor the semantics of any statement determines it to be a picture, though a statement's syntax or semantics can certainly disqualify it. The pragmatic features of when and how that statement (or thought) occurs are the significant determinant of picture-candidacy. A statement such as 'Harry is in bed' is a descriptive statement, and its meaning is determined by the function(s) it can play in our linguistic activity, including the inferences (combined with other premises) that would yield it and that it in turn would yield. Brought about in the right way (e.g. perception or memory, rather than philosophical musing or novel reading) and uttered (or thought) in the proper circumstances (which include other neighbouring utterances and thoughts as well as a particular spatio-temporal context), it can be more than a merely true descriptive statement—it can be an element in the picture developed in the organism of its environmental context. The value of such a picture derives particularly from the significant role it plays in the organism's practical reasoning. In order to manoeuvre effectively in their environment, organisms need to know what objects (and objects of what kinds) are where and when, and such information needs to be automatically and easily available for use in the modulation of behaviour in real time.

A striking discovery in cognitive neuroscience is that organisms construct maps of their local environments, contained in the brain, that play important roles in guiding their practical behaviour.[22] Indeed, well before we could localise such maps in the hippocampus, Edward Tolman had started postulating such internal maps.[23] Sellars, who was surely aware of Tolman's work, broadens the basic idea, insofar as his pictures are not restricted to the spatio-temporal properties of the pictured objects. He discusses what he calls 'animal representational systems' in the late article 'Mental Events' and describes them using the map metaphor that Tolman and later cognitive neuroscientists have also employed.

So, my interpretive suggestion is that picturing, in Sellars's view, plays a role that puts it between the purely physical and what he often called 'the intentional order'. The ability to develop the internal maps or pictures employed by animals in controlling their behaviour given their environment is, of course, the product of evolution. It is not too hard (and it is not a mere just-so/pre-established harmony story) to imagine that an animal with a more extensive, finer-grained, higher-dimensional 'map' of its world at its disposal thereby has an advantage in the struggle to survive and reproduce, if it can make use of those features.

We humans are part of that evolutionary history and have been designed by evolution to develop fairly complex maps or pictures of our environment. Because the systems by which we come to picture the world around us have been selected for, normative assessments of their performance are possible: they can perform the task for which they have been selected well or ill. Thus, it makes sense to talk of correct and incorrect pictures. In our case, however, the pictures we are able to construct of the world around us and our position in it have been recruited into another system as well, a socially shared system with significant conventional aspects to it: language, with logical operators and connectives, quantifiers, and the full expressive power of a natural language. Sellars does not believe that we lose the more primitive but also more basic animal representational system when we acquire language. Obviously, it is a question of huge interest how the animal mapping system interfaces with the acquired linguistic system available to socialised humans. That is not a question there is room enough left here to answer—given that I understood all of this well enough to have an answer. Ultimately, it will take *years* of difficult empirical research to uncover those connections.

In its earliest incarnations, human language and the conceptual framework it embodied were themselves strictly causal upshots of complex interactions between social groups and their environment—we did not reason our way to our 'original image', for there would have been no language/conceptual framework within which to do such reasoning.

But however it came about, the language we developed enabled us to represent distant and even merely hypothetic situations, to draw explicit generalisations and formulate explicit rules, and to represent our own representations. With the acquisition of those abilities, the ability to modulate and control our own behaviour achieved new levels of complexity. We could not only reason about how the world wags, but also about how we reason and the adequacy of the concepts with which we reason. These new abilities, in turn, allowed us to begin to refine, elaborate, sophisticate, and extend language, to develop both the arts and the sciences.

Evolution provided us with the ability to take up, retain, and use information about the world around us. Unlike sublingual animals, that ability in us has been further connected to the linguistic abilities we alone, for whatever reasons, evolved. Sellars's insistence on the need for pictures is an insistence that empirically meaningful languages cannot be divorced from the primitive mapping and tracking abilities common (in different degrees) to virtually all animals. The regularities that instantiate the interface rules of the language for elementary, atomic sentences coincide by and large with the regularities that produce the maps we operate with on an animal level.

But, there is one further twist to the story: changes in our language, at least some of which occur under the influence of rational, scientific investigation, come to change the pictures or maps with which we operate, as we learn to refine the conceptual responses we make to our sensory encounters with the world. We are not *stuck* with the original pictures or maps that would have been developed by beings such as us prior to the development of language. We can learn how to construct ever more fine-grained, ever more extendable, and ever more highly dimensional pictures of the world around us. These would be *better* or *more adequate* pictures, because they would enable us to better accomplish the purposes of the mapping systems, namely a more successful and more flexible modulation of our behaviour to suit our goals.

To put it in the Dennettian terms I mentioned earlier, picturing is a capacity that is salient from the design stance when trying to understand the interactions between a sophisticated animal organism and its environment. From the intentional stance, the phenomenon of picturing can get lost to sight under the connected intentional activities of observation, perception, intention, and volition (at least until good empirical science starts uncovering the conditions of such activities). But picturing or mapping should not be confused with those intentional-realm activities. It is not entirely independent of them either, however, for developments in the intentional realm—refinements and extensions of the framework—feed back into the capacities employed in picturing, enabling the generation of ever more adequate pictures. It is because the framework developed by future science will enable more adequate pictures (and thereby more facile, better controlled action) that we can say the scientific image will be "more true" or at least more adequate than our current manifest image.

Without relying on semantic *relations*, Sellars can nonetheless both tie an otherwise seemingly independent intentional realm to the actual world while also accounting for the possibility of progress in our comprehension of the world. And it is all perfectly naturalistic.

Notes

1. For instance, even Jay Rosenberg, perhaps the most orthodox of Sellars's commentators, complained about it in his (2007: 147–184), though he retracts that complaint later in his (2007), where the earlier essay is also reprinted. See also R. B. Brandom (2014: 13, 15).

2. By this I mean a naturalism that seeks a strongly reductive or even eliminative resolution to all the "placement problems"; I think it is equivalent to what John McDowell, in *Mind and World,* calls "bald naturalism".

3. I use the industry-standard abbreviations for Sellars's works.

4. See, the Stanford Encyclopaedia of Philosophy. https://plato.stanford.edu/archives/win2016/entries/naturalism/.

5. David Papineau, Ruth Millikan, and Alex Rosenberg would be examples here.

6. See the last few paragraphs of the introduction to NAO.

7. The essays are pretty much contemporaneous, so there is no question of a change in Sellars's doctrine.

8. Robert Brandom makes a related point in his discussion of the "Kant-Sellars thesis about modality" in Brandom (2015).

9. [Sellars's footnote:] For an elaboration of this point, see my essay "Empiricism and the Philosophy of Mind" (EPM(31) in SPR(53), particularly sections 35–38 (pg. 103–113).

10. See Sellars (1949).

11. I put 'relate' in scare quotes, because what can be properly described as a *relation* between mind and world turns out to be a significant issue for Sellars.

12. The significance of this distinction only emerged after the height of German Idealism, that is, after Darwin. The pragmatists were among the earliest to recognise how significant it is.

13. "There is a sense in which it is correct to say that truth does not admit of degrees. A statement in our conceptual structure is either S-assertible or it is not. (If it is in principle undecidable, neither it nor its negation is S-assertible.)" (SM, V, ¶54: 134).

14. For instance in the first paragraph of section III of PSIM. In SPR: 14; in ISR: 382.

15. It is vital that there be some sophistication in one's talk of relations here. Not everything that *appears* to be a relation is; nor is everything that appears nonrelational indeed such. "John is tall" appears not to describe a relation, but only a little philosophical reflection quickly reveals the complex relationality this assertion hides. Meaning and reference appear to be specific relations: "'Abraham Lincoln' refers to the 16th President of the U.S." is, on the surface, a relational statement. But, it is a central Sellarsian thesis that this is only appearance: there is no one relation that can be called the meaning or the reference relation. The job the sentence performs is better analysed as a kind of functional classification.

16. Sellars has a complex stance towards nominalism, both avowing a radical nominalism and trying to accommodate many of the things Platonists want to say. For interesting analyses, see R. Kraut (2010) and P. Giladi (2014).

17. This is a major lesson in Sellars (1963b).

18. Carl Sachs argues that whereas Sellars and C. I. Lewis agree that *knowledge* is not given, they disagree about whether *meaning* is something given in experience. See C. Sachs (2015).

19. Indexical predication is not as widely recognised a phenomenon as it should be. See J. Heal (1997), for a general discussion of this underrecognised aspect of language.

20. Note that the analysis of 'refer' is different from the analysis of 'meaning' or 'standing for'. This is because 'refer' is an extensional notion, unlike the other two, and adjustments need to be made on that account.
21. This amounts to a rejection of the strong inferentialist program advocated by Brandom. According to strong inferentialism, the language-internal relationships of inference and incompatibility are *sufficient* to determine the content of linguistic items. In Sellars's view, the employment of terms in interface situations is also important. He is, therefore, a *weak* inferentialist.
22. John O'Keefe, May-Britt Moser, and Edvard Moser won the 1914 Nobel Prize for Physiology or Medicine for their work on the spatial maps contained in the hippocampus.
23. Tolman 1948: 189–208.

References

Brandom, R. B. 2014. 'Some Hegelian Ideas of Note for Contemporary Analytic Philosophy'. *Hegel Bulletin* 35: 1–15.
Brandom, R. B. 2015. *From Empiricism to Expressivism: Brandom Reads Sellars*. Cambridge, MA: Harvard University Press.
Dennett, D. C. 1971. 'Intentional Systems'. *The Journal of Philosophy* 68: 87–106.
Heal, J. 1997. 'Indexical Predicates and Their Uses'. *Mind* 106: 619–640.
Kraut, R. 2010. 'Universals, Metaphysical Explanations, and Pragmatism'. *The Journal of Philosophy* 107: 590–609.
McDowell, J. 1994. *Mind and World*. Cambridge, MA: Harvard University Press.
O'Shea, J. R. 2007. *Wilfrid Sellars: Naturalism with a Normative Turn*. Cambridge: Polity Press.
Papineau, David. 'Naturalism'. In E. N. Zalta (ed.) *The Stanford Encyclopaedia of Philosophy*, Winter 2016 ed. Available at: https://plato.stanford.edu/archives/win2016/entries/naturalism/
Rosenberg, J. 1975. 'The Elusiveness of Categories, the Archimedean Dilemma, and the Nature of Man'. In H-N. Castañeda (ed.) *Action, Knowledge, and Reality: Studies in Honour of Wilfrid Sellars*. Indianapolis, IN: Bobbs-Merrill.
———. 2007. *Wilfrid Sellars: Fusing the Images*. Oxford: Oxford University Press.
Sachs, C. 2015. *Intentionality and the Myths of the Given: Between Pragmatism and Phenomenology*. New York and London: Routledge.
Sellars, W. 1949. 'Aristotelian Philosophies of Mind'. In R. W. Sellars, V. J. McGill and M. Farber (eds.) *Philosophy for The Future, The Quest of Modern Materialism*. New York: Palgrave Macmillan. [APM]
———. 1952. 'Mind, Meaning, and Behaviour'. *Philosophical Studies* 3: 83–95. [MMB]
———. 1956. 'Empiricism and the Philosophy of Mind'. In H. Feigl and M. Scriven (eds.) *Minnesota Studies in the Philosophy of Science, Vol. I: The Foundations of Science and the Concepts of Psychology and Psychoanalysis*. Minneapolis: University of Minnesota Press, reprinted as Chapter 5 in SPR. Republished in *Empiricism and the Philosophy of Mind*. 1997. with an introduction by Richard Rorty, and a study guide by Robert Brandom. Cambridge, MA: Harvard University Press. [EPM]

———. 1957. 'Counterfactuals, Dispositions, and the Causal Modalities'. In H. Feigel, M. Scriven and G. Maxwell (eds.) *Minnesota Studies in The Philosophy of Science*, vol. II. Minneapolis: University of Minnesota Press. [CDCM]

———. 1962. 'Philosophy and the Scientific Image of Man'. In R. Colodny (ed.) *Frontiers of Science and Philosophy*. Pittsburgh, PA: University of Pittsburgh Press, reprinted in SPR and ISR. [PSIM]

———. 1963a. *Science, Perception and Reality*. London: Routledge and Kegan Paul. Republished in 1991 by Ridgeview Publishing Company, Atascadero, CA. [SPR]

———. 1963b. 'Abstract Entities'. *Review of Metaphysics* 16: 627–671. [AE]

———. 1968. *Science and Metaphysics: Variations on Kantian Themes: The John Locke Lectures for 1965–66*. London: Routledge and Kegan Paul. Republished in 1992 by Ridgeview Publishing Company, Atascadero, CA. [SM]

———. 1980. *Naturalism and Ontology: The John Dewey Lectures for 1973–74*. Reseda, CA: Ridgeview Publishing Co. [NAO]

———. 2007. *In the Space of Reasons: Selected Essays of Wilfrid Sellars*. K. Scharp and R. B. Brandom (eds.). Cambridge, MA: Harvard University Press. [ISR]

Tolman, E. C. 1948. 'Cognitive Maps in Rats and Men'. *Psychological Review* 55: 189–208.

11 Rethinking Sellars's Naturalism

Steven Levine

Perhaps the most difficult issue in Sellars scholarship concerns the question of how normativity fits into a naturalistic picture of the world. On the one hand, Sellars takes it that the norms that articulate the framework of persons—the framework at the heart of the manifest image—are irreducible. On the other hand, Sellars is a scientific realist for whom the physical sciences are the ontological measure of all things. In an ideal scientific framework there are no norms. So the question is: how can Sellars square the seeming indispensability of the normative with its apparent reducibility in an ideal scientific framework? In this chapter, I examine James O'Shea's answer to this question. O'Shea ascribes to Sellars a complex view in which he defends both the conceptual irreducibility of the normative space of reasons and its causal reducibility to the non-normative entities and processes posited by the scientific image. I agree with O'Shea's reading of Sellars's strategy to fit normativity into a naturalistic picture of the world. But I argue that this strategy cannot work because the notion of causal reduction at play in it admits of two interpretations, both of which lead to unacceptable theoretical consequences. The first, which interprets the concept of causal reduction in a weak way, leads to what O'Shea calls a 'separated-off' account of persons-in-the-world, while the second stronger interpretation leads to certain paradoxical conclusions.[1]

I

At the heart of Sellars's system of thought is the idea that the 'manifest' and the 'scientific' image can be brought together to form a single synoptic vision. The possibility of bringing together these two disparate images depends on accounting for three phenomena that seem recalcitrant to treatment by the scientific image, i.e. thought, sensory consciousness, and personhood.[2] With respect to the first two cases, Sellars tries to 'save the appearances' concerning a subject's personal-level thought and sensory consciousness while showing that ultimately these capacities can be accounted for by the scientific image. Sellars's thought is here genuinely dialectical insofar as he argues that built into our manifest account of thought and sensation are pressures that transform it into one that only uses the concepts and categories of the scientific image. Here Sellars thinks the 'primacy of the scientific image' can, in principle, be vindicated. With persons, however, it is different. For "the task of showing that categories pertaining to man as a *person* . . . can be reconciled with the idea that man is what science says he is" (Sellars 1991b: 38) is far more difficult to bring about.

Sellars takes it that persons—the main concept of the manifest image—have two main features. First, persons appear to themselves as unitary logical subjects of experience, as the self-identical locus of a multiplicity of perceptions, thoughts, and intentions.[3] Second, persons are creatures that are "bound up in a network of rights and duties," (Sellars 1991b: 39) i.e. are creatures that find themselves "confronted by standards (ethical, logical, etc.) . . . to which [they] may or may not conform" (Sellars 1991b: 38). So persons, instead of simply acting on natural inclinations given by their nature, are rational agents who act in light of norms and standards that can be rejected. The difficult question for Sellars, and the one that determines the success of his synoptic vision, is whether these features of persons can be reconciled with a naturalistic account of man-in-the-world, whatever that account will turn out to be.

In recent years, James O'Shea has powerfully answered this question in the affirmative.[4] With respect to the question of the place of normativity in a naturalistic picture of the world—which is the aspect of persons that I will focus on in this chapter—O'Shea demonstrates that Sellars has a complex view in which he defends both the *conceptual irreducibility* of the normative space of reasons and its *causal reducibility* to the non-normative entities and processes posited by the scientific image. While within the manifest image the distinction between the space of reasons and the space of causes is an irreducible distinction, from the point of view of the ideal scientific framework, this distinction is a reducible distinction.

In this chapter, I argue that Sellars's '*irreducibility* cum *reducibility* position' is not successful. I largely agree with O'Shea's reading of Sellars's strategy to naturalise normativity. I think that we can find the '*irreducibility* cum *reducibility* position' in Sellars's work. But I do not think, as O'Shea does, that this particular strategy to naturalise normativity is philosophically successful. To use the language of left- and right-wing Sellarsianism, we could say that my *reading* of Sellars is 'right wing', while my *evaluation* of the position so read is 'left wing'.

My goal in making this argument is not, however, to bury the prospects of giving a naturalistic account of the place of norms in nature. Rather, I want to make the narrower case that *Sellars's strategy* to naturalise normativity is not successful. At the end of the I make some brief suggestions about how this strategy could be modified, leading to a more robust pragmatic naturalism.

II

This question about the place of normativity in Sellars's naturalistic account of man-in-the-world is difficult because he defends two theses that do not, on the face of it, cohere.[5]

On the one hand, Sellars is a scientific realist who holds that "in the dimension of describing and explaining the world, science is the measure of all things, of what is that it is, and of what is not that it is not" (Sellars 1997: 83). While current science does not have a complete description and explanation of all things, the telescoped picture of the world given to us by an ideal or completed micro-physical science—what Sellars calls "Peirceish"—provides the benchmark of the true and the real.[6] Such an ideal scientific framework will only use a vocabulary that describes and explains how things are and never one that prescribes how they ought or ought not to be. In Sellars's terminology, this naturalistic account will only give 'pure descriptions':

> The naturalistic 'thesis' that the world, including the verbal behavior of those who use the term 'ought'—and the mental states involving the concept to which this world gives expression—can 'in principle', be described without using the term 'ought' or any prescriptive expression, is a logical point about what it is to count as a description *in principle* of the world. . . . [N]aturalism presents us with the ideal of a *pure* description of the world (in particular human behavior), a description which simply says what things *are*, and never, in any respect, what they *ought* or *ought not* to be; and it is clear (as a matter of simple logic) that neither 'ought' nor any other prescriptive expression *could* be *used* (as opposed to *mentioned*) in such a description.
>
> (Sellars 1958: 283)

If such descriptions of human behaviour were possible, then we would be able to say that the world—*from the point of view of pure description and explanation*—contains no norms. From the point of view of the pure descriptions of Peirceish the norms that purportedly govern a person's thoughts and intentions will, in a sense that needs specifying, be reducible to the entities and processes described by the concepts and categories of the scientific image.

On the other hand, Sellars claims that the framework of persons is irreducible to the concepts and categories of the scientific image. To think that such a reduction is possible is, as Sellars puts it, "a mistake of a piece with the so-called 'naturalistic fallacy' in ethics" (Sellars 1997: 19). In other words, the notion that the norms and standards that govern our beliefs and intentions can be the object of an account that only uses pure descriptions seems to be equivalent to the notion that Ought is reducible to Is. And Sellars seems to think that such a reduction "is in principle impossible, the impossibility in question being a strictly logical one" (Sellars 1991b: 38).[7]

Why is this reduction logically impossible? Sellars does not say directly, but I think that we can tease out an answer from his discussion of persons. The basic issue is that a description of a person, to be true to its object, must be more than a mere description.

> To say that a certain person desired to do A, thought it his duty to do B but was forced to do C, is not to *describe* him as one might describe a scientific specimen. One does, indeed, describe him, but one does something more. And it is this something more which is the irreducible core framework of persons.
>
> (Sellars 1991b: 39)

What is this 'something more'? It is the fact that any description of a person also involves a type of *recognition* of them *as* a person who can act on intentions, and this recognition is the irreducible core of the framework of persons.

To understand why a description of persons involves recognition, and therefore 'something more' than just description, we must see that the norms and standards to which persons are subject are intrinsically *social*:

> To think of a featherless biped as a person is to think of it as a being with which one is bound up in a network of rights and duties. From this point of view, the irreducibility of the personal is the irreducibility of the 'ought' to the 'is'. But even more basic than this (though ultimately, the two points coincide), is the fact that to think of a featherless biped as a person is to construe its behavior in terms of actual or potential membership in an embracing group each member of which thinks of itself as a member of the group. Let's call such a group a 'community'. . . . [T]o recognise a featherless biped or dolphin or Martian as a person is to think of oneself and it as belonging to a community.
>
> (Sellars 1991b: 39)

The fact that persons are beings bound up in a network of rights and duties ultimately coincides with the fact that persons are members of a community because they can only be part of a network of rights and duties if there is a community of persons that *takes* those rights and duties to be rights and duties. Norms have no existence outside of their being taken as correct or incorrect—as being authoritative or not—by a community of persons. So to be a being that can take a norm to be the basis of one's thought and action requires that one be a part of a community of beings that recognises those norms and standards as having authority. As such, to think of a creature as a person and not merely a thing requires that one not only describe its behaviour but recognise that what is being described is an expression of their rational responsiveness to such community norms. But to recognise that the creature is responsive to community norms *one must oneself be subject to norms*, if not the norms of the community that the recognised creature is responsive to, then the norms of another community.

Sellars's point is this: to recognise a person, and so even to describe them, an interpreter must, like the person being interpreted, be part of a community of those who say 'We', that is, a community that accepts fundamental norms as binding on its members. In being part of such a community one is able to draw upon a type of practical knowledge of what it is to be subject to norms oneself, and it is this practical knowledge that is deployed on our recognition of other persons. In drawing upon this knowledge one does not give pure descriptions of the person interpreted but *rehearses the intentions* to which they are subject:

> Now, the fundamental principles of a community, which define what is 'correct' or 'incorrect', 'right' or 'wrong', 'done' or 'not done', are the most general common *intentions* of that community with respect to the behaviour of the members of the group. It follows that to recognise a featherless biped or dolphin or Martian as a person requires that one think thoughts of the form 'We (one) shall do (or abstain from doing) actions of kind A in circumstances of kind C'. To think thoughts of this kind is not to *classify* or *explain*, but to *rehearse an intention*.
>
> (Sellars 1991b: 39–40; emphasis in original)

We can now see why the normativity that characterises the framework of persons is irreducible. If the description of a person always involves a type of recognition of them, and if this recognition requires that one rehearse an intention, then one's recognition of a person, and so one's description, involves having thoughts in which 'Ought' is *used* rather than merely *mentioned*. So to recognise a person we cannot, as the scientific image purports to do, deploy pure descriptions that only mention the Oughts to which the person recognised is subject, rather, the recogniser must oneself rehearse an intention or act on a norm, i.e. use it. This use of norms or rehearsal of community intentions is the non-reducible core of the framework of persons.

So the question is: if the normativity characteristic of the framework of persons is irreducible in this way, how can Sellars uphold the primacy of the scientific image? This is the deep problem at the heart of Sellars's synoptic vision. There are, I think, two interrelated moves through which Sellars tries to make sense of the way in which the framework of persons is related to scientific image. I now wish to examine them in order.

III

The first move to uphold the primacy of the scientific image, while holding onto the thought that the framework of persons is irreducible, is simply to assign them different roles that are orthogonal to one another. The scientific image and the framework of persons do not compete ontologically because they have different tasks that operate in different domains. Let me explain.

Following Sellars, one can stipulate, for the reasons canvased previously, that the framework of persons cannot be reconstructed in the concepts of the scientific image. But does this mean that there is a type of basic thing (a substance) that stands outside of what science tells us there is? Sellars denies this inference. As Richard Bernstein puts it, "[e]verything that can be described and explained about persons can be described and explained in terms of the scientific image. The 'something more' that is left over is not something more to be described and explained; it involves the having and rehearsing of intentions" (Bernstein 1966a: 125). In other words, the framework of persons is concerned with a type of *doing*, with the activity of rehearsing intentions, not with representing the world. In Sellars's famous statement about science being the measure of all things, he pointedly says that it is only in the dimension of *describing and explaining the world* that this holds, leaving open the possibility that there are frameworks that have different functions than describing and explaining (see Sellars 1997: 83). And this is the case with the framework of persons. The vocabulary of this framework is not in the business of describing and explaining what there is but in the business of being used to rehearse and act on intentions. Because the 'something more' that is irreducible about the framework of persons cannot be described and explained, the

> conceptual framework of persons is not something that needs to be *reconciled with* the scientific image, but rather something to be *joined* with it. Thus, to complete the scientific image we need to enrich it *not* with more ways of saying what is the case, but with the language of community and individual intentions.
>
> (Sellars 1991b: 40)

In other words, although it is not possible to account for persons *in* the concepts of the scientific image, it is possible to expand and enrich the scientific image by joining to it the vocabulary of agency.

The second move follows from an explanatory *desideratum* left over by this first move; for can we not ask about the *ontological* status of the intentions (the principles and norms of a community) that are used or rehearsed? It is all well and good to say that they are not part of a framework that describes and explains, but this does not answer the question of whether they can be the *object* of another framework that describes and explains through pure descriptions that only mention and do not use normative vocabulary.

Sellars seems to give a negative answer to the question whether the framework of persons cannot be reconciled with, but only joined to, the scientific image. But O'Shea argues that this negative response is only half the story; that while *from the point of view of the manifest image* the normativity characteristic of the framework of persons is irreducible, i.e. cannot be reconciled with the concepts of scientific image, from the perspective of *an ideal scientific framework* such normativity admits of naturalistic treatment. As O'Shea puts it, Sellars defends "both the irreducibility of the normative space of reasons and yet, simultaneously and in another sense, its comprehensive reducibility from the perspective of an ideal scientific conception of the nature of reality and of the human being" (O'Shea 2009: 188).[8] Let us examine this strategy in detail.

IV

To make this position comprehensible we begin, as O'Shea does, by considering Sellars's early meta-ethical account of ethical Oughts. In his early paper "A Semantical Solution of the Mind-Body Problem" Sellars considers the general question of how to think about the relation of Ought to Is. On the one hand, Sellars agrees with ethical non-naturalists that Ought is logically irreducible to Is. To logically reduce Ought to Is requires that one can translate the content of statements that contain Ought into statements that only use descriptive, here meaning extensional, terms. This is not possible, Sellars thinks, because the translations will either tacitly call upon the meaning of the Ought statements they were meant to replace, or because the translations lose much of the content of the original statements, leading to unconvincing translations. To put it simply, any adequate translation of the content of an ethical assertion must itself use normative language.

In arguing that Ought statements have conceptual content Sellars rejects emotivism, the then dominant form of ethical naturalism. But while he rejects emotivism as an account of the content of ethical statements, he nonetheless agrees with the ethical naturalist that Ought is reducible in some sense to Is. It is, in his terms, *causally* reducible:

> [A] concept will be said to be causally reducible to descriptive concepts if (roughly) it . . . occurs in the antecedent of a properly constructed casual explanation only as a subordinate element in a descriptive mentalistic context. . . . Thus, a non-naturalist who holds that the only way in which moral obligation can enter into the causal explanation of human history is via facts of the form Jones thinks (feels) that he ought to pay his debt, would be holding that Ought is, in the above sense, causally reducible to Is. In traditional terminology, he

would be claiming that obligation enters into the causal order only as an element in the intentional object of a mental act.

(Sellars 1980: 222)

The idea here is that when Ought is an element of an agential attitude's intentional object, i.e. part of what is specified by a 'that-clause', one can describe facts about those attitudes without having to make Ought-assertions in *our* description of those attitudes. So while a subject could not translate 'one ought to pay one's debts' without using normative vocabulary, a description of the psychological attitude of that subject towards that statement would not need to make Ought-assertions because, insofar as Ought is part of the intentional object of those attitudes, the description will only mention and not use Ought, thereby neutralizing its normative force. So to say that Ought is causally reducible to Is, is to say that one can give a causal explanation and description of an agent's moral behaviour without that explanation or description itself making Ought-assertions.

Now that we know what a causally reductive account is, the question becomes whether it is possible to give such an account. Ethical non-naturalists, for example the intuitionists (Ross, Prichard), doubt that it is. While the intuitionists agree with Sellars that Ought enters into our behavioural economy due to its being an element of an intentional object of our mental acts, it can become such an object through moral training only because Oughts are already objective normative facts. For them it is "impossible to give a causal account of ethical thoughts without, at some stage, making ethical assertions" (Sellars 1980: 223) because on their account such objective normative facts play an "essential role in both the development of ethical concepts and the development of moral codes" (Sellars 1980: 223). In other words, when an agent, through moral training, learns to take Ought as the object of his or her mental acts, he or she learns to intuit normative facts that are already there. So when we give a causal explanation of how ethical thinking comes about, when we trace the history of how Jones came to think or feel he ought to pay his debt, we will eventually be pushed into using normative vocabulary in our description of the objective normative facts which Jones intuits. When we get to the bottom of an explanation of how Jones came to think that he ought to pay his debts we get to more normative facts, the ones to which Jones appropriately or correctly responds through moral apperception.

Sellars does not attempt to refute this intuitionist view head on. Instead, he provides an alternative account in which he tries to show that it is possible to give an explanation of how Jones came to think that he ought to pay his debts that does not need to posit normative facts. In other words, to vindicate his notion of causal reduction—of giving explanations and descriptions that only mention but do not make Ought-assertions—Sellars gives an account of the history of moral

agents that only takes recourse to dispositions and psychological uniformities that can be described in matter-of-factual terms, i.e. in terms
that only say how things are, not how they Ought to be. Here is how
Sellars puts it:

> If we use 'ethical assertion' in such a way that 'Jones ought to pay
> his debt' is an ethical assertion, but 'Jones feels that he ought to pay
> his debt' is not, then we can say that to claim that Ought is causally
> reducible to Is is to claim that one can give a casual explanation of
> the history of moral agents without making ethical assertions.
>
> (Sellars 1980: 222–223, quoted in O'Shea 2009: 196)

To understand this, let us backtrack a bit and say something more
about Sellars's general view of moral Oughts. As we saw earlier, the content and force of moral norms makes fundamental references to a community of agents who reciprocally take themselves to be bound by certain
fundamental principles, principles which are, in Sellars's terms, "the most
general common intentions of that community" (Sellars 1991b: 39). So
when an agent intends to do something (by thinking or saying 'I shall do
action A') what they are doing is taking a community intention, a We-
Shall intention, to be the basis of their behaviour. According to O'Shea, a
causally reductionist account of this will give a:

> causal explanation of the motivational efficacy of 'shall' intentions as
> socially acquired linguistic and psychological dispositions to follow
> up one's 'I shall do A' intentions and volitions, other things being
> equal, with the doing of A. Such a social-behavioral account of the
> origin, the content, and the motivational force of individual inten-
> tions, community intentions, and on that basis, of normative 'ought'
> statements, would not itself . . . involve the assertion of any 'ought
> statements'.
>
> (O'Shea 2009: 199)

I hope it is now clear why giving an account of the causal history of moral
agents is the key for the possibility of causal reducibility: we can causally
reduce Ought to Is by giving a causal explanation of how the disposition to
act on shall-intentions is acquired, not by learning to respond to objective
normative facts that are already there, but by learning to follow up on the
espousal of a shall-intention to do A with doing A. So a causal reductionist
account focuses on the acquisition of the matter-of-factual dispositions
that underlie the reliable relation between intention and bodily behaviour,
an acquisition that can be described without the describer asserting any
Ought statement.

In accounting for moral behaviour in this way, Sellars thereby replaces
a conception of moral Ought as "an intruder in the natural order" with

"the view that the causal efficacy of the embodied core generalizations of rules is ultimately grounded on the Law of Effect, that is to say, the role of rewards and punishments in shaping behavior" (quoted in O'Shea 2009: 200). In other words, instead of seeing moral Oughts as objective normative facts to be intuited (the intuitionists) or actualised by pure practical reason (Kant), we should see moral Oughts as ultimately grounded in naturalistically inculcated uniformities and patterns of behaviour that can be described in matter-of-fact terms. It is this that makes it possible to describe a moral agent without having to make Ought-assertions, and so makes it possible to causally reduce Ought to Is.

V

But what does it mean to say that Oughts are ultimately grounded in naturalistically inculcated uniformities and patterns of behaviour?

The key here is Sellars's concept of pattern-governed behaviour. Sellars formulated this concept originally to solve the problem of how one acquires the ability to follow rules without assuming that one already has that ability. Let's stipulate that learning to play a game (perhaps a language game) is learning to obey the rules of the game. Here we do what we do *because* of the rules. In playing a game, on this conception, we do not merely conform to the rules unconsciously; the rules must be involved in our making the moves we make—we must in some sense 'have them in mind'. But how do we learn *these* rules? Are there meta-rules that we must obey, and therefore have in mind, to learn these rules? Sellars thinks that this sets up a dilemma: either one embarks on an infinite regress of rules, or one posits that there is a pre-linguistic realm of demands and permissions, a realm of rules that is given rather than learned. Both horns of the dilemma are unacceptable, the first for obvious reasons, the second because a normative realm that is given in this way is not consistent with the naturalism for which Sellars is trying to argue.

Pattern governed behaviour is meant to avoid this dilemma. Pattern governed behaviour is neither rule *conforming* behaviour, behaviour that is merely caused, nor rule *obeying* behaviour. It is not rule conforming behaviour because it is not just done in conformity with the rules but *because* of the rules. But it is not rule obeying behaviour because although it is in some sense done because of the rules, it is not done because the subject has the rules 'in mind'. In engaging in pattern governed behaviour one is playing a game because of the rules of the game, but not—as with rule obeying behaviour—because one, in some sense, is also playing a meta-game.

To illustrate the concept, Sellars gives the example of a bee doing a complex dance after returning from a mission. Clearly the bee turns and wiggles in the way it does *because* it is part of a complex (signalling) dance, but does this commit us to the idea that it does so "by virtue of intending to realise the dance" (Sellars 1991d: 326)? Clearly not, Sellars thinks. And does this commit us to rejecting the idea that "the dance pattern as a whole is involved in the occurrence of each wiggle and turn" (Sellars 1991d: 326)? Again, the answer is clearly not. The bee does what it does (turns and wiggles) because it is part of the dance, and the dance is involved in the occurrence of each doing, even though the bee does not have the dance as a whole, or its rules, in mind. We can make sense of this not by drawing on the mentalistic language of intention and purpose, but by giving "an evolutionary account of the phenomenon of the dance, and hence to interpret the statement that *this* wiggle occurred because of the complex dance to which it belongs . . . in terms of the survival value to groups of bees of these forms of behavior" (Sellars 1991d: 326). In other words, the bee does not wiggle because it has a pattern of behaviour (a dance) in mind; rather it wiggles because, through natural selection, it has come to have "a 'wiring diagram' that expresses itself in this pattern" (Sellars 1991d: 326). Because we explain this wiggle in terms of the survival value of possessing this wiring diagram (which produces the dance in the right circumstances), rather than in terms of an intention and purpose, it is easy to see how the pattern of behaviour brought about by the diagram admits of pure descriptions, i.e. of descriptions that do not need to use Ought in its characterization of these patterns.

But how does pattern governed behaviour help us understand how the acquisition of rule obeying behaviour can be explained in a naturalistic fashion? It is clear that the acquisition of pattern governed behaviour itself can be explained in a naturalistic fashion. As Sellars says: "to learn to engage in pattern governed behaviour is to become conditioned to arrange perceptual elements into patterns and to form these, in turn, into more complex patterns and sequences of patterns. Presumably, such learning is capable of explanation in S-R reinforcement terms" (Sellars 1991d: 327). But how does this get us to rule obeying behaviour? Rule obeying behaviour is behaviour in which one plays "a game and a meta-game, the latter being the game in which belong the rules obeyed in playing the former game as a piece of rule obeying behavior" (Sellars 1991d: 337). Sellars's view is that since he has explained how we can learn to play the object level game in a naturalistic fashion (by learning pattern governed behaviour) then we can also explain our ability to play the meta-game in such a fashion. But it is unclear how learning two types of pattern governed behaviour, even two types that are exercised at the same time, adds up to learning to do something because of the rules— in the sense of 'because' at play in rule obeying behaviour. As Bernstein cogently puts the point:

> The central issue here is how are we to interpret the transitions between the object and meta-language. If these transitions are simply a matter of being conditioned to respond in certain determinate ways

(pattern governed behavior), we haven't come any closer to understanding rule obeying behavior: we have only a more complex form
of pattern governed behavior . . . Sellars's elaborate schema depends
on assuming that the transitions back and forth from the object language to the meta-language are not merely conditioned responses,
but the full-fledged obeying of rules. But this is the concept of rule
obeying behavior that the schema was supposed to clarify. The concept of rule obeying behavior has been presupposed rather than
explicated.

(Bernstein 1966a: 314)

Adding patterned governed behaviour that is described in matter of factual terms to patterned governed behaviour that is also described in such
terms does not add up to rule-obeying behaviour. So if one is to posit the
latter concept, it must be presupposed rather than explained.

But the problem is even worse for the partisan of causal reducibility.
For even if we could account for the *acquisition* of normative behaviour
without making Ought statements in our explanation of this acquisition
this does not establish that we can describe a *full-fledged person's* normative behaviour without making Ought statements. To use language that
Sellars introduced later in his career, persons, in their mature behaviour,
do not just conform to rules (Ought-to-be-rules) by exhibiting uniformities of behaviour, they also act *because* of the rules insofar as they are
rationally responsive to them (Ought-to-do-rules). As Sellars puts it:

One isn't a full-fledged member of the linguistic community until
one not only conforms to linguistic ought-to-be's (and may-be's) by
exhibiting the required uniformities, but grasps these ought-to-be's
and may-be's themselves (i.e. knows the rules of the language). One
must, therefore, have the concept of oneself as an agent, as not only
the subject-matter subject of ought-to-be's but the agent subject of
ought-to-do's.

(Sellars 1974: 101)[9]

To provide a causally reductive account of our being an agent subject
of ought-to-do-rules, one can't simply show how rule obeying behaviour arises out of uniformities and pattern governed behaviour, one must
show how rules and norms, as they operate at the level of reasons, *con-
sist in* such naturalistically acquired uniformities. What we need is an
account of how naturalistically acquired dispositions and uniformities of
behaviour *add up to* normative behaviour.

O'Shea recognises the explanatory burden. If one does not extend the
notion of causal reducibility in this way one will end up with what O'Shea
calls a 'separated off' account of persons-in-the-world, one which instead
of *accounting* for how Oughts operate at the level of reasons, simply

changes the subject and focuses just on the outward physical movements that are the product of acting on such Oughts. It admits that there are norms and norm obeying behaviour, but is satisfied with simply describing behavioural uniformities in causal terms. Here is how O'Shea puts it:

> [A] causal account is supposed to be more than just a trivial, subject-changing, or 'separated off' scientific explanation of various physical motions. For ideally a causal reduction of normative 'oughts' would explain specifically and exhaustively those particular psychological dispositions and complex patterns of behavior in which the practice of asserting and obeying intersubjectively valid moral assertions really consists.
>
> (O'Shea 2009: 199)

In essence, a separated off account of persons-in-the-world is a dualistic account that accepts, and does not try to explain, the distinction between normative and causally uniform behaviour. But this view does not, O'Shea thinks, respect the *"reducibility* side of Sellars's position" which is:

> supposed to apply to the *distinction of level itself*; that is, to the distinction between the normative-conceptual and the non-normative or pre-conceptual that constitutes the difference between 'man' and his 'precursors'. It is this distinction that Sellars sees . . . as a *reducible difference of level* when viewed under the regulative ideal of the final scientific image of the human being.
>
> (O'Shea 2009: 192–193)

On O'Shea's reading, Sellars is not content with merely joining the framework of persons to the scientific image; he also wants to show how the difference between persons and their animal precursors—the former being in the space of reasons, the latter not—is a reducible difference from the point of view of Peirceish, i.e. a framework that is articulated by pure descriptions. I think O'Shea is right here, that Sellars had this larger ambition and that the account of joining the framework of persons to the scientific image given at the end of "Philosophy and the Scientific Image of Man" was not his last word on the matter. It's not that the joining thesis is wrong, it's just not the whole story with respect to the place of normativity in a naturalistic account of the world. While the joining thesis articulates the irreducibility side of Sellars's 'irreducibility cum reducibility position', it does not account for the reducibility side of his position.

VI

As we have seen, to account for the reducibility side of Sellars's view—and arrive as a non-trivial conception of causal reduction—one's account of norm obeying behaviour must not only describe the *acquisition* of uniformities and patterns of behaviour without using Ought in its descriptions, but also describe the *current functioning* of Ought-to-do rules in the life of agent subjects without using Ought. Can Sellars meet this more demanding requirement?

In his 1962 paper, "Truth and Correspondence," Sellars introduces an important explanatory principle that is meant to do just this. Here is the principle:

> Espousal of principles is reflected in uniformities of performance. . . . I am not claiming that to follow a principle, i.e., act on principle, is identical with exhibiting a uniformity of performance that accords with the principle. I think that any such idea is radically mistaken. I am merely saying that the espousal of a principle or standard, whatever else it involves, is characterised by a uniformity of performance. And let it be emphasised that this uniformity, though not the principle of which it is the manifestation, is describable in matter-of-factual terms.
> (Sellars 1991a: 215–216)

Here we have a paradigmatic example of Sellars's 'no conceptual reducibility/but causal reducibility' position. On the one hand, the principle avoids a "naturalistic reduction of 'ought' to 'is' " (Sellars 1991a: 215) because it does not claim that acting on a principle *is* exhibiting a uniformity of performance. Indeed, this is a radically mistaken idea that is equal to the idea that Ought can be logically reduced to Is. The principle thus does not deny that the behaviour of the person being described is "fraught with ought" (Sellars 1991a: 212). However, in stipulating that uniformities of performance, *ceteris paribus*, follow from their espousals of principles, the principle allows one to 'bracket' these principles and norms and describe the uniformities of behaviour that result from them in matter-of-factual terms. It is in this sense that the principle allows for the causal reducibility of Ought to Is.

Notice that the use of this principle does not have to be tied to a naturalistic account of the acquisition of uniformities, for it can be utilised to describe and explain not only the behaviour of subject-matter subjects but also the normative behaviour of adult agent subjects who act in accord with their conception of rules. In using a conceptual framework that includes this principle, an inquirer steps out of the framework of persons, where the recognition and the rehearsal of commonly shared norms and rules are at issue, and adopts a standpoint that only describes what Is and never what Ought to be.

How shall we evaluate this principle? As we know, the principle, as part of an interpretive conceptual framework, applies *to* an object, i.e. to what, before the principle was applied, we called a person. When interpreted this way persons turn out to be mechanisms whose uniformities of performances can be described in matter of factual terms. But the question then emerges: is the conceptual framework that includes the principle, and which is used to interpret this object, *itself* subject to the principle? To achieve a robust notion of causal reduction it seems that we must answer this question in the affirmative. For if the explanations and descriptions generated by this framework do not apply to the inquirer and the norms that articulate *their* conceptual framework, then we will have a new type of separated off account insofar as these norms will not be subject to the principle. And this means that these norms will not be subject to causal reduction.

But there is a question of whether the principle can coherently be applied to the framework that includes the principle. There is such a question because if the principle is to apply to the framework that includes the principle its normative force cannot be neutralised (by being subject to itself), for otherwise it could not apply to the framework. But then the framework includes a principle whose normative force is not neutralised by being subject to the principle (i.e. to itself). This leads to a dilemma for Sellars's account: to bracket the normative force of the principle in this framework is to undermine the possibility of completing a causal reduction insofar as the principle is what lets us assume that espousal of principles is reflected in naturalistically describable uniformities; but to not bracket the normative force of the principle with respect to the framework of which it is a part means that there is a framework to which the principle cannot apply, leading to a view in which there is a framework that escapes causal reduction.

To avoid this dilemma Sellars must posit that the principle, when applied to the framework of the inquirer, is part of a higher-order framework. The principle must be a meta-principle. O'Shea accordingly calls it the 'norm/nature *meta*-principle'. But the problem of the normative force of the principle will simply iterate insofar as we can always ask the question of whether the normatively governed conceptual practice of the agent subject of the higher-order framework is subject to the principle. For that framework to be subject to the principle, we must posit an even higher-order framework, and so on. This regress can only stop if we posit a framework in which the principle is in force without that framework having to be used by an agent subject. But where is such a framework to be found?

At some points in *Science and Metaphysics* Sellars suggests that the final idea scientific framework, Peirceish, could be such a framework:

> Notice that although the concepts of 'ideal truth' and 'what really exists' are defined in terms of a Peircean conceptual structure they do not require that there ever be a Peircean community. Peirce himself fell into difficulty because, by not taking into account the dimension of 'picturing', he had no Archimedeian point outside the series

of actual and possible beliefs in terms of which to define the ideal or limit to which members of this series might approximate.

(Sellars 1968: 142)[10]

Now it is not likely that someone so nourished on Kant and Peirce as Sellars would think that a Peircean community need not exist because the Archimedeian point of a view is a pre-critical 'view from nowhere'. Rather, Sellars thinks that a community need not exist because within our current conceptual scheme we already have a grasp on the importance of picturing as the criterion for the correctness for our truth-evaluable assertions (see Sellars 1968: 136). But even if this is so, why say that picturing gives us an Archimedeian point *completely outside* the series of actual and possible beliefs? This conclusion is not entailed by the fact that picturing functions as a criterion, for a criterion can only be a criterion for our assertions if it is taken as a criterion in a possible framework. My argument is that Sellars needs the Archimedeian point to avoid the force of the question: 'who posits the final framework and does the norm/nature meta-principle included in it apply to this self-same framework?' If one is to avoid this question, there must be a way, after ascending to the Archimedeian point, of throwing away the ladder—meaning a way of escaping the fact that the framework from which a naturalistic explanation and description of the world is fashioned is itself governed by norms that are not themselves neutralised by the principle.

It seems to me that Sellars's 'irreducibility cum reducibility position' eventuates in one of three options, all of which are unsatisfactory. First, Sellars could offer a weak concept of causal reduction that leads to a separated off account of persons-in-the-world. Here, one would accept the 'joining thesis' as Sellars's last word concerning the status of the norms that inform the framework of persons. But then the 'reducibility side' of his view gets short shrift. Or, Sellars could offer a stronger version of causal reduction by utilizing the norm/nature meta-principle. But this leads to the dilemmas mentioned earlier: either the principle is vitiated through the paradoxes of self-reference, or these paradoxes are avoided by positing an Archimedeian point that is not in keeping with critical meta-theoretical strictures that Sellars ought to accept for his synoptic vision. What we should conclude is that Sellars's system, at its highest apex, is not stable, and this should spur us on to try to do better in thinking about the place of normativity in the natural world.

VII

There is an irony at the heart of Sellars's 'irreducibility cum reducibility position'. Although it is meant to deliver us a quite stringent type of naturalism, the position is tailored to avoid the naturalistic fallacy at all costs. Because of this Sellars is forced to say that normative vocabulary can either be used but not described or explained (the irreducible side of the 'irreducibility cum reducibility position'), or merely mentioned but not used (the reducible side of the 'irreducibility cum reducibility position'). The view that I want to counter-pose to Sellars's, which is a *pragmatic naturalism*, eschews both of these ideas.

Briefly, a pragmatic naturalism says that normative behaviour, including linguistic behaviour, is causally and not just conceptually irreducible in the sense that even in Peirceish normative vocabulary must be used and not merely mentioned to capture the framework of persons in its net. But while normative vocabulary must be used and not merely mentioned by those describing persons, we can nonetheless tell a naturalistic explanatory story about the use of *this* vocabulary, but one not told exclusively in the vocabulary of physics but in that of biology, anthropology, ethology, genetic psychology, history, etc. This story, the vocabulary of which remains fraught with ought, aims at explaining the *historical* conditions of possibility for normative behaviour itself. In this sense this story aims at grasping the historical process through which the non-normative *becomes* the normative, and at identifying the ontogenetic mechanisms in the development of agents through which normativity is anchored in their behaviour. From the first part of the story we would understand the development of the normative out of the non-normative through understanding the evolutionary development of cooperative behaviour in human groups,[11] and from the second part we would understand norms as based in the instrumental and social expectations that agents come to have concerning themselves, others, and world, which are implicit in their acquired bodily habits and skills.

The first part of the story has similarities with Sellars's notion of causal reduction. To give a causal reduction is also to give a kind of historical account of the genesis of normative behaviour, but it does not attempt to explain the emergence of the normative; for that, Sellars thinks, would entail the use of normative vocabulary. From the perspective of the framework of Peirceish there simply is no such emergence, while from the perspective of the framework of persons this explanation is impossible insofar as the transition from pre-normative to normative behaviour "was a holistic one, a jump to a level of awareness which is irreducibly new, a jump which was the coming into being of man" (Sellars 1991c: 6).[12] But the felt impossibility of explaining the emergence of the normative out of the non-normative depends on the inability to see that *normative vocabulary can be used as part of genuine descriptions and explanations*, for example, the descriptions and explanations of biology or ethology. The dominance of physics in Sellars's picture, the need to telescope the special sciences into the microphysical sciences, is here disabling.

What about the second part of the story? To grasp the importance of bodily habits for a pragmatic naturalism, let us go back to Sellars's concept of pattern governed behaviour. Although Sellars means pattern governed behaviour to mediate between mere stimulus-response behaviour and rule obeying behaviour he can't really have it serve this function because his understanding of the concept is structured, one again, by the dichotomy between things that can be described in matter of factual terms and things that cannot. Because pattern governed behaviour is on the matter of factual side of the dichotomy the addition of patterned governed behaviour to more pattern governed behaviour cannot add up to rule obeying behaviour. What we need to do to get from stimulus-response behaviour to normative behaviour is reject the dichotomy between what can be described matter of factually and what can only be recognised by acting on a norm or rehearsing an intention. We can do this by thinking of pattern governed behaviour not as mere uniformities or regularities that can be described in matter of factual terms but as bodily habits and skills that, due to training and habituation, involve a kind of rational intelligibility. Some habits *are* like merely uniformities. But to describe most habits or bodily skills as mere uniformities is to miss the fact that they, even if exercised outside of the conscious control of the agent, *have a rationale*, a rationale provided by the practice of which they are a part.[13] In drifting to the right part of the penalty box through a direct motor response to the perceived configuration of play, a skilled footballer is not exercising a mere uniformity, they are rather calling upon a deep well of know-how which is tailored to the logic of the practice. Their habits and skills involve a 'practical sense' of the situation, a sensitivity to what the situation requires, to what is right or appropriate to do. While mostly implicit in practice, this practical sense is lived through by the agent in their embodied action. This cannot be said of uniformities that can be characterised in S-R terms.

Full-fledged rule obeying behaviour—behaviour where one is an agent subject of Ought-to-do-rules—is behaviour that stems from making explicit in reflection certain of the expectations concerning self, other, and world rooted in this practical sense. Built into the habit of drifting to the right part of the penalty body are implicit expectations, based on past experience, of what will happen in the future. Such expectations are of course probabilistic and fallible, but nevertheless they guide our future behaviour. The rules of a practice, we could say, are a codification of the expectations that participants in the practice reciprocally have with respect to each other and to the common features of the situation in which they act, and rule obeying behaviour is behaviour that is consciously undertaken in light of these expectations. We cannot give a causally reductive account of rule obeying behaviour because to so much as describe the expectations upon which they are based requires that one can *recognize them*, that one oneself has a practical sense of what the situation requires. Any plausible naturalism has to accommodate this insight rather then work around it.

There is one issue outstanding. The Sellarsian is sure to say that for this picture to work that it needs to be able to explain how we not only act in conformity with rules but go against them, break them. Without this one had not genuinely gotten at the normative. The Sellarsian is able to explain that because, as we saw in our discussion of the framework of person, the norms that govern behaviour, linguistic and otherwise, are social—instituted through our mutual recognition of each other as subject to them. Because of this we are confronted by norms whose force has a kind of objectivity. This accounts for the fact that when one sees a red light when driving one *ought* to stop. But while one ought to stop, one can choose not to (as is often done in the town in which I live). A habit, in contrast, is a regularity such that when one sees a red light *one stops*. We cannot say that that one ought to stop for there is no possibility of not acting on a habit when it is triggered in response to a situation. The habit is triggered and propels us to act or it does not.

The pragmatic naturalist agrees with the Sellarsian that the rule to stop at a red light has an irreducible social component. But instead of finding it primarily in our recognition of others *as* subject to the rules, and so in a kind of cognitive attitude toward others, the pragmatic naturalist locates it in the expectations that we have about one another and the world implicit in our habits and bodily skills. They also agree that we have to make sense of our going against a rule. But this, they think, is not the product of a disembodied act of reason in which one 'steps back' from the rule and decides to do otherwise, but is rather the product of a situation in which one's habits are conflicted. Conflict may come about because the situation is novel, or because one has conflicting desires and values. In either case, the situation is indeterminate, and there are no clear expectations and so clear rule to guide our behaviour. What we must do in this case is, through a reflective and creative process, abductively arrive at a new rule, one that fits the indeterminate situation and allows action to recommence. If action does recommence one modifies to some degree one's habits and the expectations implicit in them. Usually this new rule is a small variant on the existing rules and does not conflict with them. But sometimes the new rule does so conflict. It is this this case that we says that one has gone against a rule, by which we mean that one has not acted in keeping with the standing body of expectations implicit in our collective habitual practice.

Clearly, much more would need to be said to make this alternative pragmatic picture plausible. But hopefully I have done enough to justify the idea that Sellars's naturalism with a normative turn is not the path to follow to give a naturalist account of the normative.

Notes

1. I would like to thank James O'Shea for comments on an early draft of this chapter.
2. In Huw Price's language, these are three 'placement problems'. See Price 2004.

3. I say that subjects 'appear to themselves' as logical subjects rather than sim-ply being logical subjects because Sellars argues that persons ultimately are not logical subjects. We take this up below.
4. See O'Shea 2007, 2009. Because of its clear and compact presentation of the key moves at the heart of the Sellarsian system, I focus on O'Shea 2009.
5. I say 'on the face of it' because, as we shall see, O'Shea claims that there is in fact no tension.
6. See chapter 5 of Sellars (1968) for the concept of 'Peirceish'.
7. As Sellars puts it in his early work: "The task of the philosopher cannot be to show how, in principle, what is said by normative discourse can be said without normative discourse, for the simple reason that this cannot be done" (Sellars 1980: 82).
8. The space of reasons, which involves both theoretical and practical normativ-ity, is more extensive than, and includes within it, the framework of persons.
9. This passage, which is about linguistic rules specifically, applies to moral rules as well.
10. For Sellars it is not just moral Oughts that are grounded in naturalistically acquired uniformities but also normatively governed signifying relations as well. The norms that confer meaning on our thought and speech presuppose real relations between linguistic items and the world, relations that can be described in naturalistic non-normative terms. Sellars calls these real rela-tions *picturing* relations. So any casually reductive account of norms that goes beyond the practical to the theoretical would depend on the success of this concept. For reasons of space, we cannot discuss picturing in this chapter, although what we have said in this chapter could be extended, with some modifications, to picturing. For more, see Levine (2007).
11. For the kind of account of I have in mind, see Mead 1934; Tomasello 1999.
12. Sellars argues that to deny this jump is to fall prey to the Myth of the Given, which accounts for why he tailors his naturalism to avoid the naturalistic fal-lacy. In Levine (forthcoming), I argue at length that denying this jump does not entail acceptance of the Myth of the Given.
13. For much more on habits, see Levine (2015) and Levine (forthcoming).

References

Bernstein, R. J. 1966a. 'Sellars's Vision of Man-in-the-Universe I'. *Review of Metaphysics* 20: 113–143.

———. 1966b. 'Sellars's Vision of Man-in-the-Universe II'. *Review of Metaphysics* 20: 290–316.

Levine, S. 2007. 'The Place of Picturing in Sellars's Synoptic Vision'. *Philosophical Forum* 38: 247–269.

———. 2015. 'Norms and Habits: Brandom on the Sociality of Action'. *European Journal of Philosophy* 23: 248–272.

———. forthcoming. *Pragmatism, Objectivity, and Experience*. Cambridge: Cambridge University Press.

Mead, G. H. 1934. *Mind, Self, and Society: From the Standpoint of a Social Behaviourist*. C. W. Morris (ed.). Chicago, IL: University of Chicago Press.

O'Shea, J. 2007. *Sellars: Naturalism with a Normative Turn*. Cambridge: Polity Press.

———. 2009. 'On the Structure of Sellars's Naturalism with a Normative Turn'. In W. A. deVries (ed.) *Empiricism, Perceptual Knowledge, Normativity, and Realism: Essays on Wilfrid Sellars*. Oxford: Oxford University Press.

Price, H. 2004. 'Naturalism without Representation'. In M. de Caro and D. Macarthur (eds.) *Naturalism in Question*. Cambridge, MA: Harvard University Press.

Sellars, W. 1958. 'Counterfactuals, Dispositions, and the Causal Modalities'. In H. Feigl, M. Scriven and G. Maxwell (eds.) *Concepts, Theories, and the Mind-Body Problem*. Minneapolis, MN: University of Minnesota Press.

———. 1968. *Science and Metaphysics*. London: Routledge and Kegan Paul.

———. 1974. *Essays in Philosophy and its History*. Dordrecht: D. Reidel Publishing.

———. 1980. 'A Semantical Solution of the Mind-Body Problem'. In *Pure Pragmatics and Possible Worlds: The Early Essays of Wilfrid Sellars*. Atascadero, CA: Ridgeview Publishing.

———. 1991a. *Science, Perception and Reality*. Atascadero, CA: Ridgeview Publishing.

———. 1991b. 'Truth and Correspondence', in Sellars 1991a.

———. 1991c. 'Philosophy and the Scientific Image of Man', in Sellars 1991a.

———. 1991d. 'Some Reflections on Language Games', in Sellars 1991a.

———. 1997. *Empiricism and the Philosophy of Mind*. Cambridge, MA: Harvard University Press.

Tomasello, M. 1999. *The Cultural Origins of Human Cognition*. Cambridge, MA: Harvard University Press.

12 Pragmatic Naturalism

The Authority of Reason, the Agrippan Trilemma and the Significance of Philosophising *in medias res*

David Macarthur

Although pragmatism is a form of naturalism and German idealism is traditionally seen as a form of non-naturalism, both are forms of *normativism*, that is, both involve commitments to a conception of rational normativity that is indispensable to a sense of ourselves as rational agents; and one that is not reducible to the objective causal categories recognized by scientific naturalism—essentially those that constitute the scientific image of the world often, though not always, identified with the posits of the successful natural sciences. For present purposes the term 'naturalism' only indicates a commitment to anti-supernaturalism (e.g. it is anti-theistic). Note, too, that the qualification 'scientific' is substantive. It indicates a conception of science that is not primarily aimed at tracking the use of the term 'science' as a matter of everyday usage or grammar—since this use is variable and heterogeneous—but indicates a level of success in achieving a certain form of intelligibility associated with the rise of modern science. What is at issue is a form of causal intelligibility that aims to institute an ideal of objectivity such that the data for scientific explanation and its results are available to public scrutiny and criticism (e.g. verification, re-testing, repeating the experiment). Science, on this conception, attempts to bring objective (so, publicly measurable) phenomena in both the natural and human realms under general causal laws or, at least, local causal patterns. Normativists hold that rational norms cannot be reduced to the objective causes or relations between such studied by the sciences. To put it briefly, we might say rational norms concern what *ought* to happen, whether it does or not; whereas causation concerns what does happen or, perhaps, what must happen (according to some notion of physical necessity). Pragmatism is thus a *liberal* naturalism that, unlike scientific naturalism, does not attempt to limit its view of the world to the (natural) scientific image; but attempts to also do justice to the manifest image of the world.

I

Normativism and Agrippa's Trilemma

A major difficulty confronting the normativist of either persuasion is the ancient sceptical problem known as Agrippa's trilemma, perhaps the most powerful general argument in the Pyrrhonian sceptical arsenal.[1] How can there be genuine justification if for any justification (whether put forth as knowledge or belief) one can raise a why-question for which any justification offered, in turn, raises another why-question to which any further justification raises another why-question; and so on ad infinitum. The position is aptly described by the famous Pyrrhonian sceptic, Sextus Empiricus,

> what is brought forth as a warrant for the matter in question needs another warrant, which itself needs another, and so *ad infinitum*, so that we have no point from which to begin to establish anything.
>
> (1985: 41 [Book 1, 166])

The infinite regress of reasons for reasons is vicious because at no point in the regress do we achieve what is needed, namely, a source or explanation of rational authority that is ultimately transferable to the original judgment that was called into question. From the rational point of view nothing has been established. Justification *uberhaupt* is undermined.

The trilemma is generated by reflecting on how we might attempt to avoid the infinite regress of justifications for justifications for any given judgment. If we simply refuse, at some point, to provide further justification we are making the arbitrary and unwarranted assumption that our terminating justification is a good enough justification to support the rest—a move that is clearly hopeless. Or if we find ourselves offering as a justification something that has already been called into question earlier in our chain of reasoning then we have simply argued in a fruitless circle. Again, and this is the common theme of all the three 'lemmas', no rational authority has been, or can be, established. Since the argument is content insensitive it seems no rational authority is available for any judgment whatsoever.

To see this in more detail, it is important to consider the basis of the power of the trilemma. An initial observation is that it trades on an indefinitely iterable demand for epistemic entitlement—which is, arguably, the primary sense of that multiply ambiguous term 'justification' in practice.[2] Being justified on this understanding is for one to be epistemically responsible in believing as one does.[3] It is worth noting here that the use of such deontological terms as entitlement, responsibility and blame in epistemology does not presuppose that beliefs are under our voluntary control.[4] The relevant notion of epistemic responsibility requires no commitment to voluntarism but depends on the fact that it is an internal feature of beliefs that they are responsive or sensitive to reasons.

The relevant sceptical problem arises in a reflective setting in which what is in question is one's epistemic right to one's judgments, and whether one can 'bring forth' or demonstrate the basis of one's entitlement. The present suggestion is that Agrippa's trilemma can be understood as follows:

> In order for a subject S to be epistemically entitled to his judgment that p, *S must exhibit an appropriate reason* (say q) for p that is *independent* of p. And since we can ask, in turn, about our epistemic entitlement to q, we are set upon an infinite regress of reasons for reasons which must meet these same requirements.

Two points are worth emphasising. It is presupposed that there can be no epistemic entitlement for a judgment without the exhibition of an *independent* reason for it, a consideration that counts in favour of it without presupposing its truth.[5] For each item whose entitlement is called into question what is demanded is, as Sextus puts it, "another warrant" of entitlement i.e. the bringing forth of another distinct reason.[6] And since these reasons must be *exhibited*, one must be aware of them, or at least they must be cognitively accessible once the question of justification is raised. So the entitlement in question cannot be earned by supposing that the judgment in question is formed by a reliable process that one knows nothing about. Consequently, if we accept the Agrippan requirement for epistemic entitlement, and if vicious forms of regress and of circularity and arbitrary assumption exhaust the options (as they certainly seem to), then Agrippa's trilemma is, quite simply, unanswerable.[7]

II

The Failure of Scientific Naturalist Solutions

At this point one might wonder whether scientific naturalism does not offer a way out of this difficulty, which might be thought to arise only for a normativist outlook. But scientific naturalism faces its own dilemma in confronting Agrippa's trilemma. On the one hand scientific naturalism may attempt to appeal to reliable natural processes as 'justifications' (in the different sense of evidence of truth-conduciveness) in place of the normativist's appeal to reasons. The problem here, of course, is that although one can justify (i.e. demonstrate one's entitlement to) a claim by appeal to its being formed on the basis of a reliable process, such a justification is only operative insofar as one is aware of this process.[8] But it is a central claim of the scientific naturalist that one need not be aware of the reliability of the processes giving rise to one's beliefs or claims to know.

As natural facts about us we might be completely unaware of them; that is, they are blankly external to us (e.g. they are not available to introspection). If we do become aware of them then they can become reasons but they then also become subject to the trilemma. So long as we feel the grip of the question of justification in the sense of our entitlement to what we believe or claim to know, scientific naturalism cannot avoid it in this way.

Alternatively, the scientific naturalist might attempt to block the regress by appeal to non-rational natural facts which explain why we believe or claim to know on the basis of some psychological mechanism (e.g. a habit of mind based on the operations of the imagination) rather than attempting to meet the normative demands of reason. Hume, for example, writes:

> Nature, by an absolute and uncontroulable necessity has determin'd us to judge as well as to breathe and feel; nor can we any more forbear viewing certain objects in a stronger and fuller light, upon account of their customary connexion with a present impression, than we can hinder ourselves from thinking as long as we are awake, or seeing the surrounding bodies, when we turn our eyes towards them in broad sunshine. Whoever has taken the pains to refute the cavils of this total scepticism, has really disputed without an antagonist, and endeavour'd by arguments to establish a faculty, which nature has antecedently implanted in the mind, and render'd unavoidable.
>
> (*THN*: Bk. 1, Part iv, Sect i)

Here Hume is using the term "total scepticism" to refer to a reflexive doubt of one who is "conscious of many errors in the past" which compounds the weakness of our faculty of understanding in each of its operations. But the anti-sceptical appeal to nature could surely also be applied to Agrippa's trilemma. If nature has determined us to have such-and-such a belief then the rational demonstration that it is without reason or evidence is of no consequence. The belief is unavoidable and cannot be argued away.[9]

The scientific naturalist who argues in this way, however, misses the force of the trilemma. It is not in the first instance a threat to the *maintenance* of a belief. It is a question of its epistemic credentials, our entitlement to it, whether we are responsible in holding the belief or not. In our everyday practices both the expressions of belief and claims to knowledge are matters for which we are treated as responsible; hence, as matters for which we can be criticized. To be told that we would have a belief no matter what the weight of reasons or evidence demonstrates is not an escape from scepticism but, at best, an escape from what might be thought to be (mistakenly, I think) the consequence of scepticism. Natural beliefs, understood as unbidden states of one's psychology arising passively and quite independently of one's rational capacities, cannot be seen as one's commitments or a matter that one can take any responsibility for. So if we understand the Agrippan trilemma as asking for what entitles one to one's ultimate beliefs or claims to know then Hume's naturalistic 'answer' is: nothing. But that is not a refutation or defusing of scepticism; it is, in fact, an expression of it.[10]

Hume's scientific naturalist 'solution' to the trilemma is no solution at all. The matter of responsibility for one's beliefs or claims to know cannot be so evaded by switching to a naturalistic account of belief formation and stability. Indeed, the naturalist, by arguing that we are not responsible for the regress-blocking belief leaves us in the uncomfortable position of being a victim of beliefs for which we cannot see ourselves as entitled—indeed beliefs which it is hard to understand as one's own as opposed to unwanted symptoms of a psychological affliction (akin to a form of psychosis).

Given that the problem of entitlement to our beliefs and knowledge claims arises in our everyday practices and given that scientific naturalism not only lacks the resources to adequately respond to it but makes matters worse (insofar as natural beliefs cannot be practically identified with) then the only way of satisfyingly engaging with the trilemma is on normativist ground. The question, then, is whether we should prefer a pragmatic naturalist normativism to an idealist non-naturalist normativism.[11] The key issue is one of rational authority: on what basis, or grounds, does reason have authority in one's thought and action? I hope to show the advantages of a pragmatism that attempts to defuse the threat posed by Agrippa's trilemma in contrast to an idealism that attempts to provide absolute grounds (in terms of some supernatural super-entitlement) to escape the trilemma once its force has been fully felt.

III

The German Idealist Attempt to Escape Agrippa's Trilemma

A fundamental problem of German Idealism is that of accounting for rational authority in all areas of life—everyday life, science and philosophy—given a full appreciation of the power of Agrippa's trilemma, one that has both theoretical and practical implications. Idealists hold that unless we can find an *absolute* ground for our claims to rational authority then genuine justification in any of our reason-giving practices is an illusion (Franks 2005: 8; Gardner 2007).

Although Kant saw Agrippa's trilemma as little more than an academic problem for philosophers (whose job it is to explain the obvious cognitive successes we have achieved in, say, the natural sciences and mathematics) the German Idealists who succeeded him saw Agrippa's trilemma as undermining all justification in everyday life, morality, aesthetics, law, politics, and the sciences. For them it was an existential no less than an intellectual problem. Given its devastating impact the question then becomes, how is one to respond to it?

Paul Franks (2005) has persuasively argued that the German Ideal-ists accept from Jacobi a certain conception of what is required to over-come Agrippa's trilemma—understood as a threat to "every putatively justificatory practice"—and so, of what is required to establish genuine rational authority:

> For [the German Idealists], the problem of escaping the Agrippan trilemma becomes the problem of achieving a Spinozist system that meets the holistic and monistic requirements.
>
> (10)

The holist requirement is "that every particular (object, fact, or judg-ment) be determined through its role within the whole and not through any intrinsic properties" (9–10); and the monistic requirement is "that the whole be grounded in an absolute principle that is immanent and not transcendent" (10). As Franks explains it, the German idealist strategy for responding to Agrippa's trilemma is to admit that it is completely unanswerable within the empirical realm, but that it is possible to pro-vide a transcendental (or metaphysical) grounding for empirical justifi-cation as a whole by appeal to an *absolute* (unconditional, necessary, unique) ground that is in some sense self-grounding, and so, capable of stopping the regress of reasons. The main candidate for the absolute or unconditioned ground which does not require further grounds or pre-suppositions to establish its rational authority is God—although other options are sometimes considered, e.g. Fichte's absolute "I".[12]

I shall not explore the idealists' detailed execution of this strategy but there are several general difficulties with it that are worth noting: (i) it appears to face a dilemma: either the transcendental grounding of empiri-cal justification is homogeneous with respect to empirical justification and then it, too, is subject to Agrippa's trilemma or it is heterogeneous with respect to the empirical (as Franks argues it must be in order to avoid the problem of homogeneity) in which case it cannot constitute genuine grounds for it. This problem becomes acute if one has doubts about the traditional notion of a radical separation of the *a priori* ('tran-scendental') standpoint of reflection from that of empirical experience.

Consider examples such as 'Two straight parallel lines will never meet' and 'Mammals do not lay eggs', which show that what was once taken to be *a priori* true, necessary and unrevisable, is empirically defeasible and, in these cases, false;[13] (ii) it is reasonable to wonder whether any ground can be *absolute* in the extremely demanding sense required, given that understanding anything always has its preconditions (conceptual, logical, evaluative, empirical). Moreover, even if a ground *seems to us* absolute in the relevant sense that does not show that it will continue to do so in the future especially under conditions of conceptual clarification, innovation or revolution;[14] (iii) the German Idealist strategy can be justly called a form of *mitigated* scepticism since it accepts the unanswerability of Agrippan scepticism at the empirical level even if this is overcome from the point of view of the system as a whole considered transcendentally; but, then, it can be criticised for giving far too much ground to the sceptic insofar as it accepts the conditional correctness of scepticism at the empirical level.

The present point is not that any of these difficulties are decisive, but together they do at least provide good reason to explore an alternative response to Agrippa's trilemma—one that does not require accepting its conditional correctness, i.e. when considered as undermining empirical justification across the board.

Indeed in light of these considerations, it seems reasonable to think that the *only* way to truly *escape* the trilemma (as the German Idealists are aiming to do) is to defuse its initial grip on one's system of judgment— whether prosecuted as a matter of belief or knowledge. What is required is not an absolute regress-blocking ground (however that is to be understood) but a means of challenging the problem itself and in that way earning the right not to have to respond to it. This alternative defusing strategy is one that pragmatism employs to drain the power of Agrippa's trilemma before it even gets off the ground.

Another virtue of the pragmatist approach is that it promises to be much less controversial than that of the German Idealist system, which appeals to substantial forms of *a priori* metaphysics and onto-theology. In the *Critique of Pure Reason* Kant remarks:

> By this procedure [of metaphysics] human reason precipitates itself into darkness and contradictions. . . . For since the principles of which it is making use transcend the limits of experience, they are no longer subject to any empirical test. The battlefield of these endless controversies is called metaphysics. . . . But it is idle to feign indifference to such enquiries, the object of which can never be indifferent to our human nature.
>
> (Avii)

Kant aimed through his critique of pure reason to answer the problem of metaphysics—that by way of it, human reason leads itself into "darkness and contradictions", the oscillation between dogmatism and scepticism— by showing the possibility of putting a new conception of metaphysics on "the secure path of science" (Bix). To this end Kant distinguishes *critical* metaphysics, which reflects on the possibility of experience and its transcendental conditions, from *speculative* metaphysics concerning, e.g. God, freedom and the soul, which transcends the limits of experience. But despite his insightful diagnosis of the problem Kant failed in this aim of overcoming it. Metaphysics *remains* a battlefield of endless controversies, as does onto-theology, e.g. witness the on-going dispute between theism and pantheism (which is particularly relevant in the present context given that German Idealists model the system that they require on that of the pantheist Spinoza). With regard to the *a priori*, "the difficulty," as Peirce puts it, "is that the opinions that today seem most unshakable are found tomorrow to be out of fashion" (1955: 17).

Neither field has established clear methods or results that have won anything like universal or near-universal acclaim and endorsement—even amongst those who are metaphysical and theological constructivists.[15] We might not be able to feign indifference to such metaphysical and theological inquiries but in light of the endless history of metaphysical and theological battles—one that is still with us—we have more than enough motivation to adopt a sceptical attitude towards them and any approach built on them. It is worth observing that pragmatism designed its pragmatic maxim for testing the experiential and practical upshot of concepts as a way of sifting out unworkable metaphysical and theological concepts from those that can play a fruitful role in legitimate inquiry.[16]

Of course, there will always be those, including the classical pragmatists Peirce and James (and the post–2007 neo-pragmatist Putnam), who will pursue compatibilist strategies looking for 'naturalised' forms of metaphysics or theology—philosophies which, at the very least, see themselves as compatible with the findings of modern science; and operate with a relativised form of the *a priori*. Nonetheless, pragmatism has a strong methodological motive to pursue a non-metaphysical non-theological—we could call it a 'naturalised'—response to Agrippa's trilemma. Since pragmatism puts great stock in 'scientific' consensus—or, less misleadingly, a consensus of democratically minded experimentalists in all fields of inquiry, scientific and non-scientific (e.g. ethics, aesthetics, politics)—pragmatists are concerned to defuse sceptical challenges, both ancient Pyrrhonian and modern Cartesian, without appeal to any highly controversial metaphysical or theological commitments. This is despite the fact that Peirce and James actually *do* have such commitments. It follows that pragmatic naturalists such as Dewey, Rorty and Price need not be seen as dogmatically rejecting metaphysics and theology.[17] They have good reason based on the history of metaphysical and theological dispute for their scepticism of these subjects (cf. Peirce 1955: 57).

IV

The Pragmatist Attempt to Defuse Agrippa's Trilemma

Let us, then, consider the pragmatist response to Agrippa's trilemma as it is manifest in the theory of inquiry originated by Peirce and adopted (in a somewhat revised or enhanced form) by almost all pragmatists thereafter.[18] In this context I shall understand the term 'pragmatism' broadly to include philosophers and philosophical resources from the classical pragmatists as well as more recent neo-pragmatists, linguistic pragmatists, etc.—the one common element being their commitment to the idea that epistemology is equated with (or replaced by) democratic experimentalism.[19] Furthermore, let us discuss the bearing of Agrippa's trilemma on *beliefs* (rather than judgment or knowledge) since the pragmatist theory of inquiry is focused on the fixation of belief.[20] And by 'entitlement' I shall henceforth mean to be referring to *epistemic entitlement*. To set the stage let us consider the pragmatist attitude to the holism and monism requirements that German Idealists believe are essential to escape the trilemma.

Like the German Idealists, pragmatists are semantic and epistemological holists, holding both that the meaning of a concept is determined, in large part, by its role in a system of rational inferences—what Sellars calls "the logical space of reasons" (1991: 169)—and that beliefs are justified by having a place in a "web of belief" (Quine and Ullian 1970), a complex tangle of semantic and justificatory relationships, which is adjusted in light of new experiences. I will return to this conception later.

But where pragmatists strongly disagree with German Idealism is in their rejection of the monism requirement. Pragmatists are pluralists and anti-foundationalists who reject both the idealists' demand for a unified system and its dependence on a single absolute principle or ground. Indeed, pragmatists reject the whole notion of *absolute* grounds. No ground is guaranteed *a priori* to remain a (good) ground come what may. Nor is any ground (or, for that matter any question) absolute in the sense of being presuppositionless—and, inevitably, presuppositions can be brought to light, questioned, and overturned under various conditions.

The pragmatist strategy for defusing Agrippa's trilemma depends upon exposing as a key presupposition an initially plausible—some have called it an "utterly humdrum" (Barnes 2006: 168)—account of epistemic entitlement which we might refer to as the Inferential Account of (Epistemic) Entitlement, or IAE for short. IAE holds that *entitlement can only accrue to a belief by its being inferred from an independent belief that provides a good reason for it*. The pragmatists' response is to accept that reasons can, and often do, confer entitlement inferentially, but that we fall victim to a rationalist over-generalisation if we suppose that this is the *only* form entitlement can take.

Pragmatists argue that in our everyday, professional, and scientific practices there is, in addition to inferentially derived entitlement, default entitlement, i.e. entitlement *without reason*. Indeed, entitlement is also possible without a reliable method. Sceptical scenarios such as the evil demon hypothesis or the brain-in-a-vat are good examples (insofar as they make enough sense) in which one cannot be blamed for forming systematically false beliefs.[21]

On the pragmatist's theory of inquiry our entitlements have what has been called a "default and challenge structure" (Brandom 1994: 176); in the image of Neurath's boat, entitlements as a whole figure as those parts of the boat that keep it afloat whilst it is being repaired at sea (Quine 1960: 3). In our ordinary social practices and scientific inquiries, there are many beliefs for which entitlement is the *default* status. Such beliefs are like citizens under the law, innocent until proven guilty. Their entitlement is not conferred by the exhibition of reasons from which they can be inferred. Rather, in our social practices of giving and asking for reasons we have an epistemic right to accept them as true without justification and to appeal to them, if need be, to provide reasons for other beliefs. Not only do we have no justification for such default entitlements, they do not stand in need of any.

To remove a potential misunderstanding, the pragmatist view is not that there is a fixed class of default entitlements that are to be accepted as true in all contexts. Pragmatists claim, rather, that in any given context of inquiry, *some* beliefs function like the hinges of a door (to use an image of Wittgenstein's): they are a fixed point around which the inquiry moves.[22] Their truth is accepted as a matter of course; unless or until some genuine reason for doubt arises, they are not properly subject to questions of justification.[23] In responding to Descartes's 'universal doubt' (more properly, universal doubt about things 'external' to the mind) Peirce writes:

> We cannot begin with complete doubt. We must begin with all the prejudices which we actually have when we enter upon the study of philosophy. These prejudices are not to be dispelled by a maxim, for they are things which it does not occur to us *can* be questioned. Hence this initial scepticism will be a mere self-deception, and not real doubt. . . . A person may, it is true, in the course of his studies, find reason to doubt what he began by believing; but in that case he doubts because he has a positive reason for it, and not on account of the Cartesian maxim. Let us not pretend to doubt in philosophy what we do not doubt in our hearts.
>
> (1955: 228–229)

Although officially addressed to Descartes's method of doubt, the relevance of Peirce's account of entitlement to Agrippa's trilemma is obvious. Once we have admitted the existence of default entitlements to believe—what Peirce calls the "prejudices" we bring to our inquiries, or those beliefs "it does not occur to us can be questioned"—then there is no threat of an infinite regress of justifications. From the pragmatist perspective the mere asking of a why-question does not automatically lead to a suspense of entitlement on pain of bringing forth a suitable reason from which the belief in question can be inferred. Given the rejection of

IAE it can be epistemically responsible to hold a belief to which we have a contextual entitlement in the absence of justifications, until or unless circumstances arise in which a legitimate challenge to it has been made, i.e. a "positive reason" for doubt, not the mere logical possibility of error which Descartes terms "metaphysical doubt" but which Peirce denigrates as "paper doubt" (1955: 294).

V

Reflecting in medias res and Reason's Self-Legitimation

How are we to understand the relevant notion of a default entitlement or that which Peirce refers to as "what we do not doubt in our hearts"? We are not entitled to believe in, say, astral travel, astrology, the healing power of crystals or witches. Michael Williams (2000: 611) has likened default entitlements to the legal rights and privileges that we are granted in virtue of being citizens of a democratic country:[24]

> Epistemic rights and privileges accrue to us in virtue of induction into a linguistic community, with its shared epistemic practices. . . . The process of acquiring the status of epistemic subject involves learning when and where default entitlements are defeasible. . . . Like legal rights, they exist only in so far as they are mutually acknowledged by those who are subject to them. None of us has them unless we all recognize that each of us does.

Consider historical investigation into the early convict settlement in Sydney. No matter how carefully we check documentary and other evidence of the penal colony we shall not for a moment doubt that "The earth has existed for many years before my birth." Historical inquiry depends upon *not* doubting this Moorean certainty about the extent of the past.[25] And this is not a matter of practical limitation. It is in the nature of historical inquiry. To doubt that the earth has existed for many years past would not be a further refinement of our inquiry. It would be to change the subject from historical investigation to a completely different inquiry in epistemology centred on scepticism about the past. Similar considerations suggest that it is in the nature of inquiry in physics not to raise the brain-in-a-vat doubt; and that it is in the nature of the cross-examination of legal testimony in a courtroom not to question the reliability of memory *uberhaupt*. What these examples show is that theoretical inquiry depends upon there being some things that are not in fact subject to doubt—which is not to say that they cannot be doubted as a matter of logic.

Unlike legal rights, however, default entitlements are not usually written down. Nor is one aware of them in the sense that they are usually on one's mind in the way that, say, a bad toothache or a burning thought is. Both of these features are well captured by speaking of default entitlements as *immanent* in practice. One who has been inculcated into a linguistic community has an occasion-sensitive sense of what justifies what, what sources of information to trust, whose testimony to count on, how to weigh evidence, when to be suspicious, and so on. In the mutual acknowledgement of entitlements within this setting some beliefs have the status of default entitlements across a wide range of contexts, e.g. 'The earth is a planet that circles the sun'. Their truth is the norm, and doubts about them are quite exceptional. They form part of what we might call the intellectual climate or a "style of reasoning" (Hacking 2002: 160) which we know from the history of science is liable to change, sometimes in slow subtle ways, at other times dramatically and rapidly— what Kuhn (1996), in the context of science, calls a shift in 'paradigm'. Through education what we learn is, we might say, a whole system of beliefs, as Wittgenstein (1969: §140–141) elegantly notes:

> We do not learn the practice of making empirical judgments by learning rules: we are taught judgments and their connexion (sic) with other judgments. A totality of judgments is made plausible to us.
>   When we first begin to believe anything, what we believe is not a single proposition, it is a whole system of propositions.
>   (Light dawns gradually over the whole.)

Since default entitlements are an essential element of inquiry the pragmatist philosophises in *medias res*, from the agent point of view of a participant in the midst of practice. Like Wittgenstein, the pragmatist makes essential reference to a first-person plural 'we' who acknowledge each others' beliefs as either standing in need of reasons or not. Gardner, an idealist sympathiser, objects that "[t]he metaphysical significance of the soft naturalist's [read: pragmatic naturalist's] use of the first person plural has to be shown, not merely asserted" (2007: 34). This precisely misses the idea of philosophizing *in medias res*. For the idealist it is not enough that in philosophising one articulates one's sense of being entitled to a belief on the basis of an acknowledged sense that it does not require justification. From that orientation, one must provide a "metaphysical vindication" in the form of "extra-naturalistic ontological grounds" which are further characterized as "absolute" (32, 38, 37). A pragmatist response is to say that the metaphysical demand for systematicity, complete totality, and absolute grounding leads to a mischaracterisation of the very values and norms that idealists seek to vindicate. It is a feature of our practices that one is normatively entitled to some beliefs without reason or metaphysical vindication. To say that that needs to be 'shown' (i.e. by way of a rational demonstration from a single principle in a metaphysical system) is to insist on a supernaturalist foundationalism whilst overlooking the pragmatist's naturalist antifoundational strategy for undermining rationalistic demands.

If the pragmatist attempt to defuse Agrippa's trilemma is to be viable it must be possible to reflectively claim rational authority about a belief without needing—perhaps without (then) being in a position—to provide any reason from which it could be inferred. In order to explain how it is possible to speak or think with rational authority without justification it is important to see that Peirce's theory of ("scientific") inquiry is a democratised, historicised non-apriorist version of a Kantian approach to reason's self-vindication. The method Kant articulates does not require any connection with Kant's own pure *a priori* thinking. It is not tied to Kant's transcendental standpoint or the related notion of an *a priori* which is independent of the course of experience, and capable of yielding necessary and unrevisable knowledge.[26] Kant's strategy can be equally employed at the level of experimental thinking which, although it has a relatively *a priori* aspect (say, the conceptual framework within which experimental inquiry proceeds), does not yield either necessary or unrevisable truths.[27]

The Kantian strategy as manifest in the *Critique of Pure Reason* is to avoid *dogmatism* and *scepticism* which are both pictured in Kant's political figures as forms of arbitrary individualism: 'despotism' on the one hand; 'nomadism' on the other. Their 'authority' is fundamentally private. In the case of dogmatism, it is only made public by fear or force—so, in a sense, it remains private.[28] So it is not genuine *rational* authority according to which reason is internally related to universalizability. If a consideration is a good reason for me to believe that *p* then it is a good reason for anyone in a similar situation. Rational authority is not a private matter: if it bears on anyone then it so bears on everyone. When Peirce objects to three historically significant methods of belief formation—(i) the method of *tenacity* (or conviction in one's own prior opinions); (ii) the method of *authority* (or the arbitrary authority of those with the power to force their opinions upon others through fear, intimidation and control of the sources of information); and (iii) the *a priori* method (or appealing to one's own taste in rational matters)—it is on the ground that they are based on arbitrary authority and are not sufficiently open to "the social impulse" (1955: 12).

Unlike the German Idealist strategy according to which "the *a priori* conditions of experience must be derived from a single, absolute first principle" (Franks 2005: 17), rational authority on the Kantian-Pragmatist strategy is strongly anti-foundationalist: it depends on instituting conditions that allow for the formation of an uncoerced unguaranteed consensus among free rational agents. It cannot begin with transcendental insights (e.g. mystical intuitions, speculative metaphysical claims, religious dogma) since these can be reasonably rejected. Nor can it be achieved by coercion or the dictates of some arbitrary authority (say, of church or state), as Kant explains:

Reason must subject itself to critique in all its undertakings and cannot restrict the freedom of critique through any prohibition without damaging itself and drawing upon itself a disadvantageous suspicion. Now there is nothing so important because of its utility, nothing so holy, that it may be exempted from this searching review and inspection, which knows no respect for persons. **The very existence of reason depends upon this freedom, which has no dictatorial authority, but whose claim is never anything more than the agreement of free citizens, each of whom must be able to express his reservation, indeed even his veto, without holding back.**

(A739/B767, emphasis added).

What is required is a *rational* authority understood as a recursive and public achievement that depends upon removing all obstacles to "the freedom of critique" and subjecting whatever claim, standard or method is in question—including the critique of reason itself—to a "searching review and inspection" which it is open for all to criticise without fear or favour.

Kant's model for achieving rational authority is an open debate amongst free citizens in a true democracy.[29] This is particularly apt since, for both Kant and pragmatism, the task of achieving rational authority is in many ways political, rather than narrowly epistemological. It depends upon creating certain conditions—of anti-authoritarianism, freedom to criticize, tolerance of dissent, and fair and open communication—such that any agreement achieved under those conditions counts as rationally authoritative. What makes this agreement authoritative is that it is achieved under conditions that survive their own reflective scrutiny and criticism. This is precisely what Peirce says about the rational authority achievable by practising the theory of inquiry (which he calls, somewhat misleadingly, "the scientific method") in contrast to the other methods of forming beliefs we have already mentioned (tenacity, authority, a priority): "No doubts of the method . . . necessarily arise from its practice [including its application to itself], as is the case with all the others" (1955: 18–19).

One might wonder how such a conception operates at the level of the individual thinker who has nothing to go on but a sense of being entitled to a belief without justification. On the Kantian-Pragmatist strategy the individual has to be confident that the entitlement is acknowledged as such by the rational public as opposed to being an illusion of entitlement based on a merely subjective conviction. At this point Kant appeals to a *sensus communis* which

in its reflection takes account (*a priori*) of everyone else's way of representing in thought, in order as it were to hold its judgment up to human reason as a whole. . . . Now this happens by one holding his judgment up not so much to the actual as to the merely possible judgments of others, and putting himself into the position of everyone else, merely by abstracting from the limitations that contingently attach to our own judging.

(2000: 173–174 [5: 293–294])

While pragmatism accepts the spirit of this account it rejects Kant's abstractionism. Kant is primarily interested in the conditions for a "merely possible" relation to the judgment of others. All it takes to adopt "a universal standpoint", on this view, is to hold one's judgment up to the merely possible judgments of others, thus arriving at an entitlement-vindicating agreement with notional 'others' in one's own thinking. In contrast, pragmatists think that rational authority can *only* be vindicated on the basis of the acknowledgement of others in actual practice. It is trusting in one's being an on-going participant in the intersubjective (second-personal) realm of everyday, professional or scientific practice that is fundamental. As Dewey puts it, criticizing Kant's reliance on merely logical universality, "Communication, sharing and joint participation are the only actual ways of universalizing" (1948: 206).

Pragmatists speak of following "the scientific method"—which, under the guise of the theory of inquiry, plays a vitally important role in rationally vindicating its own entitlements and results—not because they are wedded to a method exclusive to the sciences but rather because they regard natural science as the best example in human history of a community that actualises to the highest degree Kant's conception of a free and open public forum capable of rational self-authorisation. Scientific method is understood as democratic experimentalism: experimentalism because its results and methods are fallible working hypotheses, susceptible to revision or conceptual innovation prompted by new experiences and discoveries; democratic because it involves attitudes of equality, toleration, cooperation, freedom and fairness. Consequently, we can think of the pragmatist theory of inquiry as a naturalized and democratized form of Kant's epistemology of critique—one that effectively sidesteps the Agrippan trilemma.

Notes

1. The modes of argument that Sextus Empricus (1985) calls the Five Modes (disagreement, infinite regress, relativity, assumption and circularity) are attributed to Agrippa who lived 1st–2nd century CE. Agrippa's trilemma is composed of the 2nd, 3rd and 4th modes.
2. William Alston (1993: 532) has remarked, "The persistence of the disputes [about epistemic justification] leads to the suspicion that there is no unique common item concerning the nature of which people are disagreeing." And he goes on to call the deontological conception operative in Agrippa's trilemma "the most natural interpretation" of the term "justification" (533).
3. Mark Kaplan (1991: 138) writes: "In ordinary contexts, questions about whether one is justified in one's belief are questions about one's intellectual responsibility in holding the belief, about one's entitlement to persist in the belief, about the propriety of one's methodology."

4. Cf. Alston (1988).

5. I follow Tim Scanlon in taking reason as basic or irreducible and in understanding a reason for something as "a consideration that counts in favor of it" (1998: 17).

6. In the R. G. Bury translation quoted in Robert Fogelin (1994: 113) the reference is to "further proof."

7. Fogelin (1994: 119), too, notes that "the Agrippa Problem seems quite unanswerable"—although his account of the force of the trilemma is not exactly mine.

8. See, e.g. Klein (2008).

9. Peter Strawson (1985) supposes that his neo-Humean naturalism has anti-sceptical consequences: "The correct way with the professional skeptical doubt is not to attempt to rebut it with argument, but to point out that it is idle, unreal, a pretense" (19). The idea is that we have no option but to believe various things (e.g. that the external world exists, that memory is largely reliable) so that scepticism is without consequence.

10. See Macarthur (2006) for more discussion of this point.

11. Gardner (2007), following Norman Kemp Smith, remarks: "it is the great antagonism between idealism and naturalism that lies at the heart of all philosophy" (21). Both he and I see the fundamental philosophical choice as that between idealism and naturalism. But he sees this contrast, as Kemp Smith does, in metaphysically inflationary terms: a metaphysically weighty interpretation of German idealism is set against a metaphysically weighty (e.g. materialist) *scientific* or 'hard' naturalism. I argue, on the contrary, that the important contrast now is between idealism and a metaphysically sceptical liberal or 'soft' naturalism. Although there are non-metaphysical readings of idealism both Gardner and Franks provide powerful considerations in favour of the metaphysical (and, in Franks's case, theological) reading of it.

12. Franks (2005: 390) writes of "the central importance of ontotheology—notably the identification of God as the absolute first principle required for an escape from Agrippa's trilemma—for the German Idealist program in its most fundamental formulations."

13. The discoveries of Riemannian geometry and the platypus overturned these *a priori* necessary definitional 'truths'. Putnam (1975) discusses cases akin to the first of these and notes that "something that was literally inconceivable has turned out to be true" (664).

14. Putnam (Ibid., 670) remarks: "the traditional philosophical distinction between statements necessary in some eternal sense and statements contingent in some eternal sense is not workable."

15. On Franks's account, German Idealists have an explanation of their lack of universal appeal in terms of an esotericism that is an inevitable feature of their system. The present point is simply that without universal appeal there is good reason to take a sceptical attitude to the German Idealist strategy and pursue alternatives to it.

16. Peirce formulates the pragmatic maxim as follows: "Consider what effects, that might conceivably have practical bearings, we conceive the object of our conception to have. Then our conception of these effects is our whole conception of the object" (1955: 31).

17. Franks raises this worry in the following remark: "If a naturalist is someone who rejects any philosophical position with a theological dimension *out of hand and without argument*, then it is a form of dogmatism whose influence is regrettable" (2005: 392).

18. Here I mean to include such 20th-century luminaries as Quine and Sellars who prefer not to call themselves pragmatists but who, nonetheless, endorse

the theory of inquiry. In Macarthur (2016) I argue that we should regard Peirce's theory of inquiry—or what I prefer to call "democratic experimentalism"—as the most important core commitment of the pragmatist tradition. From this perspective Peirce's pragmatic maxim can be demoted to playing an auxiliary role—as opposed to the primary meaning-giving role it is typically given in discussions of classical pragmatism—say, one of sifting and operationalizing concepts for use in inquiry.

19. For further discussion of democratic experimentalism see Macarthur (2015).
20. This topic requires separate treatment. It is part of Peirce's strategy to avoid the grip of Cartesian skepticism. Pragmatism has been uneasy about the concept of knowledge ever since.
21. Semantic externalist considerations may suggest that the brain-in-a-vat is not an apt example since its beliefs are largely true given its causal environment. In that case, imagine that the brain-in-a-vat has been recently envatted so that its contents are not yet determined by its actual environment.
22. See Wittgenstein (1969: §341–343).
23. Wittgenstein remarks: "it seems impossible to say in any *individual* case that such-and-such must be beyond doubt if there is to be a language-game—though it is right enough to say that *as a rule* some empirical judgment or other must be beyond doubt" (Ibid., §519).
24. Williams takes over the analogy from Fred Dretske (2000) but develops it in a different direction.
25. See Moore (1993, Ch. 7) for a discussion of such cases. Note that I am not endorsing Moore's characterization of default entitlements in terms of things one knows with certainty to be true.
26. Kant (A11–12/B25, emphasis added) writes, "I call all cognition **transcendental** that is occupied not so much with objects but rather with our a priori concepts of objects in general."
27. See Friedman (1997) for a defence of the notion of a relative revisable *a priori*.
28. Both Kant and Peirce oppose the 'private' use of reason understood as thinking in accord with external authorities (e.g. the church) as well as the dogmatic assumption of authority. What they endorse is the public use of reason which is a matter of speaking as a member of "the society of citizens of the world" (1989: 8, 37).
29. Kant's appeal to the political metaphor of a free and open public forum (A738–739/B766–767) counters the residual authoritarianism of his earlier juridical metaphor of a legal tribunal in which judges preside (Axi–xii). Another metaphor Kant appeals to is that of builders constructing a structure without a pre-existing plan (A707/B735). I have benefited in my understanding of these metaphors and of the political implications of Kant's strategy from Onora O'Neill (1989). However, she does not make the connection that I do between Kant's epistemology of critique and the pragmatist theory of inquiry.

References

Alston, W. 1988. 'The Deontological Conception of Epistemic Justification'. *Philosophical Perspectives* 2: 257–299.
———. 1993. 'Epistemic Desiderata'. *Philosophy and Phenomenological Research* 53: 527–551.
Barnes, J. 2006. 'Review of W. Sinnott-Armstrong (ed.) *Pyrrhonian Scepticism*'. *Mind* 115: 166–169.

Brandom, R. B. 1994. *Making It Explicit*. Cambridge, MA: Harvard University Press.

Dewey, J. 1948. *Reconstruction in Philosophy*. New York: Henry Holt and Co.

Dretske, F. 2000. 'Entitlement: Epistemic Rights Without Epistemic Duties'. *Philosophy and Phenomenological Research* 60: 591–606.

Fogelin, R. 1994. *Pyrrhonian Reflections on Knowledge and Justification*. Oxford: Oxford University Press.

Franks, P. 2005. *All or Nothing: Systematicity, Transcendental Arguments and Scepticism in German Idealism*. Cambridge, MA: Harvard University Press.

Friedman, M. 1997. 'Philosophical Naturalism'. *Proceeding and Addresses of the American Philosophical Association* 71: 7–21.

Gardner, S. 2007. 'The Limits of Naturalism and the Metaphysics of German Idealism'. In E. Hammer (ed.) *German Idealism: Contemporary Perspectives*. London and New York: Routledge.

Hacking, I. 2002. *Historical Ontology*. Cambridge, MA: Harvard University Press.

Hume, D. 1975. *A Treatise of Human Nature*. L. A. Selby-Bigge (ed.), P. H. Nidditch (revised), 2nd ed. Oxford: Clarendon Press.

Kant, I. 1989. 'What Is Enlightenment?' In H. S. Reiss (ed. and trans.) *Kant: Political Writings*. Cambridge: Cambridge University Press.

———. 1998. *Critique of Pure Reason*. P. Guyer and A. W. Wood (eds. and trans.). Cambridge: Cambridge University Press.

———. 2000. *Critique of the Power of Judgment*. P. Guyer (ed.), P. Guyer and E. Mathews (trans.). Cambridge: Cambridge University Press.

Kaplan, M. 1991. 'Epistemology on Holiday'. *Journal of Philosophy* 88: 132–154.

Klein, P. 2008. 'Contemporary Responses to Agrippa's Trilemma'. In J. Greco (ed.) *The Oxford Handbook of Scepticism*. Oxford: Oxford University Press.

Kuhn, T. S. 1996. *The Structure of Scientific Revolutions*, 3rd Edition. Chicago: University of Chicago Press.

Macarthur, D. 2006. 'Scepticism, Self-Knowledge and Responsibility'. In S. Hetherington (ed.) *Aspects of Knowing*. Amsterdam: Elsevier.

———. 2015. 'A Kant-Inspired Vision of Pragmatism as Democratic Experimentalism'. In G. Gava and R. Stern (eds.) *Pragmatism, Kant & Transcendental Philosophy*. London: Routledge.

Moore, G. E. 1993. *Moore: Selected Writings*. T. Baldwin (ed.). Oxford: Routledge.

O'Neill, O. 1990. *Constructions of Reason: Explorations of Kant's Practical Philosophy*. Cambridge: Cambridge University Press.

Peirce, C. S. 1955. 'The Fixation of Belief'. In J. Buchler (ed.) *Philosophical Writings of Peirce*. New York: Dover.

Putnam, H. 1975. 'It Ain't Necessarily So'. In his *Mathematics, Matter and Method. Philosophical Papers*, vol. 1. Cambridge: Cambridge University Press.

Quine, W. V. 1960. *Word and Object*. Cambridge, MA: MIT Press.

Quine, W. V. and Ullian, J. S. 1970. *The Web of Belief*. New York: Random House.

Scanlon, T. 1998. *What We Owe to Each Other*. Cambridge, MA: Harvard University Press.

Sellars, W. 1991. *Science, Perception and Reality*. Atascadero, CA: Ridgeview Publishing Co.

Sextus Empiricus. 2000. *Sextus Empiricus, Outlines of Scepticism*. J. Annas and J. Barnes (eds. and trans.), 2nd ed. Cambridge: Cambridge University Press.

Strawson, P. F. 1985. *Scepticism and Naturalism: Some Varieties*. New York: Columbia University Press.

Williams, M. 2000. 'Epistemic Entitlement'. *Philosophy and Phenomenological Research* 60: 607–612.

Wittgenstein, L. 1969. *On Certainty*. G. E. M. Anscombe (trans.). Oxford: Blackwell.

Bibliography

Adorno, T. W., and Horkheimer, M. 2002. *Dialectic of Enlightenment: Philosophical Fragments*. G. Schmid Noerr (ed.) and E. Jephcott (trans.). Stanford, CA: Stanford University Press.

Almeder, R. 1980. *The Philosophy of Charles S. Peirce: A Critical Introduction*. Oxford: Blackwell.

Alston, W. 1988. 'The Deontological Conception of Epistemic Justification'. *Philosophical Perspectives* 2: 257–299.

Anscombe, G. E. M. 1958. 'Modern Moral Philosophy'. *Philosophy* 33: 1–19.

Aristotle. 2009. *Nicomachean Ethics*. L. Brown (ed.) and D. Ross (trans.). Oxford: Oxford University Press.

Armstrong, D. 1978. 'Naturalism, Materialism and First Philosophy'. *Philosophia* 8: 261–276.

Atkins, P. W. 1995. 'The Limitless Power of Science'. In J. Cornwell (ed.) *Nature's Imagination: The Frontiers of Scientific Vision*. Oxford: Oxford University Press.

Aufderheide, J., and Bader, R. M. (eds.). 2015. *The Highest Good in Aristotle and Kant*. Oxford: Oxford University Press.

Austin, J. L. 1962. *Sense and Sensibilia*. London: Oxford University Press.

Baehr, P. 2001. 'The "Iron Cage" and the "Shell as Hard as Steel": Parsons, Weber, and the *stahlhartes Gehäuse* Metaphor in *The Protestant Ethic and the Spirit of Capitalism*'. *History and Theory* 40: 153–169.

Baker, L. R. 2013. *Naturalism and the First-Person Perspective*. Oxford: Oxford University Press.

———. 2017. 'Naturalism and the Idea of Nature'. *Philosophy* 92: 333–349.

Balaguer, M. 1998. *Platonism and Anti-Platonism in Mathematics*. Oxford: Oxford University Press.

———. 2018. 'Fictionalism in the Philosophy of Mathematics'. In E. N. Zalta (ed.) *The Stanford Encyclopaedia of Philosophy*. Available at: https://plato.stanford.edu/entries/fictionalism-mathematics/

Barnes, J. 2006. 'Review of W. Sinnott-Armstrong (ed.) *Pyrrhonian Scepticism*'. *Mind* 115: 166–169.

Baron, M. 1996. 'Kantian Ethics'. In M. W. Baron, P. Pettit and M. Slote (eds.) *Three Methods of Ethics*. Oxford: Blackwell.

Bechler, Z. 1995. *Aristotle's Theory of Actuality*. Albany: State University of New York Press.

Beiser, F. C. 2005. *Hegel*. London and New York: Routledge.

————. 2014. *After Hegel: German Philosophy 1840–1900*. Princeton, NJ and Woodstock, NJ: Princeton University Press.

Bernardete, S. 1965. 'XRH and DEI in Plato and Others'. *GLOTTA* 43: 285–298.

Bernstein, R. J. 1966a. 'Sellars's Vision of Man-in-the-Universe I'. *Review of Metaphysics* 20: 113–143.

————. 1966b. 'Sellars's Vision of Man-in-the-Universe II'. *Review of Metaphysics* 20: 290–316.

Bilgrami, A. 2012. *Self-Knowledge and Resentment*. Cambridge, MA: Harvard University Press.

Blackburn, P., di Rijke, M., and Venema, Y. 2001. *Modal Logic*. Cambridge: Cambridge University Press.

Block, N. 1997a. 'Can the Mind Change the World?' In G. Boolos (ed.) *Meaning and Method: Essays in Honour of Hilary Putnam*. Cambridge: Cambridge University Press.

————. 1997b. 'Anti-Reductionism Slaps Back'. *Philosophical Perspectives* 11: 107–132.

Brandom, R. B. 2014. 'Some Hegelian Ideas of Note for Contemporary Analytic Philosophy'. *Hegel Bulletin* 35: 1–15.

Brandom, R. B. 2015. *From Empiricism to Expressivism: Brandom Reads Sellars*. Cambridge, MA: Harvard University Press.

Breen, K. 2013. *Under Weber's Shadow: Modernity, Subjectivity and Politics in Habermas, Arendt and MacIntyre*. London and New York: Routledge.

Brent, J. 1998. *C. S. Peirce: A Life*, rev. ed. Bloomington: Indiana University Press.

Broad, C. D. 2008. *The Mind and Its Place in Nature*. New York and London: Routledge.

Bunge, M. 2006. *Chasing Reality: Strife Over Reality*. Toronto: University of Toronto Press.

Burch, R. 2017. 'Charles Sanders Peirce'. In E. N. Zalta (ed.) *The Stanford Encyclopaedia of Philosophy*. Available at: https://plato.stanford.edu/archives/fall2017/entries/peirce/

Caddick Bourne, E. 2013. 'Fictionalism'. *Analysis* 73: 147–162.

Caruso, G. 2013. *Exploring the Illusions of Free Will and Moral Responsibility*. Lanham, MD: Lexington Books.

Cavell, S. 1979. 'Thinking of Emerson'. *New Literary History* 11: 167–176.

Chakravartty, A. 2007. *A Metaphysics for Scientific Realism: Knowing the Unobservable*. Cambridge: Cambridge University Press.

Chalcraft, D. 1994. 'Bringing the Text Back in: On Ways of Reading the Iron Cage Metaphor in the Two Editions of *The Protestant Ethic*'. In L. J. Ray and M. Reed (eds.) *Organising Modernity: New Weberian Perspectives on Work, Organisation and Society*. London and New York: Routledge.

Chalmers, A. 2009. *The Scientist's Atom and the Philosopher's Stone: How Science Succeeded and Philosophy Failed to Gain Knowledge of Atoms*. Dordrecht: Springer.

Chevalier, J-M. 2014. 'Why Ought We to Be Logical? Peirce's Naturalism on Norms and Rational Requirements'. In J. Dutant, D. Fassio and A. Meyla (eds.) *Liber Amicorum Pascal Engel*. Geneva: Université de Genève.

Chisholm, R. M. 1977. *Theory of Knowledge*. Englewood Cliffs: Prentice Hall.

Church, A. 1940. 'A Formulation of a Simple Theory of Types'. *Journal of Symbolic Logic* 5: 52–68.

Churchland, P. M. 1988. *Matter and Consciousness*, Revised Edition. Cambridge, MA: MIT Press.

———. 1996. *The Engine of Reason, the Seat of the Soul*. Cambridge, MA: MIT Press.

Churchland, P. S. 1986. *Neurophilosophy: Toward a Unified Science of the Mind-Brain*. Cambridge, MA: MIT Press.

———. 2002. *Brain-Wise: Studies in Neurophilosophy*. Cambridge, MA: MIT Press.

Ciancio, C. 2004. 'Il senso comune nel pensiero ermeneutico'. In E. Agazzi (ed.) *Valore e limiti del senso commune*. Milano: Franco Angeli.

Clericuzio, A. 2000. *Elements, Principles and Corpuscles: A Study of Atomism and Chemistry in the Seventeenth Century*. Dordrecht: Kluwer.

Colapietro, V. 2003. 'The Space of Sings: C. S. Peirce's Critique of Psychologism'. In D. Jacquette (ed.) *Philosophy, Psychology, and Psychologism*. Boston, MA: Kluwer.

Collingwood, R. G. 1998. *An Essay on Metaphysics*, rev. ed. with an introduction by R. Martin. Oxford: Oxford University Press.

Copeland, J. B. 2002. 'The Genesis of Possible Worlds Semantics'. *Journal of Philosophical Logic* 3: 99–137.

———. 2008. 'Arthur Prior'. In E. N. Zalta (ed.) *The Stanford Encyclopedia of Philosophy*. Available at: http://plato.stanford.edu/archives/fall2008/entries/prior/

Crisp, R. 2004. 'Does Modern Moral Philosophy Rest on a Mistake?' *Royal Institute of Philosophy Supplement* 54: 75–93.

Cristalli, C. 2017. 'Experimental Psychology and the Practice of Logic: Charles S. Peirce and the Charge of Psychologism, 1869–1885'. *European Journal of Pragmatism and American Philosophy* 9. Available at: https://journals.openedition.org/ejpap/1006

Darwall, S. 2006. *The Second Person Standpoint: Morality, Respect, and Accountability*. Cambridge, MA: Harvard University Press.

———. 2007. 'Law and the Second-Person Standpoint'. *Loyola of Los Angeles Law Review* 40: 891–910. Available at: http://digitalcommons.lmu.edu/llr/vol40/iss3/2

Davidson, D. 1980. 'Mental Events'. In D. Davidson (ed.) *Essays on Actions and Events*. Oxford and New York: Oxford University Press.

De Caro, M. 2015. 'Realism, Common Sense, and Science'. *The Monist* 98: 197–214.

———. 2016. 'Introduction: Putnam's Philosophy and Metaphilosophy'. In M. De Caro (ed.) *Naturalism, Realism, and Normativity*. Cambridge, MA: Harvard University Press.

———. 2017. 'On Galileo's Platonism, Again'. In R. Pisano, J. Agassi and D. Drozdova (eds.) *Hypotheses and Perspectives Within History and Philosophy of Science. Hommage to Alexandre Koyré 1964–2014*. Dordrecht: Springer.

De Caro, M., and Macarthur, D. 2004a. 'Introduction: The Nature of Naturalism'. In M. De Caro and D. Macarthur (eds.) *Naturalism in Question*. Cambridge, MA: Harvard University Press.

———. (eds.). 2004b. *Naturalism in Question*. Cambridge, MA: Harvard University Press.

———. (eds.). 2010a. *Naturalism and Normativity*. New York: Columbia University Press.

————. 2010b. 'Introduction: Science, Naturalism, and the Problem of Normativity'. In De Caro and MacArthur 2010a.

De Caro, M., and Voltolini, A. 2010. 'Is Liberal Naturalism Possible?' In De Caro and MacArthur 2010a.

Deligiorgi, K. 2012. *The Scope of Autonomy. Kant and the Morality of Freedom.* Oxford: Oxford University Press.

————. 2017. 'Interest and Agency'. In J. M. Rasmussen, M. Gabriel and J. Rometsch (eds.) *German Idealism Today*. Frankfurt: De Gruyter.

————. 2018. 'The "Ought" and the "Can"'. *Con-Textos Kantianos. International Journal of Philosophy* 8: 6–30.

————. forthcoming. '"Why Be Moral?" How to Take the Questions Seriously (and Why) from a Kantian Perspective'. In C. Yeomans and A. Lyssy (eds.) *Dimensions of Normativity: Kant on Morality, Legality, Humanity*.

Dennett, D. C. 1971. 'Intentional Systems'. *The Journal of Philosophy* 68: 87–106.

————. 1978. *Brainstorms*. Cambridge, MA: MIT Press.

————. 1991. *Consciousness Explained*. New York: Little, Brown.

————. 2009. 'Daniel Dennett'. In P. Grim (ed.) *Mind and Consciousness: 5 Questions*. Copenhagen: Automatic Press, VIP.

Descartes, R. 1984–91. *Philosophical Writings of Descartes*. J. Cottingham, R. Stoothoff, D. Murdoch and A. Kenny (trans.), 3 vols. Cambridge: Cambridge University Press.

————. 2008. *Meditations on First Philosophy*. Oxford: Oxford University Press.

deVries, W. A. 1988. *Hegel's Theory of Mental Activity: An Introduction to Theoretical Spirit*. New York: Cornell University Press.

————. 2005. *Wilfrid Sellars*. Montreal and Kingston: McGill-Queen's University Press.

Dewey, J. 1925. *Experience and Nature*. London: Allen and Unwin.

————. 1934. *A Common Faith*. New Haven: Yale University Press.

————. 1948. *Reconstruction in Philosophy*. New York: Henry Holt and Co.

Dodd, J. 2007. *Works of Music: An Essay in Ontology*. Oxford: Oxford University Press.

Donnellan, T. 1968. *Lattice Theory*. Oxford: Pergamon Press.

Dodd, J. 2007. *Works of Music: An Essay in Ontology*. Oxford: Oxford University Press.

D'Oro, G. 2018. 'The Touch of King Midas: Collingwood on Why Actions Are Not Events'. *Philosophical Explorations* 21: 1–10.

————. 2019. 'Between Ontological Hubris and Epistemic Humility: Collingwood, Kant and Transcendental Arguments'. *British Journal of the History of Philosophy* 27: 336–357.

D'Oro, G., Giladi, P., and Papazoglou, A. 2019. 'Non-Reductivism and the Metaphilosophy of Mind'. *Inquiry* 62: 477–503.

Drake, S. 1989. *History of Free Fall: Aristotle to Galileo*. Toronto: Wall and Thompson.

————. 1999. 'Galileo and the Law of Inertia'. In N. M. Swerdlow and T. H. Levere (eds.) *Stillman Drake's Essays on Galileo and the History and Philosophy of Science, Vol. 2*. Toronto: University of Toronto Press.

Dray, W. H. 1957. *Laws and Explanation in History*. London: Oxford University Press.

———. 1958. 'Historical Understanding as Rethinking'. *University of Toronto Quarterly* 27: 200–215.

———. 1963. 'The Historical Explanation of Actions Reconsidered'. In S. Hook (ed.) *Philosophy and History*. New York: New York University Press.

Dretske, F. 2000. 'Entitlement: Epistemic Rights Without Epistemic Duties'. *Philosophy and Phenomenological Research* 60: 591–606.

Dummett, M. 1993. 'What is a Theory of Meaning? (II)'. In M. Dummett (ed.) *The Seas of Language*. Oxford: Clarendon Press.

Dunham, J., Grant, I. H., and S. Watson. 2011. *Idealism: The History of a Philosophy*. Durham: Acumen.

Dupré, J. 1995. *The Disorder of Things: Metaphysical Foundations of the Disunity of Science*. Cambridge, MA: Harvard University Press.

———. 2004. 'The Miracle of Monism'. In M. De Caro and D. Macarthur (eds.) *Naturalism in Question*. Cambridge, MA: Harvard University Press.

Dummett, M. 1978. *Truth and Other Enigmas*. Cambridge, MA: Harvard University Press.

Ellis, F. 2014. *God, Value, and Nature*. Oxford: Oxford University Press.

Engstrom, S. 2006. 'Understanding and Sensibility'. *Inquiry* 49: 2–25.

Esposito, J. 2005. 'Synechism: The Keystone of Peirce's Metaphysics'. In *The Commens Encyclopedia: The Digital Encyclopedia of Peirce Studies*. Available at: www.commens.org/encyclopedia/article/esposito-joseph-synechism-keystone-peirce%E2%80%99s-metaphysics.

Everson, S. 1995. 'Psychology'. In J. Barnes (ed.) *The Cambridge Companion to Aristotle*. Cambridge: Cambridge University Press.

Ferrarin, A. 2001. *Hegel and Aristotle*. Cambridge: Cambridge University Press.

Ferrini, C. 2009. 'Reason Observing Nature'. In K. R. Westphal (ed.) *The Blackwell Guide to Hegel's Phenomenology of Spirit*. Oxford: Blackwell.

Field, H. 1980. *Science Without Numbers*. Oxford: Blackwell.

———. 1989. *Realism, Mathematics, and Modality*. New York: Blackwell.

Findlay, J. N. 1933. *Meinong's Theory of Objects*. Oxford: Oxford University Press. Expanded in 2nd ed. as, *Meinong's Theory of Objects and Values*, 1963.

———. 1941. 'Time: A Treatment of Some Puzzles'. *Australasian Journal of Philosophy*, reprinted in Flew, A. G. N. 1951. *Logic and Language, first series*. Oxford: Blackwell.

———. 1955–1956. 'Some Merits of Hegelianism: The Presidential Address'. *Proceedings of the Aristotelian Society New Series* 56: 1–24.

———. 1958. *Hegel: A Re-Examination*. London: Allen and Unwin.

Fodor, J. 1965. 'Explanation in Psychology'. In M. Black (ed.) *Philosophy in America*. Ithaca, NY: Cornell University Press.

Fogelin, R. 1994. *Pyrrhonian Reflections on Knowledge and Justification*. Oxford: Oxford University Press.

Foot, P. 1978. *Virtues and Vices*. Oxford: Blackwell.

———. 2001. *Natural Goodness*. Oxford: Clarendon Press.

———. 2004. 'Rationality and Goodness'. *Royal Institute of Philosophy Supplement* 54: 1–13.

Förster, E. 2000. *Kant's Final Synthesis*. Cambridge, MA: Harvard University Press.

———. 2012. *The Twenty-Five Years of Philosophy*. Cambridge, MA: Harvard University Press.

Forster, M. 2017. 'First Philosophy Naturalised: Peirce's Place in the Analytic Tradition'. *Cognitio* 18: 33–44.

Franks, P. 2005. *All or Nothing: Systematicity, Transcendental Arguments and Scepticism in German Idealism*. Cambridge, MA: Harvard University Press.

Frankish, K. 2005. *Consciousness*. Milton Keynes: Open University.

———. 2016. 'Illusionism as a Theory of Consciousness'. *Journal of Consciousness Studies* 23: 11–39.

———. (ed.). 2017. *Illusionism as a Theory of Consciousness*. Exeter: Imprint Academic.

Frege, G. 1897. *Begriffsschrift, eine der arithmetischen nachgebildete Formelsprache des reinen Denkens*. Halle: Louis Nebert. English translation by S. Bauer-Mengelberg. In J. van Heijenoort (ed.) *From Frege to Gödel: A Source Book in Mathematical Logic, 1879–1931*. Cambridge, MA: Harvard University Press, 1967.

Friedman, M. 2013. 'Philosophy of Natural Science in Idealism and Neo-Kantianism'. In K. Ameriks, N. Boyle and L. Disley (eds.) *The Impact of Idealism: The Legacy of Post-Kantian German Thought. Volume 1: Philosophy and Natural Sciences*. Cambridge: Cambridge University Press.

———. 1997. 'Philosophical Naturalism'. *Proceeding and Addresses of the American Philosophical Association* 71: 7–21.

Galilei, G. 1623/1957. 'The Assayer'. In S. Drake (trans.) *The Controversy of the Comets of 1618*. Philadelphia: University of Pennsylvania Press.

———. 1632/1967. *Dialogue Concerning the Two Chief World Systems*. S. Drake (trans.) Berkeley and Los Angeles: University of California Press.

Gardner, S. 2007. 'The Limits of Naturalism and the Metaphysics of German Idealism'. In E. Hammer (ed.) *German Idealism: Contemporary Perspectives*. New York and London: Routledge.

Gava, G. 2011a. 'Does Peirce Reject Transcendental Philosophy?' *Archiv für Geschichte der Philosophie* 93: 195–221.

———. 2011b. 'Peirce's "Prescision" as a Transcendental Method'. *International Journal of Philosophical Studies* 19: 231–253.

———. 2011c. 'Can Transcendental Philosophy Endorse Fallibilism?' *Contemporary Pragmatism* 8: 133–151.

———. 2014. *Peirce's Account of Purposefulness: A Kantian Perspective*. London: Routledge.

Geach, P. T. 1956. 'Good and Evil'. *Analysis* 17: 33–42.

Giladi P. 2014a. 'Liberal Naturalism: The Curious Case of Hegel'. *International Journal of Philosophical Studies* 22: 248–270.

———. 2014b. 'Ostrich Nominalism and Peacock Realism: A Hegelian Critique of Quine'. *International Journal of Philosophical Studies* 22: 734–751.

———. 2016. 'New Directions for Transcendental Claims'. *Grazer Philosophische Studien* 93: 212–223.

Giladi, P., D'Oro, G., and Papazoglou, A. 2017/2018. 'Defending Humanistic Reasoning'. *Philosophy Now* 123: 31–33.

Ginsborg, H. 2004. 'Two Kinds of Mechanical Inexplicability in Kant and Aristotle'. *Journal of the History of Philosophy* 42: 33–65.

Goodman, N. 1968. *Languages of Art: An Approach to a Theory of Symbols*. Indianapolis, IN: Bobbs-Merrill.

Goudge, T. 1947. 'The Conflict of Naturalism and Transcendentalism in Peirce'. *The Journal of Philosophy* 44: 365–375.

Griffiths, P. E. 1997. *What Emotions Really Are: The Problem of Psychological Categories*. Chicago: University of Chicago Press.

Gubeljic, M., Link, S., Muller, P., and Osburg, G. 1999. 'Nature and Second Nature in McDowell's *Mind and World*'. In M. Willaschek (ed.) *John McDowell: Reason and Nature, Lecture and Colloquium in Münster*. Munster: LIT Verlag. Available at: http://web.uni-frankfurt.de/fb08/PHIL/willaschek/mcdowell kolloq.pdf

Guyer, P. 2003. 'Beauty, Systematicity, and the Highest Good'. *Inquiry* 46: 195–214.

Haack, S. 2007. *Defending Science Within Reason: Between Scientism and Cynicism*. Amherst, NY: Prometheus Books.

Haag, J. 2007. *Erfahrung und Gegenstand*. Frankfurt: Klostermann.

———. 2013. 'Grenzbegriffe und die Antinomie der teleologischen Urteilskraft'. In J. Haag and M. Wild (eds.) *Übergänge, diskursiv oder intuitiv? Essays zu Eckart Försters Die 25 Jahre der Philosophie*. Frankfurt: Klostermann.

Habermas, J. 1987. *The Theory of Communicative Action. Vol. II: Lifeworld and System*. T. McCarthy (trans.). Boston: Beacon.

———. 1989. *The Structural Transformation of the Public Sphere*. T. Burger and F. Lawrence (trans.). Cambridge, MA: MIT Press.

———. 1992. *Postmetaphysical Thinking*. W. M. Hohengarten (trans.). Cambridge, MA: MIT Press.

———. 1996. *Between Facts and Norms: Contributions to a Discourse Theory of Law and Democracy*. W. Rehg (trans.). Cambridge, MA: MIT Press.

———. 2002. 'Modernity—An Incomplete Project'. In H. Foster (ed.) *The Anti-Aesthetic: Essays on Postmodern Culture*. New York: The New Press.

Hacking, I. 2002. *Historical Ontology*. Cambridge, MA: Harvard University Press.

Hanna, R. 2014. 'Husserl's Crisis and Our Crisis'. *International Journal of Philosophical Studies* 22: 752–770.

Hardcastle, V. G. 1999. *The Myth of Pain*. Cambridge, MA: MIT Press.

Harris, S. 2012. *Free Will*. New York: Free Press.

Hawking, S., and Mlodinow, L. 2010. *The Grand Design*. New York: Bantam Books.

Heal, J. 1997. 'Indexical Predicates and Their Uses'. *Mind* 106: 619–640.

Hegel, G. W. F. 1968. *Gesammelte Werke*. Hamburg: Felix Meiner.

———. 1969. *Science of Logic*. A. V. Miller (trans.). Amherst, NY: Humanity Books.

———. 1970. *Philosophy of Nature (Part Two of the Encyclopaedia of Philosophical Sciences)*. M. J. Petry (trans.), 3 vols. London: George Allen and Unwin.

———. 1975. *Lectures on Aesthetics*. T. M. Knox (trans.), 2 vols. Oxford: Oxford University Press.

———. 1977. *Phenomenology of Spirit*. A. V. Miller (trans.). Oxford: Oxford University Press.

———. 1991a. *Elements of the Philosophy of Right*. A. W. Wood (ed.) and H. B. Nisbet (trans.) Cambridge: Cambridge University Press.

———. 1991b. *The Encyclopaedia Logic: Part 1 of the Encyclopaedia of Philosophical Sciences*. T. F. Geraets, W. A. Suchting and H. S. Harris (trans.). Indianapolis, IN: Hackett.

———. 2007. *Philosophy of Mind: Part Three of the Encyclopaedia of the Philosophical Sciences* (together with the Zusatze). W. Wallace (trans.) and M. Inwood (rev.). Oxford: Oxford University Press.

———. 2010. *Science of Logic.* G. di Giovanni (ed. and trans.) Cambridge: Cambridge University Press.

Heidegger, M. 1962. *Being and Time.* J. Macquarrie and E. Robinson (trans.). New York: Harper & Row.

———. 1977. 'Modern Science, Metaphysics, and Mathematics'. In W. B. Barton, Jr. and V. Deutsch (trans.) and D. F. Krell (ed.) *Martin Heidegger: Basic Writings.* New York: Harper and Row.

Hempel, C. 1942. 'The Function of General Laws in History'. *Journal of Philosophy* 39: 35–48.

Herman, B. 1996. *The Practice of Moral Judgement.* Cambridge, MA: Harvard University Press.

Hookway, C. 1985. *Peirce.* London: Routledge and Kegan Paul.

———. 2012. *The Pragmatic Maxim: Essays on Peirce and Pragmatism.* Oxford: Oxford University Press.

Horgan, T., and Potrč, M. 2008. *Contextual Semantics Meets Minimal Ontology.* Cambridge, MA: MIT Press.

Hornsby, J. 2001. *Simple Mindedness: In Defence of Naïve Naturalism in the Philosophy of Mind.* Cambridge, MA: Harvard University Press.

Höwing, T. (ed.) 2016. *The Highest Good in Kant's Philosophy.* Berlin: De Gruyter.

Hume, D. 1975a. 'An Enquiry Concerning Human Understanding'. In L. A. Selby-Bigge (ed.) *Enquiries Concerning Human Understanding and Concerning the Principles of Morals*, 3rd ed. Oxford: Clarendon Press.

———. 1975b. *A Treatise of Human Nature.* L. A. Selby-Bigge (ed.) and P. H. Nidditch (rev.), 2nd ed. Oxford: Clarendon Press.

———. 2007. *A Treatise of Human Nature: A Critical Edition.* D. F. Norton and M. J. Norton (eds.). Oxford: Clarendon Press.

Hursthouse, R. 1999. *On Virtue Ethics.* Oxford: Oxford University Press.

Husserl, E. 1970. *The Crisis of the European Sciences and Transcendental Philosophy.* D. Carr (trans.). Evanston, IL: Northwestern University Press.

Hutto, D., and Myin, E. 2012. *Radicalising Enactivism: Basic Minds without Content.* Cambridge, MA: MIT Press.

Jackson, F. C. 1998. *From Metaphysics to Ethics: A Defence of Conceptual Analysis.* Oxford: Oxford University Press.

James, W. 1891. 'The Moral Philosopher and the Moral Life'. *International Journal of Ethics* 1.3: 330–354.

———. 1909. *A Pluralistic Universe.* London: Longman, Green.

Jantzen, B. 2009. 'Peirce on the Method of Balancing "Likelihoods"'. *Transactions of the Charles S. Peirce Society* 45: 668–688.

Kammareddine, F., Laan, T., and Nederpelt, R. 2002. 'Types in Logic and Mathematics Before 1940'. *Bulletin for Symbolic Logic* 8: 185–245.

Kania, A. (ed.). 2013. 'Platonism vs. Nominalism in Contemporary Musical Ontology'. In C. M. Uidhir (ed.) *Art and Abstract Objects.* Oxford: Oxford University Press.

Kant, I. 1902. *Gesammelte Schriften*, vols. 1–22 ed. Preußischen Akademie der Wissenschaften, Berlin 1902 ff., vol. 23 ed. Deutschen Akademie der Wissenschaften, Berlin, 1956, vols. 24–29 ed. Akademie der Wissenschaften zu Göttingen, Berlin 1966 ff.g.

———. 1960. *Religion Within the Limits of Reason Alone.* T. M. Greene and H. H. Hudson (trans.). New York: Harper and Row.

———. 1989. 'What Is Enlightenment?' In H. S. Reiss (ed. and trans.) *Kant: Political Writings.* Cambridge: Cambridge University Press.

———. 1998. *Critique of Pure Reason.* P. Guyer and A. W. Wood (eds. and trans.). Cambridge: Cambridge University Press.

———. 2000. *Critique of the Power of Judgment.* P. Guyer (ed.), P. Guyer and E. Mathews (trans.). Cambridge: Cambridge University Press.

———. 2004. *Prolegomena to Any Future Metaphysics.* G. Hatfield (ed. and trans.). Cambridge: Cambridge University Press.

———. 2006. *Anthropology from a Pragmatic Point of View.* R. B. Louden (ed. and trans.). Cambridge: Cambridge University Press.

———. 2012. *Groundwork for the Metaphysics of Morals.* M. Gregor and J. Timmermann (eds. and trans.). Cambridge: Cambridge University Press.

———. 2017. *The Metaphysics of Morals.* L. Denis (ed.) and M. Gregor (trans.). Cambridge: Cambridge University Press.

Kaplan, M. 1991. 'Epistemology on Holiday'. *Journal of Philosophy* 88: 132–154.

Karlberg, S. 1980. 'Max Weber's Types of Rationality: Cornerstones for the Analysis of Rationalisation Processes in History'. *American Journal of Sociology* 85: 1145–1179.

Ketchum, R. 1996. 'Peirce and Naturalism'. *Philosophia Scientiae* 1: 121–132.

Killin, A. 2018. 'Fictionalism About Musical Works'. *Canadian Journal of Philosophy* 48: 266–291.

Kim, J. 1995a. 'The Myth of Nonreductive Materialism'. In J. Kim. *Supervenience and the Mind.* Cambridge: Cambridge University Press.

———. 1995b. 'The Nonreductivist's Troubles with Mental Causation'. In J. Kim (ed.) *Supervenience and the Mind.* Cambridge: Cambridge University Press.

———. 1996. *Philosophy of Mind.* Boulder, CO: Westview.

———. 2000. *Mind in a Physical World.* Cambridge, MA: MIT Press.

———. 2003. 'The American Origins of Philosophical Naturalism'. *Journal of Philosophical Research, APA Centennial Volume*: 83–98.

Klein, P. 2008. 'Contemporary Responses to Agrippa's Trilemma'. In J. Greco (ed.) *The Oxford Handbook of Scepticism.* Oxford: Oxford University Press.

Korsgaard, C. M. 1996. *The Sources of Normativity.* Cambridge: Cambridge University Press.

———. 2009. *Self-Constitution. Agency, Identity, Integrity.* Oxford: Oxford University Press.

Kraut, R. 2010. 'Universals, Metaphysical Explanations, and Pragmatism'. *The Journal of Philosophy* 107: 590–609.

Kreines, J. 2004. 'Hegel's Critique of Pure Mechanism and the Philosophical Appeal of the *Logic* Project'. *European Journal of Philosophy* 12: 38–74.

———. 2005. 'The Inexplicability of Kant's Naturzweck: Kant on Teleology, Explanation and Biology'. *Archiv fur die Geschichte der Philosophie* 87: 270–311.

Kripke, S. 1959. 'A Completeness Theory in Modal Logic'. *Journal of Symbolic Logic* 24: 1–14.

———. 1963. 'Semantic Considerations on Modal Logic'. *Acta Philosophica Fennica* 16: 83–94.

Kuhn, T. S. 1996. *The Structure of Scientific Revolutions*, 3rd Edition. Chicago: University of Chicago Press.

Kusch, M. 2015. 'Psychologism'. In E. N. Zalta (ed.) *The Stanford Encyclopaedia of Philosophy*. Available at: https://plato.stanford.edu/archives/win2015/entries/psychologism/

Ladyman, J., and Ross, D. 2007. *Everything Must Go: Metaphysics Naturalised*. Oxford: Oxford University Press.

Lawvere, W. F. 1992. 'Categories of Space and of Quantity'. In A. Ibarra, J. Echeverria and T. Mormann (eds.) *The Space of Mathematics: Philosophical, Epistemological and Historical Explorations*. Berlin: De Gruyter.

Legg, C. 2001. 'Naturalism and Wonder: Peirce on the Logic of Hume's Argument Against Miracles'. *Philosophia* 28: 297–318.

Legg, C., and Giladi, P. 2018. 'Metaphysics—Low in Price, High in Value: A Critique of Global Expressivism'. *Transactions of the Charles S. Peirce Society* 54: 64–83.

Lemos, N. 2004. *Common Sense: A Contemporary Defense*. Cambridge: Cambridge University Press.

Lennon, T. M. 1988. 'Descartes's Idealism'. *Philosophie Et Culture: Actes du XVIIe Congrès Mondial de Philosophie* 4: 53–56.

———. 1993. *The Battle of the Gods and Giants: The Legacies of Descartes and Gassendi, 1655–1715*. Princeton, NJ: Princeton University Press.

Levine, J. 1983. 'Materialism and Qualia: The Explanatory Gap'. *Pacific Philosophical Quarterly* 64: 354–361.

Levine, S. 2007. 'The Place of Picturing in Sellars's Synoptic Vision'. *Philosophical Forum* 38: 247–269.

———. 2015. 'Norms and Habits: Brandom on the Sociality of Action'. *European Journal of Philosophy* 23: 248–272.

———. forthcoming. *Pragmatism, Objectivity, and Experience*. Cambridge: Cambridge University Press.

Levinson, J. 1990. 'What a Musical Work Is, Again'. In J. Levinson (ed.) *Music, Art, and Metaphysics*. Ithaca, NY: Cornell University Press.

Lewis, C. I. 1912. 'Implication and the Algebra of Logic'. *Mind* 21: 522–531.

———. 1914. 'Review of A. N. Whitehead and Bertrand Russell, *Principia Mathematica*'. *Journal of Philosophy* 11: 497–502.

———. 1918. *A Survey of Symbolic Logic*. Berkeley, CA: University of California Press.

———. 1930. 'Logic and Pragmatism'. In G. P. Adams and W. P. Montague (eds.) *Contemporary American Philosophy*, vol. 2. New York: Palgrave Macmillan, 31–51.

Lewis, C. I., and Langford, C. H. 1931. *Symbolic Logic*. New York: Century Books.

Lewis, D. K. 1973. *Counterfactuals*. Oxford: Blackwell.

———. 1986. *On the Plurality of Worlds*. Oxford: Blackwell.

Linsky, B., and Zalta, E. N. 1991. 'Is Lewis a Meinongian?' *Australasian Journal of Philosophy* 69: 438–453.

Locke, J. 2014. *An Essay Concerning Human Understanding*. Ware: Wordsworth Editions Limited.

Lovibond, S. 2004. 'Absolute Prohibitions Without Divine Promises'. *Royal Institute of Philosophy Supplement* 54: 141–158.

Macarthur, D. 2006. 'Scepticism, Self-Knowledge and Responsibility'. In S. Hetherington (ed.) *Aspects of Knowing*. Amsterdam: Elsevier.

———. 2008. 'Quinean Naturalism in Question'. *PHILO* 11: 5–18.

——. 2010. 'Taking the Human Sciences Seriously'. In M. De Caro and D. Macarthur (eds.) *Naturalism and Normativity*. New York: Columbia University Press.

——. 2014. 'Subject Naturalism and the Problem of Linguistic Meaning: Critical Remarks on Price's "Naturalism Without Representationalism"'. *Análisis: Revista de investigación filosófica* 1: 69–85.

——. 2015. 'A Kant-Inspired Vision of Pragmatism as Democratic Experimentalism'. In G. Gava and R. Stern (eds.) *Pragmatism, Kant & Transcendental Philosophy*. London: Routledge.

——. 2019. 'Liberal Naturalism and the Scientific Image of the World'. *Inquiry* 62: 565–585.

Macarthur, D., and Price, H. 2007. 'Pragmatism, Quasi-realism and the Global Challenge'. In C. Misak (ed.) *The New Pragmatists*. Oxford: Oxford University Press.

Macdonald, G. 2006. 'The Two Natures: Another Dogma?' In C. Macdonald and G. Macdonald (eds.) *McDowell and His Critics*. Oxford: Blackwell.

Machery, E. 2008. 'The Folk Concept of Intentional Action: Philosophical and Experimental Issues'. *Mind & Language* 23: 165–189.

Mackie, J. 1977. *Ethics: Inventing Right and Wrong*. New York: Penguin.

Martin-Löf, P. 1996. 'On the Meaning of the Logical Constants and the Justification of Logical Laws'. *Nordic Journal of Philosophical Logic* 1: 11–60.

Matthews, G. B. 1992. *Thought's Ego in Augustine and Descartes*. Ithaca, NY: Cornell University Press.

Maund, L. 2011. 'Colour Eliminativism'. In L. Nolan (ed.) *Primary and Secondary Qualities: The Historical and Ongoing Debate*. Oxford: Oxford University Press.

McDowell, J. 1994. *Mind and World*. Cambridge, MA: Harvard University Press.

——. 1996. *Mind and World*, 2nd ed. Cambridge, MA: Harvard University Press.

——. 1998. *Mind, Value, and Reality*. Cambridge, MA: Harvard University Press.

——. 1999. 'Responses'. In M. Willaschek (ed.) *John McDowell: Reason and Nature, Lecture and Colloquium in Münster*. Munster: LIT Verlag. Available at: http://web.uni-frankfurt.de/fb08/PHIL/willaschek/mcdowellkolloq.pdf

——. 2006. 'Response to Graham Macdonald'. In C. Macdonald and G. Macdonald (eds.) *McDowell and His Critics*. Oxford: Blackwell.

——. 2009. *Having the World in View: Essays on Kant, Hegel, and Sellars*. Cambridge, MA: Harvard University Press.

Mead, G. H. 1934. *Mind, Self, and Society: From the Standpoint of a Social Behaviourist*. C. W. Morris (ed.). Chicago, IL: University of Chicago Press.

Mehrtens, H. 1990. *Moderne—Sprache—Mathematik: Eine Geschichte des Streits um die Grundlagen der Disziplin und des Sujekts formaler Systeme*. Frankfurt: Suhrkamp.

Merricks, T. 2000. 'No Statues'. *Australasian Journal of Philosophy* 78: 47–52.

Merrill, K. 1991. 'Hume's "of Miracles", Peirce, and the Balancing of Likelihoods'. *Journal of the History of Philosophy* 29: 85–113.

Messer, A. 1904. *Kants Ethik*. Leipzig: Veit.

Metzinger, T. 2003a. *Being No One: The Self-Model of Subjectivity*. Cambridge, MA: MIT Press.

———. 2003b. 'Phenomenal Transparency and Cognitive Self-Reference'. *Phenomenology and the Cognitive Sciences* 2: 353–393.

Mignolo, W. D. 2011. *The Darker Side of Western Modernity: Global Futures, Decolonial Options*. Durham and London: Duke University Press.

Millgram, E. 2005. *Ethics Done Right: Practical Reasoning as a Foundation for Moral Theory*. Cambridge: Cambridge University Press.

Moore, G. E. 1899. 'The Nature of Judgement'. *Mind* 8: 176–193.

———. 1903a. 'The Refutation of Idealism'. *Mind* 12: 433–453.

———. 1903b. *Principia Ethica*. Cambridge: Cambridge University Press.

———. 1960. 'Some Judgements of Perceptions'. In G. E. Moore (ed.) *Philosophical Studies*. London: Routledge and Kegan Paul.

———. 1993. *Moore: Selected Writings*. T. Baldwin (ed.). Oxford: Routledge.

Moore, A. W. 2012. *The Evolution of Modern Metaphysics: Making Sense of Things*. Cambridge: Cambridge University Press.

Moran, D. 2008. 'Husserl's Transcendental Philosophy and the Critique of Naturalism'. *Continental Philosophy Review* 41: 401–425.

———. 2012. *Husserl's Crisis of the European Sciences and Transcendental Phenomenology: An Introduction*. Cambridge: Cambridge University Press.

———. 2013. ' "Let's Look at It Objectively": Why Phenomenology Cannot Be Naturalised'. *Royal Institute of Philosophy Supplement* 72: 89–115.

Morris, M. 1998. 'Mind, World and Value'. In A. O'Hear (ed.) *Current Issues in the Philosophy of Mind*. Cambridge: Cambridge University Press.

Moschovakis, J. 2015. 'Intuitionistic Logic'. In E. N. Zalta (ed.) *The Stanford Encyclopaedia of Philosophy*. Available at: https://plato.stanford.edu/archives/spr2015/entries/logic-intuitionistic/

Mounce, H. O. 1999. *Hume's Naturalism*. London and New York: Routledge.

Murdoch, I. 1956. Symposium: 'Vision and Choice in Morality', Aristotelian Society, *Dreams and Self-Knowledge* (Supplementary Volume XXX): 32–58.

Murphy, D., and Stich, S. 1999. 'Griffiths, Elimination and Psychopathology'. *Metascience* 8: 13–25.

Neta, R. 2007. 'Review of *Naturalism in Question* by Mario De Caro, David Macarthur'. *The Philosophical Review* 116: 657–663.

Nolan, D., Restall, G., and West, C. 2005. 'Moral Fictionalism Versus the Rest'. *Australasian Journal of Philosophy* 83: 307–330.

Offe, C. 1984. 'Ungovernability: On the Renaissance of Conservative Theories of Crisis'. In J. Habermas (ed.) *Observation on "The Spiritual Situation of the Age"*. Cambridge, MA: MIT Press.

Olafson, F. A. 2001. *Naturalism and the Human Condition: Against Scientism*. London and New York: Routledge.

O'Neill, O. 1990. *Constructions of Reason: Explorations of Kant's Practical Philosophy*. Cambridge: Cambridge University Press.

Oppenheim, P., and Putnam, H. 1958. 'The Unity of Science as a Working Hypothesis'. In H. Feigl, M. Scriven and G. Maxwell (eds.) *Minnesota Studies in the Philosophy of Science, Vol. 2*. Minneapolis, MN: Minnesota University Press.

O'Shea, J. R. 2007. *Wilfrid Sellars: Naturalism with a Normative Turn*. Cambridge: Polity Press.

———. 2009. 'On the Structure of Sellars's Naturalism with a Normative Turn'. In W. A. deVries (ed.) *Empiricism, Perceptual Knowledge, Normativity, and Realism: Essays on Wilfrid Sellars*. Oxford: Oxford University Press.

Palmer, A. 2014. *Reading Lucretius in the Renaissance*. Cambridge, MA: Harvard University Press.

Papineau, D. 1993. *Philosophical Naturalism*. Oxford: Blackwell.

———. 2015. 'Naturalism'. In E. N. Zalta (ed.) *The Stanford Encyclopaedia of Philosophy*. Available at: https://plato.stanford.edu/archives/win2016/entries/naturalism

Patterson, A. L. T. 1997. 'Towards a Hegelian Philosophy of Mathematics'. *Idealistic Studies* 27: 1–10.

Peirce, C. S. 1931–58. *Collected Papers of Charles Sanders Peirce*. C. Hartshorne, P. Weiss and A. Burks (eds.), 8 vols. Cambridge, MA: Harvard University Press.

———. 1955. 'The Fixation of Belief'. In J. Buchler (ed.) *Philosophical Writings of Peirce*. New York: Dover.

———. 1976. *The New Elements of Mathematics*. C. Eisele (ed.), 4 vols. The Hague: Mouton.

———. 1982. *Writings of Charles S. Peirce: A Chronological Edition*. The Peirce Edition Project (ed.), 7 vols. Bloomington, IN: Indiana University Press.

———. 1985. *Historical Perspectives on Peirce's Logic of Science: A History of Science*. C. Eisele (ed.), 2 vols. The Hague: De Gruyter.

———. 1992–98. *The Essential Peirce: Selected Philosophical Writings*. N. Houser, C. Kloesel, and the Peirce Edition Project (eds.), 2 vols. Bloomington, IN: Indiana University Press.

Pereboom, D. 2001. *Living Without Free Will*. Cambridge: Cambridge University Press.

———. 2014. *Free Will, Agency, and the Meaning of Life*. Oxford: Oxford University Press.

Pinkard, T. 1994. *Hegel's Phenomenology: The Sociality of Reason*. Cambridge: Cambridge University Press.

———. 2002. *German Philosophy 1760–1860: The Legacy of Idealism*. Cambridge: Cambridge University Press.

———. 2012. *Hegel's Naturalism: Mind, Nature, and the Final Ends of Life*. Oxford: Oxford University Press.

Plato. 1921. *Plato in Twelve Volumes*. H. N. Fowler (trans.), vol. 12. Cambridge, MA: Harvard University Press.

Ploucquet, G. 2006. *Logik*. Hildesheim: Georg Olms Verlag.

Pollok, K. 2001. *Kants "Metaphyiissche Anfangsgründe der Naturwissenschaft". Ein kritischer Kommentar*. Hamburg: Meiner.

———. 2014. ' "The Understanding Prescribes Laws to Nature": Spontaneity, Legislation, and Kant's Transcendental Hylomorphism'. *Kant-Studien* 105: 509–530.

Pozzo, R. 2010. 'Gottfried Ploucquet'. In H. F. Klemme and M. Kuehn (eds.) *The Dictionary of Eighteenth-Century German Philosophy*, 3 vols., vol. 2. London and New York: Continuum Press.

Predelli, S. 2001. 'Musical Ontology and the Argument from Creation'. *British Journal of Aesthetics* 41: 279–292.

Price, H. 1992. 'Metaphysical Pluralism'. *The Journal of Philosophy* 89: 387–409.

———. 1997. 'Naturalism and the Fate of the M-Worlds'. *Proceedings of the Aristotelian Society* (Supplementary Volume 7): 247–267.

———. 2004. 'Naturalism without Representationalism'. In M. De Caro and D. Macarthur (eds.) *Naturalism in Question*. Cambridge, MA: Harvard University Press.

———. 2011. *Naturalism without Mirrors*. Oxford: Oxford University Press.

———. 2013. *Expressivism, Pragmatism, and Representationalism*. Cambridge: Cambridge University Press.

———. 2015. 'Idling and Sidling Toward Philosophical Peace'. In S. Gross, N. Tebben and M. Williams (eds.) *Meaning Without Representation: Essays on Truth, Expression, Normativity, and Naturalism*. Oxford: Oxford University Press.

Prichard, H. A. 1909. *Kant's Theory of Knowledge*. Oxford: Clarendon Press.

Prior, A. N. 1957. *Time and Modality: The John Locke Lectures for 1955–56*. Oxford: Clarendon Press.

———. 1967. *Past, Present and Future*. Oxford: Clarendon Press.

Psillos, S. 2009. *Knowing the Structure of Nature: Essays on Realism and Explanation*. London: Palgrave Macmillan.

Putnam, H. 1973. 'Reductionism and the Nature of Psychology'. *Cognition* 2: 131–146.

———. 1975a. 'It Ain't Necessarily So'. In his *Mathematics, Matter and Method. Philosophical Papers*, vol. 1. Cambridge: Cambridge University Press.

———. 1975b. *Mind, Language, and Reality. Philosophical Papers*, vol. 2. Cambridge: Cambridge University Press.

———. 1981. *Reason, Truth, and History*. Cambridge: Cambridge University Press.

———. 1990. *Realism with a Human Face*. Cambridge, MA: Harvard University Press.

———. 1992. *Renewing Philosophy*. Cambridge, MA: Harvard University Press.

———. 1994. *Words and Life*. Cambridge, MA: Harvard University Press.

———. 1995. *Pragmatism: An Open Question*. Oxford: Blackwell.

———. 1999. *The Threefold Cord. Mind, Body, and World*. New York: Columbia University Press.

———. 2002. *The Collapse of the Fact/Value Dichotomy and Other Essays*. Cambridge, MA: Harvard University Press.

———. 2004a. *Ethics Without Ontology*. Cambridge, MA: Harvard University Press.

———. 2004b. 'The Content and Appeal of "Naturalism"'. In M. De Caro and D. Macarthur (eds.) *Naturalism in Question*. Cambridge, MA: Harvard University Press.

———. 2012. *Philosophy in an Age of Science: Physics, Mathematics, and Scepticism*. M. De Caro and D. Macarthur (eds.). Cambridge, MA: Harvard University Press.

———. 2015. 'Naturalism, Realism, and Normativity'. *Journal of the American Philosophical Association* 1: 312–328.

———. 2016a. *Naturalism, Realism, and Normativity*. M. De Caro (ed.). Cambridge, MA: Harvard University Press.

———. 2016b. 'Realism'. *Philosophy and Social Criticism* 42: 117–131.

———. forthcoming. *In Dialogue*. M. De Caro and D. Macarthur (eds.). Cambridge, MA: Harvard University Press.

Putnam, H., and Putnam, R. A. 2017. *Pragmatism as a Way of Life: The Lasting Legacy of William James and John Dewey*. Cambridge, MA: Harvard University Press.

Quine, W. V. 1957. 'The Scope and Language of Science', reprinted in his *Ways of Paradox and Other Essays*. New York: Random House.

———. 1960. *Word and Object*. Cambridge, MA: MIT Press.

———. 1981. *Theories and Things*. Cambridge, MA: Harvard University Press.

———. 1986. 'Reply to Putnam'. In L. E. Hahn and P. A. Schillp (eds.) *The Philosophy of W. V. Quine*. Chicago, IL: Open Court Press.

———. 1997. 'On What There Is'. In D. H. Mellor and A. Oliver (eds.) *Properties*. Oxford: Oxford University Press.

Quine, W. V. and Ullian, J. S. 1970. *The Web of Belief*. New York: Random House.

Ramsey, W. 2016. 'Eliminative Materialism'. In E. N. Zalta (ed.) *The Stanford Encyclopaedia of Philosophy*. Available at: https://plato.stanford.edu/archives/win2016/entries/materialism-eliminative/

Ratcliffe, M. 2013. 'Phenomenology, Naturalism and the Sense of Reality'. *Royal Institute of Philosophy Supplement* 72: 67–88.

Redding, P. 2010. 'Two Directions for Analytic Kantianism: Naturalism and Idealism'. In M. De Caro and D. Macarthur (eds.) *Naturalism and Normativity*. New York: Columbia University Press.

———. 2012. 'Some Metaphysical Implications of Hegel's Theology'. *European Journal for Philosophy of Religion* 4: 139–150.

———. 2014. 'The Role of Logic "Commonly So Called" in Hegel's *Science of Logic*'. *British Journal for the History of Philosophy* 22: 281–301.

———. 2017. 'Findlay's Hegel: Idealism as Modal Actualism'. *Critical Horizons* 18: 359–377.

———. 2018. 'Hegel's Subjective Logic as a Logic for (Hegel's) Philosophy of Mind'. *Hegel Bulletin* 39: 1–22.

———. 2019. 'Hegel's Treatment of Predication Considered in the Light of a Logic for the Actual World'. *Hegel Bulletin* 40: 51–73.

Régis, P. S. 1691/1970. *Cours entier de philosophie, ou systeme general selon les principes de M. Descartes, contenant la logique, la metaphysique, la physique, et la morale*. Amsterdam: Huguetan, reprint. New York and London: Johnson.

———. 1704/1996. *L'usage de la raison et de la foy ou l'accord de la foy et de la raison*. Jean-Robert Armogathe (ed.) Paris: Fayard.

Reid, T. 1983. *Inquiries and Essays*. R. E. Beanblossom and K. Lehrer (eds.). Indianapolis, IN: Hackett.

Reitan, E. A. 1996. 'Nature, Place, and Space: Albert the Great and the Origins of Modern Science'. *American Catholic Philosophical Quarterly* 70.1: 83–101.

Rescher, N. 2017. 'Philosophy as Rational Systematisation'. In G. D'Oro and S. Overgaard (eds.) *The Cambridge Companion to Philosophical Methodology*. Cambridge: Cambridge University Press.

Richards, R. L. 2013. 'The Impact of German Idealism and Romanticism on Biology'. In K. Ameriks, N. Boyle and L. Disley (eds.) *The Impact of Idealism: The Legacy of Post-Kantian German Thought. Volume 1: Philosophy and Natural Sciences*. Cambridge: Cambridge University Press.

Rickert, H. 1926. *Kulturwissenschaft und Naturwissenschaft*, 6th and 7th expanded ed. Tübingen: Mohr Siebeck.

Ritchie, J. 2008. *Understanding Naturalism*. Durham: Acumen.

Rödl, S. 2007. *Self-Consciousness*. Cambridge, MA: Harvard University Press.

Rosen, G. 2017. 'Abstract Objects'. In E. N. Zalta (ed.) *Stanford Encyclopaedia of Philosophy*. Available at: https://plato.stanford.edu/entries/abstract-objects/

Rosen, G., and Dorr, C. 2002. 'Composition as Fiction'. In R. Gale (ed.) *The Blackwell Companion to Metaphysics*. Oxford: Blackwell.

Rosenberg, J. 1975. 'The Elusiveness of Categories, the Archimedean Dilemma, and the Nature of Man'. In H-N. Castañeda (ed.) *Action, Knowledge, and Reality: Studies in Honour of Wilfrid Sellars*. Indianapolis, IN: Bobbs-Merrill.

———. 2007. *Wilfrid Sellars: Fusing the Images*. Oxford: Oxford University Press.

Rosenberg, A. 2011. *The Atheist's Guide to Reality: Enjoying Life without Illusions*. New York and London: W. W. Norton & Co.

———. 2014. 'Disenchanted Naturalism'. In B. Bashour and H. D. Muller (eds.) *Contemporary Philosophical Naturalism and Its Implications*. New York and London: Routledge.

Ryle, G. 1949. *The Concept of Mind*. Chicago: University of Chicago Press.

Sachs, C. 2015. *Intentionality and the Myths of the Given: Between Pragmatism and Phenomenology*. New York and London: Routledge.

Scanlon, T. 1998. *What We Owe to Each Other*. Cambridge, MA: Harvard University Press.

Scanlon, T. M. 2003. 'Metaphysics and Morals'. *Proceedings and Addresses of the American Philosophical Association* 77: 7–22.

Schmaltz, T. 2017. *Early Modern Cartesianisms: Dutch and French Constructions*. Oxford: Oxford University Press.

Scruton, R. 2015. 'Scientism and the Humanities'. In R. N. Williams and D. N. Robinson (eds.) *Scientism: The New Orthodoxy*. London: Bloomsbury.

Sellars, W. 1949. 'Aristotelian Philosophies of Mind'. In R. W. Sellars, V. J. McGill and M. Farber (eds.) *Philosophy for the Future, the Quest of Modern Materialism*. New York: Palgrave Macmillan.

———. 1952. 'Mind, Meaning, and Behaviour'. *Philosophical Studies* 3: 83–95.

———. 1956. 'Empiricism and the Philosophy of Mind'. In H. Feigl and M. Scriven (eds.) *Minnesota Studies in the Philosophy of Science, Vol. I: The Foundations of Science and the Concepts of Psychology and Psychoanalysis*. Minneapolis: University of Minnesota Press.

———. 1958. 'Counterfactuals, Dispositions, and the Causal Modalities'. In H. Feigl, M. Scriven and G. Maxwell (eds.) *Concepts, Theories, and the Mind-Body Problem*. Minneapolis, MN: University of Minnesota Press.

———. 1963a. 'Philosophy and the Scientific Image of Man'. In R. Colodny (ed.) *Frontiers of Science and Philosophy*. Pittsburgh, PA: University of Pittsburgh Press.

———. 1963b. *Science, Perception and Reality*. London and New York: Routledge.

———. 1963c. 'Abstract Entities'. *Review of Metaphysics* 16: 627–671.

———. 1968. *Science and Metaphysics: Variations on Kantian Themes: The John Locke Lectures for 1965–66*. London: Routledge.

———. 1974. *Essays in Philosophy and Its History*. Dordrecht: D. Reidel Publishing.

———. 1976. 'Kant's Transcendental Idealism'. *Collections of Philosophy* 6: 165–181.

———. 1978. 'The Role of Imagination in Kant's Theory of Experience'. In H. Johnstone (ed.) *Categories: A Colloquium*. University Park, PA: Pennsylvania State University Press.

———. 1980a. *Pure Pragmatics and Possible Worlds: The Early Essays of Wilfrid Sellars*. Atascadero, CA: Ridgeview Publishing.

———. 1980b. *Naturalism and Ontology: The John Dewey Lectures for 1973–74*. Reseda, CA: Ridgeview Publishing Co.

———. 1991. *Science, Perception and Reality*. Atascadero, CA: Ridgeview Publishing.

———. 1997. *Empiricism and the Philosophy of Mind: With an Introduction by Richard Rorty and a Study Guide by Robert Brandom*. R. Brandom (ed.). Cambridge, MA: Harvard University Press.

———. 2007. *In the Space of Reasons: Selected Essays of Wilfrid Sellars*. K. Scharp and R. B. Brandom (eds.). Cambridge, MA: Harvard University Press.

Sextus Empiricus. 2000. *Sextus Empiricus, Outlines of Scepticism*. J. Annas and J. Barnes (eds. and trans.), 2nd ed. Cambridge: Cambridge University Press.

Short, T. 2007. *Peirce's Theory of Signs*. Cambridge: Cambridge University Press.

Smilansky, S. 2002. *Free Will and Illusion*. Oxford: Oxford University Press.

Smithson, R. 2019. 'An Idealist Critique of Naturalism'. *Inquiry* 62: 504–526.

Spicer, F. 2011. 'Intuitions in Naturalistic Philosophy', unpublished paper presented at Lancaster Philosophy research seminar.

Spinoza, B. 1994. *A Spinoza Reader: The 'Ethics' and Other Works*. E. Curley (ed. and trans.). Princeton, NJ: Princeton University Press.

Stern, R. 2008. 'Hegel's Idealism'. In F. C. Beiser (ed.) *The Cambridge Companion to Hegel and Nineteenth-Century Philosophy*. Cambridge: Cambridge University Press.

———. 2013a. *Routledge Philosophy Guidebook to Hegel and the "Phenomenology of Spirit"*, 2nd ed. London and New York: Routledge.

———. 2013b. 'Taylor, Transcendental Arguments, and Hegel on Consciousness'. *Hegel Bulletin* 34: 79–97.

———. 2014. 'Divine Commands and Secular Commands: Darwall on Anscombe'. *Mind* 123: 1095–1122.

Stich, S. 1983. *From Folk Psychology to Cognitive Science: The Case Against Belief*. Cambridge, MA: MIT Press.

Stone, A. 2013. 'Hegel, Naturalism, and the Philosophy of Nature'. *Hegel Bulletin* 34: 59–78.

Strawson, G. 2010. *Freedom and Belief*, rev. ed. Oxford: Oxford University Press.

Strawson, P. F. 1985. *Scepticism and Naturalism: Some Varieties*. New York: Columbia University Press.

Stroud, B. 1996. 'The Charm of Naturalism'. *Proceedings and Addresses of the American Philosophical Association* 70: 43–55.

Sundholm, G. 2009. 'A Century of Judgment and Inference, 1837–1936: Some Strands in the Development of Logic'. In L. Haaparanta (ed.) *The Development of Modern Logic*. Oxford: Oxford University Press.

Tallis, R. 2017. *Of Time and Lamentation: Reflections on Transience*. Newcastle-upon-Tyne: Agenda Publishing.

Taylor, C. 1975. *Hegel*. Cambridge: Cambridge University Press.

———. 1987. 'Overcoming Epistemology'. In K. Baynes, J. Bonham and T. McCarthy (eds.) *After Philosophy: End or Transformation?* Cambridge, MA: MIT Press.

Teichmann, R. 2008. *The Philosophy of Elizabeth Anscombe*. Oxford: Oxford University Press.

Thomasson, A. L. 2007. *Ordinary Objects*. New York: Oxford University Press.

———. 2015. *Ontology Made Easy*. New York: Oxford University Press.

Thompson, M. 2003. 'Three Degrees of Goodness'. *Iride* XVI: 179–200.
———. 2004. 'Apprehending Human Form'. In A. O'Hear (ed.) *Modern Moral Philosophy*. Cambridge: Cambridge University Press.
———. 2008. *Life and Action*. Cambridge, MA: Harvard University Press.
———. 2013. 'Forms of Nature: "First", "Second", "Living", "Rational", and "Phronetic"'. In G. Hindirchs and A. Honneth (eds.) *Freiheit*. Frankfurt: Klostermann.
Tolman, E. C. 1948. 'Cognitive Maps in Rats and Men'. *Psychological Review* 55: 189–208.
Tse, P. 2019. 'Fichte's Critique of Physicalism—Towards an Idealist Alternative'. *Inquiry* 62: 527–545.
Unger, P. 1979a. 'There Are No Ordinary Things'. *Synthese* 41: 117–154.
———. 1979b. 'Why There Are No People'. *Midwest Studies in Philosophy* 4: 177–222.
van Fraassen, B. 2003. 'McMullin's Appreciation of Realism Concerning the Sciences'. *Philosophy of Science* 70: 479–492.
van Heijenoort, J. (ed.). 1967. *From Frege to Gödel: A Source Book in Mathematical Logic, 1879–1931*. Cambridge, MA: Harvard University Press.
van Inwagen, P. 1990. *Material Beings*. Ithaca, NY: Cornell University Press.
Varden, H. 2018. *A Kantian Theory of Sexuality*. Oxford: Oxford University Press.
Vogler, C. 2013. 'Aristotle, Aquinas, and the New Virtue Ethics'. In T. Hoffman, J. Müller and M. Perkams (eds.) *Aquinas and the Nicomachean Ethics*. Cambridge: Cambridge University Press.
Walker, R. C. S. 2006. 'Kant and Transcendental Arguments'. In P. Guyer (ed.) *The Cambridge Companion to Kant and Modern Philosophy*. Cambridge: Cambridge University Press.
Weber, M. 1948a. 'The Social Psychology of the World Religions'. In H. H. Gerth and C. W. Mills (eds.) *From Max Weber: Essays in Sociology*. London and New York: Routledge.
———. 1948b. 'Science as a Vocation'. In H. H. Gerth and C. W. Mills (eds.) *From Max Weber: Essays in Sociology*. London and New York: Routledge.
———. 1992. *The Protestant Ethic and the Spirit of Capitalism*. T. Parsons (trans.). London and New York: Routledge.
Wedgwood, R. 2007. *The Nature of Normativity*. Oxford: Oxford University Press.
Westphal, K. R. 2008. 'Philosophising About Nature: Hegel's Philosophical Project'. In F. C. Beiser (ed.) *The Cambridge Companion to Hegel and Nineteenth-Century Philosophy*. Cambridge: Cambridge University Press.
Whitehead, A. N., and Russell, B. 1910–1913. *Principia Mathematica*. Cambridge: Cambridge University Press.
Wiggins, D. 2009. *Ethics: Twelve Lectures on the Philosophy of Morality*. Cambridge, MA: Harvard University Press.
Williams, B. 1993. *Shame and Necessity*. Berkeley, CA: University of California Press.
———. 2006. *Philosophy as a Humanistic Discipline*. A. W. Moore (ed.). Princeton, NJ: Princeton University Press.
Williams, M. 2000. 'Epistemic Entitlement'. *Philosophy and Phenomenological Research* 60: 607–612.

Williams, R. R. 1985. 'Hegel and Transcendental Philosophy'. *The Journal of Philosophy* 82: 595–606.

Williamson, T. 2011. 'What Is Naturalism?' *The Stone*, September 4.

Wilson, E. O. 1998. *Consilience: The Unity of Knowledge*. New York: Vintage Books.

Wilson, A. 2015. 'Peirce and the *A Priori*'. *Transactions of the Charles S. Peirce Society* 51: 201–224.

———. 2016. *Peirce's Empiricism: Its Roots and Its Originality*. Lanham, MD: Lexington Books.

Windelband, W. 1915. *Geschichte und Naturwissenschaft*, in *Präludien. Aufsätze und Reden zur Philosophie und ihrer Geschichte*, vol. 2, 5th expanded ed. Tübingen: Mohr Siebeck.

———. 1980. 'Rectorial Address: History and Natural Science'. *History and Theory* 19: 169–185.

Wittgenstein, L. 1969. *On Certainty*. G. E. M. Anscombe (trans.). Oxford: Blackwell.

Yablo, S. 2002. 'Abstract Objects: A Case Study'. *Noûs* 36 (Supplementary Volume 1): 220–240.

Ye, F. 'On Extreme Versus Moderate Methodological Naturalism'. *Philosophia* 45: 371–385.

Young, I. M. 1990. *Justice and the Politics of Difference*. Princeton, NJ: Princeton University Press.

Zahavi, D. 2015. 'Husserl and the Transcendental'. In S. Gardner and M. Grist (eds.) *The Transcendental Turn*. Oxford: Oxford University Press.

Contributors

Alexis Papazoglou was Lecturer in Philosophy at the Department of Politics, International Relations and Philosophy at Royal Holloway, University of London (2015–2018). Before that, he was Affiliated Lecturer at the University of Cambridge's Faculty of Philosophy, post-doctoral teaching associate at Girton College, Cambridge, and Director of Studies in Philosophy at Jesus College, Cambridge. During the summer of 2018, he was Visiting Scholar at the Department of Philosophy at Stanford University. His research focuses on how the post-Kantian idealist tradition can illuminate new ways for contemporary philosophy to think of the relationship between mind and nature. He writes on philosophy, politics, and current affairs for *The New Republic*.

David Macarthur is an Associate Professor in the Philosophy Department at the University of Sydney. He works at the interface of contemporary pragmatism, Wittgenstein's philosophy of language and psychology, and philosophy of art. In addition to these topics, he has published many articles in leading philosophy journals and books on liberal naturalism, metaphysical quietism, scepticism, common sense, perception, language, philosophy of architecture, and philosophy of photography and film. He has co-edited three volumes with Mario De Caro: *Naturalism in Question* (2004); *Naturalism and Normativity* (2010); and *Philosophy in an Age of Science: Physics, Mathematics and Scepticism* (2012). Prof. Macarthur's volume *Hilary & Ruth Anna Putnam, Pragmatism as a Way of Life: The Lasting Legacy of William James and John Dewey* was published by Harvard University Press in 2017.

Gabriele Gava is currently a Research Associate at Goethe University Frankfurt, where he runs a project on 'Kant, Transcendental Strategies, and Philosophical Antinomies'. Previously, he was a Humboldt Foundation Postdoctoral Research Fellow at the same institution. He received his PhD in 2009 from the University of Pisa. He has published articles in leading academic journals on Peirce, Kant, pragmatism, and epistemology. His book *Peirce's Account of Purposefulness: A Kantian*

Perspective was published in 2014 by Routledge. He is the co-editor of *Pragmatism, Kant and Transcendental Philosophy* (2016).

Giuseppina D'Oro is Reader in Philosophy at Keele University. Her research interests lie at the intersection between idealism, philosophy of mind, and metaphilosophy. She is the author of *Collingwood and the Metaphysics of Experience* (2002), the co-editor of *Reasons and Causes: Causalism and Anti-Causalism in the Philosophy of Action* (2013), the co-editor of the revised edition of Collingwood's *An Essay on Philosophical Method* (2008), and the co-editor of *The Cambridge Companion to Philosophical Methodology* (2017). Her papers have appeared in many journals, including *The Australasian Journal of Philosophy*, *The British Journal of the History of Philosophy*, and *Inquiry*. She was co-investigator (with Paul Giladi and Alexis Papazoglou) on a Templeton-funded project on Idealism and the Philosophy of Mind.

Johannes Haag is Professor for Theoretical Philosophy at the University of Potsdam. He previously worked at LMU Munich and HU Berlin. He has published on early modern philosophy as well as on contemporary theories of perception and the foundations of intentionality. He is the author of *Erfahrung und Gegenstand. Das Verhältnis von Sinnlichkeit und Verstand* (2007), and the co-editor of *Übergänge—discursi oder intuitive?* (2013). His recent publications include 'Fichte on the Consciousness of Spinoza's God' (2012), 'Kant on Imagination and the Natural Sources of the Conceptual' (2013), 'McDowells Kant und McDowells Sellars's (2014) and 'Faculties in Kant and German Idealism' (2015).

Katerina Deligiorgi is Reader in Philosophy at the University of Sussex. She is the author of *The Scope of Autonomy: Kant and the Morality of Freedom* (2012), *Kant and the Culture of Enlightenment* (2005), as well as numerous articles and book chapters on Kant, German Idealism, and contemporary philosophy. She is the editor of *Hegel: New Directions* (2006) and was editor of the *Hegel Bulletin* from 2005 to 2015.

Mario De Caro teaches Moral Philosophy at Roma Tré University, and since 2000 has also been teaching at Tufts University as a Visiting Professor. He was a Fulbright Fellow at Harvard University and a Visiting Scholar for two years at MIT. He is the Vice-President of the Consulta Nazionale di Filosofia, a past President of the Italian Society for Analytic Philosophy, and an Associate Editor of the *Journal of the American Philosophical Association*. In addition to authoring about one hundred scientific articles in six languages and three books in Italian, he has co-edited with David Macarthur *Naturalism in Question* (2004), *Naturalism and Normativity* (2010), and *Philosophy in an Age of Science: Physics, Mathematics and Scepticism* (2012). Prof. De Caro also edited *Cartographies of the Mind* (2007). He was the Literary Executor for Hilary Putnam, and edited the two last collections of essays by Putnam: *Naturalism, Realism, and Normativity* (2016), and *Hilary Putnam: In Dialogue* (forthcoming). Prof. De Caro is interested in action theory, moral philosophy, neuroethics, metaphilosophy, philosophy of film, and history of early modern thought.

Nathan Haydon is currently an Instructor in Philosophy at the University of Waterloo, where he finished his PhD dissertation in 2017. His research is primarily on Peircean pragmatism, and in particular Peirce's work on the development of reason and of reasonable behaviour. Dr. Haydon has given talks on Pierce's theory of action, Peirce's ethical theory, and how Peirce avoids transcendental assumptions when grounding his theory of enquiry. Dr. Haydon is currently working to develop Peirce's logic of relations in light of contemporary applications found in cognitive and computer science.

Paul Giladi is Senior Lecturer in Philosophy at Manchester Metropolitan University, an affiliate of the UCD Centre for Ethics in Public Life, and an honorary research fellow at the University of Sheffield. He has published articles in leading philosophical journals and edited collections on Hegel, pragmatism, critical social theory, feminism, and contemporary Anglo-American philosophy. He was the co-investigator of the Templeton-funded project 'Idealism and the Philosophy of Mind' (2016–2017), and the co-editor of the 2017 special issue of *Hegel Bulletin* on Hegel and the Frankfurt School. He was also the co-editor of the 2018 special issue of *Hegel Bulletin* on Hegel and 20th-Century French Philosophy, the co-editor of the 2018 special issue of *European Journal of Pragmatism and American Philosophy* on Idealism and Pragmatism, and the co-editor of the 2018 special issue of *Feminist Philosophy Quarterly* on Epistemic Injustice and Recognition Theory. He is also the co-editor of the 2019 special issue of *Inquiry* on Idealism and the Metaphilosophy of Mind, and the co-editor of the 2019 special issue of *International Journal of Philosophical Studies* on Hegel and Sellars. Dr. Giladi has two other book contracts with Routledge: *Hegel and the Frankfurt School: Traditions in Dialogue* (2020); and *Epistemic Injustice and the Philosophy of Recognition* (2021). He is currently the Reviews Editor of the *Hegel Bulletin*.

Paul Redding is Emeritus Professor of Philosophy in the School of Philosophical and Historical Studies at the University of Sydney. He is a Fellow of the Australian Academy of the Humanities, and a Past President of the Australasian Association of Philosophy. He works mainly in the areas of Kantian and Hegelian philosophy, and the tradition of continental idealism more generally. In particular, Prof. Redding's recent interests have focused on the relationship of this tradition to the later movements of analytic philosophy and pragmatism, and on issues in idealist logic, philosophical psychology, and philosophy of religion.

He is the author of *Hegel's Hermeneutics* (1996), *The Logic of Affect* (1999), *Analytic Philosophy and the Return of Hegelian Thought* (2007), *Continental Idealism: Leibniz to Nietzsche* (2009), and *Thoughts, Deeds, Words and World: Hegel's Idealist Response to the Linguistic 'Metacritical Invasion'* (2016).

Shannon Dea is Associate Professor at the University of Waterloo, where she teaches both history of philosophy and gender theory. She has published a range of articles on classic pragmatism (especially Peirce), early modern philosophy (especially Spinoza) and early modern science in *British Journal of the History of Philosophy*, *Transactions of the Charles S. Peirce Society*, *Dialogue*, the *Journal of Scottish Philosophy*, and the *Stanford Encyclopaedia of Philosophy*. She is the author of *Beyond the Binary: Thinking about Sex and Gender* (2016).

Steven Levine is Associate Professor of Philosophy at the University of Massachusetts, Boston. His primary philosophical interests are in Sellars, neo-pragmatism, and classical pragmatism. He has published numerous articles on these topics in the *European Journal of Philosophy*, the *Canadian Journal of Philosophy*, *Philosophical Topics*, and the *Transactions of the Charles S. Peirce Society*, amongst other places. His book entitled *Pragmatism, Objectivity, and Experience* is forthcoming with Cambridge University Press.

Willem A. deVries received his degrees from Haverford College and the University of Pittsburgh. He has taught at Amherst College, Harvard University, Tufts University, the University of Vienna, and University of New Hampshire. His books include *Hegel's Theory of Mental Activity* (1988); *Knowledge, Mind, and the Given: Reading Sellars's 'Empiricism and the Philosophy of Mind'* (2000); and *Wilfrid Sellars* (2005). Despite the focus on Hegel or Sellars, there are occasional forays into other territories, in a continuing attempt to figure out how it all hangs together. He is co-editor of Routledge Studies in American Philosophy and founding president of the Wilfrid Sellars Society.

Index